Ru Jun 02

Our Monica, Ourselves

KL DEC 2009

D0040431

SEXUAL CULTURES: New Directions from the Center for
Lesbian and Gay Studies
General Editors: José Esteban Muñoz and Ann Pellegrini

Times Square Red, Times Square Blue
Samuel R. Delany

Private Affairs
Critical Ventures in the Culture of Social Relations
Phillip Brian Harper

In Your Face
9 Sexual Studies
Mandy Merck

Tropics of Desire
Interventions from Queer Latino America
José Quiroga

Murdering Masculinities
Fantasies of Gender and Violence in the American Crime Novel
Greg Forter

Our Monica, Ourselves
The Clinton Affair and the National Interest
Edited by Lauren Berlant and Lisa Duggan

Our Monica, Ourselves

The Clinton Affair and the National Interest

Edited by
LAUREN BERLANT AND LISA DUGGAN

NEW YORK UNIVERSITY PRESS
New York and London

NEW YORK UNIVERSITY PRESS
New York and London

© 2001 by New York University

Library of Congress Cataloging-in-Publication Data
Our Monica, ourselves : the Clinton affair and the national interest /
edited by Lauren Berlant and Lisa Duggan.
p.   cm. — (Sexual cultures)
ISBN 0-8147-9865-9 (alk. paper) — ISBN 0-8147-9864-0 (pbk. : alk. paper)
1. Clinton, Bill, 1946– —Sexual behavior. 2. Clinton, Bill, 1946– —
Impeachment. 3. Lewinsky, Monica S. (Monica Samille), 1973– 4. Political
culture—United States. 5. Culture conflict—United States. 6. Sex—
Social aspects—United States. 7. Sexual ethics—United States. 8. United
States—Social conditions—1980– 9. United States—Politics and government—
1993– 10. United States—Moral conditions.   I. Berlant, Lauren Gail, 1957–
II. Duggan, Lisa, 1954– III. Title. IV. Series.
E886.2 .O96 2001
973.929'092—dc21   00-012212

New York University Press books are printed on acid-free paper,
and their binding materials are chosen for strength and durability.

Manufactured in the United States of America

10 9 8 7 6 5 4 3 2 1

Contents

Acknowledgments

We would like to thank Eva Pendleton, Alison Redick, and Micol Seigel for research assistance, Sexual Cultures series editors José Muñoz and Ann Pellegrini for their enthusiastic encouragement, and Eric Zinner and Cecilia Feilla of New York University Press for technical support and editorial savvy.

Introduction

Lauren Berlant and Lisa Duggan

It was a moment of astounding incoherence. The Clinton affair—the sex, the lying, the investigation, the impeachment—was a historic public event, yet central to it was a debate about whether it was worthy of attention. Had politics and prurience become identical, and whose fault was that? All parties—the press, the public, the political parties, the president and his prosecutors—hurled charges that the others were up to their necks in corruption. People scurried to find the moral high ground, but then again it seemed that we were drowning in moral high grounds, too. In the wake of the deluge of publicity and contradictory evaluation produced by the Clinton/Lewinsky affair and its aftermath, *Our Monica, Ourselves* seeks a medium-range perspective—offering reflective, after-the-fact assessments by politically progressive journalists, scholars, and activists addressed to the questions: How does the intersection of sex and politics shape U.S. public culture? What can the alternating waves of public obsession, revulsion, and boredom generated by this scandal of sex and justice tell us about the national interest?

In another time, the sexual scandal in the political sphere that organizes this book might have taken on a mythic aura. "Did she put on his knowledge with his power/Before the indifferent beak could let her drop?" asked Yeats about Leda and

1

Zeus. But in the contemporary United States, the compromising positions of bodies in power have tended toward farce, not tragedy; ordinariness, not myth. Indeed, that very aspect of the scandal, the revelation of ordinariness where greatness should be, is at the heart of the problem the Clinton/Starr/Lewinsky/Jones follies present to us. Shocked, we were shocked. Not surprised at all, really—what did you expect about politicians in general, or Clinton in particular? The analytic challenge posed by the scandal is that so much of its implication seems "obvious." On the other hand, the whole thing defies common sense. This anthology queries the common sense that was passionately, but often incoherently, asserted during the trials of Bill Clinton.

Since the ascent of Reaganite conservatism, questions of the relation between a politician's moral and political character and that of the nation have been posed frequently, in melodramatic tones. Does the United States have an official national sexuality, and should it? Is the U.S. not secular after all, but obliged to sustain the founders' Christian vision? What is the function of the political media, other than to produce more evidence of a decline *somewhere*, in the presidency, the Congress, the courts, the media, the body politic, and/or feminism? The disaster scene was addictive, like monitoring a hostage crisis or rubbernecking on the highway. Someone else seemed always to be failing, falling. Something was always turning up, or disappearing. Startling images produced a need for clarifying wisdom. It felt imperative to have an opinion.

This anthology emerged from a number of sources of irritation with what ensued in the public sphere. One irritant was the way the sexuality of the Clinton scandal enabled long-term political differences to be played out as distinctions of moral hierarchy. It became plausible to think that moral disgust was a politically serious enough response to warrant the president's impeachment *and* the Democrats' taint by his odor of immorality, such that politicians were virtually forced to testify to their revulsion at the president, not for his reckless prevarications but for his abomination. It was also irritating to witness conservative notions of sexual normalcy and propriety taken for granted in the public sphere, when we deem them to be open for debate. Moreover, the conservative framing of what this crisis means—for the presidency, for women, for the nation—so saturated the public discussion with contrasts between the moral Republicans in Congress and the immoral president that serious questions about their political *similarity* were drowned out during the period between Paula Jones's public accusation and the impeachment proceedings.

After all, during the eight years of the Clinton administration, from 1993 through 2000, contradictory moral melodramas dominated the national spectacle. The Official First Marriage, bolstered by Clinton's support of the Congressional Defense of Marriage Act, contrasted with the adulterous details supplied through government investigation in the Starr Report. The titular head of the state, constitutionally separated from the church, attempted to repair the damage of such exposed contradiction through confession, prayer, and invocations of the redemption of sin through Christian morality. At the same time, many feminists supported the president's right to sexual privacy and insisted that his consensual affair with an intern did not constitute sexual harassment, while the open secret of the president's sexual patterns *and* many of his policies might have shaken the Sphinx's confidence in Clinton's claim to be feminist.

This schizophrenia was supplemented by the ambivalence of mass commercial culture, mainstream media pundits, and the "public opinion" said to be measured by national poll results. The classic strategies of scandal reporting allowed public denunciations of "immorality" and avowals of mass boredom to coexist with saturation publicity, highlighting every available salacious detail. Conservatives seized the opportunity to argue that sexuality should be something that happens between husbands and wives; in the absence of marital sexual constraints, they claimed that moral disorder threatens the nation. The relentless investigation and exposure of presidential sexuality led, among moral conservatives of the religious right and in the Republican party, to the public shaming and hounding of sinners, a strategy that eventually backfired on the many sinners among the faithful. Meanwhile, across the political "center" in U.S. electoral politics and mainstream media culture, the response was to call for a clear boundary between public and private—between significant questions of national policy and distracting if not trivial issues of private behavior. In the final years of the Clinton presidency, this position developed a more flexible appendage: if Bill Clinton's sexual practices and deceptions make him a bad man, that is a private matter; nonetheless, he has been a good centrist president.

We also found these instances of common sense baffling. What about "the personal is the political?" We looked for the progressive/left analysis of the Clinton presidency and its scandal-ridden denouement. Oddly but unsurprisingly, amid the avalanche of publication on these events, we have heard little from the cultural/political left in the political public sphere. It is our argument that many readers have not been able to receive the Clinton affair outside of the conventions of the corporate news media, with its particular notions of what an issue is and who is an authority.

Our Monica, Ourselves is conceived as a progressive forum for thinking through the largest cultural, political, and public-policy issues raised by the spectacle of national investigation, worldwide publicity, political contestation, sexual scandal, and congressional impeachment proceedings surrounding the Clinton/Lewinsky affair. The essays included here abundantly illustrate the lack of a common sense or consensus among the sometimes overlapping, sometimes conflicting analyses of the feminist and queer writers, progressive journalists and activists, leftist scholars, and cultural critics we solicited for this volume. Is Bill Clinton a good or a bad man, in the terms of progressive/feminist ethics? Was he a good or a bad president for the left? Where should historians begin the tale of national sexuality, morality, and political struggle that culminated in this scandal? There is no agreement among us on these points, nor even any agreement that these *are* the important points. Such disagreements are crucially productive now, as Clinton leaves office and the political public sphere narrows and entrenches the terms and focus of analysis.

We want this volume to reopen the question of the event. What is this "scandal" a case of? The case is not only about persons, the presidency, celebrity culture, or law. It is also a moment of stunning confusion in norms of sexuality; of fantasies of national intimacy—what constitutes "ordinary sex" and "ordinary marriage," let alone the relation between law and morality, law and justice. It may be a perverse eruption of Clintonian international and economic policy; a sign of the historical persistence of anti-state feeling; a moment to question the relevance of "public opinion" to the political world that solicits it; a cultural text for historians of heterosexuality, masculinity, or feminism; a keyhole into white-collar bureaucracy or feminine sexuality. It resonates historically with the coupling of political and sexual crises in many textual and geographical domains. The essays in this volume address these issues and many others. They range from short thought-pieces to in-depth analyses, and examine the nexus of politics and the state, the media and culture industries, the politics of gender and sexuality, and the clashing class and race-inflected public languages of religion and "values," love and economics, law and decorum, and feminism.

We call this volume *Our Monica, Ourselves* for a number of reasons. We arrive at this moment from a long history of feminist discussion: just as *Our Bodies, Ourselves* is a guide from a feminist health movement that enables women to encounter their sexuality away from the alienating terms of standard medical practice, *Our Monica, Ourselves* expresses a set of frustrations about the continued humiliation of anyone who is publicly sexualized in the United States. In a social context that simultaneously overvalues and devalues sex and sexuality, as ours does, there is little room in the standard media to negotiate for a sexual ethics or political analysis that includes serious respect for unfamiliar or nonnormative forms of sexuality. Part of the purpose of *Our Monica, Ourselves* is to contribute to a nonnormalizing history of sexuality, a story about sexuality that reads its implication in social forces not ordinarily associated with sex.

In part 1, historians and political and cultural theorists debate the role of the president as a foil or a spur to democratic forces in U.S. politics, and consider the place of the Clinton/Lewinsky scandal and the congressional vote for impeachment in recurring symbolic contests and national culture wars. Eli Zaretsky, Dana Nelson, and Tyler Curtain focus on the democratic/antidemocratic tensions of presidential governing, and on the psychodynamics of dominant forms of authority and citizenship. In part 2, the essays start from the traffic in tasteless jokes that extended the scandal into unpredicted spaces of everyday life. The very publicness of the sexual and legal rhetoric that saturated the airwaves enabled a proper teller to say something raunchy or punchy and then, innocently, to ask, whose fault was it anyway, whose excesses of fascination produced these jokes, as though Starr/Clinton/Lewinsky/Jones forced us to play with their exposure? Laura Kipnis's "The Face That Launched a Thousand Jokes" zeroes in on Linda Tripp; James Kincaid considers the *un*sexiness of the sex and body parts endlessly recirculated for public voyeurism; Simone Davis analyzes the circuits of pleasure energized through secrecy and exposure; and Sasha Torres hilariously recounts the tortured history of sexual norms in television broadcasting. Toby Miller considers the public meanings of the president's private member.

Part 3 refracts the Clinton presidency and the events leading to impeachment through the lens of race and class. Fred Moten and B. Jenkins narrate the complexly contradictory reception of Bill Clinton's racial politics among African Americans, while Micki McElya exposes the class dimensions of antagonism in portrayals of the excesses of the first white-trash presidency. Marjorie Garber tracks responses to Monica Lewinsky's Jewishness, and Tomasz Kitlinski, Pawel Leszkowicz, and Joe Lockard approach events through transnational fantasies of sexual intrigue and ghosts of international conspiracy. Part 4 examines the ethical and moral questions confronting progressive left, feminist, and queer cultural critics and policy analysts as we sort out the long-term meanings of the scandal-marred history of the Clinton presidency. Eric Clarke, Janet Jakobsen, and Anna Marie Smith contemplate ways that a fuller understanding of sexuality might balance our assessments of history and dreams of a collective future.

Part 5 closes the volume with an extended discussion of the feminist meanings of the Clinton/Lewinsky affair. Catharine Lumby and Ellen Willis consider the implications of the sex scandal for feminist mappings of public and private, and Ann Cvetkovich reads the Starr Report as an archive of the practice of heterosexuality in the wake of feminism. Jane Gallop explores the migrating meanings of "sexual harassment" as this concept moves from a feminist to a right-wing slogan.

These essays are casually written and densely argued, personally specific and broadly general. They represent a range of views across the political/cultural left, with a shared interest in grasping the big picture of change and conflict at once displayed, compressed, and displaced within the terms of this "sex scandal." The volume as a whole is conceived as a collective case study of a yet unfinished moment, a moment that began before the Lewinsky affair and will not come to a conclusion at its legal closure.

Part 1

DEMOCRACY AND PRESIDENTIALISM

1 The Culture Wars of the 1960s and the Assault on the Presidency

The Meaning of the Clinton Impeachment

Eli Zaretsky

The impeachment of William Jefferson Clinton was one of those extraordinary historical events whose nature historians will debate for centuries.[1] Among the problems they will have to address are the Republicans' motivations, the chasm between the electorate and the normally dominant media elites, and the Republicans' remarkable achievement—if we can call it that—in turning Clinton's Paula Jones deposition into a protracted national emergency. The problem of the Republicans' motivations is particularly vexed since, while it was unfolding, impeachment blatantly contradicted political calculations and, afterward, resulted in the collapse of the conservative movement's pretense to hegemony. Of course, any explanation will be preliminary. But in my view, it will be easier to solve these problems if we situate the impeachment in at least two overlapping historical contexts: the long-term reaction to the cultural revolutions launched in the sixties (feminism, gay liberation, multiculturalism, etc.), and a discrete series of attacks, dating from the thirties, on the presidency as the democratic moment in modern politics.

Stephen Greenblatt, Anthony Lewis, John Judis, Michael Ignatieff, and many other commentators have noted the similarities between the impeachment and the Salem witch trials of the seventeenth century.[2] The appeal of this analogy

9

lies in its attempt to explain the irrationality of the Republican actions. As Paul Boyer and Stephen Nissenbaum demonstrated in their 1974 *Salem Possessed*, those who supported the persecution of witches lived in the poorer and more remote precincts of Salem Village. While their initial targets were social outcasts they later turned to their more prosperous fellow villagers who had ties to commerce and the sea. Witches were scapegoats; the trials were an irrational, persecutory response to anxieties unleashed by late seventeenth century commercialization and individuation.[3]

Similarly, it is plausible to argue, the Republicans spoke for white, male, rural, suburban, and southern constituencies threatened by the social and cultural changes unleashed since the 1960s. Their real targets, never far from their words, but also never directly acknowledged, were women's emancipation, sexual emancipation, cultural "relativism," secularization, and pluralism. Clinton, the out-of-control dope-and-sex fiend, was their scapegoat. If they could have gotten rid of him, a whole reign of persecutions in such areas as abortion, education, and government would have followed.

While this explanation certainly has merit, there was a second current to the impeachment drive that received less attention. This lies in the specific history of the United States right wing, whose origins date to the late 1930s opposition to Franklin D. Roosevelt and the New Deal. To understand this opposition requires a perspective on the history of the presidency. It is one of the most powerful institutions ever created—and not only because the United States is powerful. Those who wrote the Constitution put the president in place of the king, as a symbol of national unity and moral identity. Whereas in parliamentary systems such as England the monarch or president divides authority with a prime minister, in the United States the president is simultaneously the chief executive officer and the symbol of the nation. Over time, due to the uniquely pluralist—multiethnic, multireligious, and multicultural—character of American society, the president emerged, along with the Constitution and the Supreme Court, as one of the few loci of centripetal authority.[4]

The intentions of those who wrote the Constitution were conservative. Contrary to those intentions, however, the presidency became the center of democratic aspirations. This shift began during the presidency of Andrew Jackson (1828–1836), but its true origins lie in the Civil War. Then, as Abraham Lincoln argued against Stephen Douglas, the nation had to take a stand on a fundamental moral issue, namely slavery. The end of the war saw the creation of *national* citizenship, by virtue of which the executive branch of government can and must intervene to guarantee due process against local or state practices. In the late nineteenth century, the mass politics that developed with industrialization increasingly focused on the presidency. The political scientist Gwendolyn Mink tells of an Italian stowaway captured while trying to enter the United States in the 1890s, who knew only one word of English: "McKinley."[5] But the most fundamental transformation of the American presidency into the vehicle of democratic strivings occurred during the New Deal.

The New Deal launched a genuine and continuing social and cultural revolution, at first centered on the working class and the immigrants. While there were nineteenth-century predecessors for the American right wing, notably in "states' rights," secession, and the Confederacy, as well as in the legal profession, the American right active in the impeachment episode was born in opposition to the New Deal and, specifically, to the enhanced role of the president that it fostered. Thus, the Republican attempt to roll back the cultural changes initiated in the sixties was part of a longer history, one aimed at retarding democratic change in general.

Republican actions, situated within this context, have also been subjected to depth psychological analysis. Following Freud's well-known argument in *Totem and Taboo*, Jonathan Lear argued that Clinton, as the first member of his generation to become president, needed to reassure his followers that he was leading from "within the group"—in other words, as one "brother" among many. Instead, many took Clinton to be foolishly flaunting his ability to transgress the rules—to avoid the draft, to smoke grass, and to possess every woman who caught his eye. Childishly brandishing "the presidential penis"—this is Lear's characterization—Clinton awakened infantile, unconscious fears of a powerful father figure who lives outside norms. Even more disturbing, he awakened omnipresent and ubiquitous desires to be that figure. Writing amid the furor of the impeachment hearings, Lear pointed to the Christian iconography that haunted it—for example, the intense anger at Clinton for failing to apologize properly, an act that would turn his antisocial exhibitionism and public soiling into a reaffirmation of the group's collective self-suppression. Only through proper contrition could Clinton bring about the ritual cleansing of what the *New York Times* obsessively called the "hallowed rooms" at the White House.[6]

In one sense, Lear's stress on paternal authority deepened the meaning of the ritual sacrifice, cleansing, and rebirth that the impeachment enacted. The scapegoating of the witches, as described by Boyer and Nissenbaum, is actually a subcase of the scenario put forth in *Totem and Taboo*. Freud's view in that work was that the murder of the primal father—the founding moment of human society and the one that institutes the incest taboo—initiated a series of ritual reenact-ments aimed at preserving the social contract. Accordingly, symbolic fathers or fa-ther substitutes—for example, sons such as Jesus—were sacrificed to affirm the rule of the church or monarch. The mass, or other rituals, reenacted the founding moment. Similarly, in Salem, the witches were scapegoated to affirm the author-ity of ministers. One particularity of the New England example, which explains its special resonance with the impeachment, lies in the *weakness* of the ministers and their cause. A fuller study would have had to explain why the vast majority of in-creasingly secular and commercial New Englanders allowed a handful of religious bigots to have their way, just as we will have to address a similar problem in the case of the impeachment. *Totem and Taboo* provides the necessary clue. The sacri-fice is tolerated because it promises to expiate a collective guilt.

In another sense, however, Lear lost a critical subtext of the witchcraft analogy. Following Freud, who portrayed the origins of society as the banding of the brothers against the father, Lear described impeachment as an all-male event. In contrast, female scholars such as Lynn Hunt, Joan Landes, and Carol Pateman have demonstrated the central role of gender difference in founding historical moments such as the seventeenth- and eighteenth-century English and French revolutions, and of the importance of misogyny in sparking the counterrevolution.[7] In my view, the 1960s were a period of revolutionary social and cultural transgression, akin to that of the great democratic revolutions and undertaken by women along with men. The conservative counter reaction to the 1960s, such as the impeachment, was importantly aimed at women and at Clinton as a man who had aligned himself with women. As in the past, the ulti-mate if unconscious aim of the counterrevolution was to reestablish the father's role as enforcer of the incest taboo, the task Clinton was perceived as abrogating in his affair with Lewinsky.

In general, then, it is worth situating the impeachment in the context of the changing meaning of presidential—and paternal—authority. In Roosevelt's time, the president led the way against a set of sacred shibboleths: the "free" market, the Social Darwinian "laws of nature," the right of the rich to their riches. Though a patrician, Roosevelt led from "within the group"—industrial workers, blacks, women, ethnics, southern whites, union members, Jews, enlightened business-men, and the like. In doing so he helped his followers overcome feelings of defer-ence, fears of authority, and systematically weakened self-esteem. The results were the almost revolutionary changes brought about by the New Deal. In the 1960s, the executive branch of government became the focal point for a new series of struggles—against racism, sexism, and homophobia—which both continued and diverged from the economic struggles of the previous epoch. A new leadership had to preserve the gains made in the New Deal era as well as repudiate additional shibboleths, for example the naturalness of a particular family norm. However, this task was complicated by a basic difference between the 1930s and the 1960s. Whereas the New Deal was the democratic response to a *unifying national* project, namely Fordist industrialization, democratic leaders since the 1960s have had to seek support among *globalized* social forces that often pushed *against* one another. Globalization actually intensified the focus on a symbolic private sphere in which the struggle between social forces seemed to be enacted. As a result, the attack against presidential authority—to which Clinton irresponsibly opened himself— and the scapegoating of Clinton as a symbol of sixties' culture converged. Or so I shall argue in what follows.

Before Roosevelt's inauguration as president in 1933, the national government, as V. O. Key later noted, "had been a remote authority with a limited range of activity. It operated the postal system, improved rivers and harbors, [and] maintained armed forces on a scale fearsome only to banana republics [*sic*]."[8] The New Deal transformed it into an active and powerful collection of offices, comprising about one-third of the national economy, able to intervene in unparalleled ways in institutions that were defined as private, but which were actually organized through tradition, the market, and the corporations.[9] The presidency was the pivot of this change. Three aspects of the transformed presidency were particularly important for understanding the Republican drive against Clinton.

First, the New Deal freed the presidency from party control, by basing the president's new powers on direct (i.e., charismatic) communication with the masses, and on command of a vast bureaucracy. Early twentieth century presidents, notably Theodore Roosevelt and Woodrow Wilson, certainly enhanced presidential authority, especially in the sphere of foreign affairs. But only with the New Deal, did the president, the focus of mass aspirations, replace Congress, the seat of party organization, in initiating and framing legislation. The budget became the instrument of national planning, and the party system began to decline. Franklin Roosevelt actually ran against his own party members when they opposed his program, thus trying to turn the national Democratic party into an ideological party—the "party of liberalism," as he called it.[10] By the time he left office the presidency had been transformed into a unique synthesis of popular rule and administrative power.[11]

Second, the president's new authority helped legitimate an enormously expanded sense of entitlement. In 1935, a recent immigrant, Mrs. Olga Ferk, wrote to President Roosevelt complaining that she had been mistreated at her relief station, was only $19 behind in her government H.O.L.C. mortgage payments, not three months as accused, and that her son's Civilian Conservation Corps check was always late in arriving. "How long is this rotten condition going to last?" Mrs. Ferk demanded. "I am at the end of the rope. The rich get richer and the poor can go to -H- that is what it looks like to me. . . . Let's have some results." Mrs. Ferk's assumption that the national government owed her family relief, a mortgage, and employment was as unprecedented as her letter, which reflected a new, personal relation to the president.[12] In fact, before 1933, one person handled all the White House mail. By 1945 there were fifty. Of course, the presidency empowered groups as well as individuals. The great mass-production union organizing drives of the 1930s—steel, rubber, oil, electricity, autos—proceeded under the slogan "the President wants you to join a union."

Finally, the New Deal tended to promote a pluralist and secular presidency. Before the New Deal, American politics, culture, and especially reform were deeply Protestant. Even the progressive reformers of the early twentieth century were preoccupied with individual virtue and vice. The New Deal, by contrast, substantially based on Catholic and Jewish ethnic voters, was essentially secular in its orientation.[13] Often misdescribed as technocratic or "pragmatic," it elevated universal, secular ideals, such as freedom from want or (later) international justice, over moralizing, quasi-Protestant slogans, such as the progressive era's "beloved community."[14] Among Roosevelt's first acts was the repeal of the quintessential progressive moral reform, namely prohibition. The Republican attack on the presidency and on the sense of popular entitlement was also an attack on freedom of religion, the original source of all liberalism.

In spite of the New Deal's universalist, secular character, however, it was conservative in regard to gender. Roosevelt was a great father figure because he could appeal to the traditional, working-class family and community, then a source of refuge and strength for women as well as men. That option was no longer available to democratic presidents who served in the wake of the 1960s. It is true that against the background of a societywide rebellion against authority in general, Lyndon Johnson's "Great Society" sought to give new meaning to the democratizing changes of the New Deal by reaching out to blacks and by creating a third vast universalist continent of entitlements alongside education and social security, namely Medicare and Medicaid.[15] Beginning with his 1964 speech at the University of Michigan, Johnson followed his mentor, Franklin Roosevelt, in seeking to place the executive in the forefront of the new forces of democratic change: civil rights, women's rights, consumer and environmental groups.

But in spite of good intentions, Johnson failed. The essential reason, as I have suggested, was the change in the social basis for democratic reform. The New Deal brought its supporters together around the goal of subjecting mass-production capitalism to limited forms of democratic control. The goal of using federal authority to regulate capitalism did not disappear in the 1960s, but the sixties witnessed the beginnings of a globalized and computerized economy, then figured as the "multinational corporations," "cybernetics," and "automation." By the seventies, the nation-state's role as the framework for collective agreements, entitlements, and redistributive policies, or what was broadly termed Keynesianism, began to weaken. Simultaneously, the traditional family, centered on paternal authority, gave way to forms of personal life that could no longer be defined by the traditional family or the economy.[16] The New Deal strategy of turning identity conflicts into economic compromises became less and less viable. The Rooseveltian coalition began to divide: white southerners from northern liberals; blacks from Jews; women from men. Toward the second half of his presidency, Johnson found himself deeply saddened by the "disconnection" that ghetto blacks felt with the rest of society, as if they "weren't part of the world as we know it."[17] The night of March 31, 1968, when Johnson announced his decision not to seek reelection, has been described as "the moment when the old coalition gave way to the new fragmentation, when the old politics gave way to the new."[18]

One other change set in motion during the 1960s is important to understanding the impeachment. The importance of coalition politics was largely replaced by the media. Much earlier, Woodrow Wilson described the "extraordinary isolation" of the presidency, reflecting the degree to which presidential power depended on the shifting foundations of public opinion and on the play of interest groups.[19] Beginning in the sixties, a vast extension of television, talk radio, direct mail, telecommunications, pollsters, media consultants, focus groups, along with the burgeoning of a culture of personal revelation, increased that dependence.[20] This was the situation when William Clinton was sworn into office in 1993, the first president since the sixties to articulate even a modest democratic agenda.[21]

Just as the New Deal presidency provides the inevitable start for understanding Clinton, so it provides the starting point for understanding his opponents on the right. Before the New Deal, there was no right-wing movement in the United

States. "Conservatism," as exemplified by such a figure as Joseph Cannon, Speaker of the House during Theodore Roosevelt's presidency, or by the "neanderthal" businessmen whom Theodore Roosevelt castigated, upheld the status quo against reform, but it was more a climate of opinion than a movement. The contemporary American right, by contrast, emerged as an oppositional movement. It was born when southern Democrats deserted the New Deal coalition during the congressional elections of 1938 over such issues as Roosevelt's toleration of the sit-down strikes, northern support for antilynching legislation, and "Wages and Hours" legislation (the immediate precipitant). Even though later figures such as Ronald Reagan and Newt Gingrich sometimes paid lip service to the New Deal, a core feature of the American right has been its attack on the presidency and on the executive branch of government.

Originally, this stance was the reason for the right's minority status. Herbert Hoover's insistence in the midst of the Depression that the New Deal was a form of "national regimentation" akin to fascism was too absurd to garner much support.[22] Although there was considerable interest in such works as Friedrich Hayek's *The Road to Serfdom* (1944), which defended the market against planning, and Russell Kirk's Burkean *The Conservative Mind* (1953), they were essentially regarded as curiosities. After all, the vast expansion of the middle classes after World War II depended primarily on government programs such as the G.I. Bill, federal mortgage insurance, the interstate highway system (which subsidized the suburbs), and the building of state and community colleges. For most Americans, to support the right's antigovernment agenda would be to saw off the branch on which they had just recently and uncertainly perched.

The first step in the right's evolution toward hegemonic aspirations was the anti-Communism of the 1950s. To be sure, the Dies Committee, the immediate predecessor to the House Un-American Activities Committee, was founded in 1938 by anti-Roosevelt Democrats. But Cold War ideology, emblematized in Whittaker Chambers's *Witness* (1952), gave the attack on the New Deal a religious basis, as well as affirming its paranoid view of government. How, other than by invoking the specter of an external enemy, could poor southern whites or working-class ethnics, desperately in need of government support, be brought into an antigovernment coalition with right-wing oil interests and Sunbelt entrepreneurs?[23] The McCarthy period also witnessed the first twentieth-century turn toward the use of impeachment as a political weapon in the right wing's campaign to impeach Earl Warren, an action aimed less at the Supreme Court than at the federal government's support for school integration and civil liberties. As an antigovernment coalition, McCarthyism also encouraged extralegal forces such as the John Birch Society and the White Citizens Councils.[24]

Even given the power of anti-Communism, the right remained a minority in American politics until the same processes of deindustrialization and globalization that destroyed the New Deal coalition created an opening for it. Richard Nixon, president from 1968 to 1974, was unusual among conservatives in that he advocated old-fashioned, Disraeli-style governmental reforms. Nonetheless, he and his advisers grasped the significance of the breakup of the New Deal. In 1972, his speech writer, Pat Buchanan, reminded him that he had to "make permanent the New Majority" that had elected him, one that combined the "Nixon South" with the "ethnic, blue collar, Catholic, working class Americans of the North, Midwest and West."[25] Equally blatant appeals to white people characterized Kevin Phillips *The Emerging Republican Majority* (1970), which attributed the collapse of the New Deal coalition to "the Negro socio-economic revolution."[26] In addition, many of those set adrift by the breakup of the New Deal were attracted to a revived and politicized Christian evangelism.[27] Superchurches, which often competed with government in providing social services such as day care, counseling and education, electronic ministries, and grassroots political lobbying, ensconced the Christian right in the Republican party. It is well known that right-wing sentiment grew in reaction to the civil rights movement, to feminism and gay liberation, and to what came to be called secular humanism, but it is not as often recognized how much the idea that the federal government was imposing these changes contributed to that growth.

Finally, globalization created not only an opening for antigovernment sentiment, but a dominant capitalist interest in the same. Of all the groups deserting the New Deal coalition, the most important was not the white South but rather business, which, led by the Business Roundtable, used the threat of global competition and "decreasing productivity" to renegotiate the relations between business, labor, and government.[28] All three strains—anti-Communism, evangelical antisecularism, and neoliberalism—converged in the Reagan presidency, the only presidency recognized by the right as its own. Its central motif was the attack on presidential power, literally incarnated in the vacuous non-person who occupied the office. In his 1981 inaugural address, no less, Reagan proclaimed "in the present crisis, government is not the solution to our problem; government is the problem."[29] In order to eliminate that problem, his administration saddled the nation with a $4 trillion budget deficit, a deficit that stretched "as far as the eye can see," in the words of his budget director, David Stockman.

In spite of Reagan's popularity, the right's attack on the federal government never attained majority status. The defeat of the nomination of Robert Bork for the Supreme Court in 1987 signaled the surprising weakness of the right. During the presidency of George Bush, free-market conservatives pushed aside social conservatives who responded by repudiating Bush for breaking his "no new taxes" pledge, supposedly a "character" issue.[30] The ending of the Cold War eliminated the right's main raison d'être. Its marginality was dramatically apparent in the broad, popular revulsion at the "pro-family," culturally conservative posturing of Pat Buchanan and the Quayles at the 1992 Republican convention. In retrospect, neither the election of a liberal/centrist Democrat as the first post–Cold War president in 1992, nor the intensely focused and deeply irrational minority assault against him, should have been a surprise.

Clinton's problem, then, was to "reinvent" the presidency in a context of massive cultural change, Democratic party factionalization, an overwhelming media presence in American life, and a resentful and angry minority. As a product of the sixties, he brought particular attributes to this task. For one thing, he had a deep, personal need for politics and for the public sphere. Ever since the sixties, the right's onslaught had been directed not only against the presidency but against politics and collective activity in general. Outside religion, everything was being privatized. Clinton's deep hunger for human contact, for deliberation, and for action in the Arendtian sense corresponded to a felt deprivation among large numbers of Americans and was a major source of his appeal, as well as a target for sarcasm and contempt.

A second attribute lay in his attitude toward morality. Clinton behaved as if morality was one consideration that must be weighed along with others such as compassion, realism, prudence, respect for difference, and so forth; it was not always and necessarily the most important. Of course, this occasionally allowed for trimming. Nonetheless, in a country that sometimes seemed polarized between left-wing political rectitude and right-wing Christianity, both of which minimized the difference between the private and the political, Clinton embodied a progressive alternative. The public's wish to have done with a politics of personality and moralism—the politics that ended Gary Hart's candidacy in 1988—had been dramatically demonstrated during the 1992 presidential campaign when, against all the pundit's predictions, it backed Clinton after the Gennifer Flowers episode, and again after his waffling over the draft. Clinton's support actually rose after the Flowers revelations. These incidents anticipated the public's ability to resist right-wing attempts to stampede it in the Monica Lewinsky affair. At the same time, both his *need* for public life and his sometimes confused explanations for his actions drew attention to his vulnerability.[31] Clinton's enemies sensed his weakness and it aroused them.

The conventional wisdom, as summarized recently by Lars-Erik Nelson, is that Clinton had "no large vision."[32] In fact, he entered Washington with far more of a vision than Franklin Roosevelt had when he was elected in 1933 on a promise to balance the budget by cutting government expenses. What Clinton lacked was not a vision, but the support of a social movement and some breathing space from the Reagan-Bush budget deficit. Clinton's view, repeatedly asserted to the Democratic Leadership Council, was that the Democratic party had been reduced to a collection of interest groups such as labor, blacks, women, and gays.[33] Clinton claimed that the party could gain broader support if it distinguished government investment, such as health, education, and research, from government spending, especially for military purposes. Situated in the context of the account of globalization laid out in Robert Reich's *The Work of Nations* (1991), and supported by many business leaders such as Democrat Felix Rohatyn and Republican John Young, Clinton proposed to attract globally mobile capital by government investment in "human capital": education, children's programs, infrastructure, worker training, health care.[34] The ending of welfare "as we know it" was originally situated in that context, and as such had genuine support from many African Americans.[35]

Accordingly, Clinton's presidency began by proposing the most extensive social program since the sixties, including family leave (albeit unpaid), economic stimulus, and national health care. But the factionalization of his core constituencies, along with his own inexperience, impulsivity, and disorganization, got him off to a weak start. He had more obligations than supporters. Much of his first year was taken up by what George Stephanopolous called "an overactive desire to appease our liberal base with appointments because we couldn't deliver on policy."[36] Clinton's desire to symbolically support the two-career family also harmed him. He campaigned on the slogan "get two for one" and promised "an unprecedented partnership, far more than Franklin Roosevelt and Eleanor."[37] However, the Roosevelts' collaboration depended on keeping Eleanor in the sphere of extragovernmental advocacy, thus allowing Franklin to use her to test the waters on "dangerous" issues such as support for Negro sharecroppers. Hillary Clinton, by contrast, was at first practically a copresident, and thus Bill Clinton could not dissociate himself from her failures. This, in turn, weakened his ability to protect her from right-wing attacks which, in turn, weakened him.

Immediately upon Clinton's arrival in Washington, all the major power groups—the military, Congress, the bureaucracy, and the press—tested him and decided he was weak. The most convincing demonstration of "weakness" came from the military and its congressional allies after a *New York Times* article provoked Clinton into making gays in the military almost his first prominent issue. (Gay groups advising the Clinton campaign had been divided over the best timing and form for action on this front, whether through Congress or by executive order.) Simultaneously, Senate minority leader Robert Dole promised to filibuster any significant new Democratic legislation, forcing the president to obtain sixty votes for passage. Dole's disingenuous reason was that Clinton had been put in office by a minority of the electorate.[38] In February, 1993, a month after Clinton took office, Democratic senator David Boren characterized the environment surrounding Clinton as "very disturbing." Referring to a meeting with senators and House members, he noted "they were patronizing to the President. They didn't show enough deference. . . . This is popping up in other areas—in the case of the Joint Chiefs, the image that they thumbed their nose at him."[39] Furthermore, Clinton owed much of his victory to extra-Washington media such as *The Larry King Show*, MTV, and Hollywood. From the moment he arrived in Washington, the political pundits and the White House press corps regarded him as an interloper.[40] As Everett Dennis, director of the Media Center at Columbia University, noted with surprise, "there's open contempt for the Presidency with T.V. reporters saying on the air what they like and don't like—as if their opinion mattered."[41]

Clinton should have expected this kind of opposition, but the mushrooming of intense extrapolitical anti-Clintonism was less predictable. I was at a research library in 1993 and watched with growing horror as a wealthy donor to the library and a right-wing employee met each morning in the coffee room to chew over the previous day's supposed misdeeds. The source of their information was generally the editorial page of the *Wall Street Journal*, which attained a national audience during the Reagan years and routinely purveyed rumors of drug use, corruption and even murder (after Vincent Foster's suicide). Talk radio, notably Rush Limbaugh's show and Floyd Brown's *Clintonwatch*, kept survivalists, private militias, patriot groups, tax resisters, homicidal abortion-clinic activists, Paul Revere newsletter writers, Christian fundamentalists, and home schoolers roiled. The tragically mishandled Waco Raid of April 1993 further fed anti-Clinton and antigovernment paranoia. Above all, Whitewater, aimed at Hillary Clinton, provided an unending source of news opportunities, leading eventually to a congressional investigation and to the appointment of an independent prosecutor, Robert Fiske. When Fiske found nothing, the right orchestrated his replacement by Kenneth Starr. Clinton failed to understand how deep the crisis of his presidency was. Heading into the 1994 congressional elections, he touted his achievements to anyone who would listen and was "certain that 'we'd beat their ass' if he could tell everyone . . . what big changes he had made."[42]

In the absence of a Republican president, Newt Gingrich, the central figure among the Republicans in the House of Representatives, became the effective leader of the right. Combining extremist rhetoric with an overstated "vision of a technologically oriented, individualist society where government would recede and private institutions would bear the burden of philanthropy and moral uplift," Gingrich sought majority status for a "party and a movement that is based on ideas."[43] His "Contract with America," prepared for the 1994 elections, was subtitled "A Program for Responsibility" and attempted to make the Republicans an ideological party, as the Democrats had been earlier. Leaving out abortion and school prayer, it emphasized deficit reduction, term limits, and shrinking government. The key idea was to neutralize the executive branch of government by gaining control of the House. The House, Gingrich and his associates believed, "was where the political realignment of the country in favor of the Republicans would be nailed down or lost." As his close adviser, Grover Norquist, explained, "Ultimately, the House sets the pace and limits on what a President can do. Even if you have fifty-one percent of the votes in the Senate you can't control it. You need sixty votes to stop a filibuster. You rarely have that."[44]

In the 1994 elections the Democrats lost eight Senate seats and fifty-two House seats amid peace and economic growth; this loss apparently confirmed Gingrich's strategy. In the first hundred days of the new Congress, Gingrich brought all ten items of the Contract with America to a vote, losing only one of them: term limits. He celebrated with a national televised address, claiming a role for himself equal to that of the president. According to Elizabeth Drew, "The House Republicans' assault on the executive branch was to be total, on every front, and without precedent." Clinton acknowledged Gingrich's newfound authority by agreeing to his proposal that they produce a balanced budget within a fixed number of years—a decision from which a great deal followed. As Drew summarized, "Clinton and the Senate were working within Gingrich's frame of reference. The direction of the government had been turned around."[45]

In fact, the 1994 defeat created the conditions for Clinton's first attempt to

21

consolidate his presidency. While support for a transformative presidency such as Franklin Roosevelt's was never strong, support for a defensive action against the right wing was. Clinton's turn toward Dick Morris, polls and "triangulation" (i.e., cooptation of Republican issues) after 1994 was widely described as opportunism. Russell Baker wrote that "since we are being followed, not led, our followers—whom we call 'leaders'—stagger along like blind drunks, trying not to bump head-first into the lampposts."[46] But while Clinton coopted right-wing themes, he changed their meaning by linking them to centralized, democratizing power. Balancing the budget was the central example. For Gingrich it meant the limitation of governmental power; for Clinton it meant governmental authority could be used again, since it was freed from the Reagan-imposed straightjacket. Clinton agreed to the most egregious Republican programs on crime, such as the limitation on the ability of death row inmates to appeal, but he tied crime legislation to gun control. Even the abolition of welfare helped legitimate government.[47]

Clinton also benefited enormously from the bombing of the Federal Building in Oklahoma City on April 19, 1995. So powerful were the resonances between Gingrichian bombast and the explosion that Gingrich had to deny the connection. As a White House aide commented: "We tried all year to say we're the mainstream and they're the extreme. Now we can show that. Until this tragedy the Republicans felt comfortable pandering to the militia types in their rhetoric."[48] Increasingly, Clinton stressed the links between support for the federal government and the revitalization of the public sphere. In the summer of 1995, in a speech at Georgetown University, he said that politics has become "just like the rest of us, pluralized. It's exciting in some ways, but as we divide into more and more and more sharply defined organized groups around more and more and more stratified issues [we do not produce] the sort of discussion that will give us the kinds of results we need."[49] His press secretary, Mike McCurry, noted: "The President has given more and more thought about what the fundamental disconnect is between him and the public right now. People tell him that much of the public is anguished about their future, and is angry about crime, decline in moral standards, and politics. They say the Democrats have shut themselves off from the subject of values, and that he'd better get in the discussion. He wants to show that the Republicans are way off to the right on values. He's setting up the argument he wants to take into next year: what is the government's role?"[50]

As early as May 1995, Gingrich had warned of a "train wreck," meaning a government shutdown, the following fall if the budget negotiations did not proceed correctly.[51] The battle over the shutdown began in November and ended the following January. The fiscal differences were small, and economic indicators already suggested that the problem had been greatly overestimated. In December, the *Washington Post* wrote "on policy matters, congressional Republicans have utterly dominated. They have set the agenda, and President Clinton has been a bit player. By contrast, the President has completely dominated the public relations struggle. He has constantly made the Republicans look mean, petty and silly."[52] But this makes it seem that what was at stake was Clinton's status in the polls. In fact, the right had tried for years to erode the collective achievements of the New Deal by encouraging the desertion of wealthier individuals and by supporting the capitalist predators who roam under the banner "privatization." In resisting a budget deal that cut social security, Medicare, education, and job training, Clinton, one of his aides commented, "discovered his center of gravity, which was pretty close to the center of gravity of the country, and that's where he stayed."[53] The resulting reversal of Gingrich's fortunes was stunning. According to Bob Woodward, "The President's greatest strength . . . emerged from having the Republican Congress go haywire before his eyes."[54] The following November, Clinton convincingly won a second term as president.

Under earlier conditions, Clinton's victory over Gingrich would have been hailed as one of the signal turn-arounds of the century, analogous to Franklin Roosevelt's transformation of the Supreme Court, which brought constitutional legality to federal economic regulation, or to Harry Truman's 1948 presidential victory, which vindicated the New Deal. In fact, politics, in the sense of the collective determination of a common destiny, had been so evacuated of meaning that the event was trivialized. Even Clinton's supporters viewed it merely as an example of political skill, a triumph purchased at the expense of principle. But that interpretation overlooked the quasi-revolutionary nature of the Republican assault on the presidency.

The lack of a coherent social-democratic left, as well as of responsible elites, that could mediate, contextualize, and put things in perspective, along with Clinton's own immaturity, had led to the personalization of his presidency. On the one hand, Clinton often ran against his own party, so that he seemed "out for himself." On the other hand, he enraged his opponents by stealing their issues: their call to make government more efficient, their insistence on encouraging entrepreneurial incentive, their recognition of the destructive character of the welfare system, and of the legitimate desire for personal security. His very victory had rendered him more vulnerable. Prophetically, as triangulation unfolded, Press

Secretary Mike McMurry warned that leaving the Republicans issueless would prove costly: "They can only win by . . . destroy[ing] Clinton as a human being. They will do everything they can to turn him into a liar [or] cheat [or] philanderer."[55]

Even Clinton's success with the economy, which followed his defeat of Gingrich, served to intensify his vulnerability. The protestant ethic taught that wealth was a reward for hard work and self-denial. But Clinton, like the sorcerer's apprentice made famous in the 1938 Disney movie *Fantasia,* had made a pact with the devil (a.k.a. Alan Greenspan), and portable computers, VCRs, cell phones, cheap transatlantic air fares, cable TV, foreign cheeses, and mutual funds seemed to fall from the sky.[56] If the *apparently* unearned character of the new wealth was sometimes accompanied by unconscious guilt, the go-go commodification of the legal, journalistic, TV, and publishing industries provided a new outlet for aggression. Although Hillary Clinton not unreasonably described her husband's attackers as "a vast, right-wing conspiracy," the impeachment also resulted from the convergence of many discrete streams, most of which sought primarily to make a buck.[57] The main tributaries include the ex-state troopers who hoped to parlay an article in *The American Spectator* into a book to be called *The President's Women;* the small-town lawyer who first took Paula Jones's case, expecting that since its target was the president, its nuisance value might net him $15,000; Michael Isikoff, the free-lance reporter who knew that stories about sex always sold; Kenneth Starr, the obsequious Washington careerist making his way up the Republican legal-judicial hierarchy; Linda Tripp, the career civil servant, desperately seeking to turn her access to the White House into a book exposing Clinton's sex life; Lucianne Goldberg, the book agent who lived for "dish"; Robert Bork, the defeated Supreme Court nominee, one of the "elves," the right wing lawyers who secretly advised Jones's attorneys from the beginning; Matt Drudge, the Internet entrepreneur, exemplar of the new economy, who first broke the Lewinsky story; and Susan McMillan, Paula Jones's protector and the self-appointed "Media Spokes Woman" of "The Women's Coalition," a public forum for such causes as chemical castration for child molesters. Most of these individuals were committed right-wingers inflamed by Clinton-hatred, but they were also the products of an environment in which nearly everyone seemed to be getting very, very rich by buying technology stocks, real estate windfalls, literary or journalistic coups, or ridiculously inflated salaries. Why then should lawyers, writers, editors, book agents, TV newscasters, or even state troopers lose out?

Of course, nothing could have occurred had Clinton not given his enemies the opening they sought. In 1997, before the Lewinsky revelations, psychoanalyst

Stanley Renshon published an excellent study of Clinton's character stressing his "object hunger," "strategic empathy," and recurrent conflicts between ambition and ideals. But nothing in Renshon's study anticipated the extraordinary pattern of self-destructiveness and self-delusion that took shape while Clinton was president. Key moments include the recklessness of the affair itself (which began on the day of the government shutdown and effectively ended with the reopening of the government three months later), his repeated refusals to settle the Paula Jones law suit when he had the opportunity, his obvious lies at the Paula Jones deposition and in TV appearances, and his quasi-subornation of his secretary Betty Curry's testimony. Apparently, Clinton convinced himself that he hadn't had "sexual relations with that woman" because he hadn't had intercourse. Apparently, too, he consistently lied to every friend (with the possible exception of Dick Morris), to his lawyers, to his advisers, to his wife, and to his daughter. This meant that between the time that Monica Lewinsky's name appeared on the Paula Jones witness list on December 17, 1997, and Clinton's grand jury testimony on August 17, 1998, he received no advice, feedback, or consolation. When his lawyer, Bob Bennett, asked about Lewinsky before the Paula Jones deposition, Clinton responded: "Bob, do you think I'm fucking crazy? Hey look, let's move on. I know the press is watching me every minute. The right has been dying for this kind of thing from day one. No, it didn't happen."[58]

By 1996 most of the pieces that made the impeachment possible were in place. There was an irreversible cultural revolution in such areas as women's rights, homosexuality, and sexual permissiveness deeply resisted by a leaderless and recently humiliated minority. Wealth was accumulating with a minimum of toil, exertion, and privation. The designated victim had been mocked and demeaned through years of deranged accusations. His wife and even his child had become objects of public derision, without his effectively defending them. (Recall that when a music critic denigrated Harry Truman's daughter's pianistic abilities, Truman punched him.) Even the president's natural allies tended to look down on him, either because they looked down on politics or because he had failed to do what they had failed to do, namely unify the progressive forces. Nevertheless, the presidency is such an extraordinary institution, and impeachment such as an extraordinary remedy (resorted to only once before and then as an aftershock of the Civil War), that something truly extraordinary would have to occur before it could even be broached.

To grasp how this occurred, we have to descend into the realm of the collective unconscious. The starting point is the *specific* act for which Clinton was impeached, namely allowing himself to be seduced by a female employee roughly the same age as his daughter, an act which, to the collective unconscious, came across as incest. Ironically, Clinton's insistence that it "wasn't sex," along with the act's furtive, pregenital, and masturbatory aspects, reinforced this perception. Clinton's role as a (flawed) incarnation of *paternal* authority was crucial. He had associated himself with the forces of cultural revolution, feminism, gay liberation and African Americans; he had fought for symbolic appointments (Janet Reno, Madeleine Albright, James Hormel), affirmative action, and abortion rights. His opponents strove to restore an older model of patriarchal authority against all that he represented. But that program could never have found conscious support among the American people who, overwhelmingly, if mostly tacitly, welcomed the cultural changes of the sixties, along with the further loosening of mores that accompanied globalization and economic growth. What gave the impeachment drive "legs," so to speak, was that it temporarily converged, through the mechanism of overdetermination, with its seeming opposite, the feminist critique of sexual harassment and, more broadly, with the overall rejection of (paternal) authority that had erupted during the 1960s.

The sexual harassment law, on whose basis Paula Jones pressed her claim, rested on the idea that any power differential between the parties made consent problematic. To some extent, all male-female relations, and certainly "father/daughter" relations, such as the quasi-incestuous relation between Clinton and Lewinsky, had come under a cloud of suspicion. The long-overdue discovery of sexual abuse in childhood had encouraged the belief that paternal incest was commonplace. Businesses, the military, and the universities had promulgated codes forbidding consensual sex between supervisors and their subordinates. In 1995, Clinton had signed the Violence against Women Act, which made an accused rapist's entire sexual history relevant to adjudicating the charges against him, and the courts were extending this to accusations of sexual harassment. When Judge Susan Webber Wright reluctantly followed these precedents in the Paula Jones case, it allowed Clinton's opponents to turn the case into the fishing expedition that turned up Lewinsky. In his grand jury testimony, Clinton repeatedly insisted that he had engaged in consensual sex, not sexual harassment, but that distinction had little standing in law and was not fully accepted by the culture.

Even the convergence of two intense and opposed currents in the American psyche, one aimed at resurrecting patriarchal authority, the other aimed at destroying it, is not enough to answer the most important question about the impeachment—namely, how it could have occurred at all. From the time the scandal broke until the Senate acquitted Clinton, approximately one year in all, the polls never wavered: 60 percent support for Clinton, 30 percent opposed, and 10 percent undecided. No new revelation—and there were many from the right, such as the dumping of the Starr Report on Congress, the Kathleen Willey affair, the rumors of rape, and of illegitimate black children—ever budged these figures. In other words, everyone knew what they thought from the beginning. Of course, the 30 percent were highly organized while the 60 percent were not, but that is not enough to explain why the drive toward impeachment took on its irresistible quality. At some level, the majority must have felt that some kind of expiation made sense. In paying lip service to the stream of hypocrisies that led to the impeachment, the majority of Americans seemed to have believed that they could continue to conduct adulterous affairs, and enjoy, or at least aspire to, a sybaritic life style so long as they also rendered some deference to the self-appointed Puritans who surrounded them. Heroes did emerge: Barney Frank, Maxine Waters, the talk-show host Geraldo. At the conscious level, most Americans were appalled. Nevertheless, at another level, a large number assumed that a homeopathic sacrifice was warranted to purify the community. This fact reflected the overwhelming moral authority of the presidency. Even the normally well-organized, self-confident, and interconnected ruling elites of the United States—party leaders, corporate CEOs, academics, judges, and establishment newspapers like *New York Times*— somehow failed to prevent what was little more than a collective, ritualized rape.

By the time the question of impeachment reached the still Gingrich-dominated House, it unfolded like a waking dream, made up of images and decontextualized sound bites. The absurdity of the charges against Clinton made them more appropriate to a Kafka novel than to the Congress of the United States. When Barney Frank, a Democratic member of the House Judiciary Committee, pointed out that the House perjury charge failed to specify Clinton's perjurious statements—"You are embarrassed to try and unseat a twice-elected president on this degree of trivia and you have therefore used obfuscatory language"—Republican congressman Bill McCullom cited Clinton's grand jury denial that he had touched or kissed Lewinsky's breasts and genitals. "That is specifically, if anybody wants to know, where the president committed perjury." Henry Hyde, the self-pitying chair of the House Judiciary Committee, can stand for the collapse of all responsible leadership. Referring to the House members as "blue collar" when things didn't break their way in the Senate, justifying Reagan's lies in the Iran-Contra affair as intended "to serve the common good," whereas Clinton's aimed at "private pleasure" (precisely why Reagan's lies were relevant to impeachment and Clinton's weren't), Hyde broke into the hearings at one point: "Have you been to Auschwitz? Do you see what happens when the rule of law doesn't prevail?"[59] The Starr Report, which excluded all exculpatory evidence, for example of Travelgate or Filegate, made manifest the sheer procedural unfairness of the proceedings as did the secret room, maintained by David Schippers, the majority counsel, supposedly full of evidence demonstrating that Clinton had raped Juanita Broaddrick twenty years earlier. This allegation was alluded to in Republican presentations, but never presented for rebuttal or debate.

Confronted by the polls and repudiated in the 1998 elections, the leaders of the Republican party tried to appease the Clinton-hating minority. Robert Dole and Gerald Ford wrote op-ed pieces urging various measures short of impeachment. Prominent Democrats and Republicans discussed censure, apology, and fine. But all attempts at compromise were blocked by the hard-right Republican base represented in the House by majority whip Tom DeLay. In a world in which voting participation was dipping below 30 percent, the Christian right had demonstrated that it could block any Republican candidate who opposed impeachment at the primary level.[60] According to Jeffrey Toobin: "Tom DeLay lived in an entirely separate universe from the fat-cat lawyers who could once privately broker deals in line with their idea of the national interest. DeLay answered to the Christian right activists who controlled the Republican Party at the grass roots. No overture from a Bob Strauss [part of the Democrats' old guard], or even a Bob Dole, was going to change their minds."[61]

Outside of the 30 percent minority, no one *wanted* impeachment. As with all processes in which the unconscious plays a major role, it unfolded in a fatalistic manner. The Christian right's control of the Republican state parties and the Republican control of the House were necessary conditions for impeachment to occur, but they were not sufficient. As in other expressions of collective hate, such as gay bashing, lynching, the persecution of the witches, or the destruction of the European Jews, there are deep psychic connections between the active promulgators of a crime and those who seem to merely tolerate it. Republican Peter King, commenting on Robert Livingston's resignation when Livingston's affairs were outed by pornographer Larry Flynt, was reminded of Jack Ruby's killing of Lee Harvey Oswald, "the sense of national vertigo, of events spinning out of control." Dale Bumpers, in his memorable defense of Clinton in the Senate, concluded "there is a total lack of proportionality, a total lack of balance. The charge and the punishment are totally out of sync."[62] But what occurred was no accident. It was a collective sacrifice instituted by a ruthless minority, whose acts were mostly tolerated by a complicit majority because they seemed to uphold morality and law.

Like the dream that it was, it was largely forgotten the moment it was over. Still, one thing is clear. Like insects that die when they sting their prey, the impeachment broke the power that the far right exerted over public debate, although not over the Republican party. The long-term questions revolve around the general crisis in authority. The enormous and deeply positive changes in family life and sexuality that characterize our times call for new, postpatriarchal forms of authority, forms that Clinton tried to represent but couldn't. Even whether new configurations of democratic authority will emerge at the national or the global level is an open question. As such questions begin to be addressed, the impeachment of Clinton will be regarded as an important milestone.

Notes

1. My thanks to Lauren Berlant, Lisa Duggan, Nancy Fraser, and John Judis for many helpful suggestions.

2. John Judis, "Washington Possessed," *New Republic*, January 25, 1999. Stephen Greenblatt, Anthony Lewis, and Michael Ignatieff all wrote *New York Times* op-ed pieces making a similar argument.

3. Paul Boyer and Stephen Nissenbaum, *Salem Possessed* (Cambridge, Mass.: Harvard University Press, 1974).

4. The unique status of the presidency may be one of the reasons that the United States has not yet elected a female president, even though it has been one of the most women-friendly societies in the world for centuries.

5. Gwendolyn Mink, *Old Labor and New Immigrants in American Political Development: Union, Party, and State, 1875–1920* (Ithaca, N.Y.: Cornell University Press, 1986).

6. Jonathan Lear, "Freudian Slip," *New Republic*, September 28, 1998.

7. Joan B. Landes, *Women and the Public Sphere in the Age of the French Revolution* (Ithaca, N.Y.: Cornell University Press, 1988); Carol Pateman, *The Sexual Contract* (Stanford, Calif.: Stanford University Press, 1988); Lynn Hunt, *The Family Romance of the French Revolution* (Berkeley: University of California Press, 1992).

8. Quoted in William Leuchtenberg, *The Supreme Court Reborn* (New York: Oxford University Press, 1995), pp. 213–14.

9. For the one-third figure, see James O'Connor, *The Fiscal Crisis of the State* (New York: St. James Press, 1973).

10. Sidney M. Milkis, *The President and the Parties: The Transformation of the American*

Party System since the New Deal (New York: Oxford University Press, 1993). According to Theodore Lowi, Roosevelt sought to modernize the Democratic party by transforming it into "a truly programmatic national party along European lines." Theodore J. Lowi, "The Roosevelt Revolution and the New American State," in Peter J. Katzenstein, Theodore Lowi, and Sidney Tarrow, *Comparative Theory and Political Experience: Mario Einaudi and the Liberal Tradition* (Ithaca, N.Y.: Cornell University Press, 1990), p. 203.

11. That the charisma of the presidency, once established, is *relatively* independent of the individual holding the office is suggested by the example of Harry Truman.

12. Lizabeth Cohen, *Making a New Deal* (New York: Cambridge University Press, 1990), p. 252.

13. Also see John Kirby, *Black Americans in the Roosevelt Era* (Knoxville, Tenn.: University of Tennessee Press, 1980).

14. Gary Gerstle, "The Protean Character of American Liberalism," *American Historical Review*, October 1994, pp. 1043–45.

15. Corresponding to a demographic revolution as well as to a revolution in attitudes toward race, it decreased the proportion of the elderly living below the poverty line from 28.5 percent in 1966 to 12.2 percent in 1987. William C. Berman, *America's Right Turn: From Nixon to Bush* (Baltimore: Johns Hopkins University Press, 1994, 1998), p. 148.

16. Eli Zaretsky, *Capitalism, the Family and Personal Life* (New York: Harper and Row, 1976; revised and expanded edition with a new afterword, 1986); Eli Zaretsky, *Secrets of the Soul: Psychoanalysis, Modernity and Personal Life* (New York: Alfred J. Knopf, forthcoming).

17. Oral history of Sherwin Markman, quoted in Milkis, *President and the Parties*, pp. 200–201.

18. Herbert S. Parmet, *The Democrats: The Years after FDR* (New York: Macmillan, 1976), p. 248.

19. Quoted in Milkis, *President and the Parties,* p. 12.

20. By the 1970s, presidents were advised that they needed to wage "permanent campaigns," i.e., to govern as if campaigning. Sidney Blumenthal, *The Permanent Campaign: Inside the World of Elite Political Operations* (Boston: Beacon Press, 1980). In 1971, Lyndon Johnson was asked about the change in political life over the previous three decades. He answered: "You guys in the media. All of politics has changed because of you. You've broken all the machines and the ties between us in Congress and the city machines. You've given us a new kind of people." Quoted in E. J. Dionne, *They Only Look Dead: Why Progressives Will Dominate the Next Political Era* (New York: Simon and Schuster, 1996), p. 232.

21. One could argue the case for Jimmy Carter on such issues as energy and consumer protection, but on balance, and given the larger political context, I think the statement stands.

22. Herbert Hoover, *Addresses upon the American Road, 1933–1938* (New York: C. Scribner's Sons, 1938), p. 138.

23. As Freud observed, it is possible to bind disparate people together "so long as there are other people left over to receive the manifestations of their aggressiveness." Sigmund Freud, *The Standard Edition of the Complete Psychological Works of Sigmund Freud,* translated from the German under the general editorship of James Strachey, in collaboration with Anna Freud, assisted by Alix Strachey and Alan Tyson, (New York: W. W. Norton, 1953–74), vol. 21, pp. 114–16.

24. It is still not a settled issue for me whether the assassination of John F. Kennedy does not also have a place in this history. On the extralegal character of the right, Tom Wicker wrote of the first right-wing candidate to win the nomination of a major party, Barry Goldwater in 1964, that his emphasis on states rights "makes the federal government sound like a foreign power." *New York Times*, July 19, 1964.

25. Quoted in Milkis, *President and the Parties,* p. 235.

26. "The Democratic Party fell victim to the ideological impetus of a liberalism which had carried it beyond programs taxing the few for the benefit of the many [the New Deal] to programs taxing the many for the benefit of the few [the Great Society]." Kevin Phillips, *The Emerging Republican Majority* (New York: Anchor Books, 1970).

27. By contrast, the late nineteenth century development of an apolitical and antipolitical evangelicism is often referred to as the second disestablishment.

28. Productivity is a problematic concept, especially in this transition to a service economy. Nonetheless, it supposedly dropped from 3.2 percent in the 1960s to 1 percent in 1975. Corporate profits went from 13.7 percent in 1965 to 8 percent during the Nixon years (Berman, *America's Right Turn,* pp. 23, 14). The Business Roundtable was established in 1972 through the merger of the March Group, made up of chief executive officers, the Construction Users Anti-Inflation Round Table, and the Labor Law Study Committee. It awaits its historian, but see Thomas Ferguson and Joel Rogers, "The Knight of the Roundtable," *Nation* 229 (1979), pp. 620–28.

29. Ronald Reagan's first inaugural address, January 20, 1981.

30. In 1988, political scientist William Schneider wrote: "The Republicans will learn that Reaganism is a spent political force." William Schneider, "The Political Legacy of the Reagan Years," in Sidney Blumenthal and Thomas Byrne Edsall, eds., *The Reagan Legacy* (New York: Pantheon, 1988). Paul Weyrich stated in 1992: "The Reagan-Bush coalition is dead. The movement that existed has been shattered."

31. Elizabeth Drew wrote, "He didn't come across as a settled person, and the public seemed to sense that." Elizabeth Drew, *On the Edge: The Clinton Presidency* (New York: Simon and Schuster, 1994), p. 97. Consider his language in the following quote. Asked in 1992 to explain his handling of the draft issue, he replied: "In terms of whether I could have handled it differently during the campaign, I think there's no question about that. You know I'd like to explain why I didn't do such a good job of it. I didn't go back through all my letters, notes, to try and put this all back together again . . . and I think I was always kind of playing catch up because I gave a lot of answers to questions off the top of my head, halfway on the run when the press would hit me. And you don't remember everything after twenty-three years, every detail and every specific." *New York Times*, October 19, 1992.

32. Lars-Erik Nelson, "Clinton and His Enemies," *New York Review of Books*, January 20, 2000, p. 18.

33. Walter Mondale was the Democratic Leadership Council's main example of a failed Democratic politician.

34. In 1983, the Reagan administration tried to coopt democratic leadership on the issue of industrial policy by appointing John Young, the CEO of Hewlett-Packard, to a commission on competitiveness. Young's report, which advocated more government spending on worker training, civilian research and education, as well as new cabinet-level departments of trade and of science and technology, was buried by the White House. John Judis, *The Paradox of American Democracy: Elites, Special Interests and the Betrayal of the Public Trust* (New York: Pantheon, 2000), p. 184.

35. George Stephanopolous, *All Too Human: A Political Education* (Boston: Little, Brown, 1999) p. 40: "When Clinton told twenty thousand African Americans in Memphis that people on welfare must work, he got the biggest applause of the campaign."

36. Ibid., p. 143.

37. "They were two great people but on different tracks. If I get elected we'll do things together like we always have." Sheehy, quoted in Stanley Renshon, *High Hopes: The Clinton Presidency and the Politics of Ambition* (New York: New York University Press, 1996), pp. 207, 216.

38. Perot won 19% of the vote in 1992 on a program of deficit reduction.

39. Drew, *On the Edge*, pp. 198–99.

40. Clinton in 1993, at a radio and television correspondents' dinner, said: "You know why I can stiff you on press conferences. Because Larry King liberated me by giving me to the American people directly." Quoted in Stephen Hess, "President Clinton and the White House Press Corps—Year One," *Media Studies Journal* (Spring 1994), p. 4.

41. Quoted in H. Brandt Ayers, "The Death of Civility," *New York Times*, July 16, 1994.

42. James MacGregor Burns and Georgia Sorenson, *Dead Center: Clinton-Gore Leadership and the Perils of Moderation* (New York: Scribner, 1999), p. 209.

43. Dionne, *They Only Look Dead*, p. 199.

44. Elizabeth Drew, *Whatever It Takes: The Real Struggle for Political Power in America* (New York: Viking, 1997), p. 2.

45. Elizabeth Drew, *Showdown: The Struggle between the Gingrich Congress and the Clinton White House* (New York: Simon and Schuster, 1996), pp. 11, 283.

46. Quoted in Burns and Sorenson, *Dead Center*, p. 166.

47. In part, Morris sold Clinton on welfare reform with poll data purporting to show that "once you deal with welfare the whole country becomes Minnesota on race." Drew, *Showdown*, p. 287.

48. Ibid., p. 202.

49. Quoted in Burns and Sorenson, *Dead Center*, p. 327.

50. Aides described Clinton's July 1995 speeches as "common-ground speeches." Drew, *Showdown*, pp. 286–87, 333.

51. Drew, *Showdown*, p. 214.

52. Quoted in Bob Woodward, *The Choice: How Clinton Won* (New York: Simon and Schuster, 1996), p. 343.

53. Burns and Sorenson, *Dead Center*, p. 208.

54. Woodward, *The Choice*, pp. 417, 340. In the Senate, Bob Dole commented, "Clinton nailed us to the mast on the government shutdown."

55. Woodward, *The Choice*, p. 210.

56. For the relations between morality and wealth see, of course, Max Weber, *The Protestant Ethic and the Spirit of Capitalism* (New York: Routledge, 1992).

57. Hillary Clinton made her famous charge on NBC's *Today* show, January 27, 1998.

58. Jeffrey Toobin, *A Vast Conspiracy: The Real Story of the Sex Scandal That Nearly Brought Down a President* (New York: Random House, 1999), p. 167.

59. Ibid., pp. 360, 357.

60. This had been demonstrated with particular force in the California primary victory of right-winger Tom Bordanaro over moderate Republican, Brooks Firestone. In the general election, Bordanaro lost.

61. Toobin, *A Vast Conspiracy*, p. 351.

62. No one should take seriously Richard Posner's argument that the Senate's acquittal redeemed the process. Richard A. Posner, *An Affair of State: The Investigation, Impeachment, and Trial of President Clinton* (Cambridge, Mass.: Harvard University Press, 1999).

2 The Symbolics of Presidentialism

Sex and Democratic Identification

Dana D. Nelson and Tyler Curtain

This essay takes the form of a dialogue, where we explore the forms and functions of "presidentialism," an (anti-)democratic practice that one of the authors recently critiqued at length. The Lewinsky-Clinton drama tested, challenged, and ultimately exacerbated antidemocratic tendencies in our political culture's insistence that the spectacle of personal interactions at the federal level constitutes the proper limits of democracy. From different critical orientations, Dana Nelson and Tyler Curtain analyze the mechanics of presidentialism—the representative mechanism that attempts perpetually to defer our hopes for democratic self-management—as a step toward disrupting its power over our imaginations and political practices.

DN: This nation recently spent more than a year being dosed with a media blitz and public opinion polls that trained us once again to substitute the aims of political change with debates over policing someone else's morality. In this "scandal," several key trends index a weakening of public power, of what Sheldon Wolin calls our "politicalness."[1] Warnings of "constitutional crisis" diverted citizens from engaging with the reemergence of a *representational* crisis (by this I'm referring to the moment that congressional leaders invoked the principles of virtual representation even as their constituents insisted on actual representation). The terms of the impeachment drama as set by political leadership and media have moved the public even farther away from a sense that we might define and redefine the terms of political action and democratic representation. We've been so obsessed with debating presidential "responsibility" as a function of personal habits that we're more glued than ever to the habit of looking to the president both to symbolize and to manage (largely through symbolization) democracy.

My position might be a little clearer here if I elaborate on that last point.[2] It is a widely regarded patriotic "fact" that the president stands for United States democracy as its only generally elected representative. The impeachment crisis provided a prime opportunity to question the democratic value of such national common sense. Presidential historian Gary L. Gregg points out that under the Articles of Confederation, there was no single executive officer, and that "this lack of a central figure within the government was more important than most commentators and historians have noticed."[3] But the obverse is also true: the transition *to* a governmental system headed by a president, a national union embodied in the single person of the president, is more symbolically important to our practice of democracy than we habitually notice. The concept of the president was useful in early nation building, not just practically but ideologically, providing an objective correlative for the political organization of a centralized nation, a vigorous embodiment of a unified national body in a time when the confederation did not yet want to be a nation.

Whatever presidential scholars might want to say about checks and balances, it's a fact that the Constitution left the office wide open for symbolic and actual expansion. Presidential scholars and analysts complain that the constitutional allotment of power actually keeps the president comparatively "weak," that the demands put on his office by public and international expectation combine with his structural dependency on other branches to create a lot of "frustration" for the president personally. Scholars call this the "paradox" or the "ambiguity" of presidential power. But the fact is, *everyone* wants to believe the president has the power—he's not called the "most powerful man in the world" over and over to register his *weakness*.

Our collective longing for the power of the president keeps this myth alive. Presidential historian Barbara Hinckley insists that this belief has real consequences for our practice of democracy. She enumerates its key features: "Presidents, factually speaking, do not manage the economy, but it is part of the symbolism of the office that they are singularly responsible for the nation's well-being.

We speak of the president's foreign policy or economic policy, collapsing a long and complex policymaking process into the work of a single individual. We use the singular—the president—in describing what all presidents do, thereby creating the impression of specialness and incomparability."[4] And it literally doesn't matter whether individual men can live up to it. As Hinckley notes, "The more individuals are blamed for mistakes and scandals the less the office is touched . . . confidence is shaken in one president but not in the presidency."[5]

Here's a polemical way to boil down my argument: it's not the president that is the problem, it's *presidentialism*. Presidentialism is a problem for democracy because it trains us to look to the president to manage democracy. But democracy, properly defined, is *our* job. Presidentialism trains what political theorist Nancy Fraser calls a "weak public," a "public whose deliberative practice consists exclusively in opinion formation and does not also encompass decision making."[6] The impeachment debate has further encouraged us to accept that democratic participation culminates in our own personal opinion about the president's personal sexual habits. It has conditioned us to be disgusted with political leadership instead of remembering the most fundamental fact of a democratic system, that democracy happens when people have, and take responsibility for, self-governing leadership.

We could stop delegating so much democratic work away from ourselves. However banal this so-called crisis was, it has offered us a clear opportunity to do just that: to dissociate democratic work from its crippling relationship to the presidency. Instead of using this crisis simply to think about and commit to redisciplining our personal sexual values, we could use it to rethink our relationship to democracy, to democratic citizenship and democratic agency.

TC: We have been asked, by both sides of this symbolic battle, to identify with certain players as a way to understand not only what is at stake for us, but what is at stake for our democracy. That identification is structured by what might be called, for lack of a better phrase, the allegorical force of presidential heterosexuality: the supposedly paradigmatic triangulation of personal and, consequentially, constitutional relations (or in this case, betrayals) among the president, the First Lady, and the Other Woman/the People.[7] Obviously, there are cognate questions. Is the Lewinsky-Clinton scandal "simply" about "adultery" and a question of character? What is the function of sexuality in the corridors of power? How does the scandal illuminate the inner workings of presidentialism? Is this drama "straight"? These questions become important not just in relation to this scandal, but to this president's (and every other president's) presumed heterosexuality. Attending to the president's presumed sexuality helps us focus on the use of normative heterosexuality to typify citizenship symbolically. The above questions also relate the practice of identifying (or what amounts to the same thing, *wanting to identify*) with the president and the "First Family" to the function of the "family" in symbolically managing democracy.

Importantly, to my mind, discussions of sexuality and presidentialism—not only of the Lewinsky-Clinton scandal but of the equally important "Don't Ask, Don't Tell" policy, and even the insidious "Defense of Marriage Act"[8]—must incorporate an understanding of the symbolic economy of individual actions and supposed harmful, national consequences. Let me explain. In the case of Don't Ask, Don't Tell, the "harm" that is attributed to same-sex sexual activity is said to be, among other things, the "breakdown" of "cohesion" of military units (distrust among same-sex armed services personnel, for example, or paranoia and distrust among a same-sex armed unit). The consequences of sex acts by a sitting president are, on the other hand, a little more difficult to articulate, even for the most paranoid of critics. *Paranoia* then becomes the scope for articulating the meaning of an action. In fact, anyone who makes the assertion either for or against the national consequences of individual sexual actions by high-ranking officials more often than not is relying on a theory where "national security" is harmed by *any* given sexual action, whatever the context.[9]

If you accept the premise that the "American family" is, by some leap of the imagination, the basic unit of American democracy (and clearly many people do), then Clinton's actions strike at our very democracy. As democracy is practiced in our country, with presidentialism at the heart of how we imagine our relationships to our own governance, any disruption in the façade of normative sexuality as exemplified by the First Family does in fact make it difficult to mobilize the "family" as the primary unit of democracy and citizenship.

DN: That's an important point. And it's absolutely true that the impeachment process did more to reignite discussions of family, monogamy, adultery, and the possibility and process of marital forgiveness than ever any national scandal! So while American families—both straight and gay from what I could see in the media—got all intense about the question of commitment-as-monogamy, we lost sight of basic, practical, political consequences. We felt "patriotic" while we talked about "love and commitment" in terms set by heterosexual, Christian culture. My own perverse response to this debate comes in my desire to keep calling attention to its overlooked assault on our already weak sense of politicalness. Obsessing over the personal life of this overly representative president concretizes not just our apolitical relationship to a monogamy that looks like heterosexual patriarchy, but also and at the same time our apolitical relationship to a democracy that looks like heterosexual patriarchy with us in the inferior position.

"Democracy" is a concept that is realized to a greater or lesser extent in a whole range of political practices and government forms. But it's founded in a couple of very basic ideals: that it is a form of "self-rule," and that it thrives insofar as "the people" can articulate political disagreement as a fundamental part of the democratic deliberation that constitutes their self-rule. Both of these presumptions promise a great deal, and it's important to remember they arouse certain basic fears and avoidance patterns: self-rule entails individual accountability and engagement, and the democratic debate that genuine self-rule demands means encountering the very things that can fracture our polity, on a regular basis. Democracy is *always* at least a little scary and dangerous, which makes it tempting to want to delegate it away from ourselves and our home/work space.

TC: I'd like to interject that unfortunately it's just such "scariness" that is often invoked as a way to "manage" minorities who come to embody the fears of pluralism and what subsequently looks like the unwieldiness of such self-rule. The dense cultural politics of presidential representivity—the way the president "stands for" for the people, conditioning civic and personal "normalcy"—uses "personal" morality to strike at not only a political foe, but at political classes—in this case, queers and women.[10] You don't have to be a president to put into play presidentialism—it is a token that is used by the media, people, Congress, pundits, and presidents alike.

DN: Exactly. For me, what's so frustrating here is how presidentialism (and we can see it in our obsessions with the Lewinsky/Clinton "scandal") works powerfully to distract and distance us from our own accountability to and embrace of the difficult work of democracy—the work of building political community across political and personal differences—in fact, it gives us incentive to avoid that work. It does that by playing on basic fears. The president symbolizes us together but only at the cost of making us forget that what binds us democratically is our willingness to keep making local community in the midst of our differences. The more we look to the president to deliver up a sense of democratic unity, the more we forget how to do that work for and amongst ourselves.

TC: This is where there is a real danger in the symbolism of presidential executive orders, such as the decree that rescinded the exclusion of queers from the armed services. It seems to me to be an open question why the desegregation of the armed services in the 1950s by Harry Truman was a sustainable catalyst for social change, while the 1992 presidential directive on lesbian and gay service personnel was met with a virulent and sustained backlash. Clearly any queer cultural critical account of the events must take into consideration the perceived "softness" of Clinton's presidency, as well as Clinton's inexpert handling of the symbolics of his presidency. The "fix" that presidentialism gives us is in part delivered by the speed with which such decisions can be made and enforced along very narrow lines of power. This is "democracy" by decree. The real (and important) changes that can be achieved through the symbolic action of the presidency are a double-edged sword. In part, such directives are the vestiges of "kingship" in the office: it is action and agency from a single source, top-down; it bespeaks a tumescent symbolics of "masculine" action that circulates well within our culture, a culture that looks to a president, and a president's body, as a "source" of democratic strength.

DN: I like it that you brought up the whole hard/soft symbolics of presidentialism. While some people read that dual symbolic as a vestige of the Elizabethan doctrine of the king's two bodies (and I don't think they're wrong to do so), we might also read the hard/soft presidential split as working out historically newer, basic conflicts in national representative democracy.[11] Our abbreviated, contradictory desires about representation-as-unity and democracy-as-individual/political difference split the symbolic president into two bodies. The hard body of the president offers us a strong guarantee for national boundaries. The soft body of the president holds out for us sensations of democratic recognition for our individuality and of equalitarian exchange.

Feminist philosopher Susan Bordo notes that Clinton's "softness"—key attributes we alternately perceive as "virtues"—are nevertheless habitually cast as feminized defects:

The fact that he is a negotiator and consensus-seeker means that his is "trying to please everyone" rather than taking a "firm" stand. His genuine commitment to diversity gets translated as "caving in" to interest groups. . . . Even Clinton's eating habits are feminized. Traditionally, a hearty appetite is a mark of the masculine. "Manwich," "Hungry Man Dinners," "Manhandlers" are products which boast their ability to satisfy men. . . . Clinton's love of food, on the other hand, continually gets represented as embarrassing, out-of-control, feminine "binge" behavior.[12]

Clinton's pudgy, not stocky, body became prima facie evidence for his various departures from the hard model of national manhood. The president who promised to feel the pain of the people elicited both longing and worry. The

NAFTA-generation electorate trained its ambivalence into fascinated anxieties about Clinton's loose bodily demeanor—and compensated by tuning alternately into the Republican right's "Contract with America," and its hard-body demeanor toward immigration, welfare, and character "reforms."

What seems to have emerged in the aftermath of Ken Starr's investigation into the "Monica Lewinsky Scandal" is that the American public did finally find a comfort zone with Clinton's "softer" presidency. At least, during the impeachment, when they had a clear choice, polls repeatedly revealed an American public very comfortable with Clinton's canny combination of hard-soft body sexual/family politics and soft-hard body economics. However loaded the 72 percent presidential approval ratings were during the trial with anger at the House and Ken Starr, it was impossible to ignore that people were flat-out fine with Clinton continuing as president.[13]

TC: I have a sense that being flat-out fine with Clinton as president has something to do with the obvious eroticization of him ("obvious" because of the media's focus on his charisma and fascination with his—of all things—thighs), but also of a sympathetic (if seldom acknowledged) identification with *Monica*. I don't want us to think that Clinton's drama of presidentialism and his psychological claim on being "representative" is simply about a play on our longing to be governed by the exemplary man. I want to talk about the possibility of sympathetic identification with Lewinsky, because I think that identification reveals some interesting dimensions of the way presidentialism works.

I believe that for presidentialism to short-circuit democratic participation, there has to be a confusion on the part of the democratic subject that a personal relationship would stand in for democratic participation. Obviously, I'm charging Lewinsky with just this confusion, but more to the point, I think that it is a mistake that anyone makes at the moment of imagining that a personal relationship with the president is a relationship with democracy. Stories were floated by some of Clinton's close allies in the months after the scandal broke that Lewinsky was delusional, that she never had access to the president's body or the president's ear in the way that she claimed to Tripp and others. Obviously she did. But in both cases the mistake is the same: that a personal relationship can "be" democratic action.

The "damage" inflicted by such actions is a result of the machinery of morality and, indeed, "constitutionality" that make sense of the actions. This is to say, the sex and its consequences can only be understood in the context of "presidentialism" itself. This is a familiar argument following Foucault's analyses of sexuality, power, and knowledge, of contextualizing "sex." I recognize in Lewinsky's de-sires, for example, the viscerally dense bind between pleasure and power, and es-pecially the status of her expectations and the nature of her claims made upon the person "in power."[14] Her late coming to the understanding was that the personal relationship to a forbidden man was itself a political relation.

Something about the Clinton-Lewinsky relationship is definitely queer: in fact, nearly all of the dense meanings and confluence of representations that are said to constitute "homosexuality" circulate within this only nominally hetero-sexual relationship precisely because of the proximity of illicit sexuality to the presidency.[15] If, as Toni Morrison has argued, there is some truth to the claim that Clinton is our first African American president, then I want to pipe up: he's our first queer one as well.[16] Monica's famous navy blue dress from the Gap was stained on a day that included the bestowal of a copy of Walt Whitman's *Leaves of Grass* by William Jefferson Clinton on Monica Lewinsky and a rim job by Monica Lewinsky on William Jefferson Clinton. Any queerly enculturated gay man will recognize the acts and the objects. Whitman has been used as a shibboleth for nonnormative sexuality since his first writings, and rimming is the religious right's new "unspeakable" crime: it's a new sodomy.

DN: This clarifies the sexual panic that pervades congressional "outrage," the im-perative to silence anything that does not speak from the normatively repressive space of the faith-demanding hetero-husband. We can draw a line from silenced "queerness" to the histrionic desire of the scolds on the right to silence Clinton politically, and raise a point that's had almost no voice in the myriad commentary on this episode, one connected to public inability to seize and develop its own terms for and analysis of this "crisis." This public inability reinforced the key af-fect of United States democracy, our fairly ubiquitous sense that what we can't make a political difference (even as making "difference" is what we all desire). And just in the moment when the media turned its attention toward the alternative analyses developing among the public, "our representatives" gave us a public les-son. Around the end of September, the Republicans publicly confronted the buck-ing public. Dripping scorn, they claimed a moral right *not* to represent the major-ity of their constituents who felt they were wasting government time and re-sources, and public monies, by continuing in the congressional investigation and impeachment.[17] In response to the polls documenting public disapproval, con-gressional leaders said things like "we are determined to do this fairly and objec-tively and not listen to the polls at all."[18]

For me, that was a breathtaking moment of political possibility, all the more stunning because it seemed as though people were fairly clear about the stakes of this "argument" against our rights to be represented. Never one to be left behind, Henry Hyde underscored McCollum's remarks, suggesting the people didn't know what was best for them, suggesting that we were like a bunch of misbehaving, sexually deviant kids. I thought: here's a moment where things can really change! People are angry about representational arrogance; they're demanding that Congress get back to political work and stop policing symbolic morality; more important, people were insisting on an active voice in political representation. Finally, I felt political hopefulness. I was excited by the idea that we could now stage some productive political disagreement that might really impact on political process in national and local government, let alone sexual practices.

But this was not to be. The public's dissatisfaction with congressional "representation" never moved beyond sidewalk/hallway/kitchen discussions into an organized political agenda—nor did it gain a coherent public analysis beyond that tiny exchange that made me feel momentarily so hopeful. One explanation for this might come in the media's increasing insistence that the impeachment debate was a "constitutional crisis." Whatever. I mean: I didn't exactly hear anyone calling for the legal maneuvers necessary either to amend or overturn the Constitution! But that terminology made us feel as though our "whole country" was at stake and kept us nervous about the specter of "disunity" instead of focused on local, concrete, political questions like what we might want to do in response to lousy representation by arrogant representatives.

Another explanation for this might come in the way that media attention was immediately diverted, with no small help from Larry Flint, to yet more bedroom revelations—those of Congressmen Hyde, Chenowith, Burton, and Barr. Returned to the familiarly antipolitical question of heteronormative "moral" hypocrisy, the public lost a crucial avenue for alternative deliberation and action, where they might have pursued the question of what constitutes adequate political representation, and whether people are happy to be virtually represented (where representatives don't have an obligation to represent their constituents' opinions but to know what's best for them), or whether they might want to insist on actual representation. This would be the kind of debate that might recharge constituents' sense of political entitlement.

Two things seemed clear in that late-September moment. First, the public was genuinely angry about congressional disdain for their political desires (I don't think there is any other way to explain the extraordinarily high presidential approval ratings in that moment). Second, as angry as they were, most people lacked a political vocabulary that would legitimate their anger in terms that could translate into political action. Without a working vocabulary about representation, bulldozed by media insistence that we were witnessing a national drama that somehow imperiled the "Constitution," and without real access to political media forums beyond polls, peoples' political expression was quickly rerouted into thumbs-up or -down opinion on the president's various behaviors. And even "revelations" about various Representatives' infidelities then worked to keep us all obsessing over marital politics as a stand-in for national politics (did Clinton *screw us too* when he lied to the grand jury?). As in a magician's trick, congressional leadership was able effectively to redirect public anger *at them* back toward a question of presidential symbolics. The public, according to them, had two choices: we could share conservative moral outrage, holding the president publicly accountable to embody conservative sexual private standards, or we could turn our backs on the spectacle, thereby certifying the conservatives' disdain to represent us.

TC: The nation's fascination with the Lewinsky-Clinton encounters are not simply salacious voyeurism. They're also a symbolic encounter with our own democracy. Given the extent to which presidentialism governs our relations to real democracy in the national imaginary, the playing out on television of one citizen's affair with the supposed living embodiment of national interest is riveting. The most common reaction I heard to the scandal by those outside the straight-male community was not a moralistic rejection of Clinton's conduct, but rather a musing on what they would have done in Lewinsky's place.

Let me just say that I identify with Monica Lewinsky. Bill is a sexy guy. I see the attraction. I probably would have been on my knees as well. I say this not simply as a strategically camp assertion, but rather as a way to understand the symbolic mechanisms of our government through sexuality, gender, presidentialism, and sentimentality. During the months of seemingly endless "investigations" into Lewinsky's relationship with Clinton, I heard a lot of people vilify her, and not a few people laugh hysterically at the thought of Monica wanting to discuss her thoughts on U.S. policy on education with the leader of the Free World. But it's fair to say that Monica got it *right*–that she understood in a deep way the traditional trade-offs of sex and power, subservience and power, one that is built into the office of the president as it is practiced in the twentieth century. If the president is representative of democracy, then it stands to reason that a personal relationship with the president is a *representative* one as well. She wanted him to represent her and her ideas. She had more than the president's ear, and she leaned on him in ways that we expect presidential wives to do; she took advantage of a close relationship in a way that we expect of the "old boys'" network, or in Clinton's case, that any FOB (Friend of Bill) would immediately recognize; she had access to the personal body of the man of power, and if you have the president's ear (or, as I'll explain shortly, the president's rear), you put your tongue and your ideas in it.

DN: So Monica "acted out" our sentimental relationship to the presidency. It's worth paying attention to the mini-battle that has been waged over the politics of presidential sentimentalism through the Clinton presidency, because it's not entirely clear yet how it's been resolved. All that is clear is that presidential sentimentalism continues to make itself useful to a variety of political agendas. It may not go without saying that presidential representivity has disciplined politics through affect from early in our nation's history. Beginning in the "cult of Washington" (the slew of memorial tracts, biographies, and dramas after his death in 1799), we can see the conservative reversal of the logic of political representation accomplished through patriotic reverence for presidents. As the itinerant preacher Mason Locke Weems—author of the best-selling biography of George Washington—instructed his readers, the aim is not to see your own political desires represented in deliberative government, but to model your personal desires on those of the presidential representative: "Since it is the private virtues that lay the foundation of all human excellence . . . give us his private virtues! In these, every youth is interested, because in these every youth may become a Washington."[19] Weems's pedagogical 1809 biography substitutes the private for the public—or, more correctly, redescribes a singular public "we" as the private "I"—and in this relocates democracy's desires for deliberation and self-governance to the apolitical, self-subordinating posture of patriotism. The emotionally patriotic relationship Weems constitutes for his readers directs their attention away from criticizing public acts to admiring (or lusting after!) personal selves in a way that demands a kind of impossible symbolic unity and consistency.

Clinton's famous ability to generate sympathy embraces and—to some extent—contests this founding mode of presidentialism. That is to say, Clinton's mode of presidential affect has been less about demonstrating that citizens should emulate him than about demonstrating that he feels for and with his constituents, that his world of feeling is constituted through his sympathetic absorption of their feelings. This absorption is accomplished through his famous physicality, his hugs and pats and touches.

TC: Indeed, from every account, his personal magnetism—what a nineteenth-century vocabulary of personality would characterize as *charisma*—is saturated by a nondiscriminating (we could say democratic) sexualized connectedness.

DN: Since I'm suggesting that Clinton's use of sympathy challenges the hierarchical pressure of traditional presidential sentimentalism, it's fair to ask whether it does so in ways that make a political difference. You might want to say it does, because it feels like a genuine reversal, a way of giving the agency of representation to the people. But viewed another way, it's fair to say it only underlines antipolitical inertia—while seeming to excite and assuage political "desire."

TC: To take a paradigmatic linguistic performance of Clinton's political charisma: the locution "I feel your pain" performs a sort of representational violence inasmuch as it assumes that you *are* in pain, or it renames your political desire to use your experiences as a basis for public change as "simply" pain, which he can recognize by absorbing.

DN: He promises to take care of us in the very act of feeling that "pain"; his sympathy distracts us from our own political agency in the very moment that he promises presidentially to represent us.

TC: This act of representivity secures Clinton's symbolically democratic body, and it does so by securing it to the symbolic body of his political constituents, i.e., "those who are in pain." This is a citizenry thus incapacitated or infantalized such that he speaks (we "need" him to speak) for "you," for "us," *for everyone.* "I feel your pain" deftly knocks aside the individual particularity of the person it seems to support. This locution is not strictly sexual, but rather sexualized in the (un)comfortable intimacy that it assumes and performs. Sentimental power makes your voice his voice; it makes your political power his political power.

DN: It is a stunning moment of representational legerdemain. And here is where there is an interesting reversal in the Washington/Weems paradigm. This doesn't necessarily increase the politicality offered by Clinton's sympathy but it does highlight a certain public desire for politicality—for Monica-ness, to adapt your analysis! The softness of his boundaries incorporates—without necessarily redressing—the hard realities of *public sentiment,* and it is the stunning economism—and eroticism—of his political sympathy, the promiscuous efficacy of his representative incorporation, that the scolds on the hard right find such a bitter pill.

TC: The promiscuity of Clinton's presidency is worth lingering over, however exhausted the subject seemingly is. The cluster of associations of softness and hardness that mediate an understanding of Clinton's relationships to power—or rather *constitute his power within a constituency that is handled or, rather, in Foucault's sense,* *"governed"*—cannot be understood outside of gender ascriptions that are pockmarked by intimations of homosexuality[20] and various epistemologies of the closet that articulate anxieties about/around sex and political power. Clinton's soft body is never quite masculine enough, just as Monica's soft white body is never quite feminine enough when it makes its claims on power. The demonization of Clinton's supposed "compulsive" sexuality—like his sneaky, feminine appetite—lift wholesale from arguments about "the homosexual's" tethering to his sexual drives: promiscuous sexuality, promiscuous representation. Clinton's presidency, like Clinton's "crime," is, if not homosexual, at the very least *sodomitical.* As commander-in-chief, he was not only the recipient of a number of blow-jobs, but he was also rimmed (oral-anal contact), a practice most often associated with gay men by the religious right. Under the Uniform Code of Conduct, such actions are explicitly termed as "sodomy."

Starr got to set the terms that retroactively defined Clinton and Lewinsky's queer engagement. As a document, the Starr Report is fairly unremarkable in its surface presentation of the facts of Monica Lewinsky's sexual encounters with Bill Clinton. The important tool for organizing the information is what Starr's congressional report called a "narrative," but what he subtitled the "Nature of President Clinton's Relationship with Monica Lewinsky." The narrative thus is a reconstruction of the nature of the relationship, which is more precisely a catalogue of names, places, dates, and the sexual acts that Lewinsky testified were performed on those dates. Again, the sexual encounters were "straight" forward: fondling, kissing, mutual masturbation, and fellatio were dutifully described.

Interestingly, however, one sexual act never made it to the surface of Starr's report: rimming. Rimming, the licking and nibbling of the butt hole of one person by another, antiseptically referred to by Starr as "oral/anal" contact, was never included in the body of the report, but lurked in multiple footnotes of the congressional reports. Public discourse—from radio station callers to newspaper op-ed pieces, from David Letterman routines to television sitcoms—implicitly and explicitly took up the president's argument that a blow job is "not sex." Nowhere was Clinton's predilection for having his butt licked by the young intern, nor her happy participation in this form of sexual intercourse, taken up by the Fourth Estate (outside of a glancing blow in a George Will column) in its confrontation with the meanings of sex, power, and the presidency.

Of course, Starr's use of the acts to punctuate nervously what he feels to be the depth of Clinton's degeneracy has a recent history in the vilification of homosexuality by the religious right. Examples are myriad, but illustrates the right's mesmerized fascination and captivated imagination around queers' celebrated eroticization of the human anus. Butt-munching, like sodomy, lurks at the center of their conceptualization of same-sex erotics. Pat Robertson often mentions rimming as one of the acts in a gay boy's standard sexual repertoire. Starr's zealous refusal to tolerate sexual plurality, and his willingness to document it with the zeal of the most dedicated of eighteenth-century pornographers, reaches a sort of horrified limit with rimming. The thought of the president, standing and delivering as it were, rivets Starr's attention and authorizes him to put into motion the efficient political and cultural machinery around narratives of sexual degeneration as a way to strike at the political left.

"Sodomy" is a nondiscriminating, equal opportunity offender category: at one time or another, one place or another, it contains just about every sexual action one could imagine. The very "softness" of the term allows for an expansiveness in representation. As president, Clinton is sodomite-in-chief, and though hypocritically in violation of the U.S. Armed Forces policies, he represents every "fellow" American who has ever participated in any nonstandard coital sexual act.[21]

DN: As prospects for Clinton's ouster from office faded, Ken Starr held out hope for one last attempt at reestablishing the purity of the White House, threatening to prosecute Clinton while he was still in it. In Starr's desire to "purge" the White House of Clinton's contaminatory softness, we can begin unpacking the alternative sentimentalist work of the Republican prosecution and its deeper history in American nationalism. In "The Housing of Gender," architectural theorist Mark Wigley historicizes the White House's role in organizing modern practices of gender division, privatized sexuality and interiorized selfhood. And he notes that "the first truly private" domestic space "was the man's study, a small locked room off his bedroom which" no family members ever entered, "an intellectual space beyond that of sexuality."[22] The White House's Oval Office stands as a national objective correlative for the privatized, purified, homosocial space of manhood: civic fraternity's *sanctum sanctorum*. This male sentimental space works to produce the affective power of our nation's whiteness qua manly purity, to reproduce that white manliness in a purified realm—and to ward off the unguarded sexuality always threatening contamination.

TC: To the right's mind, rimming literalizes contamination.

DN: And so there is the affront Clinton offered to the so-called sacred symbolics of the office, which we can see in this sense to be a threshold ritual of racially homosocial purification for the nation's disciplinarily heterosexual, white moral purity. Ken Starr's and the Republicans' morally purifying guardianship of nationalist sentiment promise to save the domestic space of the White House—the masculine heart of nation, race, and home—from contaminating impropriety. Their attack registers sentimentalist anxieties about not just Clinton's sexual improprieties but his boundary looseness, from NAFTA to campaign ("soft money") finance to health-care reform. Their attack registers their drive to remasculinize (refortify, renormatize, and repurify) sentiment at the same time it registers sentiment's flexibly productive relationship to representative democracy.

TC: The political and religious right in the United States has effectively *sodomized* (made the relations of sexuality and power sodomitical) personal relations to the presidency: every suspected sexualized relationship becomes an "abuse" of power—and not simply by the person in the "position" of power but also (perhaps primarily) by the one who wants something (a job, position, contacts, a relationship, attention, notoriety, influence).[23] Individual sexual action doubles and redoubles in this charged political space: the engine of white male sentimental presidentialism is driven in part by a phantasmatic (mis)recognition of a personal relation to the president, though it is precisely such an understanding of sexual action that we take to cement Hillary Clinton's "political" power. I throw scare quotes around "political" not to cast doubt on her very real power but rather to highlight the space where her "private" (read sexualized if not precisely sexual) relationship secures her position within our representative democracy.[24] Marriage in the space of presidentialism allows nonelected persons to take on the mantle of "representativeness." That Clinton cheerfully signed the Defense of Marriage Act is surely one of the caustic ironies of this "progressive" presidency.[25] The language of the law acknowledges that the gay and lesbian civil rights movement strikes at the heart of what amounts to heterosexual *political* power as it seeks to unmake the *Bowers v. Hardwick* formula that every private queer sex act is "public" (i.e., is under the jurisdiction of the law), whereas every public straight sex act (read "marriage") is "private" (i.e., is internal to the operation of politics though above the jurisdiction of the law).

DN: It'd be easier for me to keep believing that the retro-appeals for a "hard" president are limited to the right. But there's an awful pas-de-deux nostalgia that's developed between the right's homophobically moralistic attempt to reconstitute presidential symbolics through the Elizabethan political figure of the sodomite, and the left's morbid nostalgia for Camelot through the death of "John-John." All along, I've seen the excess of the impeachment drama and media coverage as a positive space for possibility: possibly the people were just getting tired of letting the president run our democracy; possibly they were just not expecting as much from him; possibly we'd see them react against the arrogant misrepresentation of their congressional representatives in the next election. But in the frenzy of sad-spin after JFK Jr.'s "disappearance," I saw a decisive end for the current round of possibilities. This "national tragedy" reactivated everyone's desire for the *good*/absolute leader. This leadership nostalgia reveals both the deficit in the public's democratic imaginary, and the imaginary power of presidentialism: JFK was never that president; King Arthur was never that president; and the post-mortem projection of John-John's political "career"—the one he'd repeatedly refused to pursue—could not deliver it. The president of the U.S. is only ever a figment of our antidemocratic imagination. But our clinging to that figment *really* keeps us from taking democratic power for ourselves.

TC: It seems to me imperative that the use of sexuality to cement a sympathetic identification with the presidency must be countered with the real and powerful attractions of direct (face-to-face) democratic participation. I want to believe that there is a way to reimagine sexuality in a political space as a cohesive force, something that would energize democratic participation. Monica had the right idea, just the wrong context. Instead of cruising the halls of power, she should cruise her local gay rights rally or health-care-rights meeting. Her ideas and energy would join with others, not in the exercise of extra-democratic power, but in the space where the political is local.

Notes

1. "By politicalness I mean our capacity for developing into beings who know and value what it means to participate in and be responsible for the care and improvement of our common collective life. To be political is not identical with being part of a government or being associated with a political party. These are structured roles, and typically they are highly bureaucratized. For these reasons they are opposed to the authentically political." See his *The Presence of the Past: Essays on the State and the Constitution* (Baltimore: Johns Hopkins University Press, 1989), 139. Wolin usefully indexes the constitutionally conditioned disavowal of politicalness for "democracy"—a practice which in effect remainders democracy for its citizens. See also Bonnie Honig's illuminating discussion of theories of democracy that "tend to remove politics from the reach of democratic contest" in *Political Theory and the Displacement of Politics* (Ithaca, N.Y.: Cornell University Press, 1993), 4.

2. Dana D. Nelson, *National Manhood: Capitalist Citizenship and the Imagined Fraternity of White Men* (Durham, N.C.: Duke University Press, 1998).

3. Gary L. Gregg, *The Presidential Republic: Executive Representation and Deliberative Democracy* (Totowa, N.J.: Rowman and Littlefield, 1997), 23.

4. Barbara Hinckley, *The Symbolic Presidency: How Presidents Portray Themselves* (New York: Routledge, 1990), 2.

5. Ibid., 136.

6. Nancy Fraser, "Rethinking the Public Sphere: A Contribution to the Critique of Actually Existing Democracy," in Craig Calhoun, ed., *Habermas and the Public Sphere* (Cambridge, Mass.: MIT Press, 1992), 134.

7. A fourth position, one taken up by a self-appointed manager of the crisis, occupied at times by Henry Hyde, Newt Gingrich, but paradigmatically by Kenneth Starr, might be described as the preacher's position: the preacher married us/them to the scandal, and stuck around to ensure that as much as we wanted to divorce ourselves from the muck, we were as good as married.

8. Note that all three of these examples were inflicted on us by Clinton in concert with an equal and opposite right-wing reaction.

9. Subsequently, both positions "for" or "against" the proposition that individual sex acts by the president necessarily have national consequences tend to use the same language. The language tends to be one of ownership, responsibility, and some notion of the "harm" to property or persons. Thus, in a forum such as *Crossfire*, Eleanor Clift of the national rag *Newsweek* can put into play, without irony, the terms from the same moral lexicon as those used by right-wing homophobe Patrick Buchanan ("irresponsible," "reckless," and the like), and not sound as if they are reading, if not off the same page, then from the same hymnal.

10. This argument owes much to Lauren Berlant's analysis of national rhetoric and modes of collective identification in her "Theory of Infantile Citizenship." See her *Queen of America Goes to Washington City: Essays on Sex and Citizenship* (Durham, N.C.: Duke University Press, 1997).

11. This doctrine refers to the notion that the king had one "natural body" and a second, sovereign body, wherein his body symbolically encompassed and "stood for" the body politic. For an account of the U.S. presidential absorption of this doctrine, see Michael Paul Rogin's "The King's Two Bodies" in his *Ronald Reagan, the Movie* (Berkeley: University of California Press, 1979).

12. Susan Bordo, "Reading the Male Body," *Michigan Quarterly Review* 32.4 (1993): 723.

13. Even if people were, in the end, probably most comfortable with him for "hard" reasons—for instance, because he took such great care of the economy for us throughout the scandal and provided us with the rationales we needed to let him keep managing "democracy" for us. If the economy had been in any real downturn last fall, the

public might have felt it somewhat more important to hold Clinton morally account-
able in exactly the way conservatives were scolding we should.

14. Foucault explains that "the relations of sex gave rise, in every society, to a *deploy-
ment of alliance*: a system of marriage, of fixation and development of kinship ties, of
transmission of names and possessions." See *The History of Sexuality,* vol. 1: *An Intro-
duction* (New York: Vintage Books, 1980), 106.

15. I should clarify that I do not believe that this was always the case, nor is it tran-
scultural. The expectation that men of power may have their women is said to be taken
for granted in other cultures—the French presidency is often invoked here—and cer-
tainly in our culture at another time. The paradigmatic example of this is the presi-
dency of John F. Kennedy.

16. Morrison writes, "African-American men seemed to understand it right away. Years
ago, in the middle of the Whitewater investigation, one heard the first murmurs: white
skin notwithstanding, this is our first black President. Blacker than any actual black per-
son who could ever be elected in our children's lifetime. After all, Clinton displays al-
most every trope of blackness: single-parent household, born poor, working-class, sax-
ophone-playing, McDonald's-and-junk-food-loving boy from Arkansas" (*New Yorker,*
October 5, 1998): 32. I would like to acknowledge Micki McElya's argument about the
significance of Clinton's "white trash" identity, but suggest that as a *racial* category
"white trash" (and this is to my understanding a corollary of Morrison's point) partic-
ipates in and is marked by stereotypes of blackness.

17. These declarations simply made explicit a developing disdain for the majority atti-
tudes of the U.S. public on the part of conservative leadership. As Andrew Sullivan ar-
gues, this attitude has gone beyond a simple "hatred of liberal elites" to a literal "con-
tempt for the mass of Americans" (*New York Times Magazine,* October 11, 1998, 88).

18. Bill McCollum, R-Florida. See David E. Rosenbaum, *New York Times,* September 27,
1998.

19. Mason Locke Weems, *Life of Washington*, ed. Marcus Cunliffe (Cambridge, Mass.:
Belknap Press, 1962), 4.

20. I want to acknowledge that there is a dense set of relations between sexualities, self-
identified and other-inflicted gender attributes, and representational strategies that ar-
ticulate and are articulated by such political and cultural "government." See, for ex-
ample, Eve Kosofsky Sedgwick, "Willa Cather and Others," in *Tendencies* (Durham,
N.C.: Duke University Press, 1993), 167–76.

21. Kenneth Starr cannot escape the cynosural force of these representative ascriptions:
he is most often characterized as "puffy," "effeminate," "lispy," and vilified for what
can only be called an aggressive detumescence. It is not just the left who ascribes these

attributes to Starr. He is just as often taken to task for these gender/sexuality attributes and their supposed relationships to the lack of control over his office as special prosecutor by Republican traditionalists and non-Moral Majority party members. Cartoonists and political satirists have pointed out that he is indistinguishable from the obsessed-because-jilted suitor—the stalker that Monica could only *dream* of being or becoming.

22. Mark Wigley, "Untitled: The Housing of Gender," in Beatriz Colomina, ed., *Sexuality and Space* (New York: Princeton Architectural Press, 1992), 345.

23. One has to reach back to the Henrician or Elizabethan figure of the "sodomite" to understand such sexuality so pervasively, systemically, hegemonically, in relation to the person of the "king" as a political and religious crime. During those eras, whatever the real sexual relations of a monarch to his or her courtiers and subjects, sodomy was often mobilized to strike at a courtier or king when the relationship (or person) was read as *politically* suspect.

24. The First Lady (or more properly any sanctioned Significant Other of any sitting president) is a locus classicus of a person who wields significant governmental power but who is not herself an elected official. The First Lady is an extra-constitutional entity who in a sense embodies the dense interconnections among governmental power, institutionalized heterosexuality, and the seeming ability of a spousal relation to trump any "real" political alliance. The strength of the cultural anxieties triggered by this First Lady, "*any* First Lady," is one measure of the phantasmatic power of the position. Though we may think of Hillary Rodham Clinton as the paradigmatic example of this "problem," in fact, after the nationalized health-care fiasco, her historical example dims in comparison to Eleanor Roosevelt and—spectacularly—the "presidency" of Nancy Reagan. Moreover, that Bob Dole could imagine himself as not only a potentially significant resource for Elizabeth Dole's administration but a rehabilitated former presidential candidate somehow "forgiven" by those who elected both Bill Clinton and potentially Libby Dole speaks to the potency of heterosexuality, governmental power, and presidentialism.

25. 28 USCS §1738C (1999)—the so-called "Marriage Protection Act"—records that "No State, territory, or possession of the United States, or Indian tribe, shall be required to give effect to any public act, record, or judicial proceeding of any other State, territory, possession, or tribe respecting a relationship between persons of the same sex that is treated as a marriage under the laws of such other State, territory, possession, or tribe, or a right or claim arising from such a relationship."

Part 2

BODILY IMAGINARIES AND SEXUAL PRACTICES

3 The Face That Launched a Thousand Jokes

Laura Kipnis

A friend with a penchant for gnomic remarks once said, "Ugliness is the last frontier for socialism." He could just as easily have said "for democracy." I can't now recall what prompted it (discussing some unfortunate mutual acquaintance?), but this doomy pronouncement has perturbed me ever since, or at least whenever my gaze falls upon some particularly unsightly visage and involuntarily the ruthless machinery of aesthetic judgment springs into motion. If ugliness registers with such visceral immediacy despite knowing everything there is to know about the historical and cultural variability of such standards, despite full comprehension of the damage these judgments wreak, maybe the friend is right and there will always be limits to the reformability of the human psyche, with some inequities remaining forever intractable (no doubt even after the revolution). What's worse is that we who suffer by such judgments perform them so relentlessly nonetheless: when the guilty "U" word trips into consciousness, aren't we less the willing emissaries of capricious cultural norms than their hapless vessels—harsh judge one moment, harshly judged ourselves the next? Perhaps not coincidentally, it was this same friend—self-described as no beauty, either—who gleefully related the most hilariously scurrilous Linda Tripp joke I heard during a banner year for scurrilous jokes, so many of them aimed, fistlike, at Linda Tripp's face. After all, we don't choose our preoccupations. Or our faces.

It was a hard face to ignore and a harder one to forget. For reasons that were clearly too subterranean to be ever sufficiently explained, Tripp (spurred on by the dubious Lucianne Goldberg) propelled herself headlong onto the national stage; the nation took one look and winced. It will be news to no one if I say that consensus was quickly reached in the unraveling saga of Monicagate that the descriptive "ugly" could be applied with impunity to this self-fashioned one-woman surveillance unit, and that it would be no-holds-barred in the cruel humor department. ("What's the cure for an overdose of Viagra? Linda Tripp.") Or perhaps more precisely, consensus was tacitly reached that the nation's collective disgust with Tripp's tenuous grasp of the concept of friendship would be expressed through the idiom of negative appearance assessments. An "I Hate Linda Tripp" Web page listed over forty separate looks jokes. True, many had the musty odor of Don Rickles playing the Desert Sands a couple of decades ago, like they'd been in comedy cold storage waiting for the right occasion to see daylight again. But other Tripp-inspired Web pages had the antic novelty that the revenge imperative often fuels. One reported the FBI's confirmation that Tripp and Dallas Cowboy Troy Aikman are actually one and the same person, going on to describe Tripp's news conference confirming the dark secret, at which she sobs, "I'm not a freak." Then there were the talk-show monologues (Leno: "Linda Tripp told Monica Lewinsky in those taped conversations that she hasn't had sex with anyone in seven years. That means that at some point in 1991 some guy got drunker than any man in history"); *Saturday Night Live* skits (a simpering Tripp-impersonation by the not exactly diminutive John Goodman); editorial cartoons in major newspapers (Tripp describing her television aspirations to pal Lucianne: "I could be . . . like this beautiful helpless older woman who is caught between these powerful politicians." Lucianne: "Exactly! Attracting the soccer mom audience!"); and of course, all those droll water-cooler comedians for whom the name alone could usually garner a fast laugh, or at least a lot of eye rolling.

After all, jokes are the royal road to the deepest recesses of a culture's psyche: an end run around politesse and false rectitude, the psyche's clever tactic for avoiding the censorship edicts emanating from both superego and society. Predictably, though, this often pretty hilarious Tripp-bashing produced no shortage of feminist consternation, with the more squeamish members of our sisterhood ritually flagellating themselves for guilty pleasure at the latest Trippism. The friend I regard as a feminist conscience confessed in deeply shame-ridden tones that when she saw her first photo of Linda, she thought for sure it was a transvestite. Or as she put it, "That hair!" Yes, the hair, with its big blowzy blonde ambitions of glamour and seduction was nothing if not a case study in aesthetic disharmony. Where had we seen this hair before? Wasn't it perched atop the head of the previous superannuated Clintonian intimate, Gennifer Flowers? This at least appeared to be the inference of yet another editorial cartoon, this one showing Linda with two insidious little cupids buzzing around her hairdo as she chomps down her morning cereal, one whispering in her left ear, "That pathetic Monica hasn't got a chance. He likes strong women who challenge him," while the other hisses in the right, "It's you babe, hang in there." One of the many educational aspects of having had that bevy of Clintonian girlfriends, alleged girlfriends, aspirants, and complainants camping out in the nation's living rooms during much of the nineties is that we've all become much more attuned to the semiotics of big hair: its ambitions, its class and gender connotations, its function in the Clinton sexual imagination—and perhaps in Tripp's as well.

Linda Tripp is so ugly that when she joined an ugly contest, they said, "Sorry, no professionals."

But what exactly *was* so funny about Linda Tripp's face? Or to put it another way, what makes a successful national joke? The role of the face in the course of human history is an almost imponderable subject; so, too, its salience in nation building. Nations have been constituting themselves around faces as long as there have been nations: you have your coins, your royal portraits, your news conference close-ups, your campaign posters. And if national politics is now increasingly about appearances, as we keep hearing, then we citizens are certainly going to need a far more nimble repertoire of techniques for assessing them. Jokes, at least, have always taken appearances very seriously, since jokes are ways of recirculating the contradictions that ordinary forms of language and knowledge can't reconcile. If Freud was right, jokes that don't contain some form of truth get no laughs, jokes being techniques for voicing the repressed, mostly in coded or distorted forms. Clearly, we don't choose our jokes: they choose us, which is what it means to be part of your culture—it's precisely the culture's incoherences, contradictions, and hypocrisies that are the joke's metier: everything you know but wish, at some level, you didn't. And jokes at least proffer pleasurable forms of distraction—this making them one of the more useful defense mechanisms. We don't recoil from ugliness in horror, we can laugh at it instead—and generally without being required to consider exactly why ugliness would possibly cause such hilarity.

The preoccupation with beauty and its consequences in the world is, to say the least, a deeply entangled story in human affairs, not to mention philosophy, art, romantic love, and Hollywood. It encircles our visual, emotional, and even moral universes in ways that are both banal and indelible. Appearance jokes are like the imbecilic cousin of Kantian aesthetics: borne of the same lineage but not invited to sit at the big table when the family gets together. Though Kant himself doesn't have much to say about ugliness, the ugly obviously haunts the realm of the beautiful, its banished and repudiated Other. Where would beauty be without ugliness to define its borders? But ugliness, like all disavowed and secretly formative things, is a subject attended by a certain social nervousness (and joking is nothing if not the privileged form for anxiety). When will the repressed thing come back to wreak its revenge? Who will pay?

The nation may have passed sentence on the unbeauteous countenance of Linda Tripp, but the question of what, precisely, constitutes ugliness remains troublesome. Philosophers and aestheticians are rather perplexed by it. Is it universal or individual? The opposite of beauty, or a completely different kind of category? After all, not every nonbeautiful thing merits entry into the pantheon of the ugly—most nonbeautiful things are just ordinary. Thus, is ugliness some set of identifiable characteristics (leading contenders: asymmetry; irregularity; things that protrude like warts or moles; masculinity in women), and do these properties reside in the ugly objects themselves? Or is it something about the visceral response those properties evoke in us onlookers and viewers—some sort of unsettling or queasy effect they engender? Then is the big cultural fetish for beauty actually a response to the potentially shattering power of ugliness, making ugliness really the more central and meaningful category, and beauty just a feeble defense? But if ugliness can't be reduced to the sum of its parts, how do we know it when we see it? Hence the definitional dilemma: the ways in which ugly things achieve their ugliness is remarkably diverse, and if there aren't any common properties between them, you may know it when you see it, but what is the "it" you're seeing?

It's been argued that the general reaction to ugliness carries all the symptomatic baggage of a defense mechanism. We try frantically to wash away its stain, and when that fails we avert our eyes, or mime our repellence. Ugly things do seem to take up far more space than they should, as though, unchecked, the ugly could engulf and overwhelm all else. They seem to pose some ineffable psychological threat. (And something about the maternal may enter in here: the earliest visual experience is looking into the mother's out-of-focus looming face, perhaps something to do with why, culturally speaking, ugly women seem to be more threatening than ugly men.) Watch the face of someone confronted by an ugly thing sometime. It resembles nothing so much as an expression of physical pain—all wincing and grimacing—as though encountering ugliness were some unique form of trauma.

Then we have that other ancient story about ugliness: the morality tale. The long-standing connection of beauty with the good—a gift from the gods, according to Aristotle—means that ugliness must be meant, conversely, as a special form of punishment, a connection that persists still in our godless times, if unconsciously, as an abiding moral onus on the ugly. We typically express moral judgments in the idiom of disgust and physical unattractiveness. Faced with a morally reprehensible act, we're likely to respond, "That makes me sick!" or "That was an ugly thing to do," or "Not a pretty sight." A premonition of evil or disaster lurks around ugliness's edges, the suspicion of moral or ethical violations. "Ugly as sin." And if moral failure leans on the language of ugliness, then do those whose physical appearances evoke disapproval or repugnance come to signify moral failure regardless of their actions, held morally responsible for their aesthetic insufficiencies? When an editorial cartoonist draws a series of frames featuring Linda first as a snake, then a worm, then a frog, and then a rat, it's difficult to say whether it's her actions or her appearance that makes the joke funny. A snake, a worm, and a rat conventionally symbolize betrayal; a frog is just ugly.

Tripp, therefore, poised so neatly at the intersections of moral and aesthetic failure, makes a terrific case study in the problematics of ugliness. Having so egregiously betrayed her friend—a failure of morality in a culture that hates a stool pigeon more than a murderer—and unsightly as the final affront, we're presented in Tripp's case with two separate varieties of ugliness, each refracted through the magnifying lens of the other. The optics metaphor may account for the sheer magnitude of the contempt directed her way, but still nothing quite explains the barely repressed violence (and emotional violence counts) that erupts around the subject of ugliness generally—all that ritualized atavistic aggression, as though jokes rendered the contaminant unthreatening or provided some sort of magical vaccine against catching the ugliness plague. One can't help but notice that physical attractiveness on the part of the tellers of appearance jokes seems not to be a prerequisite. This is puzzling: do the jokesters think that they themselves are somehow granted exemption from their own standards by virtue of the joke? This is either magical thinking or unbelievably optimistic. Our relation to ugliness—and clearly it runs quite deep—seems not entirely thought through.

> *Linda Tripp is so ugly she went into a haunted house and came out with an application.*

There's something both deeply confirming and deeply confusing when an ugly person does something ugly. The suspicion that surface appearances accurately reflect what's underneath dates back to day 1 of Western culture: it's a through line from Homer's *Iliad* (whose ugliest character is also the most despicable), to the Brothers Grimm, to the Wicked Witch of the West. So, of course, Tripp's unbeauteous countenance elevates the story of her ugly betrayal of her friend into a tale of satisfyingly mythic proportions, and no doubt the mythic is the conceptual grid to which even the most evolved consciousnesses return when in states of outrage or moral indignation. (As when imagining one's own rambling conversations secretly taped by a friend and broadcast to—literally—the world.) After all, if anyone really believed that beauty is only skin deep, it's not clear that its pursuit would sustain a multibillion dollar industry, or prop up so many of our language's deep-seated metaphors of worth and accomplishment.

Social progressives clearly have to treat stereotypes as lies; if they're not, then all sorts of bets about social progress are off. The road to social progress is paved with ambivalence as it is: in this tidal wave of Tripp jokes, note the eagerness to see an antistereotyping ethics lose its moral force. (Speaking of language reforms, one cartoon labels Tripp "physiognomically challenged.") The treatment of populations with physical defects by the nondefected populations is typically seen as a mark of civilization's advancement: we no longer send our malformed infants downriver on open rafts; we pass antidiscrimination bills instead, and pride ourselves upon it. But despite whatever rote displays of sensitivity may have been pounded into the population by various rights movements and language reforms, a basic aversion to physical impairment still seems to hover just beneath any surface rectitude, and if ugliness isn't the most severe form of physical defect imaginable, it may be its most paradigmatic form. Scratch the thin membrane of social politesse, and the ugly, the blemished, or any of the unfortunate bearers of what sociologist Erving Goffman called "spoiled identities" in his 1963 classic, *Stigma,* are typically held responsible for their fates. Goffman's stigmatized populations include not only those who bear various physical deformities and defects (Goffman, who reportedly stood about five foot three himself, was perhaps no stranger to his subject), but also those stigmatized by character blemishes—criminality, addiction, dishonesty, shady pasts, mental illness, and the like. But bodily abominations seem to provide the template of all stigmas for Goffman, whose opening epigraph is a letter to Nathaniel West's Miss Lonelyhearts (of the novel by the same name), from "Desperate," a sixteen-year-old girl born without a nose, and, consequently— "although I am a good dancer and have a nice shape and my father buys me pretty clothes"—is unable to get a date for a Saturday night. The letter makes you squirm: how many of us with noses would really go out with someone without one, someone with a big hole where a nose should be? For Goffman, the true affront of the stigmatized is forcing this sort of question, and obtruding on the consciousness of those he calls, a bit bracingly, "normals." The problem with the stigmatized is that you just can't ignore them.

Goffman's conclusion isn't exactly one of those well-meaning arguments for greater sensitivity. His jabbing point is that normals and the stigmatized exist on the same continuum: not two distinct social groups, but one and the same. Everyone's been stigmatized at one time or another, and we all fall short of the ideals of physical comeliness sooner or later, if for no other reason than the universality of old age and impending decrepitude. Thus, anyone who can play one of these roles has exactly the same equipment for playing out the other—though some of us may be fated to play one role more frequently than the other. It should come as no surprise, then, reports Goffman, that those who are stigmatized in one regard exhibit all the usual prejudices toward those who are stigmatized in another regard. (The stigmatized have no special corner on virtue.) We're all capable of playing both roles, and of producing virulent mean-spiritedness and cruelty toward whatever form of stigma we ourselves do not bear. Even if we play or have played the role of abuse recipient in some other regard.

As indeed we see in the case under discussion: Tripp herself had no qualms about informing poor Monica that she looked fat in "that dress," fatness, as we all know, being the winning ticket for entry into our culture's stigma sweepstakes. (And of course Tripp herself would not escape scrutiny in that regard once she'd launched herself—along with dieting-obsessed Lewinsky—into the hot glare of national attention.) Although it's anyone's guess just how self-conscious Tripp might have been about her own appearance prior to what must have been a speedy and brutal self-education at the hands of the nation's comedians, one thing is certain: even if Tripp and Lewinsky were dieting pals, every woman alive knows that telling a friend she looks fat falls somewhere on a continuum between dangerous ground and a rusty knife to the throat. Perhaps reading that remark was what made me start wondering whether Linda Tripp had gotten the face she deserved.

> *Linda Tripp is so ugly that when she was born the doctor took one look at her and spanked her parents.*

It was George Orwell who said that by age fifty, everyone has the face he deserves. Orwell wasn't alone in thinking so: psychologists whose research focuses on the face often regard facial expression, and particularly a person's most characteristic expression—how the face looks in repose or when caught in an unselfconscious moment—as composed of its owner's history. Our faces are our portable, visible biographies. Here, however, we would want to distinguish between physiognomy, that is, the physical framework of the face, and what is sometimes termed "pathognomy," from the Greek *pathos* or feeling, meaning facial expression. (Pathognomy is also a name for the branch of psychology that studies expressive behavior.) The question, when it comes to facial ugliness, should really be: *What* exactly are we describing? Perhaps it's not simply physiognomy that provokes these punitive reactions, but something more ineffable.

The face plays a massive social and psychological role in a life as lived: having a face is one of the most complicated aspects of being a person. It shades every aspect of living, from self-confidence, to love, to—studies show—material success. It's not people who interact, it's their faces. Body language may factor into our perceptions of social encounters, but primarily, we understand who people are because of what their faces reveal; they in turn, understand us through ours. Like juries, we scrutinize faces to decide if the testimonies we're hearing are true; in the private courtroom of our daily interactions, when offered opposing testimony between face and speech, we typically take the face to be the more reliable witness. Though we're probably not always entirely sure what we're looking for, we register whatever conflicting information faces signal and make determinations about character, reliability, and mate selection depending on minute and fleeting arrangements of facial features. We search the faces we meet for signs of what's "underneath"—and whether this is paranoia or emotional intelligence or metaphysics (*what* underneath?), it's a fundamental part of social interaction.

Some facial theorists regard this ability to read expressions as innate, even proposing a universality of facial expression, a line of thinking originating with Charles Darwin, who argued in *The Expression of the Emotions in Man and Animals* (1872) that all cultures display the same arrangement of facial features for the six basic emotions—disgust, joy, sadness, anger, surprise, and fear—and that all humans accurately recognize these facial expressions on the faces of others. Put a piece of rotting meat under someone's nose in Omaha or Ouagadougou and her upper lip will be raised, the lower lip extended, the brows drawn down (but not together): the face of disgust. Jump out from behind a tree at someone and his lower jaw will drop, the eyes will open wide, the brows will raise and curve, and any human observer will efficiently recognize this as the expression of a startled person. After an initial flurry of acclaim, the universality thesis fell into neglect until revived in the 1960s, when intrepid researchers actually traveled to Borneo and New Guinea to ferret out humans who hadn't yet been exposed to Western media to study their facial expressions. Would they be the same as those in the metropolises? Darwin's hypotheses proved to be, in the eyes of the new wave, essentially correct, at least according to psychologist Paul Ekman, the leading proponent of the Darwin revival as well as the de facto dean of facial research in the United States. (Ekman concedes that more complicated emotions like jealousy, pride, or guilt are culturally specific and learned behaviors.)

Though resolutely empirical, facial expression research suggests a new spin on psychoanalytic theories of identification. Psychologist Silvan Tomkins, although no partisan of psychoanalysis himself, speculated that to whatever extent we can accurately perceive the expression of anyone else, it may be that having a face is the prerequisite for "reading" a face.[1] In other words, our basic ability to discern another person begins with the embodied fact that we know what it would feel like to have that face, or wear that expression, through what are, in essence, acts of bodily identification. Indeed, we're able to interpret what is actually an extraordinary amount of information from the smallest facial response, which Tomkins suggests is made possible by this imaginary isomorphism between our own faces and others.

Tomkins, writing in the 1960s, regarded the face itself as the primary place that affects are felt. Emotion, he thought, consists of facial expression, the point being that there aren't "inner" states or emotions—the face is where emotion lives. When Tomkins zeros in on the study of a particular emotion, the technique is to describe in minute detail the behavior of the face when experiencing that emotion. In distress, for example, the mouth will open, the corners of the lips are pulled downward, the eyebrows arch, whereas in shame, the eyes are dropped, along with the eyelids, the head, and sometimes the whole upper part of the body: children will stop looking at anyone and even cover their faces with their hands. In Tomkins's often strikingly poetical accounts ("In self-confrontation, the head may also be hung in shame symbolically, lest one part of the self be seen by another part and become alienated by it"), faces take on an uncanny life of their own. He also maintains that if the face is the seat of the emotions, then feedback from the face must convey those emotions to the brain, where they're then comprehended as affective experience. So without a face, we would not be able to feel. (Although Tomkins also follows Darwin in thinking the basic emotions to be innate, like Ekman he concedes that the total set of facial responses and their interpretation are culture-bound, even class-bound: thus social mobility would involve learning new "dialects" of facial language.)

Facial researchers often break facial expression down into regions—the eye and brow combination, the mouth-jaw area, to study how the different regions of the face interact, or fail to. With the right analytical tools, facial style might tell an entire individual biography: part a story about the past, part a reaction to the present, and part an expectation of the future. A face whose disappointments have hardened into chronic resentment has a different cast than one still optimistic about the possibilities, and these interplays of contradictory sentiments can produce complicated facial expressions, though not necessarily unpleasant ones. But the face frozen in the experience of antagonistic sentiments will produce a distorted, unharmonious effect, leaving observers uncertain and even jarred. Particularly under conditions of self-deception—falseness, conflict, or competing impulses—the separate regions of the face can seem to be at war with one another, one half refusing to follow where the other half leads.

Ugliness, from this standpoint, isn't simply a physical fact, but rather a distortion of affect made physical, an involuntary subtext that tells a very visceral story. This would present certain aesthetic difficulties to an observer forced to experience that facial conflict, who, simply by virtue of perceiving the expression, also *feels* it: an unwilling and no doubt disavowed identification. (And the disavowal accounts for the massive aversion in the aesthetic response to ugliness.) To whatever extent we comprehend the language of the face, it's not only because we all have faces, but because we too are leaky vessels, better at reading the facial behavior of others than we are at controlling our own faces. We may intentionally smile at a comely stranger, but we're just as likely to break out in laughter at a funeral: having a face means we're all walking social gaffes waiting to happen. Everyone alive has been asked "Is something bothering you?" often enough to know that having a face doesn't mean that your expression is under your control. (The blank-page maneuver doesn't help either: having no expression is always a dead giveaway that something's going on "underneath.") One way to think about all this unintentional leakage would be along the lines of the parapraxis, the "Freudian slip"—something we probably do anyway. We're constantly reading intentional reactions and unintentional signals—slips of the face, so to speak—on the faces around us; conflicting signals or distorted facial expressions that can result from a failure to integrate some kind of opposing impulse. ("I love you/I hate you," "I trust you/You'll betray me . . ."—the normal gamut of human contradictions.)

Linda Tripp is so ugly the NHL banned her for life.

In the vocabulary of the face, there are involuntary distortions, but there are also conscious attempts to overmanage facial expression, which can be just as aesthetically jarring. Consider the false smile, something most of us instinctively recognize and react badly to. What makes it "false?" At some level we recognize that the smile is a mask, a substitute that forces another expression aside. An artificial expression arises because some conflict prevents the expression of another affect. Something is being repressed, the psychoanalyst would say, most likely some aggressive thought. So it's not only the falseness of the smile we're recognizing, but also the exertion of withholding another expression from surfacing. The result is often a sort of grimace: a compromise between anger and laughter resulting in distortion of the features. A face in conflict, then, is a face that lacks aesthetic unity.

In practice, though, and in real time, probably none of this is quite so comprehensible. Expressions are fleeting, visceral reactions are pushed aside out of politeness or expediency. Research on the perception of facial expression indicates that as much as we search faces for data, we're not particularly adept at processing what we're seeing. When it comes to knowing when someone is lying, mostly we don't: the cues we typically rely on to make judgments of truth telling or lies—faulty eye contact, nervous twitches, vocal hesitation—turn out to be, for the most part, totally unrelated to actual honesty.

One of the most interesting findings to emerge from the—no doubt—brooding laboratories of deception studies is that humans are actually quite terrible judges of deception. Even though people consistently report extremely high levels of confidence in their abilities to detect deception, even though our judicial system is founded on the supposed accuracy of face-to-face judgments, the success rate at detecting deception even among those trained to do so is not much better than 50 percent—in other words, not much better than complete random guessing. There is a marginally higher success rate among two groups: Secret Service agents and female spouses. (Obviously, if you assume all communication is lies, some percentage of the time you'll be right.) But ironically, the wives score better than average only at judging deception by their own husbands and aren't any better than anyone else at assessing deception by—according to an actual experiment—female friends. (No, we typically have to wait until we're cornered in the lobby of the Ritz Carlton by federal agents to learn this.) Frustrated deception researchers have been forced to conclude that humans just aren't sufficiently motivated to detect deception and have a bias against knowing the truth out of self-protection.[2] The price of skillful detection can be costly, like learning something that in the end you really wish you hadn't about yourself or others: betrayal, cheating spouses, lying friends, or everyone's fundamental ambivalence about everyone else.

Am I alone in finding these data somewhat startling? Certainly we're all trained at least to *attempt* to mask our emotions (if your face agrees to play along), perhaps making ease of detection a trickier business. And no doubt we're all highly motivated *to* deceive, deception being a basic requirement of gainful employment and general daily social interaction. But the concept that we're also motivated to *be* deceived takes some getting used to. Apparently either complete honesty or high detection rates of deception would soon bring the machinery of interpersonal relations screeching to a halt. Knowing the truth would be socially dysfunctional.

Although for the social scientists one of the compelling questions in facial research remains whether the face is a voluntary or involuntary system, the psychoanalyst would understand distortions of expression on the model of the symptom: involuntary emanations of an unconscious origin. Facial expression in psychoanalytic thinking falls under the regulation of the ego—not innate but formed in the developmental process. We grow from infants who use the entire body as an apparatus to signal emotion, squalling when unhappy, laughing rhythmically when pleased—to the use of spoken language for communication, and ever more subtle facial expressions to signal affect. For the psychoanalyst, failures of interpretation of expression would be symptomatic as well: those who interpret the expression of others badly are often "off" in their own expressive behavior.

Both social scientists and psychoanalysts agree that interacting with others means reading intentional expressions *and* the whole range of involuntary signals on display. If facial expression is indeed comprehended through an automatic process of comparison between another's expressions and one's own, as Tomkins suggests, this quite visceral apprehension of unmanaged conflict and distortion in another's face would automatically produce kindred experiences of psychical discomfort in oneself, felt, if not necessarily comprehended as such. If certain faces do nakedly display to us onlookers what is often quite well concealed from their owners, then such uncontrolled faces threaten to mirror back to us those same unsettling, even threatening contents denied access to our own consciousness. Namely, our *own* unmastered conflicts, and our own capacities for self-deception, plus all the by-product pain, resentment, or loneliness that might hover around the edges: all matters about which our knowledge, too, is likely incomplete at best. Perhaps preferably so.

This is where the question of ugliness comes home to roost. Do we have any idea what we mean when we call someone ugly? Do we have any idea *whom* we're looking at?

> *Linda Tripp is so ugly her mother had to tie a steak around her neck to get the dog to play with her.*

There did seem to be something deeply at odds in Linda Tripp's face. Something about it was just wrong. The mouth, captured in photos, was either locked in a tight, rictor-like smile, or, in the early press conference photos, opened far too wide in a distorted Munch-like cry. In the famous office photo, posed next to then-friend Lewinsky (American flag in the background), the lips are pressed together in a hard smile, but the corners turn down, as if something is hard to swallow. A pair of oversize glasses hides much of the face; the rest is veiled by that big mane of seductive blond hair. The hair says come hither, but the face seems pulled back into itself, more than a little mistrustfully. In Monica's face, by contrast, the mouth is open in a wide smile, with the eyes scrunched a bit. This is what happens in a genuine smile or laugh: the eyes narrow, laugh lines appear in the corners—the whole face laughs. In Tripp's face, though, the eyes, visible behind the glasses, are wide open and alert, staring watchfully at the camera, out of sync with the smiling mouth. It's a face in contradiction: *a two-faced face.*

Tripp began making the rounds of TV talk shows beginning the day the Senate voted to acquit Clinton, in an after-the-fact attempt to rehabilitate her corroded image. Though massively made over and media coached to within an inch of taxidermy, what defeated the carefully stage-managed new look was her mouth. The mouth wouldn't play along: it seemed to have an existence independent of the rest of the face. When speaking, it does a strange thing: the upper lip raises up to fully expose the top row of teeth, something between a snarl and a sneer. According to Tripp, her intentions toward Monica were nothing but kindly—she'd merely tried to protect her (as she'd want someone to do for her own daughter). The tones were honeyed, but the display of bared teeth was a viscerally unsettling counterpoint. But by far the oddest moment came when she was asked (on NBC's *Today* show) if she'd contacted Monica. "I know that I would not be welcome," she answered sadly, while breaking out in a wide, incongruous, mirthless smile, upper teeth bared for attack.

Facial distortion or problem dentition are things well-mannered persons are trained to overlook, and we think of ourselves as better (and classier) people to the degree that we can do so. I feel rude bringing it up. But on the other hand, skilled actors who are more than usually attractive in one role have the ability to make their faces quite ugly in another, and with the best actors it's an ugliness that works from the inside out: not makeup and prostheses, but distorted *affect*. People with big pug-ugly physical features can be renowned as sex objects, while in other cases, the same face will be worn like an ill-fitting appendage: same features, two expressions. An actor portraying a person motivated by unacknowledged aggression would give an outstanding performance by arranging his features to emulate Tripp's.

Of course, this is all post facto observation. But given the steep learning curve on deception, we're always playing catch-up here: knowledge is invariably retrospective and spotty, with no particular applicability to future cases. The ways that people wear their contradictions and what the consequences will be is too idiosyncratic to predict, like knowing which bee will suddenly decide to sting you. We're just not that astute. Knowledge, desire, anger, even friendship, transform what we see. Over-reading leads to paranoia and loneliness. We don't know what we're looking for—or at. So we live our lives as a protracted series of experiments in deception studies, constructing experimental protocols and collecting provisional data, comparing them against previous results, discarding disproven hypotheses as we go—along with lying friends, faithless lovers, and the various self-idealizations that no longer hold up, either. Let's not leave lying to oneself out of the mix. We're researchers and lab rats both: vernacular social scientists whose knowledge of the big picture is always incomplete and probably self-deluding at best. Our faces are the enduring testimony to these impossibly complicated histories of deception and betrayed trust—or deprivation and distress, or excitement and pleasure, or some clash of discordant sentiments and experiences. Sometimes so discordant as to cause others to recoil, without knowing exactly what they're reacting to.

Those who have followed the Tripp story as it unraveled will recall the archeological digs through the Tripp family dirt, much of it uncovered by Jane Mayer writing in the *New Yorker*. More retrospective knowledge: a divorced and faithless father, a mysterious teenage arrest, a troubled marriage, an adult obsession with crimes and betrayals large and small. There were continuous calls to local police to lodge minor complaints, there was an obsession with other people's sex lives. Reports (later denied by Tripp) were that our Linda was the source of those earlier rumors about George Bush's affair with another Jennifer. The latest word is a lawsuit against the White House and Defense Department for attempting to smear her reputation. A life story devoted to grievance and the search for redress. Clearly, we don't choose our obsessions (or moral failings, or disavowals) any more than we choose our faces. If we did, who would make these choices?

To bear the stigma of ugliness can only be an emotionally deforming affliction, and to be burdened with a face that wears its conflicts with such a distorted insistence is not a fate anyone would wish to live. Tripp's account of her motives for exposing and betraying her friend, recounted on the round of talk shows in February, was as contorted as her expression. First she insisted she'd done it to protect poor Monica, then she insisted that she'd been forced to do it, against her will, to protect herself. The one thing that was clear was her grievance at Clinton's sexual privilege—although precisely why this should so rile her is hardly apparent. (Or too apparent, at least according to the cartoonists.) Of course we live now in a grievance culture: all sorts of people are lining up to lodge their complaints large and small at the doorstep of the nation, or indeed, the White House. No wonder Tripp was drawn into the Paula Jones imbroglio, another out-of-scale grievance, with sexual-harassment law the big stick to protest an exceedingly minor grudge. Asked by Larry King if Tripp thought she'd played a role in reforming Clinton's sexual behavior, she nodded her head vigorously, "I think he'll think twice about it." It turns out that when Tripp isn't protesting something, she has a completely different face, and it's not unattractive. The mouth closes, she presses her lips flat together (hiding that upper row of attack teeth), and bobs her head. It's cute. After noting her own role in Clinton's supposed sexual rehabilitation, she didn't look half bad.

It's not only faces that express conflicts, of course. There are many bodily sites for symptom production. Let's not leave out symptomatic behavior, since we were treated to quite a spectacular variety of it during the Clinton presidency. In our leader's case, it seems to be other regions of the anatomy that bear the burden of his contradictions—which hardly makes him unique. (And of course the jokes about Clinton have always been aimed at his body, with all its myriad manifestations of out-of-control appetites.) It's only ironic that Clinton, whose political career was founded on his mastery of the close-up, should have been so very nearly impaled on the grievances of someone to whom the close-up has hardly been so kind. This, in fact, can be said of both the women who've chosen Clinton as a nemesis. The unhappy thing for Paula Jones and Linda Tripp, the tremulous belle and the snitch, was being so lured by the national spotlight and so myopically intent on the prospect of exposing a male miscreant—as if that would rectify some very personal injustice—they forgot that exposure is a two-way street. The nation didn't; the aftermath was a little like watching a public bloodsport and not feeling very sorry for the helpless creature getting mauled. Both women subsequently underwent extensive makeovers, reemerging with new bodies, noses, and hairdos, which did nothing whatsoever to decrease the volume of the jokes or—in this observer's aesthetic judgment—the basis for their existence.

Please don't misunderstand: I firmly believe that feminist critiques of appearance evaluations—the ranking, the impossible standards, the feminine normativity—counts as social progress for all of us. But failing to achieve beauty—of whatever version prevails in one's day—doesn't make you ugly, it only makes you ordinary. Tripp's was no *ordinary* face, and the complicated responses it evoked suggests that ugliness might be less a physical fact than a social relation, not physiognomic but pathognomic and intersubjective, rooted both in the subject's failure to integrate conflicting emotional impulses, and in the intensity of the onlooker's disidentification with the too-insistent visible evidence of those conflicts. Tripp's face didn't just launch a thousand jokes, it launched a thousand anxieties.

The question, then, would be whether aesthetic judgments such as these, norms and scorecards aside, are ways of producing social knowledge, and whether this is, perhaps, knowledge worth shielding from inducements to sensitivity. Or from our own polite denials in regard to the visceral and aesthetic responses evoked. Jokes do provide a cushion of deniability, of course, although I suspect that ugly jokes are typically made about the appearances of those toward whom there are other reasons than appearance alone to be ambivalent—power for example, or other impingements on a collective sense of social equity or justice. Jokes often function as a social corrective, and though not infrequently a conservative force, at least they have always been premised on not politely ignoring what's staring you in the face.

At the beginning of the whole imbroglio, when it started to seem as though Tripp might seriously manage to bring down a presidency, one perverse part of me cheered: *the ugly woman's revenge.* It was quite mythic, both fascinating and appalling. Tripp's repellence was aesthetically unsettling and yet somehow *pleasura-*

ble, an aversion-attraction that much of the country apparently shared. Indeed, it was quite a tangled intersubjective affair for the national sensibility. According to William Ian Miller's *The Anatomy of Disgust*, a fantastically interesting tour through the sewers of the human symbolic imagination, the theme of the loathely hag continues in various reincarnations into the present day. But it's not really that we fear intimacy with the ugly and haglike, Miller tells us. Rather, it's that we know how we see them and could not bear to be thus seen. The horror isn't in being intimate with them, it's in *being* them.

At her first press conference, when Linda Tripp protested to those assembled, "I'm just like you!" only to provoke the incredulous hoots and jeers of the nation, no one could take their eyes off her. Why the fascination? *Could* we be just like her? Who would not disavow this painful possibility—along with one's own betrayals, grievances, and self-deceptions large and small. But because we all do have faces—the prerequisite, perhaps, to knowledge of others—we do know, at some level, just how it would feel to have, or wear, or be "that face."

Notes

1. Tomkins was an early mentor of Paul Ekman's; interest in his deeply quirky work has been recently revived by Eve Sedgwick and Adam Frank's edited volume of his writings, *Shame and Her Sisters: A Silvan Tomkins Reader* (Durham, N.C.: Duke University Press, 1995).

2. One of the many ironies of the human cluelessness at detecting deception is its stymieing effect on this area of facial expression research in the social sciences. Since studies tend not to get published that display what are called "null results," that is, in which no correlation between one thing and another can be found (only positive findings interest journal editors and the funding agencies who distribute research dollars), deception research turns out not to be a hugely promising area of study. It's also a field completely constituted by moral compromise, which causes problems of conscience among its inhabitants: in order to study deception, researchers typically resort to lying, cheating, and deceiving their subjects, or inducing their experimentees—usually hapless psych students—into situations in which they're impelled to lie, cheat, or morally compromise themselves (and are then turned loose on the general population). For all of these reasons—or maybe the field just attracts offbeat types—deception researchers do seem to come up with more poignant conclusions about their object of study than one typically finds in the social sciences. The entire field seems afflicted with pathos.

Bibliography

Adorno, Theodor. *Aesthetic Theory*. Ed. Gretel Adorno and Rolf Tiedemann, trans. C. Lenhardt (London: RKP, 1984).

Cole, Jonathan. *About Face* (Cambridge, Mass.: MIT Press, 1998).

Cousins, Mark. "The Ugly." *AA Files 28* (1996), 61–64; *AA Files 29* (1996), 3–6.

Ekman, Paul, ed. *Emotion in the Human Face* (Cambridge, U.K.: Cambridge University Press, 1984).

Freud, Sigmund. *Jokes and Their Relation to the Unconscious*. Trans. James Strachey (New York: Norton, 1963).

Gilman, Sander L. *Creating Beauty to Cure the Soul: Race and Psychology in the Shaping of Aesthetic Surgery* (Durham, N.C.: Duke University Press, 1998).

Goffman, Erving. *Stigma: Notes on the Management of Spoiled Identity* (New York: Simon and Schuster, 1963).

Kant, Immanuel. *Critique of Judgement*. Trans. J. H. Bernard (New York: Haffner, 1951).

Kris, Ernst. *Psychoanalytic Explorations in Art* (New York: International Universities Press, 1952).

Miller, Gerald R., and James B. Stiff. *Deceptive Communication* (Newbury Park, Calif.: Sage, 1993).

Miller, William Ian. *The Anatomy of Disgust* (Cambridge, Mass.: Harvard University Press, 1997).

Moore, Ronald. "Ugliness." In *Encyclopedia of Aesthetics,* vol. 4, ed. Michael Kelly (New York: Oxford University Press, 1998), 417–421.

Sedgwick, Eve Kosofsky, and Adam Frank, eds. *Shame and Its Sisters: A Silvan Tomkins Reader* (Durham, N.C.: Duke University Press, 1995).

Stolnitz, Jerome. "Ugliness." In *Encyclopedia of Philosophy*, vol. 8, ed. Paul Edward (New York: Macmillan, 1967), 174–176.

Synnot, Anthony. "Truth and goodness, mirrors and masks: A sociology of beauty and the face, Parts I and II." *British Journal of Sociology* 40:4 (1989), 607–636; 41:1 (1990), 55–76.

Tomkins, Silvan S. *Affect, Imagery, Consciousness*. Vol. 1 (New York: Springer, 1962).

4 It's Not about Sex

James R. Kincaid

I

Americans are in the happy position of being able to invest just about anything with erotic desire. I say this without having recourse to studies or opinion polls by virtue of my position as a representative American,[1] not in all areas, only in sex.

My subject here is the relation of the Lewinsky-Clinton matter to our abilities to have sex or to think of having sex in response to it. Sex exists where we can find ways to talk about having sex.[2] Where we can't do that, there is no sex. Desire, then, is the same thing as sex, in that neither one exists outside of narratives, and those narratives coincide. If we can tell a story of desire, then we are telling a story that will enable us to imagine having sex, which is, for Americans, sex itself. As I say, I know.

For instance, consider what it is you do not desire. I do not mean by this the antidote to desire (Mother) or the comic grotesque (William Howard Taft and a chicken), but that which really does tend to invade desire although we wish it didn't. What do you wish wasn't around when you are thinking about sex or making up narratives about it, i.e., having sex? The right answer is: yourself. I don't mean your whole self or your mind, but your physical self, your body—the idea or, worse, the accurate image of your body. The last thing we want intruding on our sexual fantasies is us. Grant me that.

Part I: Backing Up

Why are Bill and Monica living where sexual desire isn't? That's a tasteful question, but to explore it we have to raise others that aren't. What jokes weren't told? What kind of talk was unheard around the water coolers, faculty lounges, barbershops, and garages of America? What about real flesh talk? What about those bodies?

Part II: Dismissing One Answer

One possibility is that we didn't talk about such things because we have grown sophisticated, used to it, like Europeans. We regard Bill's unfurled pecker and Monica's bethonged buttocks with bemused indifference, having seen many such and having advanced "beyond eros," like the French. Not likely. It's true that we have proved eager to "censure and move on" and that we have not produced the sort of outrage mixed with prurience we come up with when we get excited, as with JonBenet Ramsey or porn-on-the-net. Those things get our gothic juices flowing, but Bill and Monica reach no secret springs. We are agreed, though, that no honest person would call all of this "sophisticated." It looks more like avoidance to me (you).

Part III: The Kind of Sex We Do Like

The kind of sex or sex-talk we do like is in the comic or the science-fiction modes exclusively—narratives of the grotesque or of the fantastic. In terms of comedy, we can always produce terrific zany sex for any occasion; the only erotic image to emerge for this story has been in this mode: John Goodman puckering up as Linda Tripp. On the other hand, in the fabulous mode, we can fantasize about Jack Kennedy and Marilyn Monroe, about Humbert and his Lo, about anyone we haven't seen for a long time. But Bill and Monica themselves are not funny, not hazy, not available for our sexual uses. It's not that they excite oedipal prohibitions or that they are violently ugly. Were they either, we could find a way to use them, versatile as we are. I can deal easily enough with Mother and Father or with Strom Thurmond and Janet Reno in my fantasies—and so can you. It's that Bill and Monica are too close to us, too imaginable—cruelly, inescapably, and in the raw. They force their bodies—all hairy, pimpled, and blubbed—into our faces. And who wants to see that, our very selves, panting and red-faced? Nobody appears in his or her fantasies without lots of thick makeup and artful costuming. Nothing is more deadly to desire than a high-quality mental mirror.

Part IV: A Look at Bill and Monica

What do they really look like? Bill in his jogging suit is a fair image of Bill in the raw: jiggly and wet, the white whale. Monica is another story, but not a better one. Camille Paglia, who has insight into these things, says Monica disclosing to Barbara Walters looked like "a big baby; literally, all she needed was a diaper and a pacifier."[3] Monica in a diaper: there's an image that escapes any alt.binaries.pictures.erotica site. Worse are the visions she thrusts at us: *Time,* in its exclusive interview, asked her what she was thinking when she showed Bill her thong and what lay beneath. Instead of telling us what she thought, Monica told us what she *did* and gave us advice on how we too could do it: "If you put your hands on your waist and you locked your thumbs under your short jacket and just sort of lifted it, about two inches . . ."[4] Don't try it, if you want my advice. In the interests of fairness to Monica, I did and shouldn't have. Still, Monica locks her thumbs right under the reason all of this isn't sex: she is us. So is Bill. Attacks on them as "equally immature, with bottomless needs, heedless narcissism and steamer trunks full of emotional baggage"[5] are simply ungenerous descriptions of all of us. To call my own bottomless needs and heedless narcissism, yours too, "immature" is to posit a state of "maturity" none of us could reach if we wanted to, which we certainly don't. But it's not needs we're worried about; it's bodies—bodies (our own, Bill's, Monica's) we can live inside just fine so long as we don't have to watch them.

Part V: It's Not about Sex

We agree that it is not about sex. Everyone says that: Kenneth Starr—it's "about lies, not sex"; President Clinton—"I did not have sexual relations with that woman, Miss Lewinsky"; Monica—"*Do you still think that oral sex isn't sex?* Unhum [yes]"; all Baptists (Clinton being one) who know what they did was not intercourse (sex); and all the rest of us who know, even the horniest part of our population, college undergraduates.[6] What the "it" is that isn't sex shifts, of course, according to the context: anatomical, moral, legal, or casual. My point is that it always shifts so as to keep the bodies themselves out of the picture. The idea that oral sex isn't sex is just one of those refocusings.

And we all know that such professions are hokum, that even Baptists, even Kenneth Starr, knows that oral sex is sex, if it's the right people having it. The right people means somebody other than Clinton and Lewinsky or you and me. One might claim that oral sex doesn't strike us as sex because it can seem too impersonal, too like masturbation, too ungendered (a zucchini, a hole in a barrel), and so forth. But all that is beside the point: give us the right bodies and virtually anything they do will set off in our heads stories of desire, and thus sex.

Part VI: First Test—Bill/Monica Dirty Talk

What would dirty talk about Bill and Monica be like? That's a fair test of my thesis and I win. There could never be such talk, since dirty talk requires bodies and these particular bodies (ours) are banned from the erotic arena.

Part VII: Second Test—What about Their Talk?

It still might be possible to generalize the Monica-Bill affair, make it hazy and distant, like our best fantasies, and go to town on it. The problem is that what we have of their affair is their talk, and their talk is so insistently about bodies, bringing them before our eyes like slugs in a rose garden. For instance: "Nothing would make me happier than to see you, except to see you with a winning lottery ticket in one hand and a can of whipped cream in the other" (a Monica postcard to the president); or when Clinton says of coffee cups "I like big mugs," the sprightly Monica retorts, "No, you like big jugs."[7] Jugs and whipped cream are just what we do not want to think about, not here. My own favorite test case, though, is Monica's description of being mentally undressed:

And the way he looks at women he's attracted to. He undresses you with his eyes. And it is slow, from the bottom of your toes to the top of your head back down to your toes again. And it's an intense look. He loses his smile. He sexual energy kind of comes over his eyes and . . .[8]

I leave it to you, but if you think that passage doesn't go a long way to hammering in my point, go back and look at that "back down to your toes again" part and say you can live happily and erotically with that image. As the details of the undressing proceed, as Monica's garments waft upwards and downwards, leaving her bare from head to toe, nothing hidden, toes all akimbo, Bill all inflamed, any erotic idealizing we had wanted to sustain gets all glommed up in the specificity of the actual bodies. Right?

Part VIII: You Heard the One About?

As revealing as jokes are, untold jokes speak more loudly. The Monica-Bill jokes we hear are plentiful, generally bad, and always displaced, offering us a chance to practice a kind of jocular safe sex by making not only remote but invisible the bodies in question, wrapping them in condoms of steel and transporting them to some distant planet. Many of the jokes were of course about sex, but the kind of sex we like, which is not sex involving straight-on shots of Bill and Monica, me and you.

These jokes, in other words, only pretended to be about Bill and Monica. What they are about are other bodies entirely or, at most, about separable body parts: mouths attached to no face and peckers disconnected from torsos. When these jokes work, they work by artfully drawing our attention away from bodies or at least transferring our attention from the bodies of Bill and Monica to others more savory. But usually these are nonreferential jokes, generalized and requiring no visualization. Many jokes substituted numbers for anatomy: a survey of five hundred women, asking if they would make love to the President, found 87 percent of them saying "Never again!" When we *see* anything, it is likely to be displaced from the body and onto, say, the dress:

Monica walks into the dry cleaning store and tells the guy, "I got another dress for you to clean." A little hard of hearing, the clerk says, "Come again?" "No," says Monica. "Mustard."[9]

Clinton's clothes also managed to shift the focus from his flesh, even if no farther than his zipper. Usually farther: why does he wear underwear? To keep his ankles warm.

Puns take the place of bodies, as in the many knee-slappers circulating that played on harmonica/whore-Monica (Bill has given up the saxophone for—). Ditto, the jokes on head (Monica's going to Morehead University; she's the new director of the Head Start Program). Many of the jokes on oral sex carefully direct our attention to anything other than the erotic stimulation and make it sound like lunch: it's called Swallowgate because it's a full-blown crisis; Bill and Monica never had to go out because there was plenty to eat right there in the White House.

Jokes that use the visual or play with bodies do so by switching to our customary erotic possibilities, the grotesque and the fantastic. As comedy, there's Janet Reno wanting an internship program for the Justice Department and Kenneth Starr extending his probe. The fantasy jokes try to draw in bodies we really do want to look at—Hillary's and Al Gore's, for instance: somebody pee-writes "Clinton sucks" in the snow outside the White House; chemical analysis shows the pee is Gore's but (snare drums and cymbals ready) the handwriting is Hillary's.

Now, I cannot claim to have heard or read every single Clinton-Lewinsky joke, of course, but I think I have. The closest we get to bodies in any of these endless jokes involves puns on "harass," and a few dismal jokes on the president's crooked penis, jokes so bad they have to add a footnote to explain that the alleged penis-bend was reported by Paula Jones. Nobody wants to know that, though, so these laborious jokes—Nixon was a crooked pres following Johnson, and Clinton is the sitting pres with a crooked Johnson—floundered before the race started. Bad bodies are bad bodies, top to toe and in between.

More revealing are the plentiful body jokes which suggest that no bodies whatever are involved, that even Monica sees only a flabby piece of meat, and the president sees virtually nothing: "Which body part of Monica's does the president most enjoy gazing at? The top of her head." Absolutely the most revealing are those that rope in Ted Kennedy, who is himself grotesque (when will his face explode?), but also carries with him in his name and in his sad resemblance to his brother the shadow of the other erotic narrative, the fantastic. Here, in the best joke of all, we have Kennedy standing in for the frightening Clinton body but playing out the primal fantasy of eliminating bodies altogether: "What does Ted Kennedy have that President Clinton wishes he had? A dead girlfriend."

II

So why really isn't it about sex? The bodies in question are unappealing, at first glance, and so are ours. But that cannot explain everything, even if I've been suggesting that it can. After all, it really isn't true that we scream in terror if we accidentally glimpse ourselves in the mirror. I try to avoid harsh lighting or seeing myself unclothed, though once I was in an elevator that was all mirrors and a nightmare of pitiless revelations. Still, when you reach my age (roughly 24), you stop imagining that you will soon have another body and learn instead to project your fantasies maturely. That Bill and Monica both look like you and me can't account by itself for our leaving the scene of their eros. Our relationship to our own bodies and to theirs is not so simple, and what we are disavowing with one breath we are, shyly, reclaiming with the next.

Part IX: Heeeeeeeeeere's Kenneth

We all, you and me, have often found ourselves in that blessed state of loving our fellows, feeling happy to be a member of the species and not too picky about who we were rubbing elbows with. It's a Whitmanesque mood of feeling one with the bum, kin with the king, drunk on woozy human connectedness. In such a state, surely, we could find it in our libidos to be stirred by Bill or Monica, either one.

So why doesn't that happen here? Why have we refused to be aroused at this spectacle and the stories flowing from it? One reason is Ken Starr. He has stepped between us and erotic possibility here, taken up not so much center stage as the voyeur's spot behind the bushes, where we want to be. He is himself so sneakily lascivious that he sucks up the entire national supply.

It's easy to hate him for it, even if we hate Clinton too. We hate Kenneth Starr more than we used to hate the communists. Equipped with all the subtlety and tolerance for complexity of a hammerhead shark, Starr's Puritanism repulses some. But it's more his lust that we despise: he has taken lust out of the head and into the media and the courts, leaving us with very slim pickings. His own thin-lipped sexual cravings are so disgusting they embarrass our more robust voyeuris-tic sadism and cause it to shrivel. It's not because we side with the victim or be-cause, as Louis Begley puts it, Starr has "turned us into a nation of Peeping Toms";[10] it's that he has defined the sexual geography in such a blunt way as to turn it into the national dump. Only 39 percent of the people even think he acted "responsibly," and when paired with Clinton in a who-would-you-rather-have contest, he loses by at least 2-1 in the friend-and-neighbor, boss, invite-to-a-party, have-to-Christmas dinner contest; he even loses in the "have as your children's teacher" head-to-head,[11] which shows the extent of our animosity. We'll even sac-rifice our kids to spite the pharisaic ninny who throws cold water on our desire.

Part X: Even Viagara Is No Match for Banality

It's hard to keep lit a sexual fantasy when it is showered by K-Mart-quality details. Bill and Monica not only shove their bodies in our faces but their mouths against our ears. Just as Nixon's Satanism was deflated when the tapes revealed just how plain dumb the Oval Office talk was, so is the possibility of sneaky titillation de-flated here by the Monica-Bill discourse, which mixes adolescent profundity with noninsights into each other and the world, with giggly prefabricated endearments (I love you, butthead!), and jokes (the Jewish-American princess and the apple) to show how at ease they are with each other and what a special, special under-standing they share. It makes us squirm to wade through such things, so like us at our most enthusiastic and (ah) most original, so cold and lifeless there in print.

He tells her, doubtless with stupefying sincerity, "You walk around and you're always smiling and so bubbly, and there's so much sadness and pain behind those eyes," and she counts that as wisdom, telling him, in return, that he has a hard time being fulfilled, which comes from being needy. Others who meet them seem reduced to the same level. Barbara Walters, up-close and personal with

Monica, says, "I found Monica very intelligent and very open. I told her, 'You are very alive.' And she said, 'Maybe that was the appeal.'" And Billy Graham, who has experience in these matters similar to Walters's and is at least as shrewd, offered this of Bill: "He has such a tremendous personality that I think the ladies just go wild over him." There you have it, folks: Ms. Alive meets Mr. Tremendous Personality. If that isn't enough to deaden desire, their spiritual talk will do it. Here's Monica on prayer, for instance, "I think, for me, my definition of praying might be a little different. I think, for me, in some ways therapy is sort of praying. It's like what you learn in therapy and what you walk away with. You kind of think to yourself . . ."[12]

Part XI: It Really Isn't What Anyone Would Call Sex

This is just to correct what I said before about oral sex being sex if we could imagine the right people having it. That may be, but it's beside the point. When it's the wrong people having it, it simply reminds us of sex; and since we don't want to be reminded of sex in such a case, the wrong people having oral sex is something like enjoying a meal and then sneezing and having the chewed-up shrimp come out through your nose. Besides, Monica seems clear in her conversations with Linda Tripp about what sex is:

> **Linda:** What is the definition of sex?
> **Monica:** Intercourse.

Phone sex, on the other hand, does seem to fit her definition of sex. Maybe phone sex is intercourse:

> **Linda:** You're—You're so good at it. No wonder he likes phone sex with you—You're just a little Marilyn Monroe vixen. I—I would—I, I, I know in my wildest dreams I could never have phone sex.
> **Monica:** Oh, yes, you could.[13]

We can understand the distinction: in their case, phone sex *is* sex, precisely because nobody sees anything, bodies being stored away safely in the imagination.

Part XII: But Who's in Control?

I apologize in advance for the abstractions in this part, but give it a try. I think that, down deep, it's hard to imagine this story as erotic because our narratives of the affair cannot settle on who has authority, which is to say, we cannot tell the story very effectively inside Power. And since Power is the metaphysical center we worship and since everything erotic in our discourse seems sadly centered in this Power, we seem unable to imagine arousal without it.

One can watch the Republicans trying hard to make it into a clear Power story that would arouse our arousals and thus our defensive moralisms, would get us excited and thus sanctimonious. They tried, in fact, all conceivable variations. The Starr Report, as Janet Malcolm points out, idiotically portrays "the man he wishes to destroy not as the cold seducer and exploiter of youth and innocence but as the pitiable victim of a predatory female."[14] The Republicans, sensing disaster, later reversed the narrative, deciding, after viewing Monica's taped deposition, that she was "young" and fixed that label to her with as much glue as they could find: "All I can say is I found her heartbreakingly young," said Senator Susan Collins, trying hard.[15]

But few Americans found the Power stories persuasive, no matter how they were rigged. As Toni Morrison bluntly said: it was never "a story about seduction— male vamp or female predator (or the other way around). It played that way a little . . . but had no staying power."[16] The Power story had no Power, she says: it was as stirring as last week's halibut. It's a lousy thing, but we seem unable to imagine sex outside of Power, i.e., power inequalities. Our erotic imagination cannot feed except at power plants.

Part XIII: Monica May Be a Baby, but Oh You Kid!
I'll just mumble this point and slide past it, since I don't want to be thought obsessive: neither Monica nor Bill can be easily thought of as children. That means that it's hard for us to see them as enticing, our main cultural images of the arousing being the bodies of those commonly found on playgrounds, playing video games, skateboarding, and eating Lunchables. Monica does indeed project herself resolutely as a child (a great big child) but only in terms of pathology, not flesh. We've seen Shirley Temple and are not going to settle for Monica in pantaloons.

III

Maybe we deserve more credit. Perhaps it's not our inability to cast Bill and Monica in a pornographic narrative that's at issue but our more humane willingness to see them in a small and sad human drama. Perhaps it reminds us more of sit-coms than of high tragedy or good erotica. It's like glimpsing the fear inside Archie Bunker or the vulnerable Frasier or the cast of M.A.S.H. bidding farewell. The sit-com Dad, old Bill, is a good-hearted blunderer everyone else must manage: old

Lear on Walnut Street messing up again. The scene doesn't amount to a lot, but it suggests to us something too close to home to allow for much more than a sigh. We wish Bill and Monica could have it better, since their petty failings hardly deserve the stories that try to get told about them.

It's partly that the single-minded enemies of Bill and Monica, who emit what E. L. Doctorow nicely terms the "punitive lusts" of American Puritanism,[17] so overmatch them, seem to be drawn on a different scale. Even the screecher, Linda Tripp—"I'm you. I'm just like you"[18]—seems to be more at home in the soap-operatic narrative. Tripp, at least, carries on with something like admirable consistency her role of wronged truth-teller, vilified for her very virtues. If she had her way, which is to say if she were in the right plot, it'd all work. But we have refused to purchase that narrative.

We have a story forlornly looking for a genre. Whether we like Monica or not, we respond to her more as a dog-paddler lost in the mid-Atlantic than as a schemer. She can be disarmingly funny—"me only telling 10 people was being pretty discreet for me"[19]—throwing herself on our mercy without any particular design, simply because she has no other place to cast her words. She's a woman making the best of what she has, we suppose, incapable of proceeding without blundering and possessed of more spirit than wit. She sees about as little of the roots of those values that guide her as we do and is, like us, more worried about being fat than being wicked. She was, she says many times, most hurt by the comments on her weight and all those caricatures (and photographs too, I suppose). For me, the only sweet thing I can find about Bill in all this was Monica's account of how he "tried to soothe her anxiety about her weight by telling her that as a small boy he was so fat" that he never got any eggs in the Easter-egg race. We didn't either, you and me, and it's nice of him to bring it up and nice of Monica to say he did.

Bill is harder for us to like, but even he fits better as something from *Ordinary People* than as Iago or Don Juan or even Dick Nixon. And one can see in him a variousness that we can even admire: "He possesses a complexity of bearing, an openness of spirit, and a fullness of experience that allow him to embrace high ideals and at the same time trespass against convention. And it is this tolerance for ambiguity within the self," says Ethan Canin, "that distinguishes Mr. Clinton from his accusers."[20]

But I think we need not involve him in comparisons. His sins, after all, are sins of attachment,[21] which are rare enough to be virtues. He wanted to express desire somehow or other and to receive it from another. Disloyal, manipulative, heedless—yet still it is as hard to condemn as it is to be aroused by a president who will risk all for a hug, a sneak-peek at buttocks, a blow job.

It's tawdry and not what we feel, in light of conventional stories, we have every right to expect. But only in repellant moralistic stories and in only slightly less repellant porn do we get what we expect. Getting what we expect is so close to getting what we deserve—and who will 'scape whipping? Such stories as those of Bill and Monica can stir our pity and our fear, not certainly in the high Greek or Shakespearean way, but in a way appropriate to what George Eliot defined as "ordinary tragedy." Such tragedies, made up more of pity than of fear, draw us in so close we may not be able to see enough to be aroused. We may, as Eliot says, only feel our heart beat with theirs.

Or at least with Monica's, partly because that wonderful bubbler keeps on going. She admits that having a new relationship will be hard—but only for a while (a week?):

It's going to take a very special, very strong person to step up to the plate, and I don't know if the things that I want in a man and in a relationship could be balanced by someone who could do that. But I hope so.[22]

I hope so, too. What's more, I've been doing some work in the batting cage and am ready to take my cuts. I'm in the on-deck circle now.

Notes

1. I do not speak for non-Americans here. That other countries have different erotic interests and practices I do not doubt. What counts for sex in, say, Peru, Algeria, Belgium, or (especially) Canada is a mystery to me. I claim only to speak for Americans, all Americans, regardless of gender, class, sexual orientation, or race: that's what it means to live in a democracy.

I realize that my "we" may not be your "we." What I am aiming for in this use of the first-person plural is not so much your response (or mine) as a cultural and historical location, the way we are written (as we used to say) into the parts we are handed. The "we" is my sense of how the story works for us, for all of us. Now, there may be variations among actors in this story, of course, variations we wildly overstate so as to preserve the illusion of individual control. I use the "we" to counter the illusion of individuality and to point to the drama surrounding us and handing us our parts to play. You'll be quick enough to note where you are resisting the role handed down to you, so I've made no attempt to account for that. Carrying coals to Newcastle is a mug's game.

2. Frank Mankiewicz gets it exactly wrong on Bill and Monica and on this issue generally: "People don't like to talk about sex, they just like to do it" (*Newsweek*, August 24, 1998, p. 17). Mankiewicz is a consultant for the Democratic party, which is not good news for Democrats. They should hire me.

3. *Los Angeles Times* (March 5, 1999), p. B7. A poll of Americans conducted by *Newsweek* reveals that 57 percent of us agree with Paglia, seeing Monica "as a child," only 33 percent (who have never seen her) regarding her as "adult" (March 15, 1999), p. 31.

4. March 15, 1999, p. 32.

5. Margaret Carlson, *Time* (March 15, 1999), p. 41.

6. In order: *New Yorker* (August 10, 1998), p. 28; *Newsweek* (August 10, 1998), p. 25; *Newsweek* (November 2, 1998), p. 37; *Time* (March 15, 1999), p. 34; *Newsweek* (January 25, 1999), p. 28. The last results, drawn from the Kinsey Institute (a 1991 survey of a Midwestern state university's undergrads) was published in the *Journal of the American Medical Association,* landing its editor, Dr. George Lundberg, in the midst of an unedifying controversy.

7. *Time* (October 5, 1998), p. 39.

8. In the exclusive interview to *Time* (March 15, 1999), p. 32.

9. Most of these jokes are taken from the co-operative "Bill Clinton and Monica Lewinsky Joke Page": http://www.gorgon.com/users/~charlie/monica.html.

10. *New Yorker* (October 5, 1998), p. 34.

11. All figures are drawn from a Time-CNN poll, published in *Time* (December 28, 1988–January 4, 1999), p. 65.

12. Taken from, in order, *Time* (March 15, 1999), p. 34; *Time* (January 11, 1999), p. 21; *Newsweek* (December 28, 1998/January 4, 1999), p. 92; *Time* (March 15, 1999), p. 36.

13. From the phone transcripts: *Time* (October 12, 1998), p. 26. To be fair, Lewinsky later made a distinction between a "hard definition" (not sex) and "casual conversation" (is sex): *Time* (March 15, 1999), p. 34.

14. *New Yorker* (October 5, 1998), p. 32.

15. Quoted in *Time* (February 15, 1999), p. 15.

16. *New Yorker* (October 5, 1998), p. 31.

17. *New Yorker* (October 12, 1998), p. 30.

18. From her public statement read on the courthouse steps after her eighth grand jury session: *Newsweek* (August 10, 1998), p. 30.

19. *Time* (March 15, 1999), p. 32.

20. *New Yorker* (September 21, 1998), p. 39 .

21. Jane Smiley made a similar case in *New Yorker* (September 21, 1998), p. 39.

22. *Time* (March 15, 1999), p. 36.

The Erotics of Hypocrisy in the White House Scandal

Simone Weil Davis

Clinton's first apology speech in August 1998 was not entirely apologetic. Less contrite than stern, the president insisted that his errors had been private and should have remained as such, so that he could "go on with the business of running this country." Despite his patriarchal gravity that night, more Cotton Mather than François Mitterand, many of Clinton's defenders used the bon vivant dalliances of European politicians to remind us that the Puritanism of a repressed America had led in this case to the criminalization of consensual sex. These lines of defense seem commonsensical and, at first glance, just about incontrovertible to any of those who position themselves as sex-friendly. Nonetheless, I think they cast the affair in a distorted light, because they imply that in this scandal we can draw a clear divide between private pleasures, on the one hand, and the violations of an official body engaging in surveillance and censure, on the other. If you look at the Starr Report, though, at public apprehension of the entire scandal, and at Monica and Bill's sex itself (something that, rather ludicrously, we are in a position to judge), you discover that prurience and condemnation are mutually constitutive across the full spectrum of this scandal, and thus one cannot reasonably be said to be a victim of the other.

Struck by what seemed a vilification process and a merciless hounding, those who denounced Ken Starr's investigation and the subsequent impeachment proceedings often leveled the charge of "sexual McCarthyism." Although I too opposed both the spirit and the strategies of the Republicans' endeavor, I think the shoe of sexual McCarthyism just doesn't fit this end-of-millennium sexual showcase. Richard Goldstein, himself a proponent for this very analogue, wrote a *Village Voice* piece that was perhaps the most thoughtful essay along these lines that I have encountered, sensitive as he is to the sexual subcurrents that informed the McCarthy witch hunt and to those that drive the debate today.[1] Despite his insights, I will argue in this essay that the elisions required by this correspondence blind us to the deepest political significance of the scandal, and give too much credence to the ultimately false divide of partisan distinctions. The pleasure of this open secret cannot be cleaved from its discovery and denunciation nor from the hypocrisy that spawned it. Bill's and Monica's was not a witch-hunted love.

During his sexual encounters with Lewinsky (if that's what they technically were), Clinton always kept the door between the Oval Office and the adjoining private hallway several inches ajar, the Starr Report tells its avid reader.[2] The door was left open to mimic everyday appearances, to make it easier for the lovers to hear someone coming, and, one guesses, to add urgency to the panicked thrill of the forbidden exploit. As we scroll or flip through the many pages of the report, especially if we are familiar with the protocols of melodramatic intrigue, it will seem evident that the pleasure taken—and the power dynamics that unfolded—in the darkened Oval Office were intensified by the possibility of getting caught. As they pushed aside clothing, took phone calls *en dishabille*, bit hands to muffle moans, grazed genitals but avoided penetration, and always left that door cracked open, Clinton and Lewinsky invented the dangers of a probing Starr with their sex, just as Starr's soft-core/legalese treatise invents Clinton and Lewinsky *as their sex*. This porous membrane, the door ajar, brings us to the realm of the Moebius strip that double-sides power and pleasure in Foucault's *History of Sexuality*, Volume 1.[3]

The pleasure that comes of exercising a power that questions, monitors, watches, spies, searches out, palpates, brings to light; and on the other hand, the pleasure that kindles at having to evade this power, flee from it, fool it, or travesty it. The power that lets itself be invaded by the pleasure it is pursuing; and opposite it, power asserting itself in the pleasure of showing off, scandalizing or resisting. . . . These attractions, these evasions, these circular incitements have traced around bodies and sexes, not boundaries to be crossed, but perpetual spirals of power and pleasure. (45)

These "perpetual spirals" refuse to freeze or to cleave. The "sides" of a Moebius strip could never be said to oppose one another; as they *are* each other, irresolubly.[4]

We take our titillation bundled with censure in this country, as a listen to the hoots and jeers of a Jerry Springer audience will quickly corroborate. Alternate waves of mirth and disapproval from the studio spectators duet with the guests' violent, outré sexual theater. Listening to the Springer chorus and perhaps sharing their responses, who's to tell when the sneer becomes a leer and vice versa? On the Springer show the entire moral climate is tinged with farce, of course, as everyone assumes some degree of burlesque in the proceedings. Still, even at the circus, forbidden fruit can't really tantalize unless the voice of proscription sounds in. Further, for the audience to castigate the guests ("you got to take care of your baby!") actually facilitates vicarious pleasure because it puts the castigator beyond reproach, frees him or her to enjoy the antic passions unfolding on-stage guiltfree, and sets up a green light for us to do the same at home, cluck-clucking, shaking our heads, and watching the skirts ride up. Because it enables enjoyment two different ways, the condemnation itself becomes eroticized.[5]

By the same token, the furtive presidential affair cannot really be unbraided from the investigative body that hauls that affair out of the shadows for scrutiny and rebuke. To do so renders each term incomprehensible. Starr's repackaging of the testimony he received *(Penthouse Forum* meets *The Crucible)* gives us a picture of the encounters between Monica and Bill. At least prior to the Barbara Walters interview and publication of Andrew Horton's *Monica's Story* (which most of us were too spent to read by its release),[6] the cigar and the sink and the oral-anal contact only came at us via the report's legalese, its almost pulpy narrative builds, its citings of exact times of arrival and departure and its naming of crimes. The Starr Report's pornography is dependent on this coupling of dry judgment and salacious details, of outrage and graphic, novelized disclosures.

For an analyst on the left, vehement partisan battles can often seem confounding, especially when a Democratic leader like Bill Clinton so thoroughly and consistently kowtows to big business and the military industrial complex, while undercutting governmental support of economically disenfranchised Americans. What *can* they be fighting about, we wonder, wishing we could be done once and for all with the entire Republocrat apparatus. In fact, the deeper union of purpose between these two apparent foes can be felt when we read the Lewinsky scandal itself through a Foucaultian lens and discern that the "discovery" of Clinton's secret *as* sex, and the conceptualization of his sex via its forced disclosure–that these productions link the parties in the scandal as surely as are linked Foucault's confessor and his penitent sinner. Each makes sex the story and sex the revelation.

Those in our society who are sexual minorities and marginalized by class or race are under fire in a completely different way than were Bill and Monica in the aftermath of their "outing." Neither the sexual contract struck nor the sexual climate in the White House parallel the experience of America's sexual subcultures, even though the practices there violated the sodomy statutes in many American states. While the cloud of "criminality" further darkened the purported deviance of the Lewinsky scandal for some of Clinton's attackers, these antisodomy statutes, when enforced at all, are enforced *selectively;* they are used to clamp down, not on powerful white heterosexuals enjoying the fruits of their success, but on those citizens who are understood as a challenge to heteronormativity. To lean on this (non)analogue, then, is to efface the role that routine hypocrisy plays in the consolidation and maintenance of an elite sexual privilege. One of the perks that is supposed to go along with being a very successful, powerful male in this country is sexual reward, including, often enough, ready access to young employees (gender to be determined). This privilege is secured by and entirely bundled with a faked propriety: stagy, often homophobic and racist public claims about matrimonial bonds and family values create the safe environment necessary for the illicit liaisons. "Privacy" that is secured by deep and dangerously productive hypocrisy is different in kind from the vulnerable public presence of a sexual minority fighting to love idiosyncratically and without penalty. We suppress that difference at our peril, when we rush to defend the president's affairs.

Though it is not my project here, there is value, of course, in extending agency to Lewinsky, too often cast as a scarlet stalker or a "bimbo." By focusing on the president, I do not mean to dismiss (or demonize) Lewinsky's volition, in the face of male sexual entitlement. I *do* urge that Clinton's "peccadilloes" must be contextualized by his grandstanding about family values, because this grandstanding is not limited to rhetorical flourishes but generative of bad policy. As Katha Pollitt has enumerated, Bill Clinton

signed the Personal Responsibility Act, which forces poor women to name the fathers of their children as a condition of receiving welfare. . . . The same bill offered states $50 million annually for classes in abstinence for poor women. Clinton signed the Defense of Marriage Act, and has presided over the ousting of a record numbers of lesbians and gays from the military. He fired Joycelyn Elders for talking about masturbation.[7]

In further examples of poor administrative policy stemming from just this source, Clinton also played the upstanding moral arbiter when he signed the Communications Decency Act in 1996, which would have impeded the First Amendment rights of Net users. In 1997, it was found unconstitutional by the U.S. Supreme Court on just those grounds. Then in 1998, Clinton signed a new bill into law, the Child On-line Protection Act, currently being successfully staved off by the combined efforts of the ACLU, the Electronic Frontier Foundation, and the Electronic Privacy Information Center.[8] Additionally, when invited by Louisiana gay activists during campaign stumping to speak out in favor of overturning sodomy laws (finally defeated in February 1999), Clinton refused, despite his apparent enthusiasm for fellatio.

August 17, 1998. On the same day that Clinton's first apology aired, I watched a porn flick called *Deep Throat V: The Quest.*[9] Released two months earlier, the video's subtitle is "Slick Willy Rides Again!" It revolves around a vigorous, almost surrealistically debasing satire of the presidential sexcapades that had already been making headlines for several years in June 1998.

Deep Throat V brings the porn genre of the "take off" to a strange new threshold, where the mainstream entertainment being spoofed and exploited is not a Hollywood movie or a television show (such as *Sexfiles* or *The Mark of Zara*),[10] but a media-driven "news" scandal. This is a Sid Gunn production—in other words, it is populist comedy-porn, energetic, vulgar, and reveling above all in deflating pomposity. In "Disgust and Desire: *Hustler* Magazine," Laura Kipnis argues that class anger fuels *Hustler's* urge to undermine any esthetic code it reads as elite.[11] A related gusto animates *Deep Throat V,* in which "Hail to the Chief" blares proudly on the soundtrack every time Slick Willy gets some play. (Actor Kyle Stone manages a more than passable impersonation of the president while maintaining an erection, a feat that will not win him an Oscar, but which deserves kudos.) The movie's protagonist shows none of the struggling against temptation that apparently characterized Bill Clinton's interactions with Lewinsky; of course, *Deep Throat V* preceded the debut of the Starr Report by many months, so the movie could not be based on the independent counsel's findings.

In the movie's highlight, also played out to the marching tones of the presidential anthem, Willy and Hilary (spelled with one "L" to avoid litigation) dominate an intern together. The spoof depends heavily on the Hillary-wears-the-pants motif that the disenfranchised right (and the enfranchised right, for that matter) had been milking for a long time prior to Starr's emergence. Here of course, Hilary wears a strap-on and a garter, with no pants in sight, but the joke is the same. The end results of this element in the movie is that Jeanna Fine gets to turn in a masterful performance as Hilary (even though she does call Whitewater "Watergate" in one apparent snafu), and instead of the ballbuster the directors apparently mean her to be, she appears as an appealing, inspired "top."[12] Perhaps most interesting of all, the movie's First Couple seem far less alienated from each other than they had in the nonfiction saga we'd been following through the media. It's almost poignant to see them so united. Poignancy is not the operative tenor here, however: the movie begins with two bikeresque longhairs (and their Renfield, a sniveling, intellectual assistant) crashing through the breakaway wall of the Nevada State Penitentiary with a pickup truck to free Sid Gunn (the moviemaker) from the wall to which he's chained inside. Just like its opening image, the movie, committed to "bad taste" and the antigloss of cheap sets and poor lighting, crashes down the gates of privilege and hypocrisy that normally maintain a veneer of dignity around the upper echelons of both "legitimate" business and government.

What does it mean for Gunn to make this joke? In a way, the movie could be taken as proof of our postmodern descent into the sensationalist world of infotainment, a world in which the lines between news and recreational smut have blurred forever, making gate-crashing almost superfluous as the millennium drew to a close. The linkage between pornography and sociopolitical satire is longstanding, though, and not post-post, as marked by Lynn Hunt in *The Invention of Pornography*.[13] Hunt names as one key origin of the pornographic genre the sexy political spoofs that proliferated via semi-underground networks during the seventeenth through nineteenth centuries; these were generated and consumed by a disgruntled, literate elite. The milieu here, though indeed disgruntled, is anything but aristocratic. "Slick Willy Rides Again" has some of the hallmarks of a right-wing populism that many spokespeople on the left would want to eschew out of hand; its "tastelessness," I suppose, makes it just as easily dismissable by many. But what are the politics of *Deep Throat V: The Quest?* Is this the revelry of the pornographer, ceaselessly under fire by regulators, now enjoying the spectacle of the Chief regulator with his pants down? Behind that joke, is there an implicit hunger for a more traditional, "untarnished" presidency where the First Lady demurs to her man and the president reins in his appetites, or better yet sublimates them toward nationalist mastery? Or, contrarily, is the campy satire simply a leveling dig at hypocrisy and the lies that sanction the economic and political privilege of the status quo?

In his *Anatomy of Disgust* (a relevant text for understanding both the movie and the scandal), William Ian Miller discusses just these two "bases for contempt of the high. In one, the low accept the values the high espouse and resent their incompetence and knavery in failing to adhere to them; in the second, the low find the values themselves ridiculous" (222).[14] Miller argues that the first, more conservative motivation for contempt (the contemptible figure has failed to adhere to values that one shares) tends to breed "bitter and sardonic satire," and is usually "the bailiwick not of the utterly disempowered but of the middling and ministerial sorts" (222). The second basis for upward contempt, a disdain for the value system itself, he describes as resulting in "punctured pomposity," i.e., in depictions of the powerful not as "knaves," but as "clowns and fools" (223). The "misrule" that Miller here invokes certainly brings us closer to the jokey and visceral excesses of Slick Willy in *Deep Throat V* than does the genre of the satire.

What is perhaps most clear about the vulgarity of *Deep Throat V* is exactly the admixture of "disgust and desire" that Kipnis cites in the title of her chapter on *Hustler,* a cocktail also addressed in Miller's *Anatomy.* From Miller: "We might not want to oppose so-called unconscious desire to disgust at all, but see them as

Still from *Deep Throat V: The Quest (Slick Willy Rides Again).* Arrow Productions (1998).

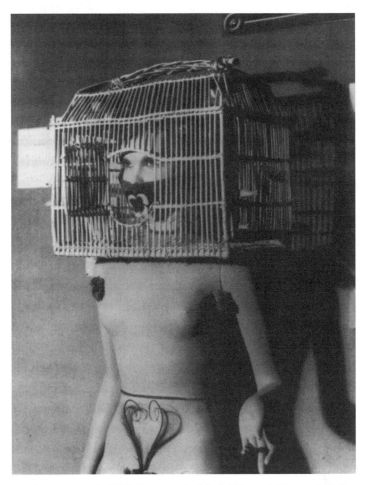

Man Ray. *Mannequin*, 1938. Photograph of André Masson's *Mannequin* at the "Exposition Internationale du Surréalisme," Galerie des Beaux-Arts, Paris, January-February 1938. © 2000 Man Ray Trust/Artist Rights Society, NY/ADAGP, Paris.

necessary to each other, part of one complex syndrome" (113). One gag that condemns Willy's lechery and callous use of women while simultaneously using them as a springboard for the viewer's own lust is the rendering of nude interns into pieces of office furniture. In a scene reminiscent of Andre Masson's 1938 *Mannequin*, which stands with a bound mouth and a birdcage on her head, three naked interns become, respectively, a lamp, a blotter, and a pencil holder.[15] More than a sudden concern about the objectification of women (unlikely at Arrow

Productions), it is probably anger at the excesses of government spending that gives the joke's surrealism its edge, as Slick Willy blithely turns tax dollars and all his attention to the task of "redecorating" his office. But the shock of this perceived waste is rendered visceral through its sexualization.

There is also the disgust . . . that has its origins in the notion of surfeit. No unconscious desires or furtive attractions there. The overindulgence in any number of foods, drinks, and activities, sexual or otherwise, for which the desire is completely conscious and acted upon, leads to disgust also—the nausea and sickness of surfeit. [T]he emotion we call disgust does not give rise to only aversive actions. The complex of judgments that are embodied in disgust, the way disgust in fact works, means that it has to get its hands dirty. (110–111)

Perhaps the number in *Deep Throat V* most emblematic of surfeit is a long sexual encounter between Slick Willy and another in a chain of interns. (Almost every female entrance is prefaced by a thwarted or reconsidered effort on the president's part to "Get Monica.") In this particular scene, the intern of the moment is placed nude in a massive "champagne glass" filled with jelly beans. As might most people in a similar circumstance, she giggles almost hysterically throughout the scene. The "monster shots" (extreme close-ups of genitals) in this case detail Slick Willy's rapture over eating jelly beans off of and out of the "intern's" vagina. This is not a bath in champagne or a cascade of diamonds—what might be typical symbols of a highroller's excess—but the juvenile, sickly sweet, brightly colored surfeit of a big boy, invoking the president's much-cited gluttony. "Oh, I like that! I like that a lot! It feels good!" cries Slick Willy. The jelly-bean scene is also about the shocking, topsy-turvy transgression of a "mouth" that isn't a mouth "eating" candy, a transgression similar in kind to the cigar incident that generated so many jokes across the continent and the world. These are "negative," "disgusting" associations, but let us not forget that the movie is a porn feature, and it offers its viewers sex scenes to augment masturbation, so its makers apparently figure they know how to strike the raunchy balance between disgust and desire that will keep its agog patrons coming back for more.

Even in realms very far removed from the purposive transgression of *Deep Throat V*, I was struck again and again by just this combined response in conversations about the scandal as it unfolded in 1998 and the winter of 1999. Prurient interest was clear—and astonishment as the details kept getting racier and racier—but in addition I cannot count the number of times I heard a friend, acquaintance, or student say, "Ewwwww!" over some little late-breaking tidbit about these "inappropriate" encounters to which the whole nation was absurdly privy. The "sexual terror" that critics cited as fueling the attacks on Clinton was perhaps more accurately described as an almost uncanny commixture of revulsion and arousal over these amazingly public revelations. This mixed, visceral response gripped, I believe, the popular imagination, not merely the minds of those interested in persecuting Clinton for sexual transgressions and sex-related lies. I remember one student writing, in an in-class thought piece on the Lewinsky scandal, September 1998, that these were details she did not want to know but that she couldn't help but tabulate, that they were faintly revolting to her, because they breached privacy, and just . . . because. In the same exercise, another student described the president as "a large, handsome man," and remarked, "I bet he smells delicious."

The "ewww" factor was probably most acute with Paula Jones's assertion, leaked from an affidavit, that she could prove that Clinton had exposed himself to her, because she knew his genitalia to have "distinguishing characteristics." In the fall of 1997, articles appeared in the *New York Times,* the *Washington Post,* and elsewhere about Peyronie's disease—a plaque-related skin condition with which our president either was or was not afflicted—that results in a decidedly bent penis. In order for her to prove her familiarity with his penis, it would be required, Jones's lawyers said, for Clinton's member to be viewed *while erect.* In this case the fascination was overdetermined: the story compelled attention in spite of any high ground we might claim; we were riveted by pathology, by arousal, and by the imagined humiliation of the great through the posited exposure, not only of private parts but of private desire.

Clinton's "overactive" sexuality had already penetrated the divide between public and private and had collapsed the "king's two bodies" into a single voracious one.[16] For his physical penis, then, to be marked with pathology, seemed the perfect metonymic symbol: fitting, fascinating, and gross. Like peering at a horror movie through splayed fingers pushed across one's eyes, we peeked with animated revulsion and curiosity at the material revelations. Among Clinton supporters (and Starr-objectors), the titillated dismay of someone who *really* feels they should not be privy to something that they're witnessing became one with the very physical details that loomed up in the press. Reactions to the prying converged with reactions to the posited penis, resulting in regular visceral responses to the news: unbidden bursts of laughter, mortified arousal at the anomalous mention of engorged organs in the *New York Times,* and a giggling disgust. In October 1997, Stuart Taylor of the *Legal Times* groaned, "Barring some deus ex machina [which did indeed arise in April of

1998], we will be treated to the spectacle of a trial exploring, ad nauseam, inter alia, whether the president of the United States when in a certain state of excitement is or ever was afflicted with an eye-catching curvature of the. . . . Well, let's just call it the Pumpkin."[17] The nausea rises in our gorge because of the proceedings' endless vulgarity, Stuart Taylor means to imply, but this repugnance is ultimately and even unwittingly extended to the "Pumpkin" as well.

Hoping to settle matters once and for all, on October 12, 1997, the president's lawyer, Robert Bennett, announced on CBS's *Face the Nation* that a urologist had been consulted and, "in terms of size, shape, direction, whatever the devious mind wants to concoct, the president is a normal man. There are no blemishes, there are no moles, there are no growths."[18] Here the mind of the licentious moralist is what deviates, or turns aside, while the penis of the president, like his recouped political past, is straight, normal, and unblemished. This shifting of the trope of bending and curvature from the physical phallus to the devious, immoral imagination is reminiscent of a conflation made by Milton in *Paradise Lost*. Hopping blithely from the Oval Office to the Garden of Eden, we find Milton linking the wily, insinuating rhetoric of the snake ("he leading swiftly rolled! in tangles, and made intricate seem straight") with the snake's sinuous body ("With tract oblique . . . sidelong he works his way") and with Eve's "wanton ringlets," "disheveled" "tresses" that are in fact merely outward signs of her own capacity for wily argumentation . . . and a rash hand.[19] One's moral stance can be read on the body, but additionally the body can be the lure, leading one astray from the proper path. The president's penis, however, is straight as an arrow, unblemished, unmarked with difference; he is "normal" and it is your mind that deviates and "swiftly roll[s]/ In tangles . . . /To mischief swift."

January 7: the first day of the impeachment proceedings in the Senate. The bodies over which we pondered in the United States during the winter of 1999 were emphatically not the dead and mangled bodies in Iraq. Years earlier, after Desert Storm, there had been, eerily, no injured bodies haunting our national imagination, even though the conflict had been brought to us with fanfare by our broadcast networks. After George Bush's Gulf War, no bodies snagged in our imaginations like they did when the television brought us the war in Vietnam. (The crying girl with the napalmed chest runs naked down the road, and behind our eyes, forever.) In 1991, the only "sex" we had to supplant the bodies injured then were the pornographic images of smart bombs penetrating airshafts—a contrived spectacle of high-tech glamor that displaced completely the many other, more chaotic impressions of physical devastation that might have circulated.

After Desert Fox, winter 1999, we did have bodies on our minds, material and vivid, riveting our attention—once again, however, they were *not* the bodies of Iraqis, starving already from the embargo and now seeking care in hospitals that had recently been bombed. Rather, we faced impeachment proceedings filled up still with the no-longer new revelations of Clinton's ejaculate on a blue dress, his masturbating into a sink, Monica's warm mouth sucking on a peppermint, Bill's cigar pushing against her labia, oral-anal contact, hands on breasts, and etcetera. Meanwhile the bombs dropped, and yet the struggle downstage, in front of the curtain, had captured our attentions almost entirely.

To say that "lying is what people do about affairs" is to *not* say that lying is what politicians do about all sorts of things, many of them far more pivotal than nine blow jobs. To say that Starr is an inquisitorial McCarthy who has dragged Clinton's secret out into the national limelight is to have this rather sorry set of sexual exchanges stand in for and supersede the many other secrets and lies in Clinton's career—and this sexy substitution is no coincidence, since Republicans, too, engage in political and economic dealings that they don't want scrutinized. The Republican right is currently not a monolith, of course, and among the Christian right and its sympathizers, the call for "moral" repression has an alarming urgency that should not be overlooked. That said, though, in order to understand the bonds that link this socially conservative segment of the right to the economic conservatives and the militarists, one needs to remember the benefits of this Starr-driven "downstage" melodrama to these other, less sexually panicked Republicans. The motivation to not break silence (conscious or not), strong enough to even make tolerable the sacrifice of Livingston and Gingrich, was shared equally by the investigator's party and that of the sybarite Chief, and it may be the ultimate "dramaturge" behind the partisan problem-play that so diverted us in the late nineties.

Notes

1. Richard Goldstein's September 1998 piece in the *Village Voice*, "Sexual McCarthyism," cited the following list of commentators who had used the term in this connection: the *Wall Street Journal*'s Albert R. Hunt, Alan Dershowitz on NBC, *USA Today* in a headline ("An Air of Sexual McCarthyism Chills the Nation's Capitol"), historian of American communism and the HUAC era Ellen Schrecker, and the French news organ *Le Monde*. See Richard Goldstein, "Sexual McCarthyism," *Village Voice*, September 23–29, 1998.

2. Here is the relevant quotation from the Starr Report's "Narrative: Section J.H.3, Steps to Avoid Being Seen or Heard":

The President ordinarily kept the door between the private hallway and the Oval Office several inches ajar during their encounters, both so that he could hear if anyone approached and so that anyone who did approach would be less likely to suspect impropriety. During their sexual encounters, Ms. Lewinsky testified, "[W]e were both aware of the volume and sometimes . . . I bit my hand—so that I wouldn't make any noise." On one occasion, according to Ms. Lewinsky, the President put his hand over her mouth during a sexual encounter to keep her quiet. Concerned that they might be interrupted abruptly, according to Ms. Lewinsky, the two of them never fully undressed.

While noting that "the door to the hallway was always somewhat open," the President testified that he did try to keep the intimate relationship secret: "I did what people do when they do the wrong thing. I tried to do it where nobody else was looking at it" (30).

And here is footnote 117, on the same topic:

Lewinsky 8/6/98 GJ at 36–37; Lewinsky 7/27/98 Int. at 2. According to a Secret Service officer who entered the Oval Office when the President and Ms. Lewinsky were in or near the study, the door leading from the Oval Office to the hallway was slightly ajar. Muskett 7/21/98 GJ at 36–37, 39. In his Jones deposition, the President was asked if there are doors at both ends of the hallway. He responded: "[There] are, and they're always open." Clinton 1/17/98 Depo. at 59. In early 1998, in the course of denying any sexual relationship with Ms. Lewinsky, the President repeatedly told Deputy Chief of Staff John Podesta that "the door was open." Podesta 6/16/98 GJ at 88–89.

3. Michel Foucault, *The History of Sexuality: An Introduction,* vol. 1 [1978] (New York: Random House, 1990).

4. In a book that is also apt in the present discussion, *Volatile Bodies: Toward a Corporeal Feminism,* Elizabeth Grosz uses the image of the Moebius strip, too, though in a different context, and cites a Lacanian reference to the image (Bloomington: Indiana University Press, 1994), xii.

5. And Springer's evenhanded "final word" at each show's end, rendered with the same patronizing calm regardless of the (staged?) melee that has preceded it, soothes and stabilizes our own sense of moral entitlement, by assuaging any freewheeling anxiety triggered by either Springer's own cruelty or the transgressive escapades we have witnessed. Significantly, it also sustains through contrast the class hierarchy that the show's buffoonery insists upon. Springer's self-righteous turn at leveling the "Law of the Father" in each show's closing moments means that we won't gag on our own excess, and thereby opens avenues for the following day's spectacle and our next round of rebukes and giggles. And yet, as Joshua Gamson argues in *Freaks Talk Back,* the show and others in the genre have nonetheless provided the sexually and economically marginalized a forum for national expression. Joshua Gamson, *Freaks Talk Back: Tabloid Talk Shows and Sexual Nonconformity* (Chicago: University of Chicago Press, 1998).

6. Andrew Horton, *Monica's Story* (New York: Norton, 1999).

7. Katha Pollitt, "Subject to Debate," *Nation* 5 October, 1998: 10.

8. For information on the CDA and COPA, and for access to the Electronic Frontier Foundation and related sites, see <homepage.interaccess.com/~driscoll/cda.html> and <www.gslis.utexas.edu/~cjyoung>.

9. *Deep Throat V: The Quest (Slick Willy Rides Again),* Arrow Productions, 1998. Director: Bud Lee; producer: Ray Gunn. According to a September 1998 review in *Unzipped,* within a month or two of *Deep Throat V's* release, a gay porn feature with the same conceit came out. *Penetration on Pennsylvania Avenue,* initially to be named *Swallow the Leader,* apparently suffers from shoddy production values and a lead actor who had to warm up to his production of Clinton's southern accent. That said, with its all-male cast, *Penetration* peels the titillation of transgressive, intergenerational, on-the-job sex entirely away from the heteronormativity that (incompletely) neutralized it in the Lewinsky scandal. Also, distinctly unlike *Deep Throat V,* it cheerfully exploits the libidinal investment of *all* the scandal's key players. Sex scenes include steamy interludes between the president and Oval Office intern "Monty Lepinski," as well as between investigator "Kevin Staff" and a witness, and the movie concludes with a group of reporters exclaiming *"bor-ing"* at the revelation that the commander-in-chief has had unconventional sexual liaisons. While director Wil Parker saw a pornographic opportunity in the whole affair, he also saw the chance to lampoon, not Clinton, but Starr and his "startling revelations." *Penetration on Pennsylvania Avenue,* XTC, 1998. See Steven Jensen's review in *Unzipped,* 29 September 1998 (pages unnumbered). Thanks to Heath Putnam and Edmund Miller.

10. *Sexfiles,* VCA/Xplor, 1998. *The Mark of Zara,* X-citement Productions, 1991.

11. Laura Kipnis, "Disgust and Desire: *Hustler* Magazine," in *Bound and Gagged: Pornography and the Politics of Fantasy in America* (New York: Grove, 1996), 122–160.

12. During the fall of 1998, a friend actually met Ms. Fine briefly and asked her about the role: she made it clear that she herself supported the president, though she conceded that it had been fun to play Hilary. Thanks to Heath Putnam.

13. Lynn Hunt, *The Invention of Pornography* (New York: Zone, 1993), 9–45.

14. William Ian Miller, *The Anatomy of Disgust* (Cambridge, Mass.: Harvard University Press), 1997.

15. See Man Ray's 1938 photo, *Mannequin,* of André Masson's *Mannequin* at the Exposition Internationale du Surréalisme," Galerie des Beaux-Arts, Paris, January–February 1938. Reprinted in Whitney Chadwick, "An Infinite Play of Empty Mirrors: Women, Surrealism, and Self-Representation," in Whitney Chadwick, ed., *Mirror Images: Women, Surrealism, and Self-Representation* (Cambridge, Mass.: MIT Press, 1998), 17, fig. 2.

16. Ernst H. Kantorowicz, *The King's Two Bodies: A Study in Medieval Political Theology* [1957] (Princeton: Princeton University Press, 1997).

17. Stuart Taylor, quoted by Maureen Dowd in "Murder of an Anatomy," *New York Times,* 18 October 1997: 15.

18. James Bennet, "Pasts Are Prologues as Jones vs. Clinton Moves Nearer to Trial," *New York Times,* 9 November 1997: 1/24.

19. John Milton, *Paradise Lost,* ed. Scott Elledge (New York: Norton, 1975). IX:; 631–632: IX: 510–512; IX: 305–306.

Works Cited

Texts

Bennet, James. "Pasts Are Prologues as Jones vs. Clinton Moves Nearer to Trial." *New York Times,* 9 November 1997: 1/24.

Chadwick, Whitney. "An Infinite Play of Empty Mirrors: Women, Surrealism, and Self-Representation." In Whitney Chadwick, ed., *Mirror Images: Women, Surrealism, and Self-Representation.* Cambridge, Mass.: MIT Press, 1998.

Dowd, Maureen. "Murder of an Anatomy." *New York Times,* 18 October 1997: 15.

Foucault, Michel. *The History of Sexuality: An Introduction.* Vol. 1 [1978]. New York: Random House, 1990.

Gamson, Joshua. *Freaks Talk Back: Tabloid Talk Shows and Sexual Nonconformity.* Chicago: University of Chicago Press, 1998.

Goldstein, Richard. "Sexual McCarthyism." *Village Voice,* vol. 43, no. 39, 23–29 September 1998: 36.

Grosz, Elizabeth. *Volatile Bodies: Toward a Corporeal Feminism.* Bloomington: Indiana University Press, 1994.

Horton, Andrew. *Monica's Story.* New York: Norton, 1999.

Hunt, Lynn. *The Invention of Pornography.* New York: Zone, 1993.

Jensen, Steve. "Penetration on Pennsylvania Avenue." Review in *Unzipped,* 29 September 1998 (unnumbered pages).

Kipnis, Laura. "Disgust and Desire: *Hustler* Magazine." In *Bound and Gagged: Pornography and the Politics of Fantasy in America.* New York: Grove, 1996.

Miller, William Ian. *The Anatomy of Disgust.* Cambridge, Mass.: Harvard University Press, 1997.

Milton, John. *Paradise Lost.* Edited by Scott Elledge. New York: Norton, 1975.

Pollitt, Katha. "Subject to Debate." *Nation,* 5 October 1998: 10.

Websites

CDA/COPA information: http://homepage.interaccess.comkAriscoll/cda.html

CDA information: http://www.gslis.utexas.edu/~cjyoung/index.html

Starr Report read at: http://www.courttv.com/legaldocs

Movies

Deep Throat V: The Quest (Slick Willy Rides Again). Arrow Productions, 1998. Director: Bud Lee; producer: Ray Gunn.

The Mark of Zara. X-citement Productions, 1991.

Penetration on Pennsylvania Avenue. XTC, 1998. Director: Wil Parker.

Sexfiles. VCA/Xplor, 1998.

6 Sex of a Kind

On Graphic Language and the Modesty of Television News

Sasha Torres

Indulge me in a fantasy, if you will. What if queer sex advisers like Susie Bright, Dan Savage, and Pat Califia had been engaged by the major networks and 24-hour cable news channels as in-house experts on the Clinton sex scandal?[1] What if, when we tuned in to ABC, say, we encountered Sam Donaldson updating us on the latest White House press conference, George Stephanopolous ventriloquizing the president's advisers, and Bright discussing the considerable overlap between the definition of sexual relations at issue in the Jones deposition and the notions of topping and bottoming that circulate within the s/m and b/d communities? One can almost hear the exchange between Susie and ABC news anchor Peter Jennings now:

> **Peter:** We go live now to Susie Bright, in New York's Greenwich Village. Susie?
> **Susie:** Hello, Peter. I'm standing in front of the East Village gay bar "The Cock" and talking to patrons here about the Jones lawyers' definition of sexual relations. You, sir, wanted to say what?
> **Patron** (clad only in jock strap and feather boa): Well, I just wanted to say that, basically, when the president claimed that he didn't have

sex with Monica, what he meant was that *she* topped *him*, and that under the definition that doesn't count as sex. It only counts as sex, according to Judge Wright, if *you're* the top.

Susie: And do you think that President Clinton is believable as a bottom?

Patron: Absolutely. And I don't think he should be impeached for it, either.

Susie: Well, Peter, there you have it. The consensus here at the Cock is that bottoming is not—should not be—an impeachable offense.

Flipping the channels to CNN, we might find sex-advice columnist Dan Savage speculating, in an interview with Judy Woodruff, about the possibility that Clinton might have been telling the truth when he testified that he had no intent to arouse or gratify Lewinsky: "Let's face the facts, Judy," he might say, "Like many men, Bill Clinton may have neither the skills nor the inclination to arouse or gratify women. He may not be a liar. He may just be a pig." Later, on MSNBC, we might encounter Pat Califia opining that the discrepancy between Clinton's grand jury testimony and Lewinsky's might stem from Lewinsky's need to ease the tension between thinking of herself as an ambitious, powerful woman and getting turned on by "servicing" the president. Imagine Califia painstakingly explaining to, say, right-wing MSNBC talk-show host and blonde bombshell Laura Ingraham, the distinction between *being servile* and *having servile fantasies*.

In indulging this little flight of fancy, I'm suggesting that the response to the Lewinsky revelations depended absolutely on the work of heteronormativity, by which I mean here a simultaneous fascination with and aversion to explicit public descriptions of sex, particularly sex other than married heterosexual intercourse. I'm suggesting as well the difference certain kinds of "perverse" sexual expertise might have made to our collective understanding of the legal and constitutional matters at stake in this affair. Additionally, I'm pointing to something about how televisual norms worked to limit the possibilities for political knowledge during this moment. Television's conventions for talking and not talking about sex impeded news organizations from analyzing a crucial element of the case: the specific content of the definition of sexual relations in use during the Jones deposition. This definition was a key element in Starr's case against Clinton, the element at stake in Starr's claims that Clinton had perjured himself both in that deposition and in his grand jury testimony. Given the centrality of the court's definition of sex to the question of impeachment, television's incompetent engagement with it is striking, to say the least. Though its aversion certainly had the effect of enabling and prolonging the case against Clinton, I locate it not in any vast right-wing conspiracy, but rather in certain historical elements of the televisual apparatus. I shall argue that television news' stunning ineloquence about sex stems from two deeply embedded elements of television's "informational" discourse; these are, first, the particular inability of the news to confront verbal ambiguity, and, second, its disinclination to speak explicitly about sex. This latter claim may seem counterintuitive to any reader who has survived a sweeps period in which local news outlets notoriously traffic in sexual allure. But we are talking about the "hard" news here, which is never supposed to be sexy.

In his January 17, 1998 deposition in the Paula Jones case, Clinton was given the following three-part definition of "sexual relations" by Jones's attorneys:

For the purposes of this deposition, a person engages in "sexual relations" when the person knowingly engages in or causes—

>   *(1) contact with the genitalia, anus, groin, breast, inner thigh, or buttocks of any person with an intent to arouse or gratify the sexual desire of any person;*
>   *(2) contact between any part of the person's body or an object and the genitals or anus of another person; or*
>   *(3) contact between the genitals or anus of the person and any part of another person's body.*

"Contact" means intentional touching, either directly or through clothing.[2]

Responding to objections from the president's council (including Bob Bennett's hyperbolic observation that "if the president patted me and said I had to lose 10 pounds off my bottom, you could be arguing that I had sexual relations with him"),[3] Judge Susan Webber Wright ruled that parts two and three of the definition were "too broad," but allowed Jones's attorneys to proceed with part one.[4]

In my survey of the transcripts of the ABC, CBS, CNN, FOX and NBC coverage of two key events in the Clinton-Lewinsky saga, the release of the Starr Report on 11 September 1998 and of the videotapes of Clinton's grand jury testimony on 21 September 1998, I was surprised to discover how seldom television commentators quoted the Jones definition directly. Indeed, in the hours and hours of coverage of the Starr Report on the 11th, only CNN's Jeanne Meserve did so:

And it might be useful here . . . to look again at that definition of sexual relations that was brought up in the Jones case. "A person engages in sexual relations when the person knowingly engages in or causes," and excuse me here, we're going to get graphic, *"if there's contact with the genitalia, anus, groin, breast, inner thigh or buttocks of any person with and intent to arouse or gratify the sexual desire of any person."*[5]

Much more commonly, reporters and anchors referred to the definition indirectly and vaguely. Sam Donaldson of ABC, for example, called it "this definition of sex that he was using that was approved by the court."[6] For CBS's Scott Pelley, it was "the definition of sex that was used in the Paula Jones civil case."[7] On NBC, Lisa Myers called it "the narrow definition of sex in the Jones case."[8] In other words, one could have watched the coverage all day long, hearing constant references to the definition, without hearing the definition itself.

The coverage of the grand jury tapes on 21 September, in contrast, forced commentators to be a bit more direct, since so much of Clinton's testimony was taken up with the question of his understanding of the definition. A bit more direct, but not much. Aside from Jim Angles's paraphrase of the definition on Fox News that morning, the conversations were more apt to sound like this exchange between Larry King and Bob Woodward on CNN:

> **Woodward:** You and I were talking about the definition that the president . . .
> **King:** He has the actual three-part definition . . .
> **Woodward:** that the president was given in his Paula Jones deposition. It's so technical, but essentially the first part of it says "was there contact with the privates?"
> **King:** Mention them all?
> **Woodward:** And it lists six areas, we'll call them the big six. And in . . .
> **King:** Item out.
> **Woodward:** And that they allowed in and it doesn't include oral sex. When you look at definition number three which says contact between the privates and any other part of the body.
> **King:** So the judge in throwing out two and three—this is the deposition throws out contact between any person of the person's body and an object, et cetera, or another. You think that he was technically correct in saying—in concept, to the one thing she left in, I did not have sex?

Even if we attribute some of the incoherence of this exchange to bad or hasty transcription, its lack of clarity is still striking. More remarkable still, given that the

Jones definition was discussed in any detail only four or five times during the cov-
erage of Clinton's testimony, King and Woodward's conversation would have to
count as one of the fuller and more sophisticated of those discussions.

Despite Meserve's coy "and excuse me here, we're going to get graphic," I
want to suggest that the reasons television news organizations balked at interro-
gating this central element of Starr's case against Clinton had to do only second-
arily with its putative sexual content. TV these days usually doesn't have much
trouble showing and naming body parts, after all, and it is hard to see what is so
terribly "graphic" about the words "genitalia," "anus," and "breast." Yet Meserve,
King, and Woodward assume that the definition is itself salacious. This anxiety
should point us toward other explanations for their hesitation.

First, there is the moral anxiety about Clinton's sexual pedantry, which
emerges from the language of the definition itself, and from legal language gener-
ally. You will remember Clinton's much-pilloried remark, during his grand jury
testimony, that the truth or falsity of one of his lawyers' statements "depends on
what the meaning of the word 'is' is." While it is not particularly my purpose to
defend Clinton—as a politician, an historical agent, or a sex partner—I am inter-
ested in defending a notion about language that was widely ridiculed throughout
this affair, namely, that *words sometimes mean more than one thing*, even within a
single sentence.

Commentators seemed to find Clinton's formulation—"what the meaning
of the word 'is' is"—risible because of the ostensible obviousness of the meaning
of "is." His lawyerly refusal to presume the commonsense definition was deemed
sure evidence for some form of guilt, whether moral or legal. In fact, the reason
this phrase accrued so much airtime was that the structure of Clinton's formula-
tion frustratingly and irresistibly both proves and disproves his point. In the sen-
tence, "It depends on what the meaning of the word 'is' is," "is" actually means
two things, working as a noun and a verb. Yet the sentence must depend on the
putative stability of commonsense understanding in order to mean anything at
all. Such dependence—the decision to strategically stabilize the meanings of
words—constitutes the linguistic positivism of legal discourse, a positivism Clin-
ton here simultaneously undermines and exploits.[9]

The "is" effect marked a crucial element of this story, because such ambigu-
ity had the potential not only to undo Starr's perjury case by reducing it to a he
said/she said contest between Lewinsky and Clinton, but also to destabilize the
notion of perjury itself. Why, then, did television news fail to cover it in its full

complexity? The answer seems to me to have to do with the medium's reluctance to engage with nuances of language.

Television relies on the same linguistic positivism that the law does, both because the pretense that ambiguity can be avoided tends to speed and simplify the production process, and, more crucially, because American television's profits are generated precisely by its traffic in common sense. The news, as a commodity traded in an increasingly crowded and competitive market, ensures its marketability via its appeal to an imaginary "general" audience for whom common sense is imagined by news workers to constitute the central ideological "optic." I use the term optic here in a literal as well as metaphorical sense, since the news imagines its task as telling stories with pictures—or "graphics," as the industry's own lingo would have it. The Clinton-Lewinsky story, though, threatened constantly to collapse the distinction between meanings of the word "graphic," even as the news scrambled to keep these meanings away from one another. They attempted this task by simultaneously hoping and fearing that the images the story evoked were already in the viewer's mind, and by evincing an enormous amount of anxiety about what the "general" audience could be presumed to know.

Television news organizations responded to the potentially contaminating proximity of their traffic in graphic images to an illicit commerce in graphic sex by focusing on their own moral embarrassment, constantly calling the scandal's details "salacious," "lurid," "explicit," "shocking," "sensitive," "embarrassing," "delicate," "sordid," "vivid," and "disturbing." Such details increased their reluctance, I think, to engage the Jones definition, as an exploration of its contradictions would have required a level of sexual candor that television news is generally unable to deploy. The 11 September coverage offers ample evidence (only a fraction of which I will cite here) of telejournalists' unease with the story.

Peter Jennings, for example, told viewers early in ABC's coverage of the Starr Report that

there's an enormous amount of graphic language contained at the very least in the footnotes of the Starr Report today. Anybody who is eager to see that graphic detail is going to find it on an internet site. They're not going to find it here. We're mindful of covering the story. We're mindful of children in the audience. We will make references to unusual sexual practices, perhaps, but you're not going to hear much graphic detail in the television coverage on ABC.[10]

CNN's Candy Crowley, on the other hand, read from the report with abandon, but interrupted herself frequently with "warnings" to "squeamish" viewers who "are offended by explicit sexual references."[11] By far the most bizarre approach to this material was to be found on CBS, where Dan Rather and his reporters dwelled deliciously on the fine line they walked between taste and transgression. When correspondent Sharyl Attkisson hesitated over the report's finding that the semen on the blue dress was the president's, Rather interrupted her:

> **Rather:** Sharyl, if I may . . .
> **Attkisson:** Yes.
> **Rather:** We want to be careful here. This is daytime television and there are children in the audience, so I do encourage you to paraphrase when there's any doubt.
> **Attkisson:** OK, I'll do my best. But we—we're seeing this for the first time, too, and we'll try to lift out the most graphic parts of it for you but give you the essence of what's contained.

Attkisson eventually rallies, throwing in pithy cautions like "This is not quite X-rated, but it's not G-rated either." But the proceedings seem quite beyond poor Bob Schieffer, who found himself in the unenviable position of translating the juicy bits of the report for the American public and his bombastic boss:

> **Bob:** While the president was on the telephone, according to her, he—let me just read this to make sure we don't—he unzipped his pants and exposed himself and—and they had sex of a kind. Again, he stopped her before, I would say, he was completed, I guess would be the way to put that. . . . Now here is another one on December 31st. He said—having lost the phone number she had given him, he had tried to find her in the phone book. According to her, they moved to the study. This is just off the Oval Office. "And then we were kissing and he lifted my sweater," and so on. And again, they had sex of a kind. Once again, he stopped her before he was finished and said he didn't know me well enough, didn't trust me enough yet. . . . So that's about it that we've been able to glean from this so far. Certainly this is living up to every expectation that it was going to be lurid, tawdry, and laid out in explicit detail. I'm trying to sort of sight-edit this as I went along, Dan, but I—it's very strong stuff.
> **Dan:** Bob, take a deep breath.

Indeed. Earlier that morning, Schieffer told Rather, "I think what is going to be stunning to people I—is the detail that we get here and how graphic some of it is going to be. . . . I think people are going to—I—there—it is going to take their breath away. They'll either be repulsed, they—or they'll say, 'How could this be?' when they see some of these details."

Bracketing personal considerations here, what made Bob so breathless?

The constriction of televisual discourse about sex is a long story, one that might be told with recourse to a number of different archives. One such archive would consist of the governmental, regulatory, and popular conversations about "sex and violence," from Newton Minow's 1961 "Vast Wasteland" speech, through the Dodd Commission hearings, right up through contemporary debates about the V-chip.[12] Another would consist of television genres representing sexual practices, paying particular attention perhaps to afternoon soap operas and the "serious," "relevant" realism we might trace from Norman Lear to Stephen Bochco.[13] For the purposes of this project, though, I am looking at the various versions of the National Association of (Radio and Television) Broadcasters' "Television Code," whose first version was written in 1952 and which went through twenty-two editions before being abandoned in 1981.[14]

The Code was a form of voluntary self-regulation produced in hopes of forestalling more official forms of censorship, along the lines of the Hollywood Production Code or the Comics Code Authority.[15] It sought to govern representations of sex, violence, and religion, as well as providing a general theory about television's social function as a "guest" in American living rooms. In regulating this visitor to the intimate sphere of national domesticity, the 1952 Code pretty much ruled sexual representation and reference out of court.[16] In particular, the Code insisted that "profanity, obscenity, smut and vulgarity are forbidden" (2), that "illicit sex relations are not treated as commendable" (2), that "violence and illicit sex shall not be presented in an attractive manner [to children]" (2), that "sex crimes and abnormalities are generally unacceptable as program material" (2), that "the costuming of all performers shall be within the bounds of propriety" (3), that "the movements of . . . performers shall be kept within the bounds of decency" (3), that "camera angles shall avoid such views of performers as to emphasize anatomical details indecently" (3), and that "morbid, sensational and alarming details not essential to the factual [news] report, especially in connection with stories of crime or sex, should be avoided."

During the next thirty years, the Code's restrictions on sexual material were highly contested and underwent numerous revisions. By the 1967 version of the Code, for example, constraints had softened somewhat: "Such subjects as violence and sex shall be presented without undue emphasis and only as required by plot development and character delineation."[17] By 1973, in the post-Lear era, the tone of the Code had shifted utterly to an emphasis on innovation, creativity, and the medium's responsibility to "expose the dynamics of social change." With regard to sex, this version stated only that "material with sexual connotations shall not be treated exploitatively or irresponsibly but with sensitivity," and deemed "unacceptable" only "obscene, indecent or profane matter, as defined by law."[18] By 1981, the pendulum had swung back the other way; this final version of the Code insisted that broadcasters

shall not broadcast any material which they *determine to be obscene, profane or inde-*
cent. Above and beyond the requirements of law, broadcasters must consider the family
atmosphere in which many of their programs are viewed. There shall be no graphic por-
trayal of sexual acts by sight or sound. The portrayal of implied sexual acts must be es-
sential to the plot and presented in a responsible and tasteful manner.[19]

Amid all these changes, only one element of the 1952 Code's regulation of sexual material remains unchanged, and that is the provision regarding television news.

If the 1952 Code's injunction against "morbid, sensational or alarming details" in the news could survive unchanged for thirty years, this can only be because the National Association of Broadcasters had no incentive to change it. From this I think it is reasonable to infer that broadcast news organizations were not clamoring for them to do so. Why not?

We get a hint, I think, from the forms that sexual discourse has taken on American television since the Code's demise, forms that we might call "network sex" and "cable sex" and which would then have to be further subdivided by genre and day-part. Cable sex is generally more explicit and generally scheduled during late night: FX's *The X Show*; MTV's *Loveline*; made-for-cable movies; Showtime's soft-core *The Red Shoe Diaries* and *Women: Stories of Passion*; HBO's *Sex in the City*, *The Sopranos*, and *Oz*.[20] Network sex is concentrated in soap operas and talk and tabloid shows during daytime, and in situation comedy and dramatic programming during prime time. With some rule-proving exceptions, these diverse representations have two things in common: an address to women (made-for-cable movies, Showtime's erotica for women, *Sex in the City*, soaps, daytime talk); and/or a tendency to treat sex as a problem, joke, or occasion for embarrassment or humiliation (*Loveline*, *Sex in the City*, *The X Show*, soaps, daytime talk, sitcoms).

Sex on television, in other words, is for women, or a problem, or, in the best-case scenario of the televisual imaginary, a problem *for* women. The feminization of sex on television produces a powerful and structural aversion to sex for the hard news, which, as a discourse that poses as rational, neutral, and disembodied, tends to shun the particular concerns of women and other special interests, preferring to imagine a general and "proper" viewer who would be either embarrassed or outraged by sexual discourse.

There are many kinds of stories of which the news likes to represent itself as a part; the genre's desire to "make itself the story" has been often remarked upon. Here, for the reasons I've suggested, the news would have liked merely to describe the Clinton-Lewinsky scandal without appearing to participate in it. But the prophylactic boundary that hard news generally maintains between itself and sexual detail was breached here by the sheer liveness—both of the event and of sex itself—and embodiedness the story seemed to produce. Suddenly everyone had a body: the president, the reporters, the anchors, the commentators. Sexually charged language was everywhere: Jennings kept calling Starr's referral "the hard report," instead, presumably, of the "hard copy of the report," while Schieffer alluded to details "kind of seep[ing] out" of "the meat of" the report.[21] In other words, the news was temporarily unable to remain above affect, to produce the tone of voice in which morality and rationality sound the same. Instead, the news became embarrassed, losing for a moment its capacity to adjudicate commonsense morality because it couldn't stop stuttering and blushing.

And thus broadcast news could not adequately cover the definition of sexual relations in the Jones deposition. To do so, they would have had to bypass one of the coverage's favorite binarisms—"Is this scandal about sex or about perjury?"—and imagine sex and perjury in this case as having everything to do with each other. They would have had to treat sex as a legitimate object of inquiry, as not the opposite of the political and the national, but as intimately entwined with them. They would have had, as I suggested whimsically in my introduction, to have called on different experts. And they would have had to engage directly the key issues at stake in the definition and in the case as a whole. For one thing, they would have had to confront the absence of any a priori correspondence between an intent to arouse or gratify someone (including oneself) and particular sexual acts. They would have had to theorize the circular nature of arousal, the difficulty of disentangling one's own arousal from one's partners'. And they would have had to inquire into the meanings of ostensibly nonnormative sexual practices among heterosexuals, to invent a sexual analytic with which to think about sexual prosthesis, topping and bottoming, fantasy and reality, the challenge of producing sexual narrative, and the valences of sexual shame, all of which were, to this observer at least, crucially productive both of the conflicting testimony and of the reactions it engendered. And to do all these things, they would have had to overcome their own flush-cheeked stammering.

Notes

1. My thanks to audiences at the MLA and Harvard University for their provocative questions; to Matthew Rowlinson, for putting me on the trail of Bob Schieffer; and to Lauren Berlant, editor extraordinaire.

Some bibliography may be useful here. See, for example, Susie Bright, *Full Exposure: Opening Up to Sexual Creativity and Erotic Expression* (San Francisco: HarperSanFrancisco, 1999); *Susie Bright's Sexual State of the Union* (New York: Simon and Schuster, 1997); *Susie Bright's Sexual Reality: A Virtual Sex World Reader* (Pittsburgh: Cleis Press, 1992); *Susie Sexpert's Lesbian Sex World* (Pittsburgh: Cleis Press, 1990); Pat Califia, *Public Sex: The Culture of Radical Sex* (Pittsburgh: Cleis Press, 1994); *The Advocate Adviser: America's Most Popular Gay Columnist Tackles the Questions That the Others Ignore* (Boston: Alyson Publications, 1991); Dan Savage, *The Kid: What Happened after My Boyfriend and I Decided to Go Get Pregnant* (New York: Dutton, 1999); and *Savage Love: Straight Answers from America's Most Popular Sex Columnist* (New York: Plume, 1998).

2. House Document 105–311, part 1, p. 681.

3. The transcripts of Clinton's deposition have not been released. I am working here from CNN's transcript of Abbe Lowell's presentation before the House Judiciary Committee on December 10, 1998, at which he showed a videotape of the deposition.

4. Hereafter, when I refer to "the Jones definition," I will be referring only to part one.

5. Cable News Network, *CNN Breaking News*, "Details of the Starr Report Emerge," 11 September 1998, transcript number 98091103V00, my emphasis.

6. American Broadcasting Company, *ABC News Special Report*, "Crisis in the White House," 11 September 1998, transcript number 98091102-j14.

7. Columbia Broadcasting System, *Special Report*, "Contents of Ken Starr's Report," 11 September 1998.

8. National Broadcasting Company, *NBC News Special Report*, "The White House in Crisis," 11 September 1998.

9. There is a confusion analogous to the "is" problem embedded in the language of the definition itself. What does "contact with the genitalia, anus, groin, breast, inner thigh, or buttocks of any person with an intent to arouse or gratify the sexual desire of any person" mean? Specifically, what do those "anys" mean? Would masturbation, performed with the intent to arouse or gratify oneself, constitute sexual relations under

this definition? It would have to, unless at least one of those "anys" really means "any other," in which case masturbation performed with the intent to arouse or gratify another would count, as would contact with another with the intent to arouse or gratify oneself. And if it is plausible to read one of the "anys" as meaning "any other"—if indeed the definition seems to require that reading then it is also plausible to read them both that way, as Mr. Clinton, certainly strategically, did during his grand jury testimony. In other words, it is possible to read the definition in a third way, as meaning "contact with the genitalia, anus, groin, breast, inner thigh, or buttocks of another person with an intent to arouse or gratify the sexual desire of another person."

10. American Broadcasting Company, *ABC News Special Report*, "Crisis in the White House," 11 September 1998, transcript number 98091102-j14.

11. Cable News Network, *CNN Breaking News*, "Details of the Starr Report Emerge," 11 September 1998, transcript number 98091103V00. Later that day, CNN aired an entire package focusing on the problems for news organizations presented by the "details" of the Starr Report; see Cable News Network, *CNN Live Event*, "Investigating the President: Aftermath of the Starr Report," transcript number 98091131V54. There was considerable print coverage as well. See, for example, Don Aucoin, "TV Outlets Say They'll Broadcast What's Fit to Air," *Boston Globe*, 11 September 1998, A29; Aucoin and Mark Jurkowitz, "Live and Uncut, Report Unfolded," *Boston Globe*, 12 September 1998, A8; Greg Braxton and Brian Lowry, "For TV News, Report Presented a Quandary," *Los Angeles Times*, 12 September 1998, A17; John Carman, "Networks Don Kid Gloves in Reporting Salacious Story," *San Francisco Chronicle*, 12 September 1998, A9; Monica Collins, "The Starr Report: Torrid Tome Plays on Television Like a Steamy, Seamy Daytime Soap," *Boston Herald*, 12 September 1998, 14; Caryn James, "Language Is a Concern as TV Covers Report," *New York Times*, 12 September 1998, A11; Howard Kurtz, "At First Blush, TV Reporters Stumble over Sordid Details," *Washington Post*, 12 September 1998, E01.

12. Newton Minow was John F. Kennedy's FCC head and author of the renowned speech to the 1961 National Association of Broadcasters Convention, which called television a "vast wasteland." The text of the speech can be found in his *Equal Time: The Private Broadcaster and the Public Interest* (New York: Athenaeum, 1964). For assessments of Minow's impact, see Mary Ann Watson, *The Expanding Vista: American Television in the Kennedy Years* (New York: Oxford University Press, 1990), and Michael Curtin, *Redeeming the Wasteland: Television Documentary and Cold War Politics* (New Brunswick, N.J.: Rutgers University Press, 1995). The Dodd Commission was a congressional committee on television violence convened by Senator Thomas Dodd of Connecticut. It met intermittently from 1961 to 1964. For accounts of the commission's work, see

William Boddy, "Approaching the Untouchables: Social Science and Moral Panics in Early Sixties Television," *Cinema Journal* 35, no. 4 (1996): 70–87, and "Senator Dodd Goes to Hollywood: Investigating Video Violence," in *The Revolution Wasn't Televised: Sixties Television and Social Conflict*, ed. Lynn Spigel and Michael Curtin (New York: Routledge, 1997), 161–184. The V-chip reads ratings information encoded in television programs and can be made to block reception of programs that have certain ratings. The FCC has mandated that half of all new television models 13 inches or larger manufactured after July 1, 1999, and *all* sets 13 inches or larger manufactured after January 1, 2000, must have V-chips. For a contextualizing account of the V-chip, see Heather Hendershot, *Saturday Morning Censors: Television Regulation Before the V-chip* (Durham, N.C.: Duke University Press, 1998).

13. For profiles of both Lear and Bochco, see David Marc and Robert J. Thompson, *Prime Time, Prime Movers* (Boston: Little, Brown and Company, 1992).

14. Surprisingly little scholarly attention has been devoted to the Code. One of the few articles I was able to find on it is Lynda M. Maddox and Eric J. Zanot, "Suspension of the NAB Code and Its Effect on Regulation of Advertising," *Journalism Quarterly* 61, no. 1 (1984): 125–156. See also Emile C. Netzhammer III, "Self-Regulation in Broadcasting: A Legal Analysis of the National Association of Broadcasters Television Code," Master's thesis, University of Utah, 1984.

15. The Production Code was instituted in 1930 as the film industry's response to calls for censorship from (among others) the Catholic Legion of Decency. The Comics Code Authority was a self-regulation effort by comic publishers formed in 1954, largely in response to the uproar produced by Frederick Wertham's *The Seduction of the Innocent* (New York: Rinehart, 1954). Wertham argued that comic books encouraged violence and perversion in their young consumers; for a fuller discussion, see my "The Caped Crusader of Camp: Pop, Camp and the *Batman* Television Series," in *Pop Out: Queer Warhol*, ed. Jennifer Doyle, Jonathan Flatley, and José Esteban Muñoz (Durham, N.C.: Duke University Press, 1996), 238–256.

16. National Association of Radio and Television Broadcasters, *The Television Code of the National Association of Radio and Television Broadcasters* (Washington, D.C., 1952).

17. National Association of Broadcasters, *The Television Code of the National Association of Broadcasters with Regulations and Procedures*, 12th ed. (Washington, D.C., 1967), 5.

18. National Association of Broadcasters, *The Television Code*, 17th ed. (Washington, D.C.,1973).

19. National Association of Broadcasters, *The Television Code*, 22nd ed. (Washington, D.C., 1981), 6, my emphasis.

20. On "cable sex," see June Juffer's chapter on "Eroticizing the Television," in *At*

Home with Pornography: Women, Sex, and Everyday Life (New York: New York University Press, 1998).

21. American Broadcasting Company, *ABC News Special Report*, "Crisis in the White House," 11 September 1998, transcript number 98091102-j14; Columbia Broadcasting System, *Special Report*, "Contents of Ken Starr's Report," 11 September 1998.

7 The First Penis Impeached

Toby Miller

[N]othing big ever came from being small.

—Bill Clinton's Second Inaugural Address[1]

There are so many reasons for the left to loathe Clinton: gays in the military, health insurance, welfare, poverty, the environment, secondary schooling, anti-socialist and pro-market rhetoric, failure to support left appointees when they were assaulted by the right (you sack the surgeon-general for recommending promiscuous hand jobs instead of promiscuous penetrative sex when that's your own M.O.?), and brutal military violence. Consider Clinton's two inauguration speeches—grotesque assortments of biblical and Catholic teaching plus clichés from the Gipper, signaling an ecumenical but strong religiosity and debts to fellow conservatives. A form of "civil religion," these addresses troped the United States as a chosen land, despite the church-and-state requirements of the Constitution.[2]

On the other side of the dime, Clinton stopped the rot, the horror of the Gipper/Bush the Elder, the unrestrained gun and tobacco lobbies, the rhetoric of anti-government, and many threats to abortion, while 1998 saw real personal incomes up by 8 percent from four years earlier.[3] He represents what Warren Beatty has appositely called "the slightly more liberal one of the two accounting firms we call our major parties."[4] Clinton is a disappointment to the left, but not our true enemy.[5] As the saying goes, "he's our bastard."

Throughout his time in national life, Clinton has been "a man whose political and personal lives conflate in the being of his erections."[6] Miraculously, "our bastard" survived the most astonishing of these assaults, impeachment. What are the cultural coordinates that might explain this staying power, in terms of both history and theory? In addressing these matters, I conclude that we need to conceive of the First Penis in the context of (a) the penis as an index of self-governance; (b) the male body as an increasingly sexualized, commodified set of signs; (c) media coverage of Clinton-Lewinsky; and (d) the public's view of (c) in the light of (a) and (b).

The Government of the Penis

Corporate America's Dirty Secret: Addicted to Sex. Forget Bill and Monica. It's a big problem for business. Companies used to wink at these troubled executives. Now they send them to desert clinics for "The Cure."   —Fortune *cover, 10 May 1999*

[T]he American president's sex organ seems to have become the center of the universe.
                                                                     —Jack Lang[7]

Saint Augustine explains Adam and Eve's post-apple physical shame as a problem of control: what had been easily managed organs prior to the fall suddenly became liable to "a novel disturbance in their disobedient flesh," homologous to their owners' disobedience of God. The result—the rest of us were left with original sin. The *pudenda*, or "parts of shame," are named as such because people now find lust can "arouse those members independently of decision." The "movements of their body" manifest "indecent novelty" and hence shame. Such feelings derive from the capacity of objects to get out of whack. The "genital organs have become as it were the private property of lust."[8] As Foucault puts it, what once were "like the fingers" in obeying the will of their owner, came to elude his control, a punishment for Adam's own attempt to evade God's will. Man exemplifies the Fall in the mutability of his penis. So Renaissance paintings of Jesus routinely depict him pointing to or touching his genitals as a sign of his human side: a begotten rather than a created Son.[9]

This appears to be Clinton's problem, "the adolescent boy-king, always in trouble, yet lovingly forgivable," as per Rob Lowe's Billy in *St. Elmo's Fire*. Clinton is unremittingly priapic and mendacious, and you can see it written all over him. Weak and trembling in the face of desire, he deals with these forces in ways that provide the world with a transparent screen of evaluation. On the surface, this priapism would suggest a massive vote of no confidence from the allegedly puritanical American public. But that never came, and it doesn't surprise me.

In Ancient Greece and Rome, the body was the locus for an ethics of the self, a combat with pleasure and pain that enabled people to find the truth, to master themselves.[10] Austerity and hedonism could be combined. Xenophon, Socrates, and Diogenes believed that sexual excess and decadence could lead to professional failure unless accompanied by regular examination of the conscience and physical training. This carefully modulated desire became a sign of fitness to govern others. Aristotle and Plato also favored regular, ongoing flirtations with excess.[11]

Five hundred years later, the sexual ethics of Ancient Rome saw spirituality emerge to complicate exercises of the self as a training for governance

within an ethics that posits that death, disease, or even physical suffering do not constitute true ills and that it is better to take pains over one's soul than to devote one's care to the maintenance of the body. But in fact the focus of attention in these practices of the self is the point where the ills of the body and those of the soul can communicate with one another and exchange their distresses; where the bad habits of the soul can entail physical miseries, while the excesses of the body manifest and maintain the failings of the soul.[12]

In place of the excesses that had preoccupied fourth-century B.C. Athens, first-century A.D. Rome was principally concerned with frailty; the finitude of life and fitness. Moral arguments were imbued with "nature and reason," with exercises of the self joined to this more elevated search for truth.[13] There are contemporary echoes in the moment when candidate Jimmy Carter advised *Playboy* that he had "looked on a lot of women with lust. I've committed adultery in my heart many times."[14] The peanut farmer's ethical combat was processual, not teleological. Clinton's very public admission of his post-Lewinsky need for spiritual uplift, courtesy of Jesse Jackson, embodied this endless search.

Clinton's apparent failure was to compromise his leadership through "a worn tale of middle-aged vulnerability and youthful appetite."[15] This "error" was central to the Republicans' strategy of appeal to public decency. But Bill's dalliance with desire, his carefully calibrated, Monigated, sense of how far he could go— what constituted sex—was in fact part of the dance of management (not denial) that characterizes high office and its organization of low desires. The high-Tory American Medical Association was onto the problem when it roundly dismissed the editor of its house journal for daring to print a paper during the controversy that showed 60 percent of undergraduates at "a large mid-Western university" (how many times have we read that expression in survey research?) in 1991 did not think they had "had sex" if it involved oral contact rather than intercourse.[16] There is evidence of similar rules among New York City teens.[17] Such research added to the sense that Clinton was not aberrant—this kind of calibration is an utterly banal and ordinary part of self-governance. Its relevance is clear from pre-impeachment transcripts of conversations between Lewinsky and Tripp in which Lewinsky says that she never fucked the Prez and so they had not "done it."[18] Perhaps Clinton's very passivity and lack of dominance in the sexual side of the relationship sent the press into frenzies of critique, and not the fact of "fooling around."[19] He didn't go all the way, and she made the moves, so he's not the complete president. But in another sense, doesn't this indicate careful lust management? When Lyndon Johnson responded to reporters' queries about why "we" were in Vietnam, he unzipped his fly, pulled out his wedding tackle, and said, "This is why."[20] Which is so presidential?

The Bright Light

Women leaving hotels following trysts with their extramarital lovers tell pollsters they abominate Mr. Clinton's behavior. Relaxed men fresh from massage parlors frown earnestly into the camera at the mere thought of such malfeasance.   —Toni Morrison[21]

[L]ittle has been made of this sentence in the Starr report: "The longer conversations [between the president and Monica Lewinsky] often occurred after their sexual contact." Is there another man alive who talks more after *sex than before?*   —Frank Rich[22]

Alongside the long-standing analogy between governance of the post-lapsarian male genital and the ability to rule the imperial presidency, Bill Clinton has also presided over a change in the public cultural economy of masculinity—equally relevant to the story of the First Penis.

The 1980s saw two crucial conferences that helped to shift the direction of global advertising: "Reclassifying People" and "Classifying People." Traditional ways of understanding consumers—race, gender, and class—were supplanted by categories of self-display, with market researchers dubbing the '90s the decade of the "new man."[23] Lifestyle and psychographic research became central issues as consumers were divided between "moralists," "trendies," "the indifferent," "working-class puritans," "sociable spenders," and "pleasure seekers." Men were subdivided into "pontificators," "self-admirers," "self-exploiters," "token triers," "chameleons," "avant-gardicians," "sleepwalkers," and "passive endurers."[24] The variegated male body was up for grabs as both sexual icon and commodity consumer. Consider the gay market under Clintonomics.

Gay magazines now circulate information to businesses about the spending power of their childless, middle-class readership—*Campaign*'s slogan in advertising circles is "Gay Money Big Market, Gay Market Big Money." The mid-1990s brought Ikea's famous US TV commercial showing two men furnishing their apartment together, and Toyota's male car-buying couple, while Hyundai began appointing gay-friendly staff to dealerships, IBM targeted gay-run small businesses, Subaru advertisements on buses and billboards had gay advocacy bumper stickers and registration plates coded to appeal to queers, and Volkswagen commercials featured two men driving around in search of home furnishings. (These campaigns are known as "encrypted ads." They are designed to make queers feel special for being "in the know," while not offending simpleton straights.) Polygram's classical-music division introduced a gay promotional budget, Miller beer was a sponsor of Gay Games '94, and Bud Light was national sponsor to the 1999 San Francisco Folsom Street Fair, "the world's largest leather event," while Coors devised domestic-partner benefits to counteract its anti-gay image of the past.[25] The spring 1997 U.S. network TV season saw twenty-two queer characters across the prime-time network schedule—clear signs of niche targeting.[26] And 1999 brought the first successful gay initial public offering, while gay and lesbian Websites were drawing significant private investment.[27] Bruce Hayes, an "out" gay man who won a swimming relay gold for the U.S. at the 1984 Los Angeles Olympics, was a key figure in Levi Strauss's 1998–99 Dockers campaign.[28]

In related developments, male striptease shows that are performed for female audiences reference not only changes in the direction of power and money, but also a public site where "[w]omen have come to see exposed male genitalia; they have come to treat male bodies as objects only." During the 1998 men's World Cup of soccer, the French Sexy Boys Band offered strip shows for "les filles sans foot" ("girls without soccer/girls who couldn't care less"). They have been performing in Paris since 1993 to sell-outs—the all-female audiences must book two weeks in advance, while the U.S. Chippendales toured northern Europe across the spring and summer of 1999 to crowds of women[29]—*The Full Monty* writ large, even though some female spectators found the reversal of subject positions far from easy.[30] The North American middle-class labor market now sees wage discrimination by beauty as much among men as women, and major corporations frequently require executives to tailor their body shapes to the company ethos, or at least encourage employees to cut their weight in order to reduce health-care costs to the employer. In 1998, 93 percent of U.S. companies featured such pro-grams for workers, compared to 76 percent in 1992.[31] American Academy of Cosmetic Surgery figures indicate that more than six and a half thousand men had facelifts in 1996. In 1997, men accounted for a quarter of all such procedures, and the following year straight couples were frequently scheduling surgery together (up 15 percent in a year). Between 1996 and 1998 male cosmetic surgery increased 34 percent, mostly through purchase of liposuction. Gay men are increasingly using steroids for cosmetic purposes, and a third of all "graying" male U.S. workers in 1999 colored their hair to counter the effect of aging on their careers. Midtown Manhattan now offers specialists in ear, hand, and foot waxing, with men comprising 40 percent of the clientele.[32] In short, Clinton has been president at a key moment of change: thanks to commodification of the male subject, he is brought out into the bright light of narcissism and purchase.

Some of that brightness shines from feminism. The independent persecutor was onto something when he portrayed Clinton as "the pitiable victim of a preda-tory female,"[33] in the sense that this downplayed his capacity to manage desire. But such a characterization forgot an intervention that problematized this issue: a thing called feminism. Journalist Nina Burleigh proclaimed that "she would be happy to give the President a blow job to thank him for keeping abortion legal."[34] Meanwhile, revelations that Lewinsky had lifted her coat from the back to reveal a thong to the president sent sales of such lingerie skyrocketing—from "the sleazy backwaters of fashion, thongs are now the fastest-growing segment of the $2 bil-lion-a-year women's panty business." Stocked by retailers from Wal-Mart to Saks, they have a big rap with women under thirty-five.[35] This was the wonton expres-sion of female desire. Even *New Yorker* columnist Rebecca Mead could see it as "progress of a kind" while joining the banal chorus about the sanctity of marriage as monogamous in describing this "freedom to flirt" as "feminism's unsought vic-tory."[36] Other sales changes came with Lewinsky's revelation that she sucked Al-toids before oral sex. The mints were increasingly to be found next to condoms in many drugstores.[37] This is not to mention the cigar-style "Monica" vibrator, which took off as well.

The right's snide accusation that feminists had abandoned women's rights in their defense of Clinton against sexual harassment legislation (which the right had hitherto loathed) did not shame feminists—it goaded them, and many others became aware of the politics of this area.[38] For William Bennett to claim that "Clinton treated Monica as a sex toy" infuriated Susan Bordo, not least given Ben-nett's own sordid history of attacking feminisms. Bordo stresses the pleasure

Lewinsky derived from oral sex, that she got a hit from Clinton's structural power—*and* that *she* seduced *him.*[39]

Clinton is also feminized by a number of qualities: his weight problems, his teariness, his physical affection, his interest in feelings, his linkage of intellectual power and emotional bravado—and his unreliable side, for all the world some throwback to the image of women as inveterate liars.[40] So when Christopher Hitchens mocks him with Paula Jones's implication that "it would have taken two of his phalluses to make one normal one,"[41] this references quite precisely the discourse long used to find fault with women's bodies. OK, Bill's is "five inches long when erect, as big around as a quarter, and bent."[42] But that is just one more point of identification with the objectification of his body, as the commodity fetish moves onto men. The same process, of problematizing masculinity, took place during the 1992 elections, when Bush the Elder accused Clinton of being influenced by "the tassel-loafered lawyer crowd." Ross Perot forbade his staff from wearing the offending shoe, and the Elder's press secretary, Toni Clarke, compared Clinton to Woody Allen.[43] A big girl, Clinton is described by friends former and current, psychoanalysts, and pol-sci mavens, as desperate to please, "seductive," and eager to hear differing points of view.[44] He is both the new man of advertising—flawed, sexy, priapic, sensitive—and the publicly humiliated, sexed body of misogyny.

The Media Penis

I still believe in a place called . . . hell. . . . Let's don't kid each other: this was an awful year. It was a year I wouldn't wish on my worst enemy. I take that back.
                                        —*Bill Clinton to a media roast*[45]

Baudrillard and Virilio triumphed in 1998–99, in the sense that intellectual mavens across the country delved farther and farther into their litany of abuse for the media as deadening the possibility of truth, imploding on their own commodity form, and transmogrifying journalists into peddlers. Clinton's *mea culpa* speech to the nation on 17 August 1998 drew 67.6 million viewers (half the numbers for the first day of the Gulf War, two-thirds of the numbers for the previous Super Bowl and O.J.'s Bronco drive, and double the figure for Diana Spencer's funeral).[46] (Keith Olbermann, the shock-jock sports comic turned talk-show host, saw his MSNBC *Big Show* completely taken over by the impeachment. All 228 episodes were dedicated to it, and his op-ed piece on the subject was entitled "The

Scandal That Ate My TV Program." But at least Olbermann did learn that Republican congressman John Kasich's careful use of the anchor's first name during an interview was assisted by "a piece of paper with 'KEITH' written in block letters and underlined twice.")[47]

The 3 March 1999 episode of *20/20* featuring Lewinsky and Barbara Walters generated a 48 percent share of the viewing audience for ABC. The biggest audience in the history of network news, it outrated the Academy Awards.[48] The network upped its commercial rates (double or fourfold, depending on whom you believe) to $800,000 a spot. Advertisers included Victoria's Secret, while ABC itself promoted a new telemovie about Cleopatra as the story of a woman who, "when she was only 20, seduced the most powerful leader in the world."[49] Lewinsky was not paid for her time in the U.S., but received a small fortune from the U.K.'s Channel Four, which gave her 75 percent of its proceeds from selling the text around the world.[50]

TV networks unleashed penis and oral-sex jokes onto sitcom viewers after the case, not to mention featuring Matt Lauer and an orthodox rabbi discussing sex toys on *Today*. Sucked in by the Lewinsky incidents and the need to compete with cable's freedom of speech, the networks were also affected by simultaneous decisions to reduce the size of their standards and practices departments to cut costs.[51]

U.S. TV devoted more airtime to Clinton's scandal in 1998 than all other news stories put together.[52] Pakistani nuclear tests? Asian economic meltdown? Fuggedaboudit. To many critics, this represented an appalling indictment of American journalism, with reporting displaced by the deprofessionalizing protocols of the Internet and cable. Matt Drudge dished the dirt, Mike Wallace became a pathetic shadow of integrity lampooned by *The Insider*, and credentials were shoved aside by populism, with neutrality a joke.[53] Toni Morrison claimed that the media had "willingly locked themselves into a ratings-driven, money-based prison of their own making,"[54] and Steve Brill lamented the "speed of today's never-pausing news cycle."[55] His *Brill's Content* magazine featured a cover with a blue Gap dress shot through with smoking bullet holes in place of DNA-laden semen stains, to make the point that Kosovo coverage followed the impeachment trend of instantaneous and indivisible reportage, analysis, and opinion. The *Wall Street Journal* proclaimed this "the climax of a generation-long trend: the melding of entertainment and politics."[56] When White House press secretary Joe Lockhart told a press room gathering that "a news magazine" was about to publish details of sexual indiscretions by Republicans, the assembled brood "howled." He edited his words, because everyone knew the identity of the periodical—Larry Flynt's *Hustler* had advertised in Kathryn Graham's *Washington Post*, offering a million dollars for evidence of right-wing "deviance." The *New York Times* called this "the Flynt Virus."[57] Across 1998, over 140 U.S. newspapers called on Clinton to resign.[58] But as we shall see, such news punditry was stunningly irrelevant to an unengaged public.[59]

The 1999 White House Correspondents' Association dinner broke with tradition. Once reserved for apparatchiks and the press corps, the guest list was extended to Jon Bon Jovi, Salma Hayek, Warren Beatty, and Sharon Stone, complete with coverage on *Entertainment Tonight*.[60] Clinton had always been providential for Hollywood, providing source material for *The American President*, *Absolute Power*, *Murder at 1600*, *Shadow Conspiracy*, *Dave*, *Mars Attacks!*, *My Fellow Americans*, *In the Line of Fire*, *Deep Impact*, *Air Force One*, *First Kid*, *Wag the Dog*, and *Primary Colors*. This textualisation coincided with the new mass-market genre of disrespectful populist prez-fiction: Erik Tarloff's *Face-Time*, Marilyn Quayle (yes) and Nancy Northcott's *The Campaign*, Newt Gingrich (yes) and William R. Fortschen's *1945*, Larry Beinhart's *American Hero*, Charles McCarry's *Lucky Bastard*, and Jeff Greenfield's *The People's Choice*. Again and again, these books portrayed affable left-wing guys who couldn't keep their dicks under control, and imperiled national security or the American way of life.[61] By the same token, liberal Hollywood supported him: David Geffen said "[e]ven though his private behavior is regrettable, his handling of the country is exemplary"; Angie Dickinson, who was reported to have some experience in these matters, offered, "We shouldn't care what a president does in his bedroom";[62] and Clinton used the services of Hollywood producer Harry Thomasson for spin surgery over Lewinsky.[63]

Clinton's product-placement of diet cola in his video testimony drew few comments—of course the president would sip from an identifiable brand. But when Tommy Hilfiger advertisements troped the scandal in mock-ups of the Oval Office, the White House complained and the offending texts were removed.[64] Following the 1998 midterms, Hillary Clinton became the only First Lady to make the cover of *Vogue*—Nancy Reagan had tried desperately, in vain. Mrs. Clinton was also shortlisted for *Time* magazine's "Person of the Year" until her husband was impeached—style was OK, current affairs were off, and much note was taken of what was termed her "I-will-survive hairstyle," itself troping Diana Spencer's post-divorce makeover.[65] *Talk* magazine got her the most publicity of all via its inaugural-issue interview that humanized the "copresident and codependent," and claimed the First Feminist and First Penis had "slowly seen a physical passion come back into their lives," thanks to the "power of ideas." Ah huh. Does that mean mind-fucking? *Talk* also reported a period of purgatory, with Clinton sent to the doghouse by his wife to seek penitence, just when she became belatedly popular as the betrayed woman rather than the policy feminist. This "regal look" has allegedly sent her husband into paroxysms: "Doesn't she look beautiful?" he has been heard asking friends; while Hillary distinguishes between venal and major sins in her support of him.[66] Attempts by friendly media outlets to humanize them aside (remember Bill the Cherokee and Hillary the Jew?), Rodham Clinton was onto something here.

The Public's Penis

We don't want to run the government based on who is a cad.   *—Jack Nicholson*[67]

We know more about the American electorate's view of Clinton than we could possibly want to. August 1998 alone saw 549 poll questions posed about him. Again and again, the results counter notions of a Republican-style permeability between public and private, as the electorate said: yes, he's a scumbag, no; I don't want to lose him as president.[68] This confounded every pollster and psephologist's understanding of the relationship between scandal and public standing, not to mention the expectations of the party of darkness.[69] How so?

In 1990, Madonna was asked what she thought of Donald Trump standing for president. Her initial response—"he can't be president if he's had sex"—softened later, as she said perhaps the U.S. electorate might be ready to choose "a guy with a dick."[70] Glenn O'Brien claimed the same year that the United States has "a ritually cyclic priapic president,"[71] while Louis Begley argued during the Clinton débâcle that the Republicans and the independent persecutor had "turned us into a nation of Peeping Toms." As per public executions, the abject had been made central to media coverage.[72] And clearly, images of a blow job while on the phone discussing Bosnia, or "shuddering over the executive washbasin," are at the outer limits. But for all the claims to wholesale public Puritanism made by self-loathing libertarian and self-loving evangelical Americans, everybody knows somebody who's been exogamous, or has done it themselves, or has broken their own moral code, or simply engaged in practices they would prefer kept secret.[73] Sooner or later, "howling after sex" implicates the people you are trying to interpellate.[74]

125

"Howling" also stands oddly alongside the condemnation by his allies and foes. Democratic congressman Rick Boucher spoke in the censure debate against impeachment, but rushed to the barricades for the sanctity of role models, the family, and truth-in-sex. Conversely, the oleaginous Henry Hyde, Republican chair of the congressional committee that recommended impeachment, insisted again and again that "sexual misconduct" is "none of Congress's business." It is "private, and ought to be left alone."[75] But when Republican congressman Bob Livingston was forced to stand aside as proto-House Speaker because he had put it about during his marriage, the Republicans played their hand—of course this was about sex.[76] Their pitiful 1998 election commercials essentially reduced the vote to a plebiscite on Clinton's morality, asking voters if they wanted to reward the president's behavior by sending Democrats to Congress.[77]

Whether the Republicans were running to the tune of the religious right, their own beliefs, or misguided psephological fantasies,[78] the fact is, they got it all wrong in terms of public strategy. Opinion polls routinely saw the public saying "enough" to both media coverage and special persecutor focus—the end of 1998 saw Clinton's approval rating at 66 percent, a record for midterm elections.[79] Suck on that, Gipper. Ratings for TV coverage on the networks were nothing special, but the cable news areas were notable successes.[80] This suggests that extremely partisan, anti-intellectual shows, like Fox News Network's right-wing populist *O'Reilly Factor*, attracted committed folks whose views it simply reinforced. But ordinary viewers were less enthralled—driven to see Clinton's and Lewinsky's accounts, but uninterested in a political corollary.

The midterm elections of 1998 *were* extraordinary: the second time since 1865 that a president's party improved its number of seats at this juncture, the end of Gingrich as Speaker, and the destruction of Republican plans for a filibuster-proof Senate majority, which they had expected based on what they delightfully called "the scarlet 'C.'"[81] The entire machinery of the American Constitution, its Byzantine checks and balances, was devised to ensure restraint of populist lunacy. All along the watchtower between elections and the execution of policy, experts stood between the mob and power. The passion of the crowd would be checked by elites. This election had the *opposite* effect, as the madness of politicians and media mavens was rejected by the voting population.[82] They clearly accepted Clinton's two catch phrases throughout the proceedings, which juxtaposed a very Weberian notion of public service. *He* was doing "the people's business." His *enemies* were engaged in "the politics of personal destruction."[83]

126

Conclusion

AFTER-THE-FACT CAUSALITY: This simple law states that having sex with an intern can cause a financial misdealing to occur twenty years prior. —Steve Martin[84]

Morrison reports suggestions from African Americans that Clinton "is our first black president," and *The Economist* agrees: working-class, single-mom, junk-food-maven (who plays the sax) and is pilloried for his sex life as a reminder that his origins will never leave him: "The Presidency is being stolen from us. And the people know it."[85] This contrasts with U.S. presidents like the Gipper, who signed a congressional enactment forbidding payment to the Contras, and then oversaw a covert operation that subsidized drug-runners to assist Nicaraguan counter-revolutionaries. (The reaction from Republicans over these matters has to be imagined—there was none.) The party of darkness also failed to recognize that Americans may expect executives to be the "alpha-male" psy-complex stereotype that Gore the Younger wanted to be in 2000—*Fortune* magazine features the fact that four CEOs of its 500 top-companies list have been treated for sexual addiction as a reason to locate the Clinton controversy inside the discourse of the powerful man with powerful appetites.[86]

In this sense, Clinton wins two ways. He wins as the underdog (for minorities), and he wins as the duelist with his own desires (for elites). The attack on him is perceived both as an assault on counterculture values and civil rights gains (still espoused by many) and on the presidency as the truly democratic face of the state. The public contains many of the non-white/poor/queer/liberal/feminist/pro-choice folks pilloried by the anti-Clinton side. Many of them benefit from the presidential centralization that the right has loathed since the Depression and the start of the Democrats' split with good ol' boys.[87] Time-series analysis demonstrates that the period since the 1970s has seen activists among the Democrats become more secular and modern, while activist Republicans have increasingly been religious and antimodern. Since 1972 and George McGovern's candidacy for the presidency, even through quasi-evangelical presidents in Carter and Clinton, Democratic partisans have been solid on abortion, queer rights, and women's issues, as have the Republicans. They are polar opposites, and the cleavage starts with spiritual versus real-world transcendence.[88]

In summary, where once the regicidal cry was "Off with his head," in the late 1990s the signifier had slipped down the body. The private parts, the Janus-faced cock that is both secreted and secreting, faced the duality of being the First Penis and Bill Clinton's own. The querying legacy of feminist critique both blurred and clarified the lines dividing these two signs. In concert with a much older legacy of structural homologies between management of one's desire and government of one's country, plus the commodification and feminization of the male body, they permitted the First Penis to stand. The public thought Clinton lied about seeking a bit of the other, and also thought he was a *good* president—exactly the way that hundreds of distinguished law professors argued was in sync with the originary logics of the Constitution's founding parents.[89] In February 1999, approval ratings for the First Penis stood at 68 percent, a mere 8 percentage points higher than the week before Lewinsky surfaced publicly in January 1998:[90] "With each new revelation, Americans became more convinced of Clinton's guilt, and less supportive of his removal."[91] Richard Posner stumbled on something correct here—that "[t]he nation does not depend on the superior virtue of one man."[92] What he missed, as ever, was why.

The maximally arch high-Tory Maureen Dowd threw her hands in the air in exasperation at Christmastime 1998: "It doesn't make sense for him to have such celestial approval ratings."[93] Not to you, Maureen, perhaps, not to you. But it may have made sense to those of us who have ever (a) lied about having an orgasm; (b) lied about infidelity; (c) held private fantasies; or (d) lied to ourselves about the meaning of a liaison. A week before La Dowd's "findings," Barbara Streisand had addressed a rally where the crowd held up a banner that read "He Lied About Sex— So What?"[94] Haven't you?

Notes

1. William J. Clinton, "Second Inaugural Address, January 20, 1997," *Presidential Studies Quarterly* 27, no. 1 (1997), p. 110.

2. John J. Pitney, Jr., "President Clinton's 1993 Inaugural Address," *Presidential Studies Quarterly* 27, no. 1 (1997), pp. 91–103.

3. Gary C. Jacobson, "Impeachment Politics in the 1998 Congressional Elections," *Political Science Quarterly* 114, no. 1 (1999), p. 33 n. 7.

4. Warren Beatty, "Why Not Now?" *New York Times* 22 August 1999, p. 13.

5. Jean L. Cohen, "The Hijacking of Sexual Harassment," *Constellations* 6, no. 2 (1999), p. 142.

6. Richard Schechner, "Oedipus Clintonius," *TDR*, no. 161 (Spring 1999), pp. 5–6.

7. Quoted in Cynthia Weber, *Faking It: U.S. Hegemony in a "Post-Phallic" Era* (Minneapolis: University of Minnesota Press, 1999), p. 105.

8. Augustine. *Concerning the City of God against the Pagans,* trans. Henry Bettenson, ed. David Knowles (Harmondsworth: Penguin, 1976), pp. 522–23, 578, 581.

9. Michel Foucault and Richard Sennett, "Sexuality and Solitude," *Humanities in Review,* 1 (1982), pp. 3–21, and Roy Porter, "History of the Body," *New Perspectives on Historical Writing,* ed. Peter Burke (Cambridge, U.K.: Polity Press, 1991), p. 206.

10. Michel Foucault, *The Use of Pleasure: The History of Sexuality,* vol. 2, trans. Robert Hurley (New York: Vintage, 1986), pp. 66–69.

11. Ibid., pp. 72–73, 104, 120, 197–98.

12. Michel Foucault, *The History of Sexuality,* vol. 3: *The Care of Self,* trans. Robert Hurley (New York: Vintage, 1988), pp. 56–57.

13. Ibid., pp. 238–39.

14. Quoted in Weber, *Faking It,* p. 119.

15. Toni Morrison, "Talk of the Town," *New Yorker* 5 October 1998, p. 31.

16. Vincent Kiernan, "Journal Editor Loses His Job over a Paper on How Students Define 'Having Sex,'" *Chronicle of Higher Education* 29 January 1999, p. A20.

17. Maggie Paley, *The Book of the Penis* (New York: Grove Press, 1999), p. 162.

18. Charles W. Collier and Christopher Slobogin, "Terms of Endearment and Articles of Impeachment," *Florida Law Review* 51 (1999), n.p.

19. Susan Bordo, *The Male Body: A New Look at Men in Public and in Private* (New York: Farrar, Strauss and Giroux, 1999), pp. 294–95.

20. Quoted in Paley, *Book of the Penis,* p. 221.

21. Morrison, "Talk of the Town."

22. Frank Rich, "What Tony Soprano Could Teach Bill Clinton," *New York Times* 14 August 1999, p. A13.

23. C. Fox, "Decade of the 'New Man' is Here," *Australian Financial Review* 21 January 1989, p. 46.

24. Sean Nixon, *Hard Looks: Masculinities, Spectatorship and Contemporary Consumption* (New York: St. Martin's Press, 1996), pp. 96–99.

25. Ronald Alsop, "But Brewers Employ In-Your-Mug Approach," *Wall Street Journal* 29 June 1999, p. B1; Ronald Alsop, "Cracking the Gay Market Code," *Wall Street Journal* 29 June 1999, pp. B1, B4; and S. Rawlings, "Luring the Big Boys," *B and T* 12 February 1993, pp. 18–19.

26. J. J. O'Connor, "Coming Out Party: The Closet Opens, Finally," *New York Times* 30 April 1997, p. C18.

27. David Bank, "On the Web, Gay Sites Start to Click," *Wall Street Journal* 28 September 1999, pp. B1, B6.

28. S. Elliott, "Levi Strauss Begins a Far-Reaching Marketing Campaign to Reach Gay Men and Lesbians," *New York Times* 19 October 1998, p. C11.

29. S. B. Barham, "The Phallus and the Man: An Analysis of Male Striptease," *Australian Ways: Anthropological Studies of an Industrialised Society,* ed. Lenore Manderson (Sydney: Allen and Unwin, 1985), pp. 51–65; Richard Dyer, *Only Entertainment* (London: Rout-ledge, 1992), p. 104; Rose Marie Burke, "Chippendales Let It All Hang Out in Europe," *Wall Street Journal* 8 April 1999, p. A16; and Fiona Harari, "The New Face of Beauty," *Australian* 18 June 1993, p. 15.

30. Emily Jenkins, *Tongue First: Adventures in Physical Culture* (New York: Henry Holt, 1998), p. 92.

31. Milt Freudenheim, "Employers Focus on Weight as Workplace Health Issue." *New York Times* 6 September 1999, p. A15; D. S. Hamermesh and J. E. Biddle. "Beauty and the Labor Market," *American Economic Review* 84, no. 5 (1994), pp. 1174–94; and M. Wells, "Slimmer Dooner Revs Up McCann," *Advertising Age* 10 October 1994, p. 50.

32. "Marketplace," National Public Radio, 3 June 1999; Joel Stein, "Only His Hairdresser Knows for Sure," *Time* 19 July 1999, p. 78; Varda Burstyn, *The Rites of Men: Manhood, Politics, and the Culture of Sport* (Toronto: University of Toronto Press, 1999), p. 217; Ellen Tien, "The More Hairless Ape," *New York Times* 20 June 1999, p. 3; Stephen S. Hall, "The Bully in the Mirror," *New York Times Magazine* 22 August 1999, p. 33; and B. Lemon, "Male Beauty," *Advocate* 22 July 1997, p. 30.

33. Janet Malcolm, "Talk of the Town," *New Yorker* 5 October 1998, p. 32.

34. Quoted in James Bowman, "Letter from Washington," *Times Literary Supplement* 12 February 1999, p. 15.

35. Asra Q. Nomani, "Brief Skirmish, or How the Thong Is Making Its Mark," *Wall Street Journal* 8 June 1999, pp. A1, A8.

36. Rebecca Mead, "Thoroughly Modern Monica," *New Yorker* 15 March 1999, pp. 29–30.

37. Paley, *Book of the Penis,* pp. 163–64.

38. Cohen, "Hijacking of Sexual Harassment."

39. Bordo, *The Male Body,* pp. 278–79.

40. Ellen Willis, *Don't Think, Smile! Notes on a Decade of Denial* (Boston: Beacon Press, 1999), p. 89.

41. Christopher Hitchens, *No One Left to Lie To: The Triangulations of William Jefferson Clinton* (London: Verso, 1999), p. 50.

42. Paley, *Book of the Penis,* p. 222.

43. Michael S. Kimmel, *Manhood in America: A Cultural History* (New York: Free Press, 1996), p. 297.

44. Stephen J. Wayne, "Clinton's Legacy: The Clinton Persona," *PS: Political Science and Politics* 32, no. 3 (1999), pp. 559–61.

45. Quoted in Francis X. Clines, "Clinton 'Singed but not Burned' at Gridiron Dinner," *New York Times* 22 March 1999, p. A15.

46. Timothy M. Gray, "'The Clinton Show': 2,406 Days Running," *Variety* 24–30 August 1998, p. 4.

47. Keith Olbermann, "The Scandal That Ate My TV Program," *New York Times* 8 December 1998, p. A27.

48. Jenny Hontz, "Media Blows Off Standards: Media Takes Up Bawdy-Building," *Variety* 29 March–4 April 1999, p. 85, and Ray Richmond, "20/20: Monica Lewinsky," *Variety* 8–14 March 1999, p. 58.

49. Francis X. Clines and Frank Bruni, "In Television Interview and in Book, Lewinsky Seizes Initiative," *New York Times* 4 March 1999, p. A22, and Caryn James, "New Monica Emerges, Feelings First," *New York Times* 4 March 1999, p. A22.

50. "Monica Misses Out in America," *Economist* 6 March 1999, p. 60.

51. Hontz, "Media Blows Off."

52. Gray, "'The Clinton Show.'"

53. James B. Stewart, "Consider the Sources," *New York Times Book Review* 4 July 1999, p. 8.

54. Morrison, "Talk of the Town," p. 31.

55. Steven Brill, "War Gets the Monica Treatment," *Brill's Content* August 1999, p. 99.

56. Gerald F. Seib, "Live from Hollywood, It's American Politics, with Warren Beatty," *Wall Street Journal* 14 September 1999, p. A1.

57. "Fighting Off the Flynt Virus," *New York Times* 24 December 1998, p. A18.

58. Hendrik Hertzberg, "Buckle Up. Here We Go," *New Yorker* 19 October 1998, p. 25.

59. James Bowman, "Letters from Washington," *Times Literary Supplement* 13 November 1998, p. 18.

60. Seib, "Live from Hollywood," p. A6.

61. Michiko Kakutani, "The Modern Political Novel as a Mirror of the Bizarre," *New York Times* 12 January 1999, pp. E1, E10.

62. Quoted in John Hiscock, "Stars Come Out behind the President," *Daily Telegraph* 7 January 1999, p. 17.

63. Seib, "Live from Hollywood."

64. "The Oval Office Collection," *New York Times* 27 December 1998, S9, p. 1.

65. Alex Kuczynski, "The First Lady Strikes a Pose for the Media Elite," *New York Times* 7 December 1998, pp. C1, C8.

66. Lucinda Franks, "The Intimate Hillary," *Talk* September 1999, pp. 167, 170–71, 173–74.

67. Quoted in Sharon Waxman and Lisa de Moraes, "Clinton's Supporting Cast: Celebrities Rally against Republican Group," *Washington Post* 17 December 1998, p. E1.

68. Jeffrey E. Cohen, "The Polls: Favorability Ratings of Presidents," *Presidential Studies Quarterly* 29, no. 3 (1999), p. 690.

69. John R. Zaller, "Monica Lewinsky's Contribution to Political Science," *PS: Political Science and Politics* 31, no. 2 (1998), p. 182.

70. Quoted in Glenn O'Brien, interview, *Interview* 20, no. 5 (1990), p. 127.

71. Glenn O'Brien, "Meanwhile, Back at the Rancho," *Interview* 20, no. 4 (1990), p. 151.

72. Louis Begley, "Talk of the Town," *New Yorker* 5 October 1998, p. 34.

73. Herzberg, "Buckle Up."

74. "The End?" *Economist* 13 February 1999, pp. 17–18.

75. Quoted in "Excerpts from Discussion of Resolution on Censure," *New York Times* 13 December 1998, p. 47.

76. Frank Rich, "Larry and Lucy," *New York Times* 23 December 1998, p. A27.

77. Bowman, "Letters from Washington."

78. Lawrence Kootnikoff, "Liberal Group Lobbies to Stop Clinton Impeachment Process," Agence France Presse, 8 January 1999.

79. Jacobson, "Impeachment Politics," p. 34.

80. Stuart Miller, "L'Affaire Lewinsky Roars On," *Variety* 30 October 1998, p. A10.

81. Jacobson, "Impeachment Politics," pp. 31, 44.

82. Cass R. Sunstein, "Dunwody Distinguished Lecture in Law: Lessons from a Debacle: From Impeachment to Reform," *Florida Law Review* 51 (1999), and Jeffrey Toobin, "Election Day Calls a Halt to the Night of the Living Dead," *New Yorker* 16 November 1998, pp. 31–32.

83. Quoted in "Bill Clinton's Luck," *Economist* 13 February 1999, p. 27.

84. Steve Martin, "Studies in the New Causality," *New Yorker* 2 November 1998, p. 108.

85. Morrison, "Talk of the Town," p. 33.

86. Betsy Morris, "Addicted to Sex," *Fortune* 10 May 1999, pp. 68–80.

87. Eli Zaretsky, "Culture Wars and the Assault on the Presidency: The Twin Stakes of the Impeachment Crisis," *Constellations* 6, no. 2 (1999), pp. 133–36.

88. Geoffrey C. Layman, "'Culture Wars' in the American Party System: Religious and Cultural Change among Partisan Activists Since 1972," *American Politics Quarterly* 27, no. 1 (1999), pp. 89–121.

89. Jacobson, "Impeachment Politics," and Sunstein, "Lessons from a Debacle."

90. Robert J. Spitzer, "Clinton's Impeachment Will Have Few Consequences for the Presidency," *PS: Political Science and Politics* 32, no. 3 (1999), p. 544.

91. Molly W. Sonner and Clyde Wilcox, "Forgiving and Forgetting: Public Support for Bill Clinton during the Lewinsky Scandal," *PS: Political Science and Politics* 32, no. 3 (1999), p. 555.

92. Richard A. Posner, *An Affair of State: The Investigation, Impeachment, and Trial of President Clinton* (Cambridge, Mass.: Harvard University Press, 1999), p. 266.

93. Maureen Dowd, "Send Out the Clowns," *New York Times* 23 December 1998, p. A27.

94. Giles Whittell, "Stars Come Out to Shine for Clinton," *Times* 18 December 1998.

Part 3

FANTASIES OF RACE, CLASS, AND ETHNICITY

8   The Return of the Oppressed

Frederick C. Moten with B Jenkins

My mom, B Jenkins, and I have spent the last couple of years talking, laughing, singing, and arguing by phone and letter about Bill Clinton. I'd like to submit to you a portion of our exchange, the collective authorship of an old ensemble, the ensemble of the recliner, in honor of Ma's blue La-Z-Boy planted right in front of the television in the den where she watches C-SPAN. There's reference here to a mode of conversation, a way of writing that cuts and augments academic conventions and the increasingly delusional style of what passes here for a public sphere. Ma's talk moves especially to break a speedup that manifests itself in products without voice/sound/tone, without phonic substance and the difference in accent that substance always carries. She makes me sound—which is to say sound different—and that sound irrupts into an automation that is, itself, reflected in complex ways in the very fact of Clinton, even though he can play off a little cry in his voice. The content of her sound also moves to critique (and critique the media critique of) the automated everyday wisdom in nonacademic discourse: in this case, the black support for Clinton which strikes us as both rational and oppressively rationalized, a discursive analog to the dangerous labor black workers performed on/as the assembly lines in Detroit in the 1960s, a regime they dubbed "niggermation." She shows the rational rigor (in spite of its denigration in the press as some intuitive and unfathomable identification) and the rationalized failure of this wisdom while noticing the links between two powerful forms of "left" social critique that find themselves in the position of supporting a war criminal responsible for a vicious attack on what was left of an always already underdeveloped welfare state.

Part I/B's notes

Spring 1996

That Bush set.[1] All I said over there was that I got pretty tired of not having a real choice when I got to vote, that I want to vote for candidates who aren't the lesser of evils in presidential, senatorial, gubernatorial, and mayoral elections, when dingy Elo asked what did I mean? Then she wanted to know what the hell did I want—we have Bill Clinton. The dictator, Q.B., took over and began to lecture me on why we need not worry, because we have it better than ever before. He alleged that I was no better than the rest of the greedy black middle class that never gets enough. He alleged that I made a drastic change when I went to Carson City to work for Dick Bryan[2] and I've been crazy as hell ever since. I asked if it ever occurred to him that maybe I learned something, particularly that the world of politics is a bundle of false impressions? Of course, he knows that, and that is why he feels so secure with Bill.

During the course of that argument his brother James called from New York, and when Qube informed him that I had gone overboard, I had to stand a questioning by him. Normally, I have always been able to inform and influence that household on matters political, but not today. They believe he will take care of us better than anyone else. Then Denby walked in talking just like them; I gave it up when he began to show me what we had in common with Bill and to warn me if Bill doesn't do it, then it won't be done.

I tried to tell them that I was pleased to see Bill come up for the candidacy, but when he began talking about moving the political goals of the weak and aimless Democratic party toward the right, I got a hunk in my throat. Then, I began to think maybe that is his plan to get by the conservative movements. Again, I failed to be reasonable about the behavior of a politician—knowing that the powerful direct their decisions, and the powerful is that small percentage of the population that controls the wealth of the Nation.

Then I said, I still had not forgotten how he had responded to Jesse Jackson in that church in Washington, D.C. It was then that Big Denby had me understand that he was sick of Jesse poking his damn head up everywhere speaking for us. I asked him, a Nevada prison guard, when was the last time he was inspired to speak for himself, or, for the rest of us at that damn prison which is moving toward contractual private management. What about "Three Strikes and You're Out"?

It was then that Sister Bush said wait 'til they get me, then I'll be singing "No Strikes!" Glynda came in and brought up that Lani Guinier appointment to the position of deputy attorney general, and how Dr. Joycelyn Elders was treated when she gave a practical reaction to birth control and venereal disease prevention and how "Lying Bill" had responded to that, which was an insult to us all. The way he handled these two prized black women was an unforgivable act for us. Of course, as I tried to tell those folk, this is common behavior for a power-hungry politician; they really have no commitments unless it helps to retrieve and maintain power. That is one thing I learned during my stay with Dick Bryan.

It was then that I wanted to know, "Just what makes Billy Boy so special to you?" Well, did I get an answer! Dr. Qube had me know we have more in common with Bill than with any other American president in history.

I came home to tell Mother what I had experienced at the Bushes, knowing that she loves Bill, and she agreed with them wholeheartedly. She says that Fred and Glynda have been influenced by my irrational thinking and that we are just like the rest of the sick minds in the country who dislike Clinton because he is a poor white boy who made it against the odds and, most of all, came from little ol' Arkansas. She is convinced that he has done all he can for the poor in this country and that they should try as hard as he has in improving their status in life. When I asked her about the plight of seniors, healthcare, Social Security, and labor unions, she sort of paused but assured me that he would certainly do more than any other candidate, and that as long as he is there, she feels quite secure, in that he has lived the life, is a Christian, and has a very stunning and captivating personality which allows him to communicate with all sorts of people. Then she started to recite Kipling's "If" and scriptures from the Bible. She began to react toward him as she always did toward me, and I am her child.

I explained to her that I didn't appreciate his economic policies and "three strikes and you're out," and that even though he had make black appointments to his cabinet, he never made an effort to get appointments for some of the finest persons. Then I decided it was useless to continue to try and help her understand that her life is being affected by Bill Clinton, and that his grinning and handshaking was only helping to make a bunch of uninformed people comfortable as he allowed them to be destroyed. I explained to her I would not be so aggravated by his actions or inactions if I didn't feel he was aware of the plight of most people in the country. I questioned why he didn't utilize his charm and grace on the people who control the wealth and power of the country, in an effort to get a more equal distribution of that wealth and power. I explained to her that working doesn't get it, for if it did, she should have no needs today—she and Daddy were hard workers. I said that I have worked hard during my career and the harder I work the poorer I become, and that if Laura and Fred aren't careful, they'll find themselves in the same condition. I have found that work is not the answer, and I am about to believe that education and preparation aren't necessarily the answer, either. My mother believes I am insane. Well, I don't.

Afro-Americans, a great number, see themselves on a personal mission to pull Clinton through to the end, because they feel we have common interests given that the system is his major enemy. The problem is, they feel, that while we have always known that the system is our common enemy, he and others like him just haven't quite figured it out.

We have young kids unable to read, graduating to the streets, falling into crime, and becoming imprisoned over and over, providing a new financial empire for government and big business to exploit. You can't make the people who are most vulnerable understand what is happening to them and that Clinton is directing this massive choir.

There is something about this man that captivates his Afro-American constituents, and they remain focused on the notion that he is as much an underdog as are they. He is a Poor White Boy from Arkansas (PWBFA) and the system doesn't want him. Hence, we must sit in the balcony and support him because he is our political Jackie Robinson. They see him as the symbol of what they wanted in those of us who had the chance to be educated, underdogs smart enough to beat the system, achieve power, and then take care of all other underdogs with grace.

November 19, 1996
Today, I mentioned Bill Clinton and his failure to speak to the real needs of the people, NAFTA and all that stuff, to "Matt Dillon,"[3] the backbone of the Laborer's and Steel Worker's, the Culinary and Teamsters Unions, here in Las Vegas, in Nevada, throughout the nation and the world. He is super-pleased with Clinton's position. At least, he says, Clinton has allowed these issues to surface; the previous presidents just let them smother and choke. He says Bill is his Man!, that they

hate him because he is a poor, smart, common, white boy from the South. I gave Matt a couple of copies of articles from my *Nation* and *Z* magazines and he subscribed to them. I noticed he is busy making copies from the publications and distributing them around the building and in the mail; at least he's reading. Of course he likes to be the first to know. Boy, if I did that, I'd be in trouble, utilizing state equipment and mail to produce and distribute controversial information. Well, there's more than one way to achieve a goal.

I ran into Helen Toland today. She has just returned from her second trip to Guinea where she previously served as a volunteer for more than a year. She is now retired, you know. When she served her first stint in Guinea, she returned to Las Vegas and got a hold of some women in a prayer band and motivated them (as only she can do) to rally and raise enough money to purchase and carry a new Toyota truck to the women in one of the villages in Africa. I guess she must have carried at least a dozen women from the Side[4] to Africa. She says, "Their lives will never be the same." I am certain she is correct.

I tried to talk with her about Clinton and how he has put a fix on the minds of black folks, seniors, the working class, and others as he destroys us, and how we are loving his misuse of power because we think he is an underdog who is trying to achieve our social and economic needs. I tried to tell her how he is using us, and she about had a fit since he, at least, doesn't ignore us. He keeps the people fully cognizant that we are real and we have not had a president do that for a long while. Because of that fact, she has to disagree with me. She has no problem voting for him. Of course, she has been captivated by Guinea and that is her interest. At least she has an interest and is working.

I really believe black folks see themselves on a personal mission to pull this man through and see him to the end. In talking with Lisa and some of the other young women who hang around my office, it seems that we have young kids unable to read and write who are graduating to the "sad streets"[5] with high aspirations, economic that is, and following crime as a career path. Of course, once arrested and imprisoned, some of these kids feel there is no other way for them. Many of them are mothers with three, four, and even five kids. Mothers the age of Lisa. It is unbelievable.

When I try to tell my peers about this, they feel it is solely the fault of the kids. They believe that Bill is trying to help them, that is why they like him so. Mother has concluded that he was born out of wedlock himself and that is why he tries so hard to help others like himself. They don't seem to understand the concept of multiple causation one bit.

They never see that once the kids fall by the wayside, they become imprisoned over and over, thus serving as fodder for a more and more productive financial empire. They refuse to accept the fact that Clinton has only contributed to this even though jails and prisons are being built and expanded right here in Clark County, even though the municipalities are busy contracting private managers to run them just like the managed-care organizations in healthcare. They either say, "What does Bill have to do with it?" or "He can't do it all," or "When is the movement going to start, when are you going to teach and explain it to the people, when are you going to get busy doing your job of helping us to understand?" I just say, "When are you going to try to read and become reasonable so you can understand what people are saying? When are you going to try and understand that there is more to it than financial growth? When are you going to try to understand what financial growth really is? These guys really feel they are better off financially. Maybe they are, but I am not. I think sometimes that I am doing it wrong.

Mike came over here and during the conversation, he informed me that he had been told by Helen that I am not a Clinton supporter. Now here is a person who is captivated by the concept of black superiority, but he wants Bill Clinton because he is "the best of the choices, a PWBFA who should do something because they (The System) don't care anymore for him than they do for us." For Mike it's not about Clinton but about resistance to The System.

I asked Mike what about education, crime, welfare, labor, downsizing, Clinton's economic and foreign policies, his strong support of big business and lukewarm support of affirmative action, and Mike yelled at me that I was just like Maya Miller. Maya and Kit had been down and I went over to Helen's to see her and found that she also sees Billy Boy as a jerk who is taking advantage of the masses, leaving them happy because he can grin and talk.

I spoke with my eighty-seven-year old friend Alice Key, always perceptive and forward thinking, about the Man, and she too supports him. She says she does so because he can win and he is the lesser of evils. She said he keeps the problems before the face of the system. She feels he is doing all he can do at this time in America. When I mentioned once again my displeasure with how he had handled the appointments of Lani Granier and Dr. Elders, she said he had no choice. She feels he should be praised since he has made more black appointments than anyone else in the country's history. She wonders what is wrong with me? Well, I am about to begin to wonder myself; it seems nobody else feels as I do.

Meanwhile, Matt Dillon is too pleased with the outcome of the election. He feels it is the Republicans and conservative, right-wing, Christian klan that have been defeated. They are the ones who have taken everything from Labor. I said to him that they are also the enemies of blacks, women, gays and lesbians, Hispanics, and others and wouldn't it be great if we could form a merger and defeat them? He said, yeah, he hadn't thought about it that way, but it sounds good to him. Since he likes to be the first to know, maybe he will begin to preach that theory.

So Bill got reelected, and all of his supporters are highly pleased that he did; they know he will do his best. The one thing they feel that people should realize is that he is not a dictator and doesn't have the power to make laws and to implement them. They see Congress and Newt Gingrich as the problem, because they know if it were left to Clinton, he would knock down so many of the barriers that have made our lives miserable. He would do so because he knows what it's all about. These people are true believers that Bill Clinton is just like them and that he cares about their welfare.

My poor mother is so overwhelmed by Bill that you'd think he was a member of her family. She loves the fact that with all his success he still accepts God into his life. When she sees him go to church with that Bible, singing in the pews, she just can't see why anyone would criticize him. She says he is personable and impressive and that the problem with people is only that he is a PWBFA, most likely conceived out of wedlock. He came out of lil' ol' Arkansas and they just can't stand the notion. She says she is going to support him, regardless.

Spring 1999

When the story broke about Monica Lewinsky, Mother knew it was a dirty lie and that they were trying once again to defeat him, all in an effort to block his plans to help poor people, all because he came from lil' ol' Arkansas. She feels that anyone with common sense would know that he didn't bother that lying gal. She just wishes she could have a personal conversation with him to encourage him and make him aware of what is happening to him. Of course, the Bushes feel that it's a lie, and if he were going to take a risk of that kind, we could certainly believe it would never be with a common drowsy broad like her. They all were convinced that it was a lie created by the Republican party.

Each time Glynda and I would tell them we felt he did it, I thought I would have to run away. They truly believe that it was a scheme, and they were doing it only because he was a PWBFA. The more they accuse him, the more Mother is going to praise and support him. She just wants to meet him face to face and tell him how it is.

Funny, when he finally admitted that he had some sort of an affair, or relationship with Monica, the amazing thing was how Mother and others became so forgiving and understanding as to why he allowed himself to fall into that pit. I never knew that Mother had such knowledge of the human mind. She began to point out all the others who had done the same thing with nobody making an issue out of that. When he went to church with that Bible, that just did it absolutely.

I don't know about myself; I never thought I would become a Bill Clinton supporter. I'm not a supporter of Bill, I'm a supporter of the people.

But, when I came to be a supporter of him during the hearings, did I gain popularity with them—even though my reasons for support had nothing to do with him being a PWBFA. For me it was all about how the powers of government were destroying the rights of a citizen. This is a threat to all of us and it troubles me. I don't think I have ever been able to make them know what I'm really talking about.

Surprisingly, Glynda is pulling for Bill also.

Can that damn Bill do an act? He looks so sad, abused, and mistreated. I wonder what black consultants have trained him to do this? Or maybe his relationships with blacks have been so abundant and deep that he learned to do it. Bill is tough!

Out here everybody is ready to fight about the way they're treating him; on the radio the preachers are praying for him; they believe that he has helped them. They believe that he is being abused by the same powers who have abused us because he has tried to help the downcast—blacks and everybody else who has been overlooked by government. It's funny, but Jesse Jackson is now a champ, as far as the Bushes and Denby are concerned.

Driving along the other day listening to Bobby Bland belt out *Sad Streets,* I thought about taking an offering from the Bushes, Matt Dillon, and Denby to buy Bill a copy of the CD and send it to Washington. It could be very useful to him if he would substitute "the Republican party" or "The System" or "Kenneth Starr" everywhere Bobby says "woman" or "lover." It could be therapeutic if he did. He should forget about Monica and the other women; its about himself and The System. I'm speaking of songs like "Double Trouble," "God Bless the Child," "I Wanna Tell You about The Blues" and "My Heart's Been Broken Again." They give a message.

Things have come to a halt out here. The last two weeks of the hearings. Q.B. won't answer the telephone during the broadcast, and Matt Dillon won't come to work. Boy! The beauty shops are unbelievable. It's a religious problem. They know the people who abuse Bill will reap what they sow. These people believe in that man. We got them registered yet, they didn't vote because they don't know whom to vote for. Wow!

Part II/Fred's notes

1. *"Did you call Mimi?"*

—So I'm happy to know that my mother is so lenient. Now I know I have the freedom to be free. 'Cause she understands Bill Clinton.

—*[White] folks have him cryin' and goin' on:*

—*Did you ever think he might be a great actor?*

—*He's from Arkansas, bred and born.*

—So was Orville Faubus.

—It's a question about Bill's birth. I assume he was born out of wedlock as much as anything else. I feel, son, for him 'cause I know how he must feel.

—Today if you ain't born out of wedlock you ain't nobody.

—*Something mysterious about his birth; I don't have to ask nobody; I know he come up rough; they fixed it so his daddy died before he was born; it's something fictitious about the whole thing.*

I'm "son," some kinda sad-ass third term, the mediator between the usual Christmas round of mother-daughter torture. I want to get that sound in the writing, too, the sound of something muffled but not repressed or not only repressed, the sound of the oppressed recorded or rerouted like a telephone call. "Did you call Mimi? Mother is driving me crazy." All these women's voices and telephone calls got to be ringing in Bill's ear. Mimi says if she can just *talk* to him and let him know what they're trying to do. Ma called and asked him, "Did you call Mimi?" It's annoying that this mug has something to do with me.

The Arkansas Department of Health used to go down in the country, out from Kingsland, out from New Edinburgh, and shoot up the whole Broughton Settlement with penicillin.

Mimi, on the other hand, hired and fired preachers like Steinbrenner, checked Ma every month, saved up for that piano, cooked for and cleaned up after Miz Campbell for them candlesticks and that milkglass, picked cotton on Johnny Cash's uncle's farm to get Ma ready for school, kept packing when she said she didn't wanna go to Fayetteville. They put her in the basement of an empty dorm and on Saturdays she had to walk past this ol' shriveled-up white man holding a dollar in the air talking 'bout "You see this; It's yours" till Reverend Hunter married her to my silent father. Mimi cried all day.

The sexual history of my family rises up behind him.

2. Recline against the Speedup: A Manifesto

My friend Steve Harney and I have been interested in the question of identification and how it is manifest in attempts to understand black support of Clinton (and we find it interesting that there hasn't been much of an attempt to understand left academic support of Clinton, as if such support were entirely natural and to be expected from "tenured [and untenured] radicals").[6] Confusions of identification produce an effect that renders the distinction between left and right meaningless, so that the left critiques itself for not being critical enough while tracing the movement of categories that have disintegrated. There is no clear demarcation between left and right in the absence of unembarrassed or undiscouraged revolutionary theory, critique and practice. The point is how to get out of this morass where confusions of identification and categorization are operative at the level of what is enacted as criticism and at the level of the diagnosis of that enactment since that diagnosis is also an enactment. The idea of such extrication might seem romantic, something that doesn't recognize the movement and force of certain historical and material laws. But we can reject the speedup that produces these misidentifications. That we were driven to defend him, that we were driven into some kind of illusory identification with him, is all bound up with our illusory identifications with one another. This is to say that we've got to assert (at least hope for) and question "we" and "our." We would then assert our identity as a function, at least in part, of our political commitments. If we did this we wouldn't attach ourselves to Clinton in some fake pragmatic way. *He is Jesse Helms at least as much as he is black or a black woman.*

These illusory modes of identification come about as modes of confusion, fictive affiliations borne of alienation: that alienation is a function not only of a certain detachment or lack of control over (the value of) what we produce, but also as a function of our relations of production. The whack absence of voice/accent/sound in academic writing comes about as a function of alienation in production: a complex interplay of the intense and individualistic separation of academic workers—the total immersion in a collective process that is experienced as noncollective and which is, as such, almost completely outside of the worker's control—and the massive deindividuation which manifests itself precisely in the

146

fact that often everybody sounds the same and says the same things about the same things. A collective authorship, a writing infused with speech, with the internal differentiation of accents, would resist this a bit. And it would hearken back or forward to other modes of political conversation, a mode of conversation that might give us a glimpse at what a proletarian or proletarianizing public sphere might be: a truly antinomian political discourse, a discourse of rantings, of the nights of labor, Saturday Night Functions or Fishfries. This is to say a discourse against or after the fact of the speedup, an arrhythmic kind of writing, a genuine screeching and honking on the other side of certain reifications of the vocalized horn because *Clinton doesn't really play the saxophone, being black like Kenny G.*

This writing will work as the artist imagines it, exhibiting the eros that we mistakenly attach to Clinton in our involuntary defense of him, as if puritanical fundamentalism and whiggish priggism weren't essentially replicated by him in his policies, where it really counts (remember his homilies against promiscuity) as well as in his practices, the intensity of their privacy, the heterosexist/capitalistic imperative/invocation of privacy, nobody's business but his own, outside of, or rather the palest echo of, any authentically grained assertion, one naturally echoplexed by the real President of the Saxophone, that "tain't nobody's business if he does," where the immediate publicity of the assertion, the out declaration of the outest of practices, throws radical publicity like a spear, a sphere. His kinkiness is only the image of kinkiness; his is the fetishization of fetishization and we ought to recognize that by way of a genuinely loud writerly erotics. Why support his sexual assertion as if it were our own and in the mildest of tones when we can talk dirty *through* him? All this is to say that we ought to concentrate as much on what we repress in our confused identification as on what he represses, namely us. Deeper still, what do Todd Gitlin and Michael Moore repress?[7] I think it's the blackness he is somehow attached too, the out, cut and cutting surplus of identifications (non-white, female, queer) that they want to silence. They repress these by way of his repression of them. They repress what the "right" hates because they hate it, too. They join Clinton's oppression of the repressed while repressing his necessary attachment to the repressed. Of course what is ultimately the most unspeakable thing is precisely what Ma knows best, what Gitlin and Moore repress most deeply in their assertions of love, concern and admiration (all sounding a lot like the evil lionization of "The Greatest Generation"): that Clinton is, in her terms, a po' white boy from Arkansas (PWBFA: her abbreviation). The question is why the repressed/oppressed support him.

Anyway, a dirty tone or sound, growls and moans and squalls and so forth, is what we mean to index in this ensemble. We want to infuse academic writing with some leisure and we don't want to turn that leisure into work. We don't want to finish anything, but we don't really want to read, either. We want to write about stuff we talk about when we eat together; but we don't want that writing to constitute work in some old high way of work. So we want it to be work as the artist—which is to say both the artist in general and The Artist Formerly Known as Prince—would imagine it. Work like Monk would imagine it but nothing that would replicate the terms and conditions of the monastery (the location of the end—or, more precisely, an iconic location of the closure—of sex and the beginning of the university). We want to write like friends, not superfriends. Like supafriends or supastars. Break up and avoid the star system with the spirit of another studio, United Sound, United Artists. Irruptive soundtrack of a B-movie, a B-boy symphony complete with bells, stooges, modern guys in modern times or Jazz at the Philharmonic. We want to sound like Detroit, like we got a lust for life. We want to sound communist like Elvin Jones. We want to improvise the industry with independence of hands and feet in public ownership. We want to break up the line. "We can rely on each other." From one corner of the house to another. Uh-huh (with too-sweet overtones of n and a). *We are, on the other hand, not—which is to say way more than—Bulworth even if we acknowledge the value of a weak, but good, example.*

3. What Is Bill Clinton?
The voice of authority is, as usual, hysterical, this time in duet: Sam Donaldson and Cokie Roberts, rejects from the summer of love embarrassed to ask questions about blowjobs. What does that tell us: perhaps that the sixties were, for some—like these old sad converts to puritanical, neo-Victorian moral values, these tight-shouldered defenders of the institution of marriage—a massive excercise in repression, mass repression, more precisely, on a scale that only Adorno (or maybe Foucault or maybe you, Ma, severest critic of white folks' recent discovery of sex) would be able to deal with, to Marcuse's dismay. This explains Gitlin, for instance, Moynihan's secret sharer. *How the quest for libidinal fulfillment devolves into a crypto-fascist sex negativity is just one interesting sidebar to the whole Clinton thing.*

And he could never simply say, I love sex, me and Hillary got an understanding, because this walking impulse, who in the old days, yesterday, would be called womanly in his inability to keep himself in check and his house in order, would have to account for Hillary's surplus sexuality which is the essence of the real problem: namely, the fact of a mug who, though politically committed to whatever repressive policies will keep him in office, is in some weird personal sense capable not only of a kind of patriarchalism that passes for its opposite but of intimacy with black people as well. Call this a kind of Hot Springs + Oxford— hick cosmopolite—phenomenon that, say, my grandmother recognizes and valorizes. Publicly evil and privately "progressive" in these lone but crucial respects, he's the embodiment of the image neoliberal power has been trying to sell: fiscally conservative, socially liberal. But, in the end, Cokie don't play that, shrew with marbled, marble hair and garbled rhetoric (Sam, superior as always, buys his hair, somewhere in Texas, somewhere where they make *real* boots). What does it mean to live in a country in which the presidency is diminished by active sexuality? The proximity of power, in this country, to fascism is asymptotic. *And power's distance from femininity is necessary.*

And don't get me wrong. Clinton is the biggest and worst kind of razorback. Again, a walking impulse whose first and faintest moments of rationality always lead him to a kind of proto-fascist expedience and instrumentality. It's just that he *can* be intimate with Vernon Jordan; he *can* think of Hillary as a kind of partner. These, in themselves, constitute a massive threat to the ancient and persistent configuration of American power and ideology and cannot be tolerated in the WHITE/HOUSE, physical embodiment, ill synechdoche, of the conflation of white supremacist patriarchy in the domestic and public spheres *(props to bell hooks, who I'm sure is firing off, even as we speak, a book she is uniquely qualified to write).*

4. Bill Clinton Is a Black Woman. Bill Clinton Is Not a Black Woman

Sister Souljah, Lani Guinier, Joycelyn Elders, every "welfare queen": Clinton's long and valiant effort to distance himself from that to which he was destined to devolve is over. The return of the repressed is the return of the oppressed, and he's become the black woman that every piece of poor white male trash holds deep within. The vaunted ability to compartmentalize is a sham. He couldn't control himself long enough even to take it out of the whitehouse. Unlike his licentious idol JFK only in that he got caught while alive, he's messed up the symbolic purity of the place. We should get Angela Bassett, or better yet Dr. Vaginal Davis, to play her in the movie. The first drag president, perpetrating a powerful realness for so long that he ain't even got a house. Washington is burning. Only a black woman would do a Jewess in the oval office. I think the CEOs and pundits and Sam/Cokie saw it in him all the time—the danger of his succumbing to, if not unleashing, that black feminine force. Only the utter absence of principles sustained him for this long. Bessie Smith burst out of his body, an excess or expense of spirit in a waste of shame, devil in and on a blue dress, he is and is attracted to the dark lady, fake-ass fair youth, Lady Soul.

Only he could have won it back for the Democrats in the first place: who else could violate the principles of its core constituencies and retain their support. Not love, but the absence of that visceral and hateful revulsion for women, blacks, and Jews makes him unique in the annals of American politics. Maybe Jefferson and Johnson are precursors. But where danger is, there the saving power also lies. Lloyd Bentsen must have smelled that populism of the genes, populism in the jeans, which can only be held back for so long. He just wants to be loved; is that so wrong? Yeah, it is. Because that weakness, manifest in a style that is structured precisely by the violation—on a purely personal level—of the anti-black racism and misogyny that is the ground of the American Ideology, has called forth this recent, very American, attempted coup.

Bill Clinton enacts modes of behavior that are tied both rightly and wrongly to the image of black women and that are, by way of the critical force of perform- ance, radically misappropriated by black women. To the extent that he indulges in inadequate critique and embarrassed, desperate disavowal of that identifica- tion, Clinton violates the spirit of such performance and estranges himself from those radical possibilities embedded in that misappropriative identity. Welfare queens or blues women or critical race theorists are linked, then, to a certain re- curring eruption out of or irruption into Bill Clinton of the black woman in image and reality. The danger to the state of this irruption/eruption is indexed in and by the identity and energy of the folks who are after him.

Bill Clinton is a black woman. Bill Clinton is not a black woman. This is clear in his moralizing invocations, his sad apologies, and, above all, in his policies. Note that the constructions above mark the open and openly political nature of my personal, historicist, and extra-strategic essentialism.

5. Letter to Lara

He's not black and he ain't a woman but he holds a space that's close to these or carries a trace of these and that this is true seems to me most clearly reflected in the viciousness of the media attack on his ass from every position in the "legiti- mate American political spectrum." The prophetess Amanda Irving, a radio preacher in Las Vegas who my mom used to have pray for me on the air when I was in college, is praying so hard for Clinton, according to Ma, that she's running over her allotted time Sunday mornings on KCEP. This is, to me, a phenomenon that is worthy of thought. I think this is some of what Toni Morrison[8] is after, and it's important because it allows us to think about how identity works in relation to politics, a necessary but not sufficient condition for resistance. I'm interested in the political implications of the possibility of Clinton's blackness or black femininity. I was reading Grace Lee Boggs's autobiography last night. What is the politico-economic and sexual weight/force of blackness? There is no blackness without that weight and force. This is to say that blackness, as I understand it, is an active political disruption and upheaval, an insurgent and expansive political ensemble, resistance at the level of an ongoing dis/organization as Boggs and James and Dunayevskaya might, at a certain fleeting moment, have understood it: dis is to say another, future, organization. There is in Clinton, or Clinton embodies, no such weight and force but there is, nevertheless, at the level of a kind of identitarian affiliation, a style or affect in or to him that folk recognize and either love or hate. He carries nothing more than a certain affinity, but look at the effect that affinity has produced!

Though actually existing American democracy is 99 percent whack, there is a coup going on; he's a lecherous harasser but it is obviously important and weird to have an openly sexual president; he's a racist and a sexist who has butchered black and poor and female people, but he doesn't seem personally to hate or, at least, be sickened, by the presence of black people or women, by the idea of their having, within the whack American paradigm, influence and power. A president with these attributes is unique in the history of this place. Working through the implications of all this is not a top of the head project. *Whereof one cannot speak, thereof one must remain silent, for the moment.* Silent march. This is a vow.
Love,
Fred

6. I Can't, I Can't, I Can't Stop Singing

Part of what's going on here is the revelation of certain cracks or fissures in the structure of straight white male bourgeois American power: that it must continually assert and renew affinities and affiliations with the very folk and the very energies it must also repress, suppress, and oppress. The prophetess knows this when she prays for this man, her tongues irrupting into a carefully crafted symbolic discourse that works in the oscillation between closeness to and distance from the oppressed. The right understands the political necessity of this closeness more than the left, in spite of leftist rhetoric. The right knows how affinity and affiliation work. The generality of blackness remains a powerful political possibility in the face of the "white power structure." Ma says we got to get over before we go under. She needs to be the governor. Ma can't explain, though, why for her it might as well not matter that the bastard bombed Iraq again and that, in the realist sense, he'd have done it under any circumstance and not just those of his impeachment. This is a function of the policy of expansion, updating and eclipsing George Kennan's containment, a policy articulated first by way of Warren Christopher, the new trilateralism that Chomsky now calls the new military humanism.[9] Ma is right to see the impeachment as a new moment in the crisis of democracy, but that crisis is most clearly articulated not in what they are doing to Clinton but in what he is doing and has done to us and the rest of the world. Ma understands the battle against impeachment as a kind of last stand, holding back the right, which will, in doing what they are doing to Clinton, now be unleashed and emboldened to do it to everybody. This, of course, reverses the chronology of their aggression. They, *which is to say him*, have been doing it to us forever and now play for a minute at eating one another up. Again, a certain contradiction regarding affiliation that one can't help but find interesting. So for me a certain excitement predicated by the almost imperceptible shadow of some future self-destruction of American power; for Ma, terror at the vision of the total control and mobilization of American fascism. But if the Trilateral Commission and the White Citizens' Councils (in the form of Bob Barr and Trent Lott) are already in power, then the future is now. Ma, of course, understands the infinite capacity of things to get worse better than me.

Ma says he should know better.

7. Bill Clinton Is a Pervert

Someone had to buy this man a house!

It's OK to say that he is a degraded thing through which people can represent the most degraded commodity of all, one who lets us know that even at its worst there's something radical in the commodity, that degradation opens distance and dislocation. His perversion is privacy, a whack desire for propriety even if all it is is something to sell, the commodity's refinishing. The only thing he's ever done is sell himself. The first president without property (but for his tarnished whiteness, his endangered maleness) in a country where the ruling class was defined from the start by property ownership and whose very subjectivity was articulated through the interinanimation of rule and ownership. A president without properties, absorptive of every possible quality, like tofu. A man without property can only become president by selling himself. He doesn't have, he *is,* property. So instead of Phineas Finn we get the president's black veil. Black veil is a kind of paint. Phineas finally married property, the dark-haired pretty Jewess. Clinton just wanted some leg or, in lieu of that, the sound of some. Clinton, on the other hand, married Lady Laura, but this time she had no money, just cultural capital. She was a little too strong, a little too tall; her feet were too big. By marrying him she staved off any danger of a latent passion, as far as we know. The veil is paint, she says. "He's got make-up on 'cause he's my bitch!" He balances the budget, goes to McDonald's, has safe sex, touches people without revulsion, and sells that tactility (the public familiarity of the hug can only be sold if no specter rises behind it—after the fact of the revelation of what went on behind closed doors, the public hug will always be suspect, is no longer on the market), speaks properly with just a hint of an accent which is, itself, charming, seductive, marketable. *This is to say that the Democratic Leadership Council is an assertion of southern accent in Democratic party politics, a Nixon/Atwater voice-over, an anti-black, homophobic, pro-family aurality.*

If Lockean subjectivity is fundamentally bound up with property and ownership, it is necessary to point out that the object of ownership is the self. Self-possession is the essential form of possession. But the bourgeoisie has degraded to the point that self-possession is not even a possibility, in lieu of which we have, now, the absolute necessity of home ownership. *The massive self-marketing as self-alienation that Clinton symbolizes is essential to and irreconcilable with contemporary American power.*

Think Jeffersonian radicalism or radical republicanism as the effect of a black feminine, pre (black) Jacobin, tone, one picked up by way of a certain proximity to blackness, to blackness as black femininity, a proximity that manifests itself not only in desire for the black woman but in that black femininity which has been given as the mark of a certain overly sentimental inability to rationally resist sexual desire. *Monica Lewinsky as Sally Hemings in a telephonic revival of an old love story.* William (Thomas) Jefferson Clinton is the producer, director, and starr. Star.

Clinton's (proximity to an equally phantasmic) Jewishness acts itself out here, too, and on another register. Here you'd have to work through Trollope, Eliot, Dickens, Disraeli, and a set of protocols embedded in the nineteenth-century English novel. This concerns Clinton's stewardship over the economy, stupid, his utility for captains of industry, robber barons and the like, who, in spite of his institution of policies that make them even richer—by way of a certain violent if incomplete disavowal of the phantasmic black woman, the placement of her (specter) under a set of measures of austerity—maintain an intense hatred of him.

8. Return of the Oppressed

I wanted to think about Ma's notes—which reveal, among other things, a kind of secret, the secret of a particular sexuality, that uplift A.M.E. prudishness (stuff Du Bois preached even if he didn't practice, though perhaps his praxis moved through such preaching) as a part of the discourse of the other black woman, the discourse that moves in opposition to the myth of black female sexual insatiability, the myth my ma and my grandma have always worked against to their own deprivation (I think: what do I know?). Mimi's, and later Ma's support of Clinton cannot be separated from this. Perhaps what they understand in and of him is the cost not only of oppression but of repression as well. Anyway, thankfully, uplift is what they taught at Arkansas A, M, & N and its embedded in her missionary zeal, moving from the beauty shop to the New Town Tavern with a good and bad kind of missionary love, trying to cut Clinton up to the point at which it becomes absolutely necessary to support him.

"Damn," says Gitlin: "~~race~~, class, ~~gender~~."

"I don't know what you want with this mess; you have interfered with my freedom. You know I don't like to write for you, professor, so I don't want to hear one criticism."[10]

Notes

1. Not Barbara and George but Eloise and Q.B., two of Ma's oldest friends from Arkansas. The conversation recorded here took place around their dining table at 1948 N. "D" St. in the heart of the West Side of Las Vegas, Nevada where, almost every Sunday, like a sacrament, the Bushes, their children Valorie, Dalorie, and Tony, Mr. Bush's mother Queentilla, my grandmother, Marie Jenkins (Mimi), Ma, and, whenever I'm in town, me, gather to renew, by way of argument and the best food in the world, a family friendship that goes back over a century.

2. Former U.S. senator (and former Nevada governor) Richard Bryan, for whom B Jenkins worked in the early eighties.

3. Ma's nickname for a former coworker at the State Industrial Insurance System in Las Vegas, Nevada, whose personal style is reminiscent of the fictional guardian of Dodge City, Kansas, on the long-running television series *Gunsmoke*. SIIS, an agency that provided insurance and compensation for injured workers in Nevada, has recently been privatized.

4. AKA the West Side, the historically black community of Las Vegas, Nevada.

5. This refers to a recording by Bobby Bland called *Sad Streets*, Malaco Records, B000001L24, 1995. The music will come up again a bit later.

6. If you're interested, see our "The Academic Speed-up," *Workplace: The Journal for Academic Labor* (http://www.workplace-gsc.com), vol. 2, no. 2, November 1999, and "Doing Academic Work," in Randy Martin, ed., *Chalk Lines: The Politics of Work in the Managed University* (Durham: Duke University Press, 1999).

7. I cite them as representative of a strain of the so-called left that would return to so-called universalist principles, thereby moving out of the slough of identity politics. See Gitlin's *The Twilight of Common Dreams* (New York: Metropolitan Books, 1995), or watch Moore's series *TV Nation* on Bravo.

8. See "The Talk of the Town," *New Yorker*, 5 October 1998: 32.

9. Noam Chomsky, *The New Military Humanism* (Boston: South End Press, 1999).

10. 17 April 2000: My mom died last night on her sixty-sixth birthday. She was visiting one of her oldest and dearest friends, Gwendolyn Jackson, in Waycross, GA. She told me on the phone that its pine trees reminded her so much of her home in the small town of Kingsland, in little ol' Arkansas. She had just visited my wife, Laura Harris, and me in New York and took great delight in meeting our friends, in lovingly demanding of them, "OK, now what are ya'll gonna do!? You know we need you!" and in climbing two long flights of stairs at Judson Church (quite a feat for her) to see and hear Angela Davis and Robin Kelley, one an old heroine of hers, the other a new hero. She spent that night conspiring with my sister Glynda White on how to get them out to Vegas to "tell the people." Now Glynda and my brother, Mike Davis, Mr. and Mrs. Bush, and Laura and I are planning her memorial service. Tomorrow we'll have some of the folks she met in New York over and listen to some of her favorites—*Count Basie Swings, Joe Williams Sings*; Duke Ellington and Mahalia Jackson's "Come Sunday"; Betty Carter re-arranging "Every Time We Say Goodbye." We'll figure out some way to tell Mimi that her daughter has gone ahead of her. Eventually I'll take her ashes down home. We'll go one last time on the road from New Edinburgh to Kingsland, past Mr. Puterbaugh's dairy farm and down that hill she loved, that she wanted me to write a poem about. I'll spread some of them under the pines my grandfather planted when she told him she was pregnant with me and lay the rest next to him. What if the first president from Arkansas had been B Jenkins?

Mama is a star. I don't have one criticism.

9 Trashing the Presidency

Race, Class, and the Clinton/Lewinsky Affair

Micki McElya

> Here, again, Clinton seems an exaggeration of the norm.
>
> —David Maraniss, *The Clinton Enigma*, 40

When Toni Morrison suggested in the *New Yorker* that Bill Clinton continued to hold the support of African Americans throughout the unfolding of the Lewinsky scandal because they understood him to be America's first black president, she provoked significant controversy. Morrison asserted: "Clinton displays almost every trope of blackness: single-parent household, born poor, working-class, saxophone-playing, McDonald's-and-junk-food-loving boy from Arkansas."[1] In making this claim, Morrison highlighted a central element of the scandal—she exposed the interplay of race and class narratives in representations of Bill Clinton. While doing this important work, however, she woefully misnamed this construct as "blackness." Far from being a black president, the boy from Arkansas she described is best understood as particularly white. He is, in fact, a white trash president.[2]

The effect of Morrison's misidentification is both to highlight and elide whiteness as a racial category. The tropes she lists all point to elements of white trash stereotyping—a grotesque melding of poverty, kitsch, excessive sexuality, danger, and disposability that lurks *within* the category whiteness. As an "internal" Other, white trash serves to define normative whiteness by absorbing attributes most often ascribed to "external," racial Others, in effect sustaining the racialization of difference.[3]

In popular, capitalist narratives of a classless America, poverty is ostensibly something one can move out of through individual initiative, hard work, sacrifice, and the benevolence of elites. In this account of class fluidity, the failure of an individual to "rise" is the mark of an inherent, naturalized, personal deficiency, rather than a result of systemic barriers. Among whites, "white trash" signifies the location of this "natural" failure, and renders normative whiteness unmarked and un(re)markable. Locating Bill Clinton within this discursive framework illuminates core assumptions driving the Lewinsky/impeachment scandal. A focus on the scandal's animating white trash stereotypes also exposes the normalizing practices of whiteness, which both produce and rely upon "trash" Others. To many of his critics, Clinton's affront has been bringing his so-called trashiness into that most sacred of places in American political culture—the White House. From the moment he announced his candidacy in 1991 to his impeachment in 1998 and beyond, assaults on Bill Clinton's character have centrally involved charges of sexual impropriety framed within the terms of "trash" narratives of race and class. These trashy improprieties have then been framed as a significant danger, not only to the high office of the presidency, but to the nation at large.

Within this language of the presidential threat, which reached a fever pitch in the drive for Clinton's removal, the "nation" is synonymous with the entwined constructions of white universality, family values, and freedom through capitalism. Summed up most precisely in the title of William J. Bennett's best-selling impeachment text, *The Death of Outrage: Bill Clinton and the Assault on American Ideals*,[4] this notion of the nation in peril masks the white, bourgeois, heteronormative specificity of the construct by calling it simply "America." This essay will trace the white trash discourses at work in such popular depictions of Clinton's history and present behavior in order to illustrate the processes by which racial, regional, sexual, and class particularities are identified and expelled to define and protect this national "abstraction."

The supposed Clinton threat to "national values" is distinct from other challenges to this construct made by people of color, feminists, queers, and labor activists, among others; it is far more slippery (slick?) and difficult to pinpoint. As a president whose New Democratic policies and compromises have so often been *anti*-progressive, Clinton has been widely perceived as a threat from *within* the very nationalist vision he is said to disrupt. Just as the category "white trash" absorbs people and practices that menace white normativity and racial invisibility, insistent assertions of Clinton's own trash subjectivity mark his deviance and his particular danger.

Clinton's mainstream centrist and conservative detractors point to his seemingly normative, empowered, white, male body and charge that he is not what he appears. These accusations are all the more persistent because Clinton is not only empowered through his gender, race, and sexuality, but he is the president. As both icon and political actor, the presidential body is imbued with immense cultural power. His critics fear that if he is not exposed as deviant, his behavior and background could be accepted as normative. The discourses of impeachment operated both to identify and expunge this threat while simultaneously saying to the American people, "We told you so."

But events did not proceed as hoped. Independent Counsel Kenneth Starr and the House managers increasingly fell out of favor in national polls while approval ratings for Clinton soared. Incredulity mounted and panic grew. Recall lead-manager Henry Hyde's ultimate insistence that, above all, we must impeach "for the children." In other words, for the sake of heroic whiteness, for American "ideals," we must impeach the white trash president. Assertions of Clinton's trashiness have circulated widely, in a variety of media, during his entire political life. A close reading of several impeachment texts reveals an overriding theme of the president's perverse heterosexuality emerging from his regional and family background. Organized by the tropes of uncontrollability and excess, critics and supporters alike have explained Clinton's behavior as the inescapable result of an inherent trash nature.

As a study in white trash stereotyping, these common representations of Bill Clinton expose the primacy of southern geography to this construction, despite the prevalence of white poverty throughout the country. Moreover, enduring perceptions of the South as uniquely backward, mysterious, and corrupt underpin constructions of white trash deviance. White trash certainly is not unique to the South, but this particular discourse cannot be removed from the regionalism that informs it.

A White Tangle of Pathology

The slippage between white trash and blackness evident in Morrison's analysis reveals the persistent equation of race and poverty in American political culture, grounded in a dominant understanding of race as singularly belonging to people *of color*. It is not coincidental that white trash stereotyping bears remarkable similarity to racist narratives of deviant blackness, the most obvious connections being to debates about the "underclass" and welfare policy. Rather, it reveals the inextricable intermingling of racialization and class formation through discourses of cultural dysfunction and abnormality. Constructions of deviant sexuality emerge as a primary location for the production of these race and class subjectivities. Policy debates and public perceptions of welfare and impoverished Americans have focused relentlessly on the black, urban poor—blaming nonnormative family structures, sexual promiscuity, and aid-induced laziness as the root causes of poverty, and mobilizing the stereotypes of welfare queens, teen mothers, and sexually predatory young men to sustain the dismantling of the welfare state. In this way, naturalizing discourses of black cultural traits obscure the mutually constituting effects of racism, class exploitation, and sexual and gendered inequalities.[5]

The virtual erasure of the white poor and rural and suburban poverties from these national discourses is a critical component of the racialization of class. Not only does this silence enable the equation of whiteness with bourgeois universality, it absorbs white poverty into a separate, marked racial formation—white trash. Rather than disrupt these deep racial and class assumptions, the creation of white trash subjects reiterates them through the production of a white culture of poverty. Once again, naturalizing narratives of deviant sexuality and aberrant family structures mark the point of production, and the reproduction, of this culture. White trash stereotyping abounds with in-breeding, honky-tonk sluts, child brides, incest, compulsive philanderers, and the unforgettable, drooling, hillbilly sodomites of *Deliverance*.

Queer scholarship and activisms shed light on the sexual demonization intrinsic to white trash stereotyping. In part, this work exposes the ways in which the dominant organization of sexual practices and gendered behaviors into static, cohesive identities distributes power and enables regulatory oppression. Representations of excessive and uncontrolled sexuality signify practices which must be expelled from the category white, literally as trash, because they endanger the heteronormative alignments of sexuality and gender which center whiteness, and heterosexuality, as supposedly abstract cultural norms. Some of this scholarship and activism has fallen short of its radical aims, however, making it incapable of fully addressing the persistent marginalization of so-called white trash heterosexuality. Too often, queer methodologies have recapitulated the hetero-homo binary they seek to disrupt by naming as "queer" only practices that are *not* heterosexual. Cathy J. Cohen illustrates this problem in her analysis of queer scholars' failure to understand constructions of "underclass" pathology as placing many black people outside the bounds of empowered heteronormativity. Within such a framework, Cohen explains, there remains an "unchallenged assumption of a uniform heteronormativity from which all heterosexuals benefit."[6] This assumption conceals the ways in which supposed deviant heterosexualities become a primary nexus of oppression and marginalization for impoverished and racialized Others. This recognition is critical to locating the white supremacist technologies of power and preservation at work in white trash stereotyping.

While constructions of divergent white trash sexuality and family formation necessarily resemble and are informed by white supremacist narratives of pathological blackness, charges of in-breeding among poor whites (you know you're a redneck if there are no forks in your family tree) point to a unique racial panic within whiteness. In popular representation, much of this toxic, trash sexuality proliferates within the family, but outside the bounds of the marital relationship—among parents and children, sisters and brothers, first cousins, uncles and aunts with nieces and nephews, and so on. Where white superiority is presumed to be the offspring of glorified, bourgeois, heteronormative culture, these common stereotypes of hillbilly incest locate deviant reproduction as the genesis of white bodies that are flawed because they are racialized. The white trash family is a queer family, not because it fails to reproduce heterosexually, but because its supposedly warped reproduction produces failures. Moreover, this particular stereotype of abusive nonnormative behavior acts as a sort of cloaking device. By focusing only on individual families and personal dysfunction, it refuses to situate sexual and physical abuse within the larger contexts of economic, political, and cultural dislocation as well. Simultaneously, this stereotype obscures the fact that all of these things also occur within elite and middle-class families of all races, yet remain more easily denied or hidden because these families do not experience the same levels of surveillance.

It is precisely this framework of deviant heterosexuality and imperiled normative whiteness that informs common representations of Bill Clinton as white trash. That he can be so powerful and empowered, yet still be understood as such suggests that the category can be separated culturally from the material conditions of poverty which produce it. Like other racializations, trashiness stays with a person. You can educate Bill Clinton, dress him up, and even make him president, but you can't take the trash out. In fact, it is the possibility that all that gloss may hide the trash "truth" that makes Clinton, and others like him, so threatening to his detractors.

Clinton's racialized class position, similar to that of Elvis Presley with whom he has so often been associated, is based upon a trash subjectivity not wholly related to day-to-day material realities. Both figures became financially secure and gained political and/or cultural power yet never extricated themselves from their so-called southern trash sensibilities, often appearing to glory in them. Clinton's Georgetown and Yale degrees, Rhodes scholarship, and political and financial successes have not been enough to negate assertions of his trashiness. The Elvis analogy is illuminating as it actually performs this work of separating white trash subjectivity from actual impoverishment to foreground cultural attributes and behavior. As Gael Sweeny has argued in her article on Presley and the "aesthetics of excess," to link the president with the King is to recall that Elvis poured his money into jeweled, polyester capes, Graceland, peanut butter and bacon sandwiches, and various other addictions.[7] He was no longer poor, but in popular representation he was still ludicrously and fatally trashy. As a racialized set of attributes, behaviors, and desires, trash culture is detached from tangible poverty and becomes mobile—traveling from generation to generation as pathology, even when poverty is left behind. In this framework, inherent attributes produce inequalities, not systematic oppressions. But even those who beat the system cannot escape their "natures."

First in His Class

Like other national spectacles produced in the age of the Internet-CNN-Fox News Channel, twenty-four-hour news cycle, the Clinton scandal created a mini-industry of commentary and analysis. Included were many "experts" on the character and motivations of the president who sought to explain why Clinton would risk his office for a quickie in the bathroom, and why he could not deny himself the furtive pleasures of a relationship with a young intern in the Oval Office. Contrary to the persistent attempts of Starr and the House managers to cast Monica Lewinsky as a vulnerable, young victim of the inappropriate advances of her older boss, dominant narratives of the affair quickly revolved around Monica, with her "presidential kneepads" and thong underwear, as pursuer, instigator, or aggressor. The question then became, Why didn't he just ignore her, if for nothing else than to avoid the political risk? The most common response: Clinton just can't help himself.

In the repeating loop of commentators and authors, one of those most often heard on these questions was David Maraniss. After winning a Pulitzer Prize for his coverage of Clinton the candidate in 1992 for the *Washington Post*, Maraniss began work on a biography of the newly elected president—the most official of the unofficial biographies published to date. He organized his story around the figure of Bill Clinton, first representative of the generation shaped by the civil rights movement, cultural upheavals of the 1960s, Vietnam, and Watergate to attain the highest political office in the country. He summarized this account in his title, *First in His Class*. Yet Maraniss's choice of titles reveals a more complicated meaning when read in the context of the white trash representations of Clinton that saturate his biography (a double meaning mobilized by some critics, most obviously in a book review titled "Usually First, Not Always Classy").[8] Coupled with his hastily published analysis of the Lewinsky scandal, *The Clinton Enigma: A Four-and-a-Half-Minute Speech Reveals this President's Entire Life*, Maraniss has produced a sort of uber-narrative of white trash Bill Clinton, locating the answers to this presidential puzzle within his region and his family and, ultimately, his inability to fully "overcome" this tangle of pathology.

Every story of Clinton's life, whether told by himself or others, begins with his identity as a southerner. Throughout his campaign for national office, Clinton struggled against dominant perceptions of a backward, corrupt South while simultaneously relying upon romanticized images of the region to carve out a distinct national persona. He strategically positioned himself as a new breed of antiracist, progressive-but-pragmatic, southern politician from outside the Beltway, dripping with down-home folksiness and disarming the public with his soft-drawled charm. Yet as effective as this approach often was, Clinton was never able to distance himself from the ubiquitous nickname "Bubba," mobilized by detractors and skeptics to expose the fat, white, redneck underbelly of all that charisma. Though it is common regional slang for "big brother," the term also conjures the image of a southern-fried cracker, so that "Bubba for President" evoked the danger and hilarity of a Clinton presidency. Playing on the notion of Big Brother, that single word performed significant discursive work. At once, it insinuated that Clinton was far too trashy to be the public face of the nation, too seedy, flawed, and incompetent to lead, and, ultimately, so unscrupulous, corrupt, and wily—such a Good Ole Boy—he would do immeasurable damage to the office and the nation.

Both representations of Clinton, the corrupt, cracker politician and the soft, intelligent, southern charmer, are at play in Maraniss's texts. In *First in His Class*, nearly half of which is devoted to Clinton's high school and college careers and time as a Rhodes scholar and Yale law student, Maraniss marvels at Clinton's sincere love of his region and roots and of his ability to parlay that identity into success in arenas (Georgetown, Oxford, Yale) where it might have first seemed a liability. He suggests that Clinton's national regionalist strategy of the 1990s was proven on these earlier terrains where his obvious drive and ambition were tempered by folksy friendliness, self-deprecating charm, and a seeming inability to conceal motive. Maraniss also suggests, however, that cultural traits innate to Clinton's region and class were inherent character flaws and the root causes of many of his political setbacks, laying the groundwork for this explicit argument in his impeachment text, *The Clinton Enigma.*

Although Hope, Arkansas, anchored the regionalist mythology of the presidential campaign as the candidate's birthplace and metaphor for change, Clinton actually grew up in Hot Springs, a small resort community. Then known primarily for its accessible, illegal gambling houses and nightlife, Maraniss makes much of Hot Springs, which he calls a "town of secrets and vapors and ancient corruptions."[9] Clearly drawing upon gothic images of the South, he locates Clinton's character within this regional mist of illegality and mystery. By 1998, Maraniss's take on the town is harder, far less romantic, and more indicative, in his eyes, of Clinton's innate flaws and hubris: "Hope is largely a myth in the Clinton story. Hot Springs explains the Clinton enigma. Virtue and sin coexisted there; the largest illegal gambling operation in the South operated side by side with dozens of Baptist churches, some of them funded with gambling money."[10] In this picture, the virtue is so tainted by vice as to be laughable, if, for Maraniss, it were not so deeply troubling.

While Hot Springs positions Clinton within a moral geography, the central figure marking his racial, class, and regional identity in this trash narrative is his mother, Virginia Kelly. It is through her body that Hot Springs joins race and class to produce the white trash president. Maraniss writes:

Virginia Clinton, a nurse anesthetist, layered her face with make-up, dyed her hair black with a bold, white racing stripe, painted thick, sweeping eyebrows high above their original position, smoked two packs of Pall Mall cigarettes a day, bathed in a sunken tub, drank liquor, was an irrepressible flirt, and enjoyed the underbelly of her resort town, with its racetrack and gaming parlors and nightclubs.[11]

Maraniss depicts her physical presentation as cheap, theatrical, and outlandish, implying a stark contrast to an unnamed set of standards of bourgeois femininity based on subtlety and "natural" beauty. Her trashiness, and subsequently her son's, is revealed by her failure to meet that ultimate bourgeois standard: Good Taste. For Maraniss, Bill Clinton often failed this test as well: "At times it seemed like Clinton stood out like a multicolored plaid sports coat in . . . [an]

atmosphere of subdued tweeds."[12] Assertions of lacking taste predominate in the construction of a derogatory aesthetics of white trash. The very term, with its suggestion that one can inherently taste what is "classy" or appropriately pleasing, just as one tastes sweetness or salt, positions the failure to do so as abnormal, or an embodied disability—Bad Taste. In effect, this normalizes and naturalizes an arbitrary standard based on bourgeois consumption patterns and capitalist status desire. Moreover, it marks white trash consumption as the scene of excess and uncontrollability.

In its entirety, this picture of Virginia situates the white trash culture from which Clinton emerged and grew. Compounding the discursive power of Maraniss's physical description of her is his detailed account of Virginia's attitudes, loves, and addictions: cigarettes, nightclubs, liquor, gambling, flirting, and a sunken tub. In a similar description in *The Clinton Enigma*, Maraniss adds to this list of things he calls "exotic": sunbathing, convertibles, and halter-tops.[13] Maraniss asserts Clinton's essential trashiness by locating these attributes within his mother. This is critically reminiscent of another southern narrative of maternity and culture—race follows the mother—produced by a society organized historically around the one-drop rule and the panicked denial of interracial sex, forced and otherwise, between white men and black women. Just as this discourse was intended to assert the "truth" of race in the face of profoundly unsettling appearances to the contrary, so detailed descriptions of Virginia's trashiness stand as a constant reminder of Bill Clinton's deviant whiteness, even when it's not always apparent.

This construction comes full circle in *The Clinton Enigma* as Maraniss seeks to answer that question, why did he do it, or, as the author eventually puts it, why couldn't Clinton stop himself from doing it? In his analysis of the president on the eve of his admission of an "inappropriate relationship" with Monica Lewinsky, Maraniss literally transforms Clinton into the embodiment of his mother: "His image on the television monitor looked pinched, his face blurry, his features slightly distorted and misplaced, more like his late mother, the oddly exotic Virginia, than I had ever noticed before."[14] Where his trashiness was once signified through Virginia while often unreadable upon his own, apparently normative, empowered, white, masculine body, Clinton has now overspilled those boundaries. "Blurry," "distorted," and "misplaced," his grotesque features testify to the class and racial "truth" which Maraniss and others hold had always been there.

The absence of Clinton's birth father and a series of troubled or tangential relationships to his mother's next three husbands enhance the centrality of Virginia Kelly to this narrative. Recalling assertions of the racialized, deviant, matri-archal family that saturate black, "underclass" discourse, Virginia represents the primary source of affection and support, as well as discipline and guidance, the latter being a particular misplacement of gendered authority outside the boundaries of the normative nuclear family. For Maraniss, she is also the primary site of danger. He suggests that through her refusal to leave a philandering, abusive, alcoholic husband and her own alleged history of promiscuity, Virginia put her children at risk and taught them dysfunctional cultural standards. He explains Clinton's extramarital sex life as the result of behavior learned from her: "There was little history of sexual restraint in Bill and [his brother] Roger's family culture, no puritanical sense that sexual propriety was the barometer of goodness and morality. Suspicious gossip and mystery were always part of the sexual mix."[15] The gossip and mystery of which Maraniss speaks here refers to rumors dating back to Clinton's first run for governor of Arkansas—rumors that his father's identity is actually unknown. In a chapter that opens tellingly with "Nature or nurture: what does a father mean in the development of character?" Maraniss chooses to report, rather than insinuate, this gossip in *Enigma*.[16] While still unsubstantiated, Maraniss clearly believes this information crucial to an understanding of the behavior that led to Clinton's impeachment. This raises a question: Even if it were proven that William Blythe was not his father and that Clinton was conceived in an extramarital encounter, why does it matter? What could this possibly have to do with his character, performance as president, or decision to have an affair with Monica Lewinsky? Within the white trash narrative of inherent dysfunction that Maraniss constructs, absolutely everything. This "fact" bespeaks the toxic commingling of white trash nature and nurture at the very moment of Clinton's conception. Ultimately, Maraniss claims that the president's supposed uncontrollable lusts—for food, sex, and power—were genetically and circumstantially encoded when he was born the probably bastard child of a trashy widow.

Trash Act

If Clinton's family and regional backgrounds produce and locate his racial and class identity in popular representation, the constant reports of his voracious appetites, particularly for food and sex, attest to the behavioral "proof" of his continued white trash subjectivity. Couched within pathologizing narratives of addiction, assertions of Clinton's inability to control himself, whether confronted with a cheeseburger, sex, or an easy lie, label his behavior as the product of a white trash culture he cannot escape; they are the enactments of that culture, or trash acts.

One of the most prominent assertions of Clinton's excess and uncontrollability is his supposed gluttony. For example, in Joe Klein's political tell-all/novel *Primary Colors* and its popular film adaptation, the Clinton figure constantly speaks through donut glaze-encrusted lips and devours platters of barbecue.[17] The president's love of Big Macs was such a dominant theme in his first national campaign that some even suggested a boost in burger sales for McDonald's based on the free advertising.[18] Critically, not only is Clinton's appetite deemed trashy, but so are the foods he desires: pizza, Big Macs, barbecue, donuts, etc. In this narrative of excess, compulsive eating is easily linked to, and often acts as a signifier for, compulsive sexuality, or as Maraniss puts it, "a lack of normal standards of self-control."[19] Assertions of his out-of-control eating and sex life, of his excessive and warped consumption, identify Clinton's trash acts. Along these lines, Kenneth Starr, the House managers, and the media constructed his affair with Monica Lewinsky (linked to the alleged harassment of Paula Jones and Kathleen Willey, and accusations of his rape of Juanita Broderick) as his ultimate trash act.

I use the phrase "trash act" with some hesitation, for it suggests a certain performative agency and desire to radically disrupt oppressive, normalizing discourses that I would never attribute to Bill Clinton.[20] This notion of the trash act is more appropriately applied to writer-activists such as Dorothy Allison and Jim Goad,[21] or the countless others who lack access to publication but daily resist the imperative to assimilate and the pressure of humiliation imposed to police this "failure." I stick with the idea, however, for two reasons. First, Clinton's impeachers read his behavior as an aggressive act against the norm, or the national body. In their eyes, as white trash with presidential power, Clinton had the ability literally to destroy the nation through his degradation of the office. He could warp and unsettle normative standards by replacing them with his own cultural dysfunction. This position was clearly advanced in William Bennett's assertion that Clinton's "assault on American ideals" resulted in "the death of outrage" among an American people so numbed to his perversities and crimes they were no longer alarmed by them.

Second, I employ "trash act" to highlight the centrality of behavior, or individual acts, both to the production of white trash stereotypes as well as panicked resistances to the hostile gazes that deploy them. Within the category of whiteness, the (color) line between trashy and simply poor is a slippery and treacherous one to maneuver. Ultimately, strategic performances of worth and normalcy produce the only distance between demonized, racialized Otherness and normative invisibility. Confronted with the racialization of poverty, white skin privilege is not so easily conferred or assumed, but must be earned. Some of the labors that bring the wages of whiteness include constant vigilance in maintaining a "neat" appearance, piety, and heteronormative domesticity through strict adherence to dominant understandings of gender, sexuality, and bourgeois notions of privacy. The terrible psychic cost of such self-policing and surveillance should not be underestimated.[22]

One result of this work is a pronounced hostility for those who fail to do it. In large part, the performance of disgust and accusation enables claims by poor whites to normative whiteness based in a shared venom for the trash Other. As many have struggled to understand the righteous fervor and extreme determination Ken Starr brought to his special prosecution of Bill Clinton in the face of near-certain failure and many compromises of the law, one factor must be his own lifelong effort to avoid performing trash acts. The son of a fundamentalist preacher in rural Texas, Starr's own regional and familial background was drenched with the desire to claim and sustain heteronormative whiteness, and a moral compulsion to ensure that others did as well.[23] His self-fashioned position as policeman cannot be separated from his experience as one similarly policed.

The case for impeachment that Ken Starr constructed in his Referral to the House, known immediately as the Starr Report, narrates the sexual relationship between Clinton and Lewinsky and its subsequent coverup as acts so egregious, so disgusting, and so denigrating to the office as to merit the punishment of removal. And while it was attempts to hide the affair that actually formed the basis of the legal charges against the president, the report dwells upon the sex as the primary offense. Capitalizing on the trash tropes of uncontrollability and excess that have circulated throughout the Clinton presidency, Starr and his team presented the case that Clinton's sex with Lewinsky amounted to an extreme trash act.

Far from being a simple chronological recounting of the president's relationship with Lewinsky, or a list of sexual acts, the narrative of the Report was crafted with common themes, characters, and a plot, building to the ultimate, and already known, exposure of the affair. One of the most prominent themes, instrumental to constructing the relationship as a trash act, was the narrative of heterosexual deviance that fueled the "case" against Clinton. Two events stand out in this respect: Lewinsky's testimony that she performed oral sex on Clinton while he conducted presidential business, and the now infamous "cigar incident."

On two separate occasions, according to the Starr Report, Clinton received a blow job while speaking on the phone to a member of Congress or the Senate. In both cases, this piece of information is superfluous to the report of fact at hand. The first instance is marked parenthetically and is unsubstantiated: "(Ms. Lewinsky understood that the caller was a Member of Congress or a Senator)."[24] The second is recounted more dramatically. Allegedly, while the two were talking in his office, Clinton received a call. "Ms. Lewinsky recalled that the caller was a member of Congress with a nickname. While the President was on the telephone, according to Ms. Lewinsky, 'he unzipped his pants and exposed himself,' and she performed oral sex."[25] The decision to include this information serves a variety of purposes given the different audiences at which the report was aimed. Foremost, it was a referral to the House of Representatives, which would decide whether to impeach and, if (when) they chose to, prosecute the case before the Senate. The immediate intent was to alarm the representatives by suggesting that Clinton held so little respect for them and the business they conducted together that he was having sex while talking to them. One can only imagine the legislators trying to figure out if they had spoken to him on those particular days, or to which one of their nicknamed colleagues Lewinsky was referring.

The House committee's decision to publish the Starr Report broadly on the Internet and in the press produced a much larger audience for the text, however. The bigger picture constructed through the narrative of these two events was to argue that the president's extramarital sex life directly impacted his ability to perform the functions of his office, his excesses being so pronounced and beyond control that he could not wait or stop for a phone call. Moreover, the second account of his answering the phone and then unzipping insinuated that it could be presidential business that fueled his desire. It was to suggest: This is what you get when you elect white trash to the presidency. Rather than being interested in the business of state, he just gets off on the power, literally.

While these oral sex stories spoke directly to Clinton's lack of fitness for office and his inability to perform his job, the "cigar incident" was intended to spotlight his perversity. As probably the most titillating piece of information about sex in the report, the insertion of a cigar into Monica as a single act rivaled blow jobs and kisses for repetitions in the narrative—over forty-seven times by one journalist's count.[26] The narrative builds to the act, mentioning the president's cigars or Monica's desire for a cigar twice before actually relating: "At one point, the President inserted a cigar into Ms. Lewinsky's vagina, then put the cigar in his mouth and said 'It tastes good.'"[27] Again, these details bear very little significance to the ostensible case for impeachment, yet are crucial to framing the scandal as Clinton's performance of his white trash subjectivity. The report transforms a moment of sexual play, through repeated reference and an appalled tone, into an act of heterosexual deviance.

This narrative of deviance constructed in the Starr Report was compounded by the press's overwrought, highly publicized attempts to figure out how to report the details. The discourse of unspeakability and constant warnings of offensive content that surrounded the report and Clinton's grand jury testimony (re)produced the salaciousness of the acts. Notably, many newspapers refused to print the portions of the Starr Report quoted above in deference to the assumed values of their readerships. Instead, they editorialized their omission of the "pornographic," "explicit," and "dirty" details. The media's dramatic struggles to report tastefully upon phone sex, blow jobs, cum stains, and the "cigar incident," transformed relatively mundane sexual practices into a series of perversities. This was perhaps best illustrated by Barbara Walters's request that Monica explain the exotic practice of phone sex to a supposedly confused American viewing public.[28]

Conclusion: Hillary Talks

While white trash stereotyping has most obviously been mobilized against Clinton to suggest his unfitness for office, his supporters have deployed racialized representations of the president as well. Toni Morrison's discussion of his blackness, which opened this essay, was made in the context of an argument against impeachment. In that same *New Yorker* piece, Morrison also refers to the number of lynching analogies made by anti-impeachment speakers to describe the activities of the independent counsel and the House managers.[29] E. L. Doctorow elicited a standing ovation with one such comparison at a highly publicized New York–based anti-impeachment rally in December 1998. There, Doctorow concluded his remarks with a suggestion that the impeachment fervor drew to mind the image of the president being dragged through the dust from the back of a pickup truck surrounded by a vicious mob. The description bore unmistakable similarity to the Texas lynching of James Byrd, Jr., as one of his accused murderers was going to trial at the time of the rally, save for one crucial distinction—Byrd was African American.[30]

Calling Clinton's impeachment a lynching incorporated this symbol of citizenship brutally denied and of political criminality to frame impeachment as a rogue abuse of the system, driven by hate. Given that lynching has operated historically to police citizenship through claims of uncontrollable black sexuality and extreme violence,[31] the analogy underscored the centrality of presumed sexual impropriety at the heart of the scandal and located the regional discourses circulating throughout. But above all, while victims of lynching have never been uniformly black or male, the analogy served as a persistent assertion of Clinton's essential blackness.

Proponents of the lynching comparison accessed a multivalent, national, historical memory, locating the impeachment within a long history of racial violence and false accusation. But they also referenced the more recent deployment of the narrative in the Anita Hill–Clarence Thomas sexual harassment case.[32] The appalling success of Thomas's claim that he was the victim of a "high-tech lynching" in shutting down challenges to his Supreme Court nomination lurked heavily about the use of the term to describe attempts to remove Clinton. The president promoted this allusion himself in his grand jury testimony when he compared his own situation to Thomas's.[33]

Like Morrison's "tropes of blackness," these lynching narratives cannot be removed from representations of Bill Clinton as white trash. While the analogy promotes his racialization, it is grounded in a preexisting assumption of Clinton's nonnormative subjectivity. Where Thomas deployed the history of lynching to locate himself racially and to alter the dynamics of the confirmation hearings, the description seems ill-fitted to the impeachment of a white, second-term president of the United States. That it was used at all suggests the wide embrace of the notion that Bill Clinton is actually not so white himself. The lynching comparison inherently relies upon the very same constructions of a racialized, trash culture that drive the arguments of Maraniss and Starr, but highlights them to radically different ends.

From all sides of the impeachment crisis, people sought to explain Clinton's behavior and responses to it as the product of his distinct cultural history. Once again, the deployment of the lynching narrative by Clinton's supporters both acknowledged yet fundamentally misrecognized the forces of race and class construction at work in dominant depictions of the president. Their recourse to metaphors of blackness belies a profound inability to describe whiteness as a contingent racial category within popular discourse. Additionally, it foregrounds the demonization of particular heterosexualities in negative relation to white heteronormativity, yet leaves the latter unremarked upon and still privileged.

Because the specific demonization of Bill Clinton's sexuality has elicited such intense scrutiny of his marriage, that heteronormative centerpiece, it seems appropriate to give Hillary Rodham-Clinton the last word here. Throughout the scandal and its aftermath, no one but the president's daughter, Chelsea, garnered more sympathy than his wife. Emerging from her newfound popularity as First Victim to make a probable run for a U.S. Senate seat, Hillary spoke of her husband's troubles and advanced reasons for his infidelities. In a startling testament to the wide presumption of Bill Clinton's white trash subjectivity, she suggested that it was this very cultural dysfunction which drove him into Monica's arms. In the premier issue of *Talk* magazine, Hillary made a plea for understanding and called her husband's affair a "sin of weakness" which could be traced back to his family life, particularly to his mother, Virginia, and her mother. In this brief portion of the interview, Hillary constructed a narrative of deviance, or "weakness," traveling from generation to generation along the lines of the mother—a narrative strikingly similar to the maternal, trash culture of poverty described by David Maraniss. Yet, where others had refused to position his political success as a story of against-the-odds-uplift, Hillary claimed: "Yes, he has weaknesses. Yes, he needs to be more responsible, more disciplined, but it is remarkable given his background that he turned out to be the kind of person he is, capable of such leadership."[34] So, she argued, we should commend Clinton for doing as well as he has, given the circumstances, and not vilify him for slipping every now and then. Once again, she tells us, the president couldn't help himself. He is, after all, still just white trash.

Notes

1. Toni Morrison, "The Talk of the Town," *New Yorker* (5 October 1998): 32.
2. In the flurry of responses to Morrison's assertion, both positive and negative, two commentators I am aware of noted that Clinton is more appropriately understood in terms of white trash. In a flippant, derogatory remark, Christopher Hitchens suggests this in "What Do Jefferson and Clinton Have in Common (Besides Randiness)?" *Salon* (18 November 1998): www.salon.com. Marita Sturkin provides a more thoughtful analysis in "The Taint of Trash, Beltway Never Accepted Clinton," *Denver Post* (27 December 1998): G2.
3. For white trash as an "internal" Other see, Annalee Newitz and Matthew Wray, "What Is 'White Trash'? Stereotypes and Economic Conditions of Poor Whites in the United States," in *Whiteness: A Critical Reader,* ed. Mike Hill (New York: New York University Press, 1997), 168–84. Other sources on the production of white trash stereotypes include Dorothy Allison, *Skin: Talking about Sex, Class, and Literature* (Ithaca, N.Y.: Firebrand Books, 1994); Jim Goad, *The Redneck Manifesto: How Hillbillies, Hicks, and White*

Trash Became America's Scapegoats (New York: Touchstone, 1998); the essays collected in *White Trash: Race and Class in America,* ed. Annalee Newitz and Matthew Wray (New York: Routledge, 1997); and Patricia J. Williams, "The Ethnic Scarring of American Whiteness," in *The House That Race Built: Black Americans, U.S. Terrain,* ed. Wahneema Lubiano (New York: Pantheon Books, 1997), 253–63.

4. William J. Bennett, *The Death of Outrage: Bill Clinton and the Assault on American Ideals* (New York: Free Press, 1998).

5. With the publication of Daniel Patrick Moynihan's *The Negro Family: The Case for National Action* (Washington, D.C.: U.S. Department of Labor, 1965), the phrase "tangle of pathology" entered popular discourse to describe the supposed black family disorganization said to (re)produce the black, urban "underclass," or culture of poverty. Known since as simply the Moynihan Report, this document set off decades of debate concerning the roles of the family, gender, race and sexuality in dominant understandings of American poverty and welfare policy. The literature on these narratives and their destructive impacts, which I have summarized here, is extensive, but includes Wahneema Lubiano, "Black Ladies, Welfare Queens, and State Minstrels: Ideological War by Narrative Means," in *Race-ing Justice, En-gendering Power: Essays on Anita Hill, Clarence Thomas, and the Construction of Social Reality,* ed. Toni Morrison (New York: Pantheon Books, 1992), 323–63; Gwendolyn Mink, "The Lady and the Tramp: Gender, Race, and the Origins of the Modern Welfare State," in *Women, the State, and Welfare,* ed. Linda Gordon (Madison: University of Wisconsin Press, 1990), 92–122; Rickie Solinger, "Race and 'Value': Black and White Illegitimate Babies in the U.S., 1945–65," *Gender and History* 4 (1992): 343–63; and Hortense Spillers, "Mama's Baby, Papa's Maybe: An American Grammar Book," *Diacritics* 17, no. 2 (Summer 1987): 65–81.

6. Cathy J. Cohen, "Punks, Bulldaggers, and Welfare Queens: The Radical Potential of Queer Politics?" *GLQ* 3 (1997): 452.

7. Gael Sweeny, "The King of White Trash Culture: Elvis Presley and the Aesthetics of Excess," in *White Trash,* 259–60.

8. Jonathan Alter, "Usually First, Not Always Classy," *Washington Monthly* (March 1995): 41.

9. David Maraniss, *First in His Class: A Biography of Bill Clinton* (New York: Simon and Schuster, 1995), 146.

10. Maraniss, *Enigma,* 52.

11. Maraniss, *First,* 13.

12. Ibid., 133.

13. Maraniss, *Enigma,* 54.

14. Ibid., 28.

15. Maraniss, *First,* 425.

16. Maraniss, *Enigma,* 44.

17. Anonymous, *Primary Colors: A Novel of Politics* (New York: Random House, 1996), and the film *Primary Colors* (1998).

18. Richard Gibson, "Back to Fat: Too Skinny Burger Is a Mighty Hard Sell, McDonald's Learns—McLean Deluxe Wins Kudos but Not Many Customers as Mega Mac Hovers Near—A Burger Fit for a President?" *Wall Street Journal* (15 April 1993): A1.

19. An anecdote from Maraniss's experience on Clinton's second national campaign trail, relayed in *Enigma,*22, reveals that the president's handlers and strategists were well aware of this slippage between depictions of his appetites and responded accordingly. Noting that he was not getting access to the candidate, Maraniss writes that Press Secretary Mike McCurry "informed me that the Clinton entourage was unhappy with a letter from the campaign trail I had written for the *Post* in which I had described Clinton on a roll as a man with a voracious and barely restrained appetite. . . . Harold Ickes, the deputy chief of staff, complained that I was using appetite as a code word for sex." Maraniss denied that this was his intent. On "normal standards of self-control," see ibid., 43.

20. Here, I refer to the term "act" as Lisa Lowe has used it in *Immigrant Acts: On Asian American Cultural Politics* (Durham, N.C.: Duke University Press, 1996), 9, where she explains: "'Immigrant acts' names the agency of Asian immigrants and Asian Americans: the *acts* of labor, resistance, memory, and survival, as well as the politicized cultural work that emerges from dislocation and disidentification."

21. Allison, *Skin; and* Goad, *Redneck Manifesto.* Newitz and Wray discuss Allison's and Goad's radical identifications as white trash in "What Is 'White Trash'?" 170.

22. Patricia Williams explores this pain in the context of immigration and urban, white, ethnic assimilation, in "The Ethnic Scarring of American Whiteness," 254.

23. For descriptions of Starr's regional and family backgrounds, see "Starr's Report Recalls Views of a Preacher," *New York Times* (13 September 1998): A1, 37; and Peter Applebome, "Two Dueling Sons of the South," *New York Times* (13 September 1998): D5.

24. *The Starr Report: The Findings of the Independent Counsel Kenneth W. Starr on President Clinton and the Lewinsky Affair* (New York: PublicAffairs, 1998): 51.

25. Ibid., 53.

26. Joel Achenbach, "Dreary Prose, Silly Plot. Can't Put It Down," in *Starr Report,* xlvii.

27. The "incident" is foreshadowed; *Starr Report,* 54–55 and 57; and then actually detailed in ibid.,62.

28. Monica Lewinsky gave her first, televised, American interview to Barbara Walters for ABC's *20/20* (3 March 1999).

29. Morrison, "Talk of the Town," 32.

30. On Saturday night, June 6, 1998, James Byrd, Jr., was abducted from a Jasper, Texas, roadside, taken into the woods, and beaten, then chained to the back of a pickup truck from which he was dragged two miles down a road to his death. Of the three white men accused of his murder, John William King was the first to go to trial at the time of Doctorow's comment. In February 1999, King was found guilty of capital murder and sentenced to death. Lawrence Russell Brewer and Shawn Allen Berry were later found guilty and sentenced to death and life in prison, respectively.

31. Some recent studies of lynching, citizenship, and sex are Sandra Gunning, *Race, Rape, and Lynching: The Red Record of American Literature, 1890–1912* (New York: Oxford University Press, 1996); Martha Hodes, *White Women, Black Men: Illicit Sex in the Nineteenth-Century South* (New Haven: Yale University Press, 1997); Bryant Simon, "The Appeal of Cole Blease of South Carolina: Race, Class, and Sex in the New South," *Journal of Southern History* (February 1996): 56–86; Robyn Wiegman, *American Anatomies: Theorizing Race and Gender* (Durham, N.C.: Duke University Press, 1995).

32. For analysis of the race, gender, and sexual narratives at play in the Anita Hill–Clarence Thomas sexual harassment case and the confirmation controversy generally, see the essays collected in *Race-ing Justice, En-gendering Power*.

33. Subpoenaed by Kenneth Starr, Bill Clinton testified before a federal grand jury concerning his relationship with Monica Lewinsky and the Paula Jones sexual harassment case, 17 August 1998. Congress later released the videotaped testimony to the public.

34. Lucinda Franks, "The Intimate Hillary," *Talk* (September 1999): 174.

Marjorie Garber

moniker, slang. Also monarch, monekeer, monica, monick(er), monniker, etc. [Origin unknown.] A name, a nick-name; also (rare), as *v. trans.*, to apply a name to (a person).

"Why don't we hear very much about Monica Lewinsky being Jewish?" joked comedian Emily Levine at a Los Angeles fund-raiser for the Morning Star Commission, a group of professionals from the media and academia who have organized to combat the stereotype of the "Jewish American Princess." (The group gets its name from the eponymous heroine of Herman Wouk's fifties novel, *Marjorie Morningstar*, about an aspiring Hollywood star who changed her name from Morgenstern.) "A Jewish girl with oral sex? I don't believe it," quipped comedian Jackie Mason to a Florida audience. "An oral surgeon, maybe, that's what a Jewish girl wants."[1]

The question of Monica's Jewishness, and her mother's name change from Lewinsky to Lewis, was hardly glanced at in media accounts in this country. (In Israel, interestingly, there has been more attention, pro and con.) When I asked a well-known conservative columnist why, he said it might be because there were so many other interns who had been involved with Bill Clinton; Monica was the only one who'd gotten caught. The implication was that Clinton was an equal opportunity seducer, fairly "catholic" in his tastes. Monica, by this account, was just a "Jane Dubinsky," the Jewish Jane Doe. Yet the deep (throat?) structure of the Monica story does have fascinating resonances with Jewishness, and with the historic narratives, fact, fiction, and stereotype, of the seductive "Jewess" and her political role.

Overseas, in Europe and in the Middle East, Monica's Jewish identity was very much part of her story. As we will see shortly, it made her, in some eyes, an obvious Zionist spy and in others a cultural heroine. In the United States, however, her Jewishness was seldom mentioned, except when she herself brought it up. When it was reported that Monica had given the President a copy of *Oy Vey! The Things They Say! A Minibook of Jewish Wit*, for example, one journalist cited Henry Kissinger's "Power is the great aphrodisiac!" as a particularly apposite selection.[2] But the fact that Monica was Jewish—something she herself was frank and joyous about in many of her comments, both to the President and to her biographer—was largely ignored by the American press and politicians. Ignored—or displaced into other frames of reference. Her signifying traits were distributed across a whole spectrum of discussions. She was "pushy"; she was "ambitious"; she was "zaftig"; she was "typical Beverly Hills." She was physically mature for her age. She was sexy and seductive, "the femme fatale in the soap opera of sex and betrayal."[3] She was rich. She had designs on a political or policy role. She lacked moral gravitas. She led a weak Christian man astray.

It is not entirely an accident, I believe, that the moral "hero" of the Clinton sex scandal was the Senate's single (and first-ever) Orthodox Jew, Joseph Lieberman of Connecticut, a Democratic liberal and longtime Clinton friend. Lieberman was widely praised for his courage in speaking up about the effect of the scandal "on our children, our culture, and our national character."[4] As the man who persuaded the Senate to discontinue voting on Jewish festivals and holding sessions on Jewish High Holy Days, Lieberman had enormous moral clout. After his speech the national media wrote admiringly about his daily Torah study and prayer and his seven-mile walk from Capitol Hill to his home in Georgetown when the Senate meets on Friday night, since Orthodox Jews may not ride on the Sabbath. So far as I can tell, Lieberman never commented publicly—or for all I know, privately—about Monica Lewinsky's Jewishness. His opprobrium was aimed at the President, who had failed as a moral leader. But the fact that this story was anchored at one end of the moral scale by Bill Clinton's relationship with a young Jewish woman ("disgraceful and immoral")[5] and at the other end by his relationship with a high-ranking and highly respected Jewish man in public life ("a Jewish hero")[6] is evidence of its overdetermination in the public sphere.

Although some of the story's "Jewish" elements went unnamed and unmarked, they powerfully and uncannily reinscribed the story of Jewish-American assimilation and its late-twentieth-century discontents. For just as Senator Lieberman's "heroism" was almost predictable, given the ingredients of this underlying cultural narrative, so was the public fascination with the behavior and desires of a sensual young woman named Lewinsky. When Al Gore chose Lieberman as his vice presidential running mate, he was widely regarded as trying to distance himself from the perceived moral turpitude of the Clinton scandal. In this case the tacit hope was that the "good" Jewish man could sanitize the stain of the "bad" Jewish girl. The flood of speeches and articles that publicized his Jewishness said nothing, of course, about hers.

Precisely because it went largely unmentioned in the American press during the course of the scandal, Monica's Jewishness was, in a sense, everywhere. It became the cause behind the cause, the story behind the story. And it tapped into old stories, and cultural fantasies, that created a logic of their own. Mentions, when they did occur, were oblique and knowing, tapping into the same reservoir of erotic and sentimental stereotype, an ambivalent overestimation of the object that imbued Lewinsky with particular seductive power.

In the midst of the impeachment hearings, novelist John Updike, the nation's most famous chronicler of WASP culture (his fictional protagonist Rabbit Angstrom has been described as "a WASP antihero")[7] published a jaunty little poem in the *New Yorker* called "Country Music." "Oh Monica, you Monica/In your little black beret," it began:

> *You vamped him with your lingo,*
> *   Your notes in purple ink,*
> *And fed him "Vox" and bagels*
> *   Until he couldn't think.*[8]

Updike, whose novel *Couples* (1968) offered an early depiction of oral sex as an American way of life, stands in what might almost be considered a godfatherly relation to *Vox*, the "phone sex" novel notoriously presented by Lewinsky to the President. One of his greatest admirers and disciples is Nicholson Baker, the author of *Vox*. And Updike is himself somewhat intrigued by the phenomenon of the older man and the sexy Jewish girl.

After the Rabbit books, Updike turned to a series of books about Henry Bech, described as a "moderately well-known Jewish writer," whose lovers became younger as he grew older. "Bech had a new sidekick," begins a chapter in the 1998 *Bech at Bay*. "Her moniker was Robin. Rachel 'Robin' Teagarten. Twenty-six, post-Jewish, frizzy big hair, figure on the short and solid side." And of course, sexy. "The energy of youth plus the wisdom of age," Bech congratulates himself.[9]

"*Vox* and bagels" is a good joke, an apt telescoping of Monica's seductive charms. And while the "lingo," the purple ink, and even the phone sex might conceivably be generic Beverly Hills mall rat, the bagels (and the slightly occluded lox) hint at the specificity of "Lewinsky"—a name that does not appear in Updike's ballad of careless White House love.

Zaftig

"This demure but zoftick freshman, with a brain rivalling Spinoza's encased in the body of a Lollobrigida."   —*S. J. Perelman*, Baby, It's Cold Inside *(1970)*

"An independent-minded odalisque, unshackled from sexual modesty and constantly celebrating her *zaftig* sensuality,"[10] is how one critic characterized the response of women's magazines like *Glamour* to Lewinsky's erotic persona. (The occasion was an editorial entitled, with deliberate double entendre, "Why We Should All Get Down on Our Knees and Thank Monica Lewinsky.")

However sex-affirmative *Glamour* and its sisters *Cosmopolitan* and *Marie Claire* may be, *zaftig* is not a word one regularly finds in their pages. *Zaftig* (from the German for "juicy") is the closest term we have today to the somewhat outmoded, regionally nonspecific "buxom," denoting someone, or something, plump and well-rounded. ("*Zaftig* describes in one word what it takes two hands, outlining an hourglass figure, to do.")[11] The same word means provocative, seminal, germinal—"*zaftig* ideas." "Hourglass figure" is a term as much associated in this century with Mae West or Dolly Parton as with delectable Jewishness. (Does Elizabeth Taylor count as a Jew in this connection?) But if *zaftig* makes a comeback in the fashion world—and who can doubt that it will, sooner or later?—Monica Lewinsky will have played a role in its revival.

An odalisque is a female slave or concubine in an Eastern harem, so that the orientalism of "Jewish looks" here encompasses both Turkey and Israel, by way of Byron and nineteenth-century French painting. The lush Jewish woman is sexual and sensual, but with a mind of her own. No sex slave ("unshackled"), she is free to enjoy her own pleasures.

But on the other hand, the "book" on Jewish girls is that they are neurotic and even phobic about sex, and that—as Jackie Mason so delicately hinted— there are some things a "nice Jewish girl" just doesn't do. "My friend Riva is very upset," wrote humor columnist Anne Beatts in the *Los Angeles Times*. 'Monica Lewinsky crossed a line,' she says. "This oral sex thing—everyone knows Jewish girls don't do that. Now she's ruined it for the rest of us.'" Beatts comments, "I happen to be Jewish, and I believe Riva is operating on a false assumption. But then again I'm only a convert, so maybe that rule was something they forgot to let me in on."[12] A *New York Times* article on television stereotypes of Jewish women, published the same week as Lewinsky's ABC interview with Barbara Walters—but making no reference to her—was accompanied by a photo display that neatly summarized the issues: it read "Role models: The sexless (Bebe Neuwirth, 'Frasier'), the dependent (Jennifer Aniston, 'Friends'), the garish (Fran Dreschler, 'The Nanny') and the intrusive (Cynthia Harris, 'Mad About You.')"[13] Symptomatically, the article's headline offered three other categories for Jewish girls: Princesses, Punishers, and Prudes.

The paradox of the Jewish girl as temptress and siren, on the one hand, and marriage-minded upwardly mobile virgin on the other, is far older than the postwar cliché of the "Jewish American Princess," a term whose disparaging acronym, JAP or Jap, indicates something of the same mechanism of displacement and abjection. "Jap" is an insult when applied to a person of Japanese origin. Applied to a Jewish American Princess, "a pampered and usually wealthy young woman who feels she deserves special treatment," it's just an affectionate little joke.

The *Jewish American Princess Handbook* (1982) includes a glossary of "Jewish Jargon" that runs the gamut (not, incidentally, a Yiddish word) from "*shagits*" ("blond haired, blue eyed forbidden fruit who ends up marrying a *shiksa*") to "guilt" ("Jewish hereditary disease. Symptoms include a churning stomach and feelings of deep-seated anxiety. Highly contagious, especially when the Princess spends too much time in the company of her mother") and "money."[14] As Sander Gilman points out, "Such lists were standard in all of the anti-Semitic literature of the late nineteenth and early twentieth centuries."[15] For the end of the twentieth century, these terms mean differently—or do they? How much self-irony is protection enough for the minority group that coined the phrase "self-hatred"?

"The woman, the Jewish woman as JAP, has replaced the male Jew as the scapegoat," observes Evelyn Torton Beck, "and the Jewish male has not only participated, but has, in fact, been instrumental in creating and perpetuating that image." Beck rightly sees this as a mechanism of displacement.[16] "All the [fantasied] characteristics he cannot stand in himself are displaced onto the Jewish woman." The old slurs about Jews—that they are "materialistic, money-grabbing, greedy, and ostentatious," that they are "manipulative, crafty, untrustworthy,

unreliable, calculating, controlling"—resurface in postwar fiction and popular cul-
ture as typical qualities of the Jewish American Princess.

Princess

"They could see she was a real princess and no question about it."
—*Hans Christian Andersen, "The Princess and the Pea"*

In October 1997, according to what she told Andrew Morton, Monica and the
President had a phone conversation in which "they started swapping dirty jokes—
a Lewinsky specialty—mainly on a Jewish theme. One of Monica's ran, 'why do
Jewish men like to watch porno films backwards? So that they can see the hooker
give back the money.' The President responded in kind: 'What do you get when
you cross a Jewish American Princess with an Apple? A computer that won't go
down on you.'"[17]

So it seems that Jackie Mason was right in his estimate of the do's and don'ts
for nice Jewish girls. (Who would have guessed that Bill Clinton even knew the
phrase "Jewish American Princess"?) Monica Lewinsky's story is certainly the tale
of a princess. But which princess? There seemed to be several competing for the
starring role.

There was, for example, the (non)-coincidence that the task of writing her
biography was given to the same man who canonized Princess Di, the thinnest
and blondest of royals. "It is no accident," *New York Times* television critic Caryn
James observed, "that Ms. Lewinsky's forthcoming book is called *Monica's Story* or
that it is written by Andrew Morton, the author of the best-selling *Diana: Her True
Story*, which so effectively spun the sympathetic image of an emotionally
wounded Princess. (Not an easy sell when you think about it.)"[18]

Monica Lewinsky's videotaped testimony, played before the Senate and the
world, elicited, perhaps predictably, its own set of stereotypes. "Wearing a sensi-
ble suit, pearls, heavy makeup and a semi-lacquered hairdo, Ms. Lewinsky was
well-spoken, used no slang and showed only trace evidence of the Valley Girl of
her taped phone conversations with Linda R. Tripp," said the front-page article in
the *New York Times*. "Even her voice seemed different now, more modulated, less
high-pitched and breathy." The *Times* suggested that Lewinsky, referred to "sim-
ply as Monica" by the House prosecutor throughout the deposition, seemed in
"appearance, voice and vocabulary" to be "all grown up—and even a little bit
hard."[19] Here the division between Valley Girl and JAP, or, we could say, between

"Monica" and "Lewinsky," is making itself felt as a cultural divide. The "Jewess" of old, mature beyond her years, "businesslike," ironic, sexy, savvy, and sage (with too much makeup and a throaty voice), vs. the young, vulnerable female "victim."

"They make her seem like she's typical Beverly Hills," said a woman who works in a Rodeo Drive clothing store, reflecting on the Monica phenomenon, "and in a lot of ways I'd have to say that's true. It's the whole rich, snobby thing, which is a stereotype but isn't really. I mean you can just spot them by their attitude."[20] *Them*? Californians? Rich people? Or . . . ?

"You can see some life in her, a little snappy something," said a man in a health club watching Monica on CNN as he pedaled on his stationary bike, "not a ditzy Californian as many people have made her out to be."[21] Other articles called attention to her "go-getter's quality" (read: pushy?) and cited her self-description as a "pest" in putting the pressure on Vernon Jordan to help her find a job.[22] (The President's secretary, Betty Currie, was also quoted as calling her "a little bit pushy" and a "pain in the neck.")[23]

Reviewing Andrew Morton's book in the *New York Times,* Michiko Kakutani struck the same familiar chords, noting that "Mr. Morton tries to present Ms. Lewinsky in this book not as a ditsy Valley Girl or pushy tart but as a die-hard romantic who loves roses and shabby chic furniture."[24] So Monica was not California (ditsy) or New York (pushy) but, as Morton tried to tell her, much to the astonishment of many, "classic Boston."[25] The Boston mayor and the Boston media, none of whom had apparently ever heard of "shabby chic" (the title of a book and a design store) took offense at the "shabby," disavowed the "chic," and announced to Monica that she was not really their kind of girl.

But there was a Boston girl in the Monica story after all, as it turned out. Consider the following characterization, from a prominently placed media account: "Despite a popular stereotype as a spoilt Jewish-American princess, she emerged as a fiercely independent and driven young woman, determined to make her way in television, and attracted to power." She had become "a national celebrity."[26] The subject of this analysis was not Monica Lewinsky, but rather the woman she would choose, with uncanny aptness, as her television interviewer: Barbara Walters. And Walters, who emerged in the course of the interview both as Monica's unwitting double and as her clucking, affectionately reproving "mother," was born in Boston.

Barbara Walters, the daughter of Lou and Dena Selett (née Seletsky) Walters lived as a child in Brookline, Massachusetts, and grew up in circumstances that alternated between wealth and poverty. She attended the tony Fieldston and Birch

Wathen schools, and graduated from Sarah Lawrence. Her father was an entertainment entrepreneur, the man who founded the Latin Quarter nightclub in New York. By the time she was eleven, he had bought her a mink coat. The family moved to a succession of penthouses, then lost all their money.

Like Monica, Barbara says she and her mother were exceptionally close and that she felt more distant from her father. Like Monica, too, she is described as "insecure" and "peculiarly vulnerable"—the words are those of CBS's Mike Wallace.[27] And like Monica she enjoys confiding in her female friends. "She is," announced a celebrity profile interview in the *New York Times*, "a woman's woman who loves the telephone and having lunch with the girls. Not least, she is an excellent gossip."[28]

In 1977 Walters arranged the first interview between Egypt's president Anwar Sadat and Israel's prime minister Menachem Begin. *Saturday Night Live*'s Gilda Radner immortalized her as Baba Wawa, impersonating her speech, with its soft l's and r's that sound like w's. "This isn't journalism, this is a minstrel show," complained old-line TV journalist Fred Friendly. "Is Barbara a journalist or is she Cher?"[29] (If Barbara Walters was the media's Cher Sarkisian Bono Allman, was Monica Lewinsky its Cher Horowitz? Clued-in, or totally *Clueless?*)

At a New York Friars Club dinner in 1994, Walters was saluted by her supposed arch-rival, now her *20/20* colleague, Diane Sawyer, who sang, to the tune of Judy Garland's "You Made Me Love You," a parody that contained the following lyrics:

You made me ruthless. I didn't want to do it, ambition drove me to it. You made me greedy. I couldn't bear that you net $3 million more than I get.

Desperate to beat you, I thought I'd do what you do, I slept with Roone [ABC news chief Roone Arledge] and Hugh [Downs], too, scheming for interviews.

As the punch line of her song, Sawyer wound up with this: "I even married a Jew—hoping to be more like you." The Jew Sawyer married was, as everyone knew, director Mike Nichols. Was the "more like you" line intended to refer to marriage (Walters has been married to three Jewish men, Robert Henry Katz, theatrical producer Lee Guber, and television executive Merv Adelson; in college she dated Roy Cohn) or identity?

Indeed, Walters had been the forerunner of Lewinsky in yet another way. Here's how she reported her encounter with Lyndon Johnson when they met in the Oval Office. "Our conversation had been so disarmingly friendly that I felt courageous enough when it ended to say, 'Mr. President, do you suppose [I] can ask to kiss a president? . . . I've had such a splendid time, and I would like to kiss you on the cheek.'"[30] An early apostle of flirtation as a way of getting ahead ("My own opinion is that there is far too little flirtation in our country as it is,"[31] she wrote in a 1970 book), she had tempered her views, at least for public consumption, by the time she got Monica to describe flashing her thong underwear at the President as a "small, subtle, flirtatious gesture."

The Monica-Barbara television interview attracted some 48.5 million viewers, and many of those watching were impressed. But not all. "If I want to watch two princesses gossiping, I can stop in at Zabar's," complained Lucianne Goldberg, the literary agent who counseled Linda Tripp.[32] (Goldberg had a lot of attitude about Monica Lewinsky, and some of it was expressed in anti-princess mode. When a wire news service asked for predictions about Lewinsky's future—"What next for Monica?"—Goldberg suggested she should go back to California and marry a Beverly Hills dentist 'with more gold chains than he can swim in.'"[33] She claimed some expertise on the subject, having married a Jew; her husband, Sidney, runs a news syndication service, United Media. "I raised two Jewish kids—and, boy, do I understand the type.")[34]

Bigmouth

Pisk (Yiddish, from Polish: "mouth")
1. The mouth of an animal or human.
2. (Colloquialism). An eloquent or garrulous speaker.
3. A brusque slang word for "mouth," used in expressions such as "shut your trap."
The diminutive, piskel or piskeleh, is often applied admiringly to a child who speaks precociously. "Does he have a piskeleh."   —Leo Rosten, The Joys of Yiddish

"You told 10 other people you had this relationship with the President," Walters chided Lewinsky, almost affectionately it seemed. "I mean, Bigmouth! Why did you want people to know?"[35] "Bigmouth!" seemed a curiously colloquial interjection from the usually more decorous Walters, but then of course Monica's big mouth was, in every sense, the real topic under discussion and on display.

My haircutter, a woman of excellent judgment and forward-looking politics, said she'd watched The Interview for only the last fifteen minutes or so, but long enough to see for herself what was hardly news: "She's so *oral*." The camera repeatedly sought out her mouth, and her exceedingly white and gleaming teeth.

"What's with the Vaseline on her teeth?" asked Lucianne Goldberg. "Can we get a little closer to her mouth with the camera, please! They're gonna go down her throat any minute. Maybe we'll get to see her uvula!"[36]

The ABC website on the night of the interview logged more inquiries about Monica's shade of lipstick than about any other single matter. (It was Club Monaco's "Glaze," and—once the answer was revealed on ABC's *Good Morning, America* by Charlie Gibson and Diane Sawyer—the net obligingly listed major stores in New York and California where it might be found. "We went out to find a tube of this stuff, and it was sold out," said Gibson. "It was literally sold out everywhere in New York.")[37] What she had done with her mouth, and to whom, was what the whole country wanted to know. Indeed, the interest was not confined to the United States; a BBC broadcaster labeled her "Hot Lips," and described her appearance on Channel 4 as "pure televisual Viagra." Almost all women, he contended, "regard Lewinsky with tight-lipped distaste," while men have considerable affection "for louche ladies who hold out the prospect of uncomplicated oral sex."[38] The broadcaster in question was Charles Spencer, the brother of Princess Diana. "Bigmouth!" If it's not a translation from the Yiddish, perhaps it should be. For Jewish girls with big mouths are some of the ambivalent superstars of our culture.

As always seems to be the case with images of Jewishness, and especially of Jewish women, they cross boundaries: between homeliness and beauty; between Jewish mother and wayward daughter; between fat and thin; between proper and raucously improper.

Sophie Tucker, weighing in at two hundred pounds, became the red-hot *Yiddishe Mamme* with a patter that was both racy and sensual. As Eddie Cantor remarked, "Sophie's style and material are hardly what you'd want at a Holy Name breakfast. . . . She has no inhibitions. . . . She sings the words we used to write on the sidewalks of New York."[39] Belle Barth, the "doyenne of the dirty line," was another "pudgy Jewish woman" with an uninhibited approach to sexual comedy. ("Only two words you have to learn in the Yiddish language and that is *Gelt* (money) and *Schmuck* (penis). Because if a man has no, he is.")[40] Comedienne Totie Fields (born Sophie Feldman) poked fun at her own size—she was 4'10" and weighed 190 pounds—and continued to joke about it even after a long bout of phlebitis forced doctors to amputate her leg, and she dwindled to 120 pounds. Her particular "brand of prosthetic humor"[41] blended pathos with wisecracking. These Jewish comediennes deliberately distanced themselves from seductiveness, stressing their weight and their sexual misadventures as a way of seeking stage legitimacy.

Singer and entertainer Fanny Brice, later the subject of the musical *Funny Girl*, came out of the same Jewish comic tradition (her original surname was Borach), and her "Yiddish facial grimaces" were pictured in an early newspaper spread. "Lips seemed to push and pull in different directions," wrote a recent biographer. "The rubber-faced Brice for whom Protestant prettiness was clearly unattainable was performing very much in the dialect comedy tradition."[42] When she had a nose job in 1923, the event was headline news in the *New York Times*: Fanny Brice "feels she has got all she can out of her nose and mouth and wants new ones to fit her for the comedy roles to which she aspires."[43] Brice felt that she was "too Jewish" for Hollywood. Dorothy Parker (born Rothschild, the daughter of a garment manufacturer, and herself never happy about being Jewish)[44] quipped acerbically that Brice had "cut off her nose to spite her race."[45] The new nose—and expensively capped teeth—did not keep *Variety* from speculating (accurately) that her "distinct Hebrew clowning"[46] made her "too New York" to succeed in America's heartland.

But a direct descendant of these Jewish "funny women," Joan Rivers (born Joan Molinsky and raised in Brooklyn), "defied the somatype," as Sarah Blacher Cohen points out, becoming "not a caricature of a femme fatale, but a femme fatale herself."[47] Rivers's signature phrase, "Can we talk?" defines her principal role as *yente* or scandal-monger, dishing the dirt, at the same time that she developed her antitype as "Heidi Abromowitz," a joyous sexual transgressor whose career encompassed the stages of "Baby Bimbo," "Toddler Tramp," "Teen Tart," and "Career Chippy"—all titles of chapters in Rivers's best-seller, *The Life and Times of Heidi Abromowitz*.[48] Heidi, according to Rivers, "did things with her pacifier that most women haven't done with their husbands."[49] Readers of the Starr Report who noted Monica Lewinsky's inventiveness with a cigar might find Heidi an enlightening guide.

And in the current generation of "big-mouthed" Jewish women entertainers, sexuality is a clear asset, no longer in conflict with assimilation or acceptance. "This 43-year-old Jewish mother with the mouth that other mothers might wash out with soap" is how the New York *Daily News* described wide-mouthed comedienne Sandra Bernhard.[50] The *Los Angeles Times* led with the mouth in its own celebrity interview: "Sandra Bernhard, at 5-foot-10, looks like a slimmed-down Barbie with a mouth like an Edsel grill. It's a mouth that never stops as Bernhard tells erotic and neurotic jokes, discusses sexuality, [and] banters with the crowd. . . . At some point, she usually ends up standing around in her underwear."[51]

The big-mouthed Jewish diva is a staple of the musical stage, from Bette Midler to Barbra Streisand. "Barbra does this thing with her mouth. She pulls the top of her mouth over her teeth when she sings," says celebrity impersonator Eddie Edwards. "It's the smallest detail, but people will come and say, 'You captured that about her,'" he says, noting that he's also figured out how to tighten his throat muscles the way she does.[52] (Streisand is known for her wit as well as her *chutzpah*, cracking after the London opening of *Funny Girl* that if she'd been nicer to Prince Charles, "I might have been the first real Jewish princess.")[53]

Even in Lewinsky's own age cohort, the Jewish mouth does double duty. "Alicia Silverstone's pouty mouth and slouchy poses make her the girl Hollywood is most eager to corrupt today," announced the *Boston Herald* in a feature piece about the actress who starred as Cher Horowitz, the Jewish American Princess of Beverly Hills, in the hit film *Clueless*. Alicia (like Monica Lewinsky) "actually attended Beverly Hills High School, but far from being the Coolest Chick on Campus, she recalls: 'I didn't have the right clothes. I was a misfit.'"[54] "Silverstone's mouth is a wavy wet line that wriggled when she talks," declares a feature piece in the London *Guardian*. The *Guardian*, in fact, seems fascinated with her mouth: we read that in her next film, *Excessive Baggage*, male lead Benicio Del Toro "thrust[s] his fingers in Silverstone's mouth to retrieve the car keys she's hiding." (Says Silverstone, "when he's got his hand down her throat, that's a love scene," explaining why she's not interested in doing conventional sex "stuff" on camera. Asked what she means, she "spreads her legs and lets her eyelids flop and her mouth slacken.")[55] In *Clueless,* her character offered the following seduction advice: "Anything you can do to call attention to your mouth is good."

Is it necessary here to underscore the connection between sexy, provocative, "smart-talking," Jewish women and "big-mouthed" sex?

Sex and the Jewish Girl

"'Is she also a typical Rumanian beauty?' 'I think . . . she is a typical little Jewess.'"
—*John Updike,* Bech: A Book, *35*

The story of the dangerously seductive Jewess is, of course, a very old story in Europe, and is often linked with the stage.

The mother of the French actress Sarah Bernhardt was a courtesan, whose Jewishness "did nothing to hinder her career. On the contrary, it was a promise of carnal pleasure in a city where every self-respecting bordello offered at least one Jewish girl and one black girl for connoisseurs of exotica."[56] Bernhardt herself, the model for the actress Berma in Proust's *A la recherche de temps perdu*, had numerous affairs with rich and titled men, and was the object of anti-Semitic caricatures and allegations about her "vile Jewish habits" throughout her life.[57] (Unlike the weight-obsessed Monica, Sarah was preternaturally thin—and equally unfashionable in her time for being so.)

Bernhardt's predecessor on the French stage, sometimes credited as the first stage actress to achieve "international stardom," was Rachel (Elisa) Félix, a celebrity so well known that she did not use her last name, but became simply Rachel. (Félix, a translation of the Hebrew *Baruch*, or blessed, was a common Jewish name.) The daughter of poor Jewish peddlers, with an ambitious stage father much ridiculed in the press (Heinrich Heine wrote that "Père Rachel preens himself with the success of his daughter"),[58] Rachel became the "Jewish queen of tragedy," inspiring characters in novels by Disraeli and George Eliot; her "reputation for taking and dismissing men at her pleasure made her a formidable image of sexual voracity."[59] Other Jewish actresses at the time—Mlle Judith, Mlle Nathalie—likewise used only their *prénoms*, or (what are sometimes called in English) "Christian names." Rachel became *la grande Rachel*. Rachel's looks were unconventional for beauty; she was small and dark with a large head and deep-set eyes.

In fact, the sultry "Jewess," a first-order cultural fantasy, became, in part through the agency of fiction and the theater, the very type of sexual desire. Significantly, in literature as in life, she is often paired or partnered by her father, who serves as a foil.

The seductive beauty of Jewish daughters in two famous Elizabethan plays, *The Merchant of Venice* and *The Jew of Malta* is, essentially, taken for granted; it's not a surprise that young gentile men fall in love with them, despite the fact that these same young men detest and revile their fathers, Shylock and Barabas. In Marlowe's *Jew of Malta*, Mathias, "a young gentleman," and Lodowick, the governor's son, rhapsodize about "fair Abigail, the rich Jew's daughter."[60] Using his daughter as bait, Barabas, the Jew of the title, schemes to entrap them both, and the hapless Abigail, who loves Don Mathias, sees her two suitors slaughter each other for her sake.

In Scott's *Ivanhoe* (1819), Rebecca the Jewess, the daughter of the wealthy

Isaac of York, is a woman of far more character and charm than her Saxon counterpart, Rowena. When Ivanhoe chooses Rowena, Isaac and Rebecca leave England for the Continent.

Balzac's *Le cousin Pons* (1847) describes yet another father-daughter pair, the daughter "a beautiful girl, like all Jewesses who incarnate the Asian type in all its purity and nobility."[61]

But of course the paradigm case for the Monica story is a much earlier instance, the story of Queen Esther—a story newly made popular in twentieth-century France through Marcel Proust's repeated citation of Racine's *Esther* in *À la recherche du temps perdu*. "Even today," literary critic Eve Kosofsky Sedgwick wrote in 1990, "Jewish little girls are educated in gender roles—fondness for being looked at, fearlessness in defense of 'their people,' nonsolidarity with their sex—through masquerading as Queen Esther at Purim; I have a snapshot of myself at about five, barefoot in the pretty 'Queen Esther' dress my grandmother made [white satin, gold spangles], making a careful eyes-down toe-pointed curtsey at [presumably] my father, who is manifest in the picture only as the flashgun that hurls my shadow, pillaring up tall and black, over the dwarfed sofa onto the wall behind me."[62] Sedgwick and I are roughly of the same (Long Island) generation, and my mother sewed for me a costume that sounds very like hers. Without question, Esther was a heroine and role model as well as a leading costume-part to the junior Jewish set. And the plot of the book of Esther is a story of palace intrigue.

Esther, the beautiful ward of her uncle Mordecai (the "father figure" of the story), is brought by him to the palace of King Ahasuerus. Ahasuerus, displeased with his wife Queen Vashti, who had disobeyed his order that she display her beauty before his courtiers, divorces Vashti and chooses Esther as queen in her stead, selecting her from the "many maidens" who are brought to the king's palace at his decree. Esther, on Mordecai's advice, conceals her Jewishness from the king, until a crisis arises: Haman, a court favorite and an enemy to the Jews, had conceived a plot to kill them. Esther reveals her true identity to the king, pleads eloquently on behalf of the Jews, and secures not only their rescue but preferment for Mordecai, who had once saved the king from assassins.

It is quite true, as Sedgwick notes, that one of the secondary lessons of this story for Jewish girls in the fifties was that the "proud" Vashti, who disobeyed her husband, deserved what she got. I don't remember any discussion of what it meant for her to refuse to "show the people and the princes her beauty, for she was fair to look on" (Esther 1.11). The Book of Esther is quite clear on the political consequences: "For this deed of the queen shall come abroad unto all women, so that they shall despise their husbands in their eyes, when it shall be reported, the king Ahasuerus commanded Vashti the queen to be brought in before him, but she came not" (1.17). So far were we from seeing this as a laudable act of feminist self-assertion, I think we saw it instead as an intergenerational rivalry: the "bad" queen, a mother figure like all queens, was banished and replaced by a "maiden," a "young virgin"—one of us. No wonder Sedgwick is flirting at her father and his camera. This is the story of the young girl who gets the king.

And the king, in this case, is—*o tempora, o mores*—Bill Clinton. The play casts itself: Hillary is Vashti, the headstrong proto-feminist queen, feasting on that occasion with the women in the royal house, unwilling to drop everything to display herself for his friends. And Monica, it is needless to say, is Esther, the beautiful Jewess.

The Israeli right wing saw the connection right away, calling Lewinsky a "modern-day Esther." "Like Esther," according to this analogy, "Monica allegedly slept with the head of state at a time when the people of Israel were in grave peril. And like Esther, her intervention has averted a danger—the likelihood of President Clinton embarking on a personal Middle East peace initiative," forcing Israeli Prime Minister Netanyanhu to give up more West Bank land to the Palestinians.[63]

But the political message might as easily be read the other way. The nineteenth-century Austrian playwright Franz Grillparzer wrote a tragedy, left complete but unpublished at his death, called *The Jewess of Toledo* (1855). In it a king falls passionately in love with a young Jewess, and only regains his sense of responsibility to his country after she is killed at the queen's command.

Next Year in Jerusalem?

"And why should you plead for them, Jewess?"   —*Eugene O'Neill*, Lazarus Laughed

"The Palestinian Authority can be forgiven for thinking that Monica Lewinsky was a Mossad plant (though I personally doubt they would have chosen anyone with such an obviously Jewish name)," wrote a reporter for the *Jerusalem Post*.[64]

Was Monica a spy? A number of people seemed to think so. Nation of Islam leader Louis Farrakhan appeared on NBC's *Meet the Press* and declared that Monica Lewinsky might be part of a Zionist plot to undermine the Mideast peace negotiations.[65]

A popular Chinese magazine proposed, in a plot not unlike *The Manchurian Candidate*, that Lewinsky had been sent to Washington when she was a child as a

Cold War agent on a mission to entrap the President and destabilize the government. "Is Lewinsky with the KGB?" inquired the headline. "Information has exposed Monica Lewinsky as a spy assigned to the former Soviet Union. Her mission was to drag a U.S. president through the mud!"[66] Meantime, the Syrian defense minister, too, announced that the affair was a Zionist plot. "Monica Lewinsky is a young Jewish girl that Mossad hired and pushed into working as an intern in the White House." Since it was a "Jewish lawyer who disclosed the scandal to Ken Starr," said General Mustapha Tlass to the United Arab Emirates *Al-Khaleej* newspaper, "all this definitely proves that worldwide Zionism and particularly American Jews" are working for Israel. "President Clinton has said it is a conspiracy but unfortunately he did not say by whom."[67] A Syrian newspaper declared that "Netanyahu stands behind the Lewinsky affair."[68] Palestinian commentators noted that many of the principals in the scandal were Jewish: not only Monica Lewinsky, but also lawyer William Ginsburg and literary agent Lucianne Goldberg, who persuaded Linda Tripp to do the taping. The fact that Vice President Al Gore has been favorably inclined toward Likud, Netanyahu's party, led some to think that the impeachment of Clinton would benefit the Israeli hardliners—another clear sign of conspiracy.

Other biblical analogies were also possible, of course: Monica could be seen as "a careerist Delilah."[69] A Los Angeles rabbi drew an analogy between the Clinton-Lewinsky liaison and the story of David and Bathsheba, citing a fifteenth-century Spanish philosopher who had said, "David sinned as a man and not as a king."[70]

An article in the *Jerusalem Post* took what might seem to be an unusual tack: it lamented the fact that American Jewry had become so assimilated that the Lewinskys preferred to send their child to Washington rather than to Israel. "Given the choice, how many Jewish parents in America would opt for an internship in the White House for their child rather than a scholarship from the Hebrew University?" The writer, a former director general of the Israeli prime minister's office, said, "It seems to me that the behavior and norms that motivated Monica Lewinsky and her family, which emerged from her detailed testimony before the Starr commission, were entirely, if not typically, American."[71]

"Israel has never really forgiven Monica Lewinsky," observed a commentator in the London *Guardian*. "The Jewish heroine of the Washington potboiler had once promised to flee to Israel if the pressures of fame became too great in Washington."[72]

But other Israelis were wary of both ethnic and national stereotyping. A correspondent to the *Post* was dismayed at a columnist's description of Lewinsky as "the Jewish American Princess who allegedly made it with the president," calling this a "denigrating description" used almost exclusively by "self-hating" Jews.[73]

Meanwhile, at home in the United States, some Jews felt protective, and others vulnerable. After the scandal hit, Bernard Lewinsky "had to listen in helpless, silent indignation as local Orthodox Jewish elders discussed the possibility of using religious law to cast Monica out from the faith," reports Andrew Morton.[74]

The Lewinsky family rabbi, David Wolpe of the Conservative Sinai Temple in Los Angeles, told his congregation a story about his nine-year-old niece, who had blurted out that she never wanted to be President Clinton's religion. Wolpe, the author of *Teaching Your Children about God, Why Be Jewish?* and *The Healer of Shattered Hearts,* said of the President, "He was a brilliant, talented, extraordinary child, and for the leader of the United States we need an adult."[75] Two former congregants now residing in Israel promptly wrote to reprove the rabbi for meddling in the moral instruction of a Southern Baptist, and urging him to look closer to home. "Monica Lewinsky attended Temple Sinai's religious school. Perhaps Rabbi Wolpe should review the school's curriculum to learn whether it includes lessons on proper behavior, including feminine modesty, by the Temple's boys and girls."[76] Another Israeli reader chimed in to say, "My nine-year-old daughter says she never wants to be the same religion as that of Monica—Conservative Jewish. With a student like Monica coming from his synagogue's religious school, it would be wise for the rabbi to examine exactly what is and is not being taught there."[77]

Although it was never mentioned specifically by the mainstream media in the United States, Lewinsky's religious affiliation had, perhaps inevitably, some effect upon political oratory and public discourse. Gary Ackerman, a Democratic congressman from Queens who is himself Jewish, declared that it was "unsavory" and an "outrage" for the House of Representatives to release a videotape and documents of the testimony of Bill Clinton in the Monica Lewinsky scandal on Rosh Hashanah. The item was reported in the *New York Post* and (once again) picked up by the *Jerusalem Post* (no relation to the New York paper). Non-Jewish congressmen representing largely Jewish districts reported the same concern: "I have heard from scores of constituents who are outraged that the testimony would be released during one of the holiest days in the Jewish calendar," wrote Representative Carolyn McCarthy to the House Judiciary Committee. Neither Ackerman nor McCarthy alluded to Monica's religion, though some implication of a connection seemed possible. Would it have been equally outrageous to Jewish sensibilities if the testimony, with its "sexually graphic details," had been that of Paula Jones or

Kathleen Willey? Perhaps, but the unwelcome—and unstated—fact that the woman testifying was Jewish must have added to the cultural embarrassment of the occasion. Six of the fifteen Democrats on the House Judiciary Committee were Jewish. None of the Republicans was. "Jews Rip Rosh Hashanah Tape Release" said the New York *Daily News* breezily. Again there was no mention of Monica, just of the holiness of the holiday and the inappropriateness of releasing sexually explicit materials on a day of prayer and reflection. But Abraham Foxman, director of the Anti-Defamation League, had another view, observing that the material didn't pertain to the Jewish community. Monica's Jewishness was not, for him, part of the scandal or the story. And Rabbi Ismar Schorsch, chancellor of the Jewish Theological Seminary, saw a silver lining, noting that observant Jews would not see the tape until after the holiday: "Our level of discourse will remain elevated a bit longer than [that of] the rest of America," he said.[78]

Meantime, Bill Clinton read a passage on repentance from the Yom Kippur liturgy at a White House prayer breakfast of 150 clergymen. It had, he said, been recommended by a Jewish friend.[79]

Prostheses

"Cleopatra's nose, had it been shorter, the whole face of the world had been changed."
                                                                —*Blaise Pascal, Pensées*

The Jewish-temptress theme has had a number of fascinatingly displaced effects in the playing-out of the Clinton sex scandals. I wonder, for example, if it has occurred to anyone to note that it was Paula Jones, Clinton's undeniably non-Jewish alleged playmate, who underwent a highly publicized, and publicly ridiculed, nose job. For the rhinoplasty is a time-honored puberty ritual of American middle-class Jewish girls.

Jones's plastic surgeon—paid incidentally, by an anonymous donor, and not by Jones herself—was the same man who has performed surgery on Michael Jackson and Barbra Streisand.[80] And her new nose was unveiled, like Monica, on ABC television, and in the midst of the Lewinsky scandal, as if it were a new bid for the public's attention. Fantastically—and fantasmatically—it was as if Paula Jones had had to reenact one of the secular rites of passage of surburban Jewish culture in order to rival Monica Lewinsky for the fickle attention of press and public.

The history of cosmetic rhinoplasty begins at the turn of the last century, with an operation performed by Jacques Joseph in 1898 on a male patient, thereby inaugurating what Sander Gilman calls "the craze for nose jobs in fin-de-siècle Germany and Austria."[81] "Joseph was very charitable," said a woman who benefited from his work in the early thirties, "and when he felt that someone suffered from 'a Jewish nose' he would operate for nothing."[82] "Suffering" from a Jewish nose was of course a self-fulfilling diagnosis.

Joseph, a German Jew who had changed his first name from Jakob when he undertook his medical training, died in 1934 before the full scenario of Nazi anti-Semitism and genocide had unfolded, but his procedure, an instrument for cultural invisibility and passing, became itself a rite of passage among many postwar American Jews. The objective was not so much the obliteration of a cultural heritage—most of those who changed their noses did not also change their names—but a kind of esthetics of passing, assimilating Jewish looks into the WASP mainstream. The nose job, or nose bob, became a signifying tradition of a certain subset of suburban Jewishness. Once a sign of (attempted) invisibility, the rhinoplasty had become a triumphantly, if somewhat paradoxically, visible sign: a sign of parental ambition for their children, a sign of the endorsement of "universal" concepts of beauty, a sign of affluence and of materiality. And although the first clients for this treatment in Germany and Austria were men, the preponderance of mid-twentieth-century new noses went to women. In the 1960 and '70s, the nose of choice was the "button," which went out in the early '80s in favor of a more "natural" look.

It's ironic that Paula Jones, an Arkansas native with no links to Jewish culture, felt that her nose job itself was both desirable and forbidden. "I have enough people screaming at me, talking about my new nose," Jones told *Inside Edition*'s Deborah Norville. "Everybody else has plastic surgery, and has noses done . . . but I don't have a right, I'm not pretty enough."[83] *Los Angeles Times* television critic Howard Rosenberg took note of the general risibility in the media (and on late-note talk shows) about Jones's nose:

Noses having been used historically to demean Arabs and especially Jews with Hitler's Third Reich and the old Soviet Union using such caricatures to dehumanize and isolate an entire people. In the German weekly Der Stuermer *from the 1930s, for example, you find ugly cartoon after cartoon of Jews depicted as the enemies of humanity, their most prominent feature being beak-like noses that droop almost to their thick lips.*

In my case, I recall vividly how some of the older kids in my elementary school would stroke their noses when they passed me in the halls, just because a guy named Rosenberg was obviously Jewish.

I was Jewish trash; Jones is trailer trash—making us both fair game in our respective generations.

It's a stigma she may never outlive, no matter how many times she tries to reinvent herself. And this new nose business is just another reminder, just as some of its coverage brings to mind the ever-closer ties between mainstream media and tabloids.[84]

Jones was neither a WASP (like Norville?) nor a JAP (like Monica); in the shifting hierarchy of entitlements, her nose was news.

The uncanny displacement of the "nose job" story from the Jewish Monica Lewinsky to the gentile Paula Jones was, I want to suggest, part of a larger mechanism of displacement in the U.S. media, which regularly shied away from any direct acknowledgment of Lewinsky's Jewishness. Although Britain's Jon Snow could elicit from her a televised declaration that she feels "being Jewish is my culture and my heritage," and that her grandparents' experiences in the Holocaust "have instilled in me a sense of courage,"[85] neither Barbara Walters nor any other U.S. commentator went near the topic. The "Jewish American Princess" label was occasionally trotted out by print journalists, but again it was often displaced onto other—non-American—speakers or thinkers, like biographer Andrew Morton (from a Montreal review: "Very early on, Morton identifies what he calls Lewinsky's 'high sense of entitlement,' a rather elegant euphemism for Beverly Hills brat, or Jewish American princess")[86] or young Arab onlookers at a London book signing ("To these boys she was a spoiled Jewish American Princess, a hate figure, and they didn't bother to hide their contempt").[87]

"The nice Jewish girl from Beverly Hills whose lips launched a thousand quips,"[88] said the *Irish Times*. Notice again that the overseas press, favorable or unfavorable, was far less skittish than the American media at mentioning the obvious. Which was *not*, in this case, "as plain as the nose on her face." But which was quite clearly declared—if you knew enough to see it—in her name.

Monikers

Their vicinitie, and mutual entercourses, made the Jews passe under their neighbors names.
—Theophilus Gale, The Court of the Gentiles *(1669)*

Lauren Bacall was born Betty Joan Perske, in Brooklyn.
Paulette Goddard was born Marion Levy.
Judy Holliday was born Judy Tuvim.

Shelley Winters was born Shirley Shrift.
Barbara Hershey was born Barbara Hertzstein.
Barbara Walters was born Barbara Walters.

Whoopi Goldberg was born Caryn Elaine Johnson.

This list of stage names or pseudonyms seems harmless enough in the present day, a mere reminder of another prosthetic performance of assimilated Jewishness, like the nose job. And indeed the name, like the nose, was sometimes merely bobbed, or shortened, or in some cases translated, to make it fit into mainstream American culture. Asa Yoelson became Al Jolson; Issur Danielovitch, the son of a Russian Jewish immigrant ragman, became Kirk Douglas; Eddie Cantor, taken through immigration by his grandmother, whose surname was Kantorowitz, was given, by bureaucratic fiat, an abbreviated version of her name. A typical narrative is that of novelist Irving Wallace: "Born the son of Jewish parents who emigrated from Russia as teen-agers and met and married in the United States, his real name should have been Irving Wallechinsky. But an Ellis Island immigration officer shortened the name. (Years later when Irving's son, David, heard the story, he changed his name to Wallechinsky.)"[89]

To change your name, or to have "had it changed at Ellis Island" as family lore sometimes reported (thus rendering the name change not an act of voluntary cultural disavowal or erasure but a timely accident of fate), was just another step in becoming American. Or so Jews might have thought, until the days of HUAC and the Hollywood blacklist. Then, suddenly, a changed name was a deception, a lie, perhaps even a treasonous act. Here is Senator John Rankin of Mississippi, a member of the House Un-American Activities Committee, naming Jewish names on November 24, 1947. The performers he singles out are all signers of a petition protesting against limits to the right of free association.

One of the names is June Havoc. We found out from the motion-picture almanac that her real name is June Hovick.

Another one was Danny Kaye, and we found out that his real name was David Daniel Kaminsky. . . .

Another one is Eddie Cantor, whose real name is Edward Iskowitz.

There is one who calls himself Edward Robinson. His real name is Emmanuel Goldenberg.

There is another one here who calls himself Melvyn Douglas, whose real name is Melvyn Hesselberg.[90]

The revelation or unmasking of the "real name" made the "stage name" false, an apparently deliberate deception, a potentially criminal attempt to pass. To pass, that is, as not a Jew. To pass as, instead, an American. It was unimaginable, in those days, that a non-Jewish performer might someday *choose* a Jewish name, like Whoopi Goldberg—or that a popular blond television character might bear a name that is soul-sister to Whoopi's—"Dharma Finkelstein."

"I bet you don't even remember my name," an "insecure" Monica is said to have said to President Clinton two days after their first sexual encounter, "to which he answered," according to Andrew Morton, "'What kind of a name is Lewinsky, anyway?' 'Jewish' was her immediate riposte."[91] Leaving aside whether this qualifies as a "riposte," it's of some interest to note that to Bill Clinton of Arkansas, Yale, and Oxford, "Lewinsky" was not a clear and overt signifier of Jewish identity.

If there was anyone (else) in America who had somehow remained unaware of the fact that "Lewinsky" was a Jewish name, enlightenment came quickly within the pages of *Monica's Story*. In a chapter called "My Little Farfel" (Bernard Lewinsky's baby name for his daughter, from the German/Yiddish word for "noodle"), the reader learns about her father's family's flight from the growing power of the Nazis in the Germany of the 1920s, and her mother's father's flight from Lithuania during the Stalinist purges of the '30s. Marcia Vilensky married Bernard Lewinsky in 1969, the family moved to Los Angeles in 1976, and at age six Monica, "a bright, lively Jewish girl," began attending the academically and socially prominent John Thomas Dye School in Bel Air, characterized by Morton as "a quintessential example of WASP culture."[92] We read of Monica's resistance to the strict Sinai Temple (she "wanted to attend a less orthodox synagogue with her schoolfriends")[93] and her desire for a fancy Batmitzvah party ("it is customary in Beverly Hills for Jewish children to have very elaborate Bar/Bat-mitzvah parties at the age of thirteen, usually held in a ballroom or the reception room of the temple with friends and parents' friends: 'like a wedding for one,' recalls Monica").[94]

Morton assures the reader that "Marcia Lewis" was a "pen name," adopted when Monica's mother began to write a monthly column for the *Hollywood Reporter Magazine*. The clear implication is that she hadn't adopted a new name, or disguised her Jewishness, for anything other than professional reasons. (The implication *behind* the implication was that "passing" for personal reasons—or separating herself from her husband's obviously Jewish name—would have been less admirable or understandable.) In the midst of the impeachment hearings, one Hollywood journalist wondered in print whether Lewis would have thought twice about changing her name if she had known her daughter was going to be so famous.[95]

Yet it is the first name, as well as the last, which has become famous. Note that Morton's book was called, simply, *Monica's Story*. The first name, standing alone, reinforced the analogy with that other princess, Di, but it also signaled fame pure and simple. Her "Lewinsky," we might say, was in rhetorical terms "understood," just as her Jewishness, so readable if you had the clues, was, in the lexicon of poststructuralism, "under erasure." "Monica," say the baby-name books, is a name of uncertain origin. It has been linked to words meaning "alone" (from Greek *monos*), "adviser," "pure," and "nun"—all, inevitably, telling and even comical associations in the present case. "Monica" is also a variant spelling for "moniker"[96]—which is how Lewinsky's first name would have been pronounced in the Long Island neighborhoods of my youth, or indeed in some districts of present-day Boston. During the course of the scandal, Monica's "monica" became itself a powerful signifier. Like the Valley-speak terms of *Clueless*, "a Betty" and "a Baldwin" (denoting a sexy, attractive woman or man), "a Monica" appeared to the media to be a type as well as a person. Her Jewishness—so readable to the rest of the world, and to American Jews—would, as we have seen, render her (for history does indeed repeat itself as farce) a suspect for both heroism and treason.

But to Bill Clinton she was an exotic. "What kind of a name is Lewinsky?" he wanted to know. The cluelessness of Bill Clinton, surrounded as he was by numerous male Jewish advisers (Sidney Blumenthal, Robert Rubin, Alan Greenspan, Samuel Berger, James Rubin), may stand as our final, Ahasueran, symptom. Clinton, a relatively sophisticated man who knew not only Jews but Jewish jokes, looked at Monica Lewinsky and both saw and failed to see. His relationship with her, retold by the press and the special prosecutor, re-created the stereotype it did not name ("pushy," "ambitious," "seductive") and dispersed it to the Diaspora and to the world.

Notes

1. John Fleming, "All's Well with the Shakespeare of Standup." *St. Petersburg Times* August 31, 1998, p. 1D.
2. Barbara Hoover, "What's New." *Detroit News* October 10, 1998, p. C1.

3. Mary Leonard, "An Uncertain Second Act for a Scandal Figure." *Boston Globe* September 19, 1998, p. A9.

4. Joseph Lieberman, "Character and Values and Consequences," excerpt from Senate speech, September 3, 1998. *San Diego Union-Tribune* September 13, 1998, p. G5.

5. Lieberman, quoted in Andrew Morton, *Monica's Story* (New York: St. Martin's Press, 1999), p. 260.

6. Jonathan Rosenblum, "Joseph Lieberman, a Jewish Hero." *Jerusalem Post* September 18, 1998, p. 9.

7. David Streitfeld, "Updike at Bay." *Washington Post* December 16, 1998, p. D1.

8. John Updike, "Country Music." *New Yorker* March 8, 1999, p. 25.

9. John Updike, *Bech At Bay* (New York: Knopf, 1998), p. 152.

10. Alex Kuczynski, "Enough about Feminism. Should I Wear Lipstick?" *New York Times* March 25, 1999, sec. 4, p. 4.

11. Leo Rosten, *The Joys of Yiddish* (New York: Pocket Books, 1968), p. 452.

12. Anne Beatts, "What Jews Don't Do Besides, Well, That." *Los Angeles Times* February 8, 1998, p. E8. "Part of the mythology is that the Jewish woman will suck, but she won't swallow," observes Evelyn Torton Beck in her account of the JAP stereotype. Evelyn Torton Beck, "From 'Kike' to 'JAP': How Misogyny, Anti-Semitism, and Racism Construct the 'Jewish American Princess,'" in Fred L. Pincus and Howard J. Ehrlich, eds., *Race and Ethnic Conflict* (Boulder, Colo.: Westview Press, 1994), p. 166.

13. Joseph Hanania, "Playing Princesses, Punishers and Prudes." *New York Times* March 7, 1999, p. 35.

14. Debbie Lukatsky and Sandy Barnett Toback, *Jewish American Princess Handbook* (Arlington Heights, Ill.: Turnbull and Willoughby, 1982), pp. 142–143. Quoted in Sander Gilman, *The Jew's Body* (New York and London: Routledge, 1991), p. 32.

15. Gilman, *The Jew's Body*, p. 32.

16. Beck, "From 'Kike' to 'JAP,'" pp. 163, 167.

17. Morton, *Monica's Story,* pp. 139–140.

18. Caryn James, "Video Shows an Image Sympathetic and Human." *New York Times* February 7, 1999, p. 26.

19. Melinda Henneberger, "Public Hears Lewinsky's Story as Videos Are Played in Senate." *New York Times* February 7, 1999, p. 1.

20. Lynda Gorov, "On Rodeo Drive, Something Familiar about Lewinsky." *Boston Globe* February 7, 1999, p. A27.

21. Michael Prince, quoted in Susan Sachs, "Some Compassion for Lewinsky, but Fleeting Interest by Viewers." *New York Times* February 7, 1999, p. 26.

22. "Lewinsky Confident and Cool in Her Deposition." *New York Times* February 6, 1999, p. A8.

23. Mary Leonard, "What's to Become of Monica?" *Boston Globe* September 19, 1998, p. A9.

24. Michiko Kakutani, "Books of the Times." *New York Times* March 5, 1999, p. B54.

25. Fred Kaplan, "She's Classic Boston." *Boston Globe* March 5, 1999. "She's classic Boston," Andrew Morton told the interviewer, "that sort of shabby chic, roses, a mix of urban and country—she loves that."

26. Susan Ellicott, "The Lady's Not for Spurning." *Times* March 8, 1991, Features section (n.p.).

27. Quoted in Elisabeth Bumiller, "So Famous, Such Clout, She Could Interview Herself." *New York Times* April 21, 1996, sec. 2, p. 1.

28. Ibid.

29. David Lugowski, "Barbara Walters." In *Celebrity Biographies*, Baseline II, 1999. See also *The Complete Directory to Primetime TV Stars* and *Contemporary Theatre, Film and Television*, vol. 6.

30. Barbara Walters, *How to Talk with Practically Anybody about Practically Anything* (1970), quoted in Rebecca Mead, "Thoroughly Modern Monica." *New Yorker* March 15, 1999, p. 29.

31. Ibid., p. 30.

32. Maer Roshan, "'Oh, Barbara! Your Dignity!' Lucianne on the Monica Show." *New York* March 15, 1999, p. 16.

33. Muriel Dobbin, "What Next for Monica?" Scripps Howard News Service, *Pittsburgh Post-Gazette* February 14, 1999, p. A25.

34. Charles Laurence, "'I'll Eat Hillary Alive.'" *Daily Telegraph* (London), March 25, 1999, p. 25.

35. March 3, 1999, ABC *20/20* interview. Cited in Linda Matchan, "Can We Talk? Lewinsky Not Alone in Confiding Intimacies." *Boston Globe* March 5, 1999, p. A1.

36. Roshan, "'Oh, Barbara! Your Dignity!'" p. 16.

37. "Want Lips Like Monica Lewinsky?" *NewsNet5*, March 5, 1999.

38. Charles Spencer, "Pure Televisual Viagra as 'Hot Lips' Melts Snow." Electronic *Telegraph* Friday March 5, 1999 (Issue 1379).

39. Eddie Cantor, *Take My Life*, p. 34, quoted in Lewis A. Erenberg, *Steppin' Out* (Westport, Conn.: Greenwood Press, 1981), p. 196.

40. Sarah Blacher Cohen, "The Unkosher Comediennes." In Cohen, ed., *Jewish Wry* (Bloomington and Indianapolis: Indiana University Press, 1987), p. 112.

41. Ibid., p. 114.

42. Barbara W. Grossman, *Funny Woman: The Life and Times of Fanny Brice* (Bloomington: Indiana University Press, 1991), p. 56.

43. *New York Times* August 2, 1923, p. 10. Grossman, *Funny Women,* p. 146.

44. Brendan Gill, introduction to *The Portable Dorothy Parker* (New York: Penguin Books, 1976), p. xxiii.

45. Grossman, *Funny Woman,* p. 149.

46. *Variety*, December 26, 1928 p. 11. Grossman, *Funny Woman,* p. 178.

47. Cohen, "Unkosher Comediennes," p. 115.

48. Joan Rivers, *The Life and Times of Heidi Abromowitz* (New York: Delacorte Press, 1984), table of contents. Quoted in Cohen, "Unkosher Comediennes," p. 121.

49. Rivers, *Life and Times* p. 10.

50. Bill Bell, "Nothing to Hide: In Her New One-Woman Show, Sandra Bernhard Reveals (Almost) Everything." *Daily News* (New York), November 1, 1998, Sunday "Extra" section, p. 18.

51. Bill Locey, "Queen of Outrageous Comedy Is Heading to Ventura." *Los Angeles Times* May 4, 1995, p. J6.

52. Betty Beard, "Twin Impersonators Bette You'll Get the Joke." *Arizona Republic* February 2, 1996, p. D2.

53. Monique Polak, "A Star is Revealed" (review of Ann Edwards, *Streisand: A Biography*) *Gazette* (Montreal) May 10, 1997, p. J1.

54. Bart Mills, "Model Teen: Alicia Silverstone Is More Clued than in the Roles she Plays on Screen." *Boston Herald* July 21, 1995, p. S3.

55. Emma Forrest, "Alicia in Wonderland." *Guardian* November 14, 1997, Features, p. 2.

56. Arthur Gold and Robert Fizdale, *The Divine Sarah* (New York: Vintage, 1992), p. 13.

57. Ibid., p. 275. The quotation is from her former friend Marie Colombier's thinly veiled novel, *The Memoirs of Sarah Barnum.*

58. Quoted in S. S. Prawer, *Heine's Jewish Comedy* (London, 1983), p. 755. Rachel M. Brownstein, *Tragic Muse: Rachel of the Comédie-Francaise* (New York: Knopf, 1993), p. 87.

59. Brownstein, *Tragic Muse,* p. 82.

60. Christopher Marlowe, *The Jew of Malta.* New Mermaid edition, ed. T. W. Craik (New York: W. W. Norton, 1966), 1, 2, 376, 381–82, 289, 400.

61. Honoré de Balzac, *Le cousin Pons* (Harmondsworth: Penguin, 1968), p. 143.

62. Eve Kosofsky Sedgwick, *Epistemology of the Closet* (Berkeley: University of California Press, 1990), p. 82.

63. David Horovitz, "Latter-day Esther a Boon to Jewish Right." *Irish Times* January 26, 1998, p. 15.

64. Jonathan Rosenblum, "Joseph Lieberman, a Jewish Hero." *Jerusalem Post* September 18, 1998, p. 9.

65. Frank Rich, "The 'New News'" *New York Times* October 28, 1998, p. A29.

66. "Is Lewinsky with the KGB?" *Guandong Writer.* Cited in John Hiscock, A Scandal in the White House: Monica's Rabbi Tells President to Cleanse His Soul." *Daily Telegraph* September 17, 1998, p. 20.

67. Hiscock, "Scandal in the White House," p. 20.

68. Cited in Horovitz, "Latter-day Esther," p. 15.

69. Amelia Richards and Jennifer Baumgardner, "Why Young Feminists Should Support Monica." *Nation* December 20, 1998, p. A13.

70. Ari Hier, "Why David Was Not Impeached." *Denver Post* January 29, 1999, p. F5. Reprinted from *Los Angeles Times.*

71. Yossi Ben-Aharon, "Lewinsky, for example." *Jerusalem Post* October 8, 1998, p. 10.

72. Julian Borger, "At Last, Israelis Can Enjoy Their Own Lewinsky." *Guardian* July 18, 1998, p. 16.

73. Tessa L. Auman, "Denigrating Description." *Jerusalem Post* February 6, 1998, p. 8. Greer Fay Cashman, "Forced Insomnia." *Jerusalem Post* February 3, 1998, p. 12.

74. Morton, *Monica's Story,* pp. 225-26.

75. Associated Press report, "Lewinsky's Rabbi Blasted Clinton for His Behavior." *Star Tribune* (Minneapolis), September 16, 1998, p. 10A.

76. Wendy and Alec Roth, "Inappropriate Rabbinical Behavior." *Jerusalem Post* September 20, 1998, p. 8.

77. Sam Abrams, "People in Glass Houses." *Jerusalem Post* September 18, 1998, p. 8.

78. *Jerusalem Post* staff, "Congressman Objects to Clinton Tapes on Rosh Hashana." *Jerusalem Post* September 22, 1998, p. 1; David L. Greene, "Democrats Question Release of Tape on Rosh Hashana." *Baltimore Sun* September 19, 1998, p. 6A; Tara George, "Jews Rip Rosh Hashanah Tape Release." *Daily News* (New York), September 19, 1998, p. 4.

79. "A Theatrical Repentance" editorial, *Denver Rocky Mountain News* September 13, 1998, p. 2B.

80. New York plastic surgeon Dr. Thomas Loeb. Alen Hall, "Cosmetic Surgeon and Rich Admirer Give Paula Jones a New-Look Nose for Scandal." *Scotsman* July 20, 1998, p. 7.

81. Gilman, *The Jew's Body,* p. 185.

82. Paul Natvig, *Jacques Joseph: Surgical Sculptor* (Philadelphia.: W. B. Saunders, 1982), p. 95. Cited in Gilman, *The Jew's Body,* p. 187.

83. Corky Siemaszko, "TV Questioning Turns Paula Off." *Daily News* (New York), November 18, 1998, p. 18.

84. Howard Rosenberg, "A Nose for News, from Tabs to TV" *Los Angeles Times* August 17, 1998, p. F1.

85. Calev Ben-David, "My Evening with Monica." *Jerusalem Post* March 5, 1999, p. 1. Jon Snow interview with Lewinsky, Channel 4 (Britain).

86. Carole Corbeil, "Monica's Story: Sacrificed on Misogyny's Altar." *Gazette* (Montreal) March 13, 1999, p. J1.

87. Robert Winder, "Rubber-Necking at the Monica Freak Show." *Independent* (London) March 14, 1999, p. 12.

88. Christopher Reed, "However She Handles Herself, Lewinsky's Fame Is Guaranteed." *Irish Times* September 12, 1998, p. 14.

89. Burt A. Folkart, "Irving Wallace: Prolific Writer Reached Billion Readers." *Los Angeles Times* June 30, 1990, p. A38.

90. Neal Gabler, *An Empire of Their Own: How the Jews Invented Hollywood* (New York: Doubleday, 1989), p. 372. From HUAC transcripts.

91. Morton, *Monica's Story,* p. 66.

92. Ibid., p. 22.

93. Ibid., p. 24.

94. Ibid., p. 25.

95. Anne Beatts, "A Proposition for the Sake of Science." *Los Angeles Times* February 15, 1998, p. E10.

96. Jack London, *The Road* (New York: Macmillan, 1907), p. 169: "His 'monica' was Skysail Jack."

11 Monica Dreyfus

Tomasz Kitlinski, Pawel Leszkowicz, and Joe Lockard

A specter haunted more than one continent last year, the specter of Monica Lewinsky. Stories about Monica did not remain stories: they mutated into political facts and explanations. Repetition transformed and localized stories, and another story emerged reinterpreted from the husk of its forebear. We live in an economy of stories where trading has been globalized, an economy where we seek the embodiment of power within these globalized mystery stories interwoven with images.

As the stories swirl, interpretation descends into conspiracism. Conspiracy lives within an empty shell of factuality, a shell that has long been deserted here by the self-sufficient simplicity of sexual attraction as explanation. Desire for an alternate world of cause and effect creates the image of conspiratorial desire, an image tinged with both attraction and loathing. A story of a secret and of desires becomes the story of how political power operates. Minimal factuality feeds maximal interpretive fantasy. Monica Lewinsky's absent presence spread everywhere; she appeared in the most unlikely contexts. According to news reports, in Serbia both pundits and public graffiti repeatedly linked Clinton, the NATO bombing campaign, and sex with Monica. For insult, antiwar graffiti on a Montmartre wall in Paris read "Adolf Clinton Aime Monica Chirac." For pseudoanalysis, in the words of one Russian tabloid, *Moskovsky Komsomolets*, Clinton's support for the Kosovo campaign stemmed from sexual frustration after ending his affair with Lewinsky.[1] "Bill without Monica has become a complete beast," it declared, obviously forgetting Monica's testimony that the president held a telephone discussion of U.S. infantry deployment in Bosnia while receiving fellatio. Even as Clinton's sexual memory, Monica remained an explanatory power.

Lewinsky became part of the fabric of hidden social meanings, as she was ever since first being identified in the media. While American public opinion grappled with the implications of the Lewinsky-Clinton affair, opinion in the Middle East reinterpreted the story in a radically different form. We'll first examine Monica Lewinsky as the "dark stranger" within American media imagery; then look at Clinton-Lewinsky in Middle Eastern public opinion; and finally use that comparison to speak about conspiracism and political analysis.

Domestic Monica

Who is Monica Lewinsky? The American media propagated concatenated images of her: a femme fatale, different from All-American girl power, an abused but exuberant upstart. Behind these images lurks a suspicion: Monica is a stranger. Lewinsky does not belong to the genteel, self-controlled, and rational "us," but rather is an external, alien presence; she constitutes a threat to a known and honored order, a menace to sanitized American politics.

Monica blazes with the energy of exotic sensuality: raven-haired and swarthy, thick-lipped with tons of diabolical lipstick. With her foreign, if not Gypsy mystique, she becomes an ominous Dark Lady. You can almost feel the musk-scented heat of the Bohemienne, glowing, drenched in perspiration. Lewinsky's erotic charm made her the Cosmopolitan Lady, easily suspected as a plotter. Photographs in the *National Examiner* depicted her as a sultry dominatrix clad in a pitch-black dress with a necklace of pearls. Is she not an unmeltable Slav, an ex-Soviet, or a Jew? These elements represent superstitious, backward, and irrational forces devoid of the internal conscience reserved for Protestants.[2] No wonder that, in unison with Puritan prejudice, both the white militias and black extremists pigeonhole Jews, Catholics, and sexual minorities.[3]

With her elemental desire for sex, Lewinsky challenged pure America. The Dark Lady poisoned the purest of the symbolically pure, the White House. She was also out to stain other national sanctuaries and, according to the *National Examiner*, invaded the "prestigious Smithsonian Institute"—the newspaper seems to mean the Institution—to "hunt for men." The *National Examiner* drafted her into a political bestiary as a "sex-crazed vixen," a woman "who would stop at nothing to satisfy her insatiable lust," and who—expanding into zoomorphization—uses sex to "keep her claws" in men. She was alternately a man-eater, a praying mantis, or just an immature nymphomaniac with her "oversexed teen's scheme." Monica's "non-stop stalking" gratified her desire for power; she plotted to "get the supreme representative of the People"; she became one of his "crutches"; and eventually "graduates from his seraglio."[4]

The mystery and menace branded onto Lewinsky perpetuated itself far beyond the tabloids. If not as an aggressor, Monica appeared as a freak in the tradition of attitudes toward strangers as the eccentric, the anomalous, the entertaining. Here belong the photographs by Herb Ritts featured in *Vanity Fair*: wearing a pseudo-*Empire* chiffon dress and exaggerated makeup, she awkwardly smiles and embraces a pink poodle. A bestiarium theme reemerges as the Monica kitsch matches the cheap glitz of the dyed dog. In traditional iconography, a dog stood not necessarily for fidelity, but for dirty sex (as in Netherlandish art). A different, arch-decorous painterly quality dominated Annie Leibovitz's photos of Hillary Clinton for *Vogue*: high-brow, studied, sophisticated, reading (not a newspaper), brooding, doing nothing (not even smiling) in a more expressionless than nonchalant manner. It was a long way from the dowdiness of a "hyper law-student mode, intense and bookish"[5]—Paglia's diagnosis—through the image of a southern belle and into a regal serenity. The preciosity-ridden photos of the 1998 Christmas issue of *Vogue* were coupled with a boring, apologetic text that seems to sing an anthem: "Her Majesty Hillary I deigns to reign with clemency and style." What a contrast to the uneasiness and character of the parvenue assigned to Monica. *Vanity Fair*'s jocular caption verges on the offensive: "We're stuck with her," comments the magazine on her half-wanted presence. Moreover, in a rare practice with style magazines, *Vanity Fair* hastened to publish a trial photo of Monica where she resembles a Stakhanovite (or Hillary before her public bloom): defeminized, if not beefy, with legs clumsily apart, clad in a modest, war-years ensemble, ready to fight, work, and be funny (the caption reads: "Employee of the Year").

For the media then, when Monica was not a beast, she was a comedian. An antidote to the everyday tedium of the mainstream, she fit that category which, as Hannah Arendt wrote, responds to the "demands of society, to be strange and exciting, to develop a certain immediacy of self expression and presentation [of] people whom society has always half denied and half admired."[6] Eccentric, out of place, and gauche, Lewinsky became desirable because she was different, unpredictable, and attractive. In what nearly amounted to a Year of the Affair, she was denied voice, remaining an aphasic statue, a suspicious mute, far from the chirping All-American girl power. Foreign words surrounded Monica's characterization. *New York Times* used *"zaftig"*; *Time* described her as a "Schmosnia" kind of girl;[7] journalistic coverage gave us her father's description of "my little *farfel*";[8] and readers puzzled over the Yiddish anatomy of Monica's *pulkes* to figure out just where family friend and attorney William Ginsburg had kissed her as a baby.

Barbara Walters extricated Monica's own schmooze and in the process overacted her lack of understanding, not only of phone sex, but also of Monica's out-of-control passion and irrationality. On a photograph to advertise the TV interview, a spectral, unpredictable woman in black was juxtaposed with Barbara Walters in pale blue, an image of the reasonable and self-controlled American citizen. The implicit contrast was not hard to interpret: barbarian adventurousness versus propriety. Ambiguous, lush pictorialism versus obvious restraint.

Walters manifested a deeply American faith in the objectivity and dispassion within the media, not only regarding public life, but in its reportage of private life. Through compassionate questioning and public confession, the effects of Monica's sensual intervention into public life might be controlled. If the entanglement of private and public life could not be reversed, then the Walters interview performance suggested that submission to a confessional examination could reveal the simple humanness of history. Nathaniel Hawthorne might have scripted the conflict between evidentiary narrative and human passion embedded in the Walters interview. Monica, ethnic but deethnicized for the immediate appearance, was assimilated into an old American performance: like the mystery surrounding Hester Prynne, this mystery too could be resolved.

Conspiracy theorists have another version of this performance: they insist that the Beast was present, that it remains an animating force, and that it has a specific and exorcisable address. They have found the specter, the secret agent at whom it is necessary to spit repulsively even while repressing and denying their own desires. Their stories focus on an alleged subject and theories of causation which they perpetuate, whether using "right" or "left," "Western" or "Oriental" perspectives. When Hillary Clinton diagnosed the Affair as part and parcel of a "vast right-wing conspiracy," Monica's biographer Andrew Morton wrote that "these are sentiments with which Monica, in the front line of the war, entirely agrees."[9] The "war" consisted of each side identifying, blaming, and denouncing "malicious" and "evil-minded" forces—in the First Lady's version—or the "dysfunctional" and "sociopathic,"—in the anti-Clintonite rhetoric. This moral struggle became an invisible contest for control of a society that was presumed not to recognize its own best interests. It is the patent invisibility of that cultural contest, together with a need for its simplification, that drives conspiracists into social reductionism.

Michael Parenti, one of the leading representatives of left conspiracist thought, argues in *Dirty Truths* that conspiracism and structural analysis are not mutually exclusive dynamics, and that political and corporate elites rely on often-hidden "planning" and "strategizing" as a form of conspiracy to maintain their power.[10] To the contrary, conspiracism distinguishes itself from political critique based on structural analysis in that it privileges one action (even an actual conspiracy) within a multitude of acts that constitute the political environment. Historically, that focus has devolved on individual actors with stereotypical roles designated by gender, sexual, race, ethnic, religious, or class markers. Domestic Monica is such a creature, one who diverts us away from a right-wing deployment of constitutionalism in the service of a rear-guard culture war. Domestic Monica served as a tactical gloss for this culture war, the location of an insidious internal corruption that needed illumination from the righteous.

That reductionist conversion into a social singularity relies on conceptual contractions, not perspectival expansions. The least complicated theory of human subjectivity was that advocated by Kenneth Starr. As Cynthia Ozick observes about his report-narrative, its motivation is one-dimensional. "All the President wants is 'fondling Lewinsky,' all that Monica does is 'seeking Clinton,' and all that Starr says is one obsessive sentence."[11] The riches of personality are reduced here to flat, stock characters. No one in the universe of Starr, including himself, has any inner life, dilemmas, dreams, or hesitations. Everybody is a closed circuit of public function and boredom. Paradoxically, it was due to a cruel investigation that human complexity returned when Clinton was seen as "a suffering individual" (Bobbie Ann Mason in the *New Yorker*).[12]

Open ideologies expose a maze of humanity where good and evil, violence and benevolence, rationality and sensuous bodies mingle. Puritanism, by contrast, assumed a perfectionist vision of humanity and attempted to found a sanitized world. The Puritan interrogators of conspiracy today do not want to admit the openness of personality. Their monological view has been perpetuated not only by the "independent" counsel, but also by seemingly more independent political commentators throughout the political spectra.[13]

Enemy Sluts

The Egyptian city of Port Said celebrated today its spring feast in its special way, as it has manufactured dolls of the personalities they hate. In a huge public celebration they burned dolls of US President Bill Clinton and his alleged mistress Monica Lewinsky as well as burning a doll of Israeli Prime Minister Benjamin Netanyahu. Clinton, who supports Israel, is considered the first US president whose doll has been burned by the people of Port Said, while Netanyahu's doll was burned last year.

—Egyptian news report, April 20, 1998[14]

Conspiracism inevitably attends to the potentialities of ethnic difference. While there was occasional crossover into the U.S. media between the domestic and foreign versions of conspiracism—as in October 1998, when Louis Farrakhan suggested to a clearly startled Tim Russert on *Meet the Press* that Lewinsky was a Zionist agent—the Foreign Monica rarely appeared in the United States. Conspiracy reductionism thrives on local knowledge and commonly finds framing through preexisting social conflicts. For Monica abroad, domestic allegations of vague social conspiracism become the springboard for foreign elaborations of the story.

Writing in February 1998 in *Al-Ahram*, Edward Said endorsed Hillary Clinton's characterization of the Lewinsky and Jones cases as a right-wing conspiracy.[15] Said contextualized this within a nexus of American ultraconservative forces, which he suggested had used the scandals to seize a weakened Clinton as hostage. Said concluded that "temperamentally and ideologically pro-Israel anyway, Clinton is not about to risk a full-scale battle with both the Christian and Jewish right-wing over a mere matter of Palestinian right," and he predicted a diversionary war against Iraq.

Said's analysis couched itself in an analysis of abstract political forces that had gained power by exploiting the fallibility of an individual leader. Clinton became the pawn of a divided yet monolithic bloc of right-wing Christians and their right-wing Zionist allies who were pushing him into a disastrous war scheme both to finish off Iraq and Clinton's own political career. Stripped to its central points, Said's interpretative essay for the Egyptian public offered a conspiracy theory of opportunistic warmongering, or a plan to kill Saddam Hussein and Bill Clinton with the same stone. Building from plausible political observations on American conservatism—for, in hindsight, the entire Clinton-Lewinsky affair was the manufacture of right-wing anti-Clintonism—Said hoisted the affair into the realm of international conspiracies, with Monica Lewinsky in an invisible supporting role.

Said phrased his political reading in moderate and rationalistic language in comparison to many other voices in the Arabic-language press, beginning early last year when the story began breaking. His analysis of the Lewinsky affair situated itself within a lengthy spectrum in Middle Eastern public opinion, ranging from the attribution of an inchoate, opportunistic, and indirect conspiracism to the positing of an orchestrated, targeted, and direct conspiracy against Clinton.

Exemplifying this transition into specificity, a columnist in Syria's flagship government newspaper *Tishrin* asserted that the conspiracy's source lay in diplomatic tactics by the Israeli government: "Netanyahu pre-empted his visit to Washington by fabricating the sexual scandal against President Clinton so as to weaken his position and prevent him from exerting any pressure on him. . . . Zionism has submerged the US administration in crises to force her to relinquish any effective and positive role in the peace process and has started threatening to oust President Clinton."[16] The Arabic-language press noted repeatedly that the *Washington Post* broke the Lewinsky story on January 21, 1998, when Netanyahu was meeting alone with Clinton for difficult talks (cyberjournalist Matt Drudge actually broke the story four days earlier).

Arguments in the Arabic press for an anti-Clinton conspiracy varied between those who believed the scandal was generated in response to an emergent White House opposition to Israeli expansionism and those who viewed Clinton's misfortunes as political cash being converted by the Jews. The degree of unanimity concerning the existence of a conspiracy prompted one writer to observe that Arab analysts differed only on whether Israel's Mossad was behind the conspiracy or whether it was the responsibility of the American Jewish lobby. The former explanation finds currency in Gordon Thomas's recent book, *Gideon's Spies: The Secret History of the Mossad*, which states categorically—without evidence beyond anonymous hearsay and the author's say-so—that Mossad operatives taped Clinton's telephone conversations with Lewinsky and held them as a reserve blackmail weapon to prevent further searches for their White House mole, code-named "Mega."[17] The latter explanation, assigning responsibility to American Jews, reverberated, with one Palestinian report alleging that the stained blue dress came straight out of the Anti-Defamation League's closets. *Babel,* Iraq's leading daily, blamed both Israel and the eponymous Jewish lobby, accusing them of conspiring to install a new and more pliable puppet: "The basic Zionist game plan has become clear . . . that Clinton's scandal was aimed at replacing him with Vice President Al Gore from the Democratic Party who is known for his pro-Zionist stand."[18] Picking up this theme in the January 1999 edition of *Palestine Times*, Erik Paul concluded that the Monica Affair most benefited Al Gore and his silent partners: "The more appropriate title for Operation Desert Fox is Operation Monica. But even Bill Clinton was not able to divert attention for long from his own inevitable impeachment. What is even scarier, is that Vice President Al Gore, a Jew in hiding, will take Clinton's place if the American Senate decides to send him to trial and then Israelis and Zionists can really have a field day. There will be nothing to stop them."[19]

Palestinian journalist Fawaz Turki critiqued this mode of conspiracy journalism, writing of his contempt at seeing "the public debate in the Arab media this time turn to a simple fantasy about Bill Clinton whose removal from office is being engineered by anti-Arab groups operating in tandem with the Jewish lobby in Washington. . . . [We cannot] make our imaginations outfly reality or whimsically reorder that reality to make it conform to some delusional visions we harbor in the recesses of our so-called minds." Turki added with a sour, brutal, and accurate note that "unfortunately, the West Bank does not mean so much to power brokers in this very powerful city that they would mount such an elaborate scheme."[20] News of Monica Lewinsky became a key explanatory device as Arab political comment grappled with its frustration at a lack of palpable progress given Hillary Clinton's favorable reference to Palestinian statehood in January 1998, together with the ever-poorer image generated by Netanyahu's unsuccessful visit to Washington and the Israeli government's stalling tactics against a second-round territorial withdrawal under the Oslo accords.

Major world figures subscribed openly to the prevailing conspiracy theories. Referring to what was at that time still an emerging scandal, Rafik al-Hariri, then-prime minister of Lebanon, informed his parliament that "it's not a joke. The Zionist lobby is twisting the arm of the president of the greatest country in the world." Sheikh Ahmed Yassin, the spiritual leader of Hamas, which represents a quarter to a third of Palestinian opinion, concurred: "The Zionist lobby creates disasters for anyone who may cause it problems. Its aim is to prevent the U.S. president from exerting pressure on Israel. So they pushed him into a sex trap."[21] Farouk al-Shaara, Syria's foreign minister, stated that Lewinsky was a Mossad agent.[22] And so, unable to escape the clutches of a Zionist oralist, poor Bubba found himself a sex slave to a Jewish dominatrix.

In an editorial article, Brigadier General Khaled al-Musmar of the Palestine National Authority and a secular opponent of Hamas, echoed the same opinion, that Clinton had been bludgeoned into submission by "the power which was clearly revealed in the Zionist American Congress which led to the terrorizing of the American President and the administration, through threats of sex and morals scandals which are disseminated by the obedient media in the US."[23] Other senior Palestinian officials, like Bassam Abu Sharif, voiced similar notions.

Discourse of this sort makes intercommunal conflict the refracting lens that separates the narrative elements of this story in order to facilitate its retelling. Power—its presence, or the reasons for its absence—becomes the inevitable moral of the political storyteller, and sex becomes a cynical act of power. In such interpretive retellings, Clinton's sexuality represents the point of his subversion and control, the point at which political puppetry begins. This mode of historical explanation represents gains and losses through the erotic temptation of vulnerable men. It is hardly a fresh source of explanation in Middle Eastern politics. For example, in his autobiographical account and history of the 1952 Free Officers Revolt, *Revolt on the Nile* (1957), Anwar Sadat wrote that the two German officers he hid in 1943 "were betrayed by two amiable young Jewish women with whom they were found dead drunk," leading to his own arrest the next day for collaboration with the Nazis. After Camp David, when Sadat had become a respectable Nobelist and published an updated statesman's autobiography, *In Search of Identity* (1978), this traitorous pair had become deethnicized "dancers."[24]

Betrayal by an enemy slut, an everlasting version of Samson and Delilah, provides the basis for a masculinist conversion of sexual desire into a heroic and justifiable failure. The woman who gave too much pleasure to be resisted, and whose body is available, emerges in the end with a secret political agenda. The evil of her political masters finds a mirror in the evil of her body. Monica Lewinsky, in this antagonistic understanding, was no more than an enemy slut serving corruption on her knees. Bill Clinton was doomed from the moment he capitulated to Monica's enticements, because virtue, whether lapsed or absent, was his only defense against a far more profound and ancient corruption than his own.

On the opposite side, within Israel's theofascist settler movement, commentators heroicized Lewinsky's sexuality through biblicization. Given the weakening of the American presidency and a belief that Clinton was now unable to push for greater territorial concessions, right-wing Israelis compared Lewinsky to Queen Esther, the heroine of Purim who enchanted Persia's King Ahasuerus and prevented his wicked minister, Haman, from destroying the Jewish people. Salvation might arrive in regrettable form, but preservation of the Land of Israel was the greatest good.[25] Using a double entendre, more secular Israelis joked that this news was only more evidence that Clinton would never turn his back on the Jewish people. One mainstream peace group, rather pitifully, erected billboards with a Hebrew message, "We Support You, Friend," echoing Clinton's funeral speech for Rabin,

"Shalom, Friend." Whereas Israel's right-wing annexationists rejoiced, its enfeebled peace camp lamented that secret sex meant an end to secret pressures. Israeli politics have pursued a lengthy decline into antirationalism; moreover, the moralisms upon which religious fundamentalism thrives have little personal meaning for Netanyahu, whose intraparty rivals some years ago leaked a videotape of Bibi frolicking in bed with his mistress. With a thirty-plus-year occupation that can be justified only by biblicism, ethnic supremacism, and cumulative national psychic and budgetary investment, the political mysticism that generates susceptibility to conspiracism beshrouds Israel no less than its neighbors.

By attributing significance to Lewinsky as a locus of sex, ethnicity, and political power, both Palestinians and Israelis acknowledged the ascendancy of the U.S. presidency in the peace process, irrespective of whether they were antagonistic or welcoming toward that American presence and its outcomes. It is precisely this political assumption of American centrality that needs to be challenged. The Oval Office is not what determines the everyday lives of Israelis in the Mahane Yehuda market or Palestinians sitting unemployed at the Gaza Beach camp, nor does sex in the same Oval Office. Absent concrete evidence to the contrary, sexual conspiracism is a diversion into political antirationalism. A preoccupation with social absences and narrative lacunae, critical to Said's theory of contrapuntal analysis, emerges as another form of conspiracy theory. The evidentiary search for marginalized voices rendered invisible becomes conspiracism's search for an invisible and controlling marginality. And an absence of an identifiable central intelligence becomes irrefutable evidence of its presence.

Rendering Invisibility

But aren't there reasonable grounds for suspicion? Given that the Mubarak and Netanyahu governments resulted from successful assassination conspiracies against Sadat and Rabin, and that Assad and Hussein's totalitarian governments in Syria and Iraq emerged from successful politico-military conspiracies, a reasonable observer in the Middle East might easily believe conspiracy to be a feature of normal political life. Further, given that human nature functions with rough equivalence throughout human societies, why should we exempt the United States from the same form of political analysis? The doors onto the search for formative conspiracies open wide.

Conspiracy obsessions are the end-time of the politics of reason, a nebulous world where explanations are the abject servants of faith. Conspiracism begins in the realm of empirical reasoning and then moves on to credit the unsubstantiated ends in a dark zone of exponentially expanded interconnections and fantasized possibilities. It is a form of suppositional faith that legitimates preconceptions, often preconceptions which arrive with substantial evidence and truth. To assert that major business interests and the Central Intelligence Agency have played far too large a role in U.S. policy decisions is one class of argument; to assert that Big Business and state security operatives conspired to assassinate Kennedy is quite another class of argument. The availability and nonavailability of positive evidence separates the arguments. Any leap between the two relies on a faith that an invisible hand guides history, a faith that remains immaterialist despite its attempt to substantiate itself in a materialist history. That faith, in turn, encapsulates and expresses a visceral alienation, a reaction to the foreignness that Monica the Dark Lady embodies. Conspiracism is the unending pursuit of satanic animation to the world.

Why did Edward Said, in his profound sophistication, fall victim to a mild version of Monica conspiracism by characterizing it as political entrapment of Clinton? In discussing contrapuntal reading, Said writes in *Culture and Imperialism* that, given a historiographically invisible history of anticolonial resistance and the absorption of imperial facticity within cultural production, "we must therefore read the great canonical texts, and perhaps the entire archive of modern and premodern European and American culture, with an effort to draw out, extend, give emphasis and voice to what is silent or marginally present."[26] Thus, references to Australia in *David Copperfield* and India in *Jane Eyre* become starting points for intellectual explorations of power and the appropriations of imperialism. Or, as Said continues, "in reading a text, one must open it out both to what went into it and to what its author excluded." This critical approach and its methodologies have generated a massive wave of cultural reinterpretation characterized by a new engagement with the subjects of narrative exclusion, or those who have been made invisible. It is one of the most ethical developments in cultural criticism, and one in whose practice we share.

The search for invisible subjects within ruling narratives or resistant discourses made invisible through colonialism, however, can be confused with a hypothesization of power's invisibility. Throughout its varieties, power remains manifestly visible, even if not transparent; indeed, power cannot ultimately instance itself without visibility. By confusing the invisibility of overruled subjects (Said's original sense) with invisible forces, channels, or means of rule (Said's error), the emancipatory possibilities of counterreading invert themselves:

conspiracism now cannibalizes reason. Said and other participants in Monica Conspiracism seized on the private moments of two lives, revealed in the midst of a national panic attack over presidential sexuality orchestrated by right-wing political forces, to reinterpret personal acts as aiding realizations of their political fears or visions. If Monica was an unconscious subject, under the terms of a relatively rational Saidian contrapuntal reading, her appearance might be believed to have created propitious circumstances for instigation of a major diversionary war. For less rational contrapuntal readings, those with looser consonance with facticity or plausibility, Monica was a conscious and evil agent seeking control of U.S. policy as much as of Clinton's dick.

Monica Lewinsky, in her humanity, became the invisible subject.

Imagining Monica Dreyfus

The idea of the subject underlying conspiracy theories is that of identity reduced to strict belonging to one and only one grouping. It was in the context of the Dreyfus Affair that Marcel Proust analyzed the Hamletian dilemma as having changed into "to be or not to be one of them . . . the question is not as for Hamlet, to be or not to be, but to belong or not to belong."[27] Proust's diagnosis of the change of being [*être*] into being one of them, belonging [*en être*], was developed by Hannah Arendt and Julia Kristeva.[28] Although it was formulated around the time of the Dreyfus Affair, where Proust was not only a witness, but also a participant, it defines the human condition of today. The logic of belonging forces us into the strict and unchangeable membership of a nation, gender, profession, sexual preference, of a "plot." What matters is admittance to a clan, an alliance that brings status, image, and power over opinion.[29] This is how we lose ourselves in the social, this omnivorous and reductive Blob, against which Arendt warned,[30] and where—to return to Hegel and Kojève—a dialectic of master and servant rules. Closing ourselves off from inner life, we enter a game of capital and spectacle and a political order where politics is devalued and individuality is not only neglected, but absent.

Conspiracy theories plunge their adherents into a restricted realm of the social, as opposed to a public sphere of freedom that would cherish singularity. Conspiracism glorifies sameness—the same as "us," the ones who belong among our identity—and lives transfixed by fear, opposition, and repulsion for the different. Conspiracists look with elation toward social connections between the "ours," while the names of enemies, both past and present, domestically and worldwide, are filed away. Hospitality for the fellow-guests of this world is out of the question for conspiracists. Theirs is a style of insider knowledge, social bonding, exclusivist cultivation of togetherness, and the esprit de corps of followers. Conspiracy adherents stress the feelings of menace, embattlement, victimization, and demand the loathing of and resistance to any repugnant sect or to "those people." To fight the "them," theorists and practitioners of conspiricism cannot but follow closely the alleged strategies of their putative rivals. Conspiracism employs wars of words, moratoria on outsiders, and a "prosecutorial culture" (Arthur M. Schlesinger, Jr., apropos the Lewinsky Affair).[31]

With speed and zeal, conspiracism reproduces, by both budding and cross-fertilization, a Hegelian co-optation. Conspiracists enter a love-hate relationship and depend on one another in an ideology that needs and cannot survive the death of the enemy. There can never be one without the other. They absorb tricks in the detection and interpretation of the other and are unable to break out of encircling suspicions. The only objective of a conspiracist is to outmaneuver another conspiracist who turns out to be his double. Only the Manichean vision of the good "us" and the evil "them" is duly reversed. Both sides believe that they are acting in good faith and to make barbarians more similar to the "us." To discover and announce the traces of conspiracy becomes an act of public benefit, which joins such disparate and multidirectionally opposed figures as Hillary Clinton, Edward Said, Ahmed Yassin, and Michael Parenti.

Conspiracies are then hatched to oppose and imitate conspiracies, spiraling ever downward toward the level of Stalinism and the Doctors Plot. An extreme semiotics emerges: each and every political development is taken as a sign of the conspiracy. Nothing remains insignificant. Conspiracists desperately need one another for traces, exhibits, leaks, testimonies, or files of *eminences grises* whom they despise and adore. Theirs is a semiotics akin to such critical techniques as close reading, pla(y)giarism, intertextuality, and Derridean deconstruction, except that their use of these techniques is crude, uncreative, and epigonic. Their analysis of a body of evidence centers on conspiracist readings, as if all roads toward understanding led only to this one possibility. Their social personality approaches that of Dostoevski's Underground Man, living in a polarized consciousness where politics mean either "a hero or dirt" and where the truest revelations would speak to a profoundly unpalatable self.[32]

A conspiracist as omniscient ideologue identifies, reveals, or denounces the omnipotent villain. The detective-like objective is to exalt, enlarge, and humiliate the allegedly all-empowered agents who can be proven to weave webs everywhere in macro- and micropower, who can change the world into Benthamite/Foucauldian panopticon and use the space for military purposes, and who can take hostage psyches and the collective imaginary. History and individual fate are to serve the One powerholder. He is the exclusive history maker, a cruel world paterfamilias. Everyday reality fills with imperialist traps, ambushes, and torture machines to make us into docile bodies. Such a vision not only characterizes extreme-right thinking, but is also representative of Foucault, Chomsky, Edward Herman, Zygmunt Bauman, and Said's "art of suspicions" and sociologies of invisiblized knowledge.[33]

Whether conspiracism advocates "reasonable" sexual control or "liberatory" exposure, it is equally obsessed with *Kabale und Liebe* as they dwell on sex, erotic stereotypes, lovers spurned, and frustrations. In the view of conspiracists, perversions do not belong to their own territory, but to the foreign; hence the ascription of raving sensuality to Monica. A point of comparison here would lie in the medical discourse of von Krafft-Ebing, who "diagnoses" an "abnormally intensified sensuality"[34] in the others, in the Jews, as Sander Gilman points out in his extraordinary analyses.

At the same time, conspiracy theories present themselves as those that cannot be more rational and empirically proven since their aim is to disclose "things as they are." Their mutual base is to be the chain of cause-effect, closed logic, and exposure of the tyranny of conventional logic, all of which sustain an illegitimate will to power. Their language of obviousness ("everyone knows that") leads to apparently commonsensical demands ("this is the only way for betterment") which are trapped in a militaristic thinking that divides the world into villains and good people ("this is their dirty war and our holy one").

In the canons of conspiracism, stories and images of the illuminati and the counter-enlightened are used to spark intellectual and emotional militancy, which can make very different ideologies strange bedfellows and comrades-in-arms. With a nose for perverse strangers, the voice of an emancipatory intelligentsia agitates for an end to all plots. But simultaneously, the erotic imaginary and seemingly rational framework of conspiracy theorists of different breeds quench a thirst for at least a little "perversity" and logic alike in the political spectacle. Thus the social phantasmagoria continues.

With the persona of a sharer of secrets and a gossipy friendship with Linda Tripp, Monica Lewinsky is not another Dreyfus. Yet like Dreyfus in fin-de-siècle France, if ethnicity was nominally irrelevant to public issues of fact, it remained inescapably formative to Lewinsky's media representation. Conspiracism inevitably attends on the potentialities of ethnic difference, imaginary like any imagined communities and their menace. The thinking style of conspiracism makes only kith and kin matter, while the distant and strange are a little less human or eternal enemies. Instead of human ethos, ethnos becomes the leitmotif in the ever-multiplying image-ridden stories.

The Dreyfus case instanced a failure of French modernity to come to terms with a changing internal ethnos that contradicted purist understandings of national identity, a failure that France continues to repeat at this turn-of-the-century in relation to its citizens of North African origin, newer "dark strangers." Representations of the Domestic Monica captured an American engagement with its own increasingly multiethnic self-identification. The contrasted nature of this identificational question was immediately apparent at the House Judiciary Committee hearings: an almost all-male and all-white Republican majority faced a vociferous Democratic minority composed of blacks, women, a Jewish homosexual, and a couple of white men. A new-old heterogeneity faced an older political hegemony: a once-foundational sense of the American political nation has been under prolonged challenge, and the Domestic Monica incorporates suspicions over the cultural outcome. Monica, simultaneously assimilated and yet alien to an older order, became a harbinger of its worrisome future.

At the end of the nineteenth century, the Panama and Dreyfus Affairs were presented as part of the threat of an international conspiracy in both rational and erotic terms, with Proust on one or Barrès on the other extreme. As the twentieth century began with sentencing Captain Dreyfus to Devil's Island, it ended with desecrating or adulating the image of Monica in the corners of the globe, conspiratorially blaming her for all manner of evils or turning her into a heroine. The image of Dreyfus the spy continues to inform attitudes towards "the strange, the exotic, the dangerous,"[35] quoting Arendt's analysis of French attitudes to the Jews at the turn of the century. When media insinuate or bluntly portray Lewinsky as a sexual curio of the rootless internationalist tribe, the logic of sadomasochism toward the not "one of us," the not "belonging in here," starts its game.

Yet within the public workings provoked by the Dreyfus Affair, Arendt reveals a parallelism between the tricks of opposing camps, a "disturbing similarity between Dreyfusards and Anti-Dreyfusards." Both were in constant search and mobilization against secret centers of power: "a secret Judah and a secret Rome." As Arendt points out, the anti-Dreyfusards had a monopoly on neither nationalism nor nihilism. Many of French socialists and Dreyfusards spoke in the same idiom. Supporters of Dreyfus would easily have agreed with the editorial opinion of the Catholic journal *La Croix* that "it is no longer a question whether Dreyfus is innocent or guilty, but only of who will win, the friends of the army or its foes."[36] The culture war that swirled about Dreyfus, rather than any facticity within the accusations against him, rendered a symbol of national passion into an invisible human. The fight over the Captain provided an opportunity for winning and hardening opinion, settling scores, and closing off dialogue. A war of stereotyped pictures, a clash of opposed contrapuntal stories, and a facile compartmentalization were practiced. Instead of a civil society, *Gemeinschaft*-spirited cliques and a siege mentality of political encirclements monopolized the scene. "Belonging" was the battle cry. The nationalist Maurice Barrès portrayed Zola, in his role as a leading Dreyfusard and author of the open letter *J'accuse*, as one of the uprooted aliens: "It is fatal: deep inside—through his roots—he is not French because his father and a series of his ancestors are Venetian—he thinks differently from us."

There were suspicions that a romance of a high-standing official of France with a woman spy for Germany was at the genesis of the Dreyfus Affair. A series of cover-ups followed, first with the accusation of the Jewish officer, followed by accusations against Esterhazy (of Hungarian origin). The arch-serious *Magazine littéraire* repeated this hypothesis of an *écran fumé* in an issue marking the centenary of *J'accuse*. Both affairs, Dreyfus and Lewinsky, uncovered the forces of extremism, of refusal to compromise, of commitment to a belonging based in republican nationalism. Instead of fostering democracy as an everyday way of living in social polyphony, conspiracy theories decoyed public argument away from communication and negotiation. An intolerant reduction to sameness and national identity protectionism usurped the political arena. Obsessions with sexuality, national honor, and false public ethicism were driving forces in both affairs. The quality of identification with and defense of those fallen from grace, the accused and the excluded, was equally lacking in each affair.

In the unforgiving triangle of world police (Clintonites), sex police (anti-Clintonites who would otherwise be world police), and authoritarian police nations (Saddam Hussein, Slobodan Milosevic) whose revolution generates continual crises, we forget ourselves amid conspiracy theories. But crisis does not stop at destruction; it can be creative, promising, and rewarding. Declines bring renovation, revival, and new life. Where there are ordeals, apocalypse, revivals—in creative crisis—there is still hope. When biblical prophets accuse Jerusalem of adultery and prostitution (Joycean Whorusalamin), they hasten to add that the city of sin will be saved. Augustine, too, knew the whirls of evil and realized that one does not reach the City of God without a spell in Babylon. These valorizations of crisis are not remembered by the pundits of American politics who are so fond of invoking both the prophets and the Founding Fathers; such moralists disregard these same earlier visions of the perplexity of human nature, of humanity in perpetual crisis. It is critical that politics and subjectivities become more elastic, heterogeneous, and inclusivist. Politics based on frozen identity crystallizations, like the politics of conspiracism, contradict open and tolerant comprehensions.

The political encompasses both rationality and sensuousness; it is a cross between ideas and body. It must not be empty discourse, but a living experience that does not rule out any sphere of humanity or emerge as a sanitized set of rules and maxims. Perhaps the Lewinsky Affair and Clinton's "fall" will be of ultimate help in achieving this social realization. A new civic self-awareness that emphasizes sexual tolerance as critical for social well-being—one that refuses imputations of foreignness, hidden agendas, and conspiracy, recognizing these as the spectral darkness of Roger Chillingsworth—can help us arrive at a humane world where "the capital A might have been thought to mean Admirable."[37]

This essay, slightly altered in its present version, originally appeared in *Bad Subjects,* no. 44 (April 1999). It is reprinted here with permission of the authors.

Notes

1. After the story first appeared, linkage of Clinton's sex life to control over U.S. foreign policy became a regular feature of Russian and European political comment. One of the high points occurred in December 1998, when the Russian parliament passed a resolution appealing to Monica Lewinsky to help stop U.S. bombing attacks on Iraq. The motion read, in part, "The State Duma appeals to Ms. Lewinsky to undertake corresponding measures to restrain the emotions of Bill Clinton." "Russia May Ask Lewinsky for Help," Associated Press, December 17, 1998.
2. The social centrality of Puritan conscience that we posit here is informed by Andrew Delbanco, *The Death of Satan: How Americans Have Lost the Sense of Evil* (New York: Farrar, Straus and Giroux, 1995), pp. 32–40.
3. On the ideology and practice of the militia, see Kenneth S. Stern, *A Force upon the Plain: The American Militia Movement and the Politics of Hate* (New York: Simon and Schuster, 1996). On the hatred of the "other" in the language of Khallid Abdul Muhammad, see Peter Noel, "One-Man March," *New Yorker,* September 7, 1998, pp. 20–27.
4. "Monica: A Diary of Lust," *National Examiner,* October 13, 1998, pp. 22–23.

5. Camille Paglia, "Kind of a Bitch: Why I Like Hillary Clinton," in *Vamps & Tramps: New Essays* (New York: Viking, 1994), p. 177.

6. Hannah Arendt, *Antisemitism: Part One of the Origins of Totalitarianism* (San Diego: Harcourt Brace, 1979), p. 67.

7. Margaret Carlson, "The Story within the Story," *Time*, March 8, 1999.

8. Andrew Morton, *Monica's Story* (New York: St. Martin's Press, 1999), p. 19. The phrase also provides the title for chapter 1.

9. Ibid., p. 204.

10. Michael Parenti, *Dirty Truths: Reflections on Politics, Media, Ideology, Conspiracy, Ethnic Life and Class Power* (San Francisco: City Lights Books, 1996).

11. Cynthia Ozick, *New Yorker*, October 12, 1998, p. 32.

12. Bobbie Ann Mason, ibid., p. 33.

13. See Richard Morin and David S. Broder, "Worries about Nation's Morals Test a Reluctance to Judge," in *The Starr Report: The Findings of Independent Counsel Kenneth W. Starr on President Clinton and the Lewinsky Affair, with Analysis by the Staff of The Washington Post* (New York: Public Affairs, 1998), p. XLIX. Morin and Broder's text, whose title matches the clumsiness of Starr's subtitles, concludes with citation of a representative citizen's complaint that "there are very few values left." The authors include homosexuality among "threatening" social trends. Although Morin and Broder attempt to hide their moralistic tone behind the ciphers of polling, they return to a nineteenth-century concept of sexual minority.

14. "Port Said Residents Burn Likenesses of Hated People," ArabicNews.com report, March 20, 1998.

15. Edward Said, "Power Vacuum, War Machine," *Al-Ahram*, February 6–9, 1998.

16. Mohammed Khair al-Wadi, "Netanyahu Visit and Flagrant Facts," *Tishrin*, January 26, 1998. In a similar vein, Abdulmun'em Ebrahim, managing editor of Bahrain's semi-official *Akhbar al-Khalij*, wrote: "Whenever the Zionist lobby wants to put pressure on the American President Bill Clinton, it activates the Paula Jones issue. . . . We should not be surprised to know that this 'Paula' is a Jew who cares about one thing only: winning $2,000,000 in compensation for her 'lost dignity'!" (January 21, 1998). In Morocco's opposition *Al-Alam*, Abdeljebbar Shimi asserted that "U.S. women have launched one of the ugliest kinds of terrorism against men under the banner of 'sexual harassment'" and suggested that "the entire story might be the work of the Israeli lobby targeting the most powerful man in the world. I would not be surprised to see Chairman Yasser Arafat returning from his U.S. trip with no results after the Zionist lobby used the 'sexual harassment card'" (January 24, 1998). Against this school of conspiracist interpretation in the media, Taher Udwan, editor-in-chief of Jordan's *Al-Arab al-*

Yawm, wrote: "Those Arabs who want to turn a love affair into a political struggle in order to justify their political, military and economic failure and who want to say that a woman can turn their destiny upside down are silly and can only be believed by those who lost their strength and dignity and have nothing left but to invent stories and unhappy coincidences. I don't believe that the Middle East has anything to do with the U.S. president's love affairs" (January, 26, 1998).

Reporting these and other reactions to the then-breaking Clinton-Lewinsky story in the world and Arabic-language press, the United States Information Agency stated that a majority of Arabic-language media opined that the affair emerged from a Zionist plot. "Daily Digest: Foreign Media Reaction," USIA Office of Research, Washington, D.C., January 26, 1998. *The Hindu's* Bahrain correspondent, Kesava Menon, concurs with this estimate on the prevalence of Lewinsky-Zionist conspiracy theories "even [in] responsible sections of the media in Arab countries" ("West Asian View of l'Affaire Clinton," *The Hindu*, January 27, 1998, p. 16). Susan Taylor Martin reports that the Lewinsky-Zionist plot allegation continued to characterize public discussion in Syria later that year in "It's an Interesting Time to Be in Syria," *St. Petersburg Times*, October 13, 1998.

17. Gordon Thomas, *Gideon's Spies: The Secret History of the Mossad* (New York: St. Martin's Press, 1999).

18. *Babel*, August 18, 1998.

19. *Palestine Times* [http://www.ptimes.com/].

20. Fawaz Turki, "Arab Conspiracy Theorists Run Amok," *Arab News*, February 12, 1998.

21. Al-Hariri and Yassin quotes: untitled Reuters report, January 23, 1998. Also David Landau, "Divine Act or Coincidence? Israelis Ponder Sex Scandal," Jewish Telegraphic Agency, January 26, 1998. Two regional English-language newspapers provided similar stories. In an editorial entitled "Will Clinton Be Impeached?" the conservative *Teheran Times* began: "The melodrama, for which the script was written by top Zionists, has come to an end. Leading role was played by a Jewish Monica Lewinsky. President Bill Clinton was forced to play the role of a villain. But Clinton's crime was that he simply put pressure on the Zionist regime" (August 19, 1998). Earlier in the year, the *Syria Times* printed a similar editorial opinion (quoted in *Middle East Times*, February 1, 1998).

22. Akiva Eldar, "Now It's Bibi's Turn to Be Taken Care Of," *Ha'aretz*, August 24, 1998. Such assertions arise in the context of a predisposition within Syria's political leadership to accept Jewish conspiracy theories. Most notably, defense minister Mustafa Tlass published *The Matza of Zion* (Damascus: Dar Talas, 1988), a history of the Damascus Trial of 1840 which concludes that Jews use non-Jewish blood for ritual purposes.

23. *Filistin al-Yaum*, August 21, 1997.

24. Anwar Sadat, *Revolt on the Nile* (New York: J. Day Co., 1957), pp. 55–56 , and *In Search of Identity: An Autobiography* (New York: Harper and Row, 1978), p. 34.

25. Lewinsky herself participated in using ethnic history for exaggerated self-heroiza- tion. In Morton's biography, she identifies with Anne Frank because she "live[ed] in constant fear" of prosecutor Kenneth Starr (198) and reports that anti-Nazi parachutist Hannah Senesh served as a role model while enduring the legal process (pp. 26–27, 180).

26. Edward Said, *Culture and Imperialism* (New York: Knopf, 1993), p. 66.

27. Marcel Proust, *Sodom and Gomorrah,* vol. 4 of *In Search of Lost Time,* translated by C. K. Scott Moncrieff and Terence Kilmartin, revised by D. J. Enright (New York: Modern Library, 1999), p. 572. Proust's formulation is: "La question n'est pas comme pour Ham- let d'être ou ne pas être, mais d'en être ou de ne pas en être."

28. Arendt, *Antisemitism,* p. 84; Julia Kristeva, *Le temps sensible: Proust et l'expérience lit- téraire* (Paris: Gallimard, 1994), p. 203.

29. For a developed discussion of the sadomasochism of social life and the Dreyfus Af- fair, see Kristeva, *Le temps sensible,* ibid., pp. 178–203.

30. See further Hanna Fenichel Pitkin, *The Attack of the Blob: Hannah Arendt's Concept of the Social* (Chicago: University of Chicago Press, 1998).

31. Arthur Schlesinger, Jr., "How History Will Judge Him," *Time,* February 22, 1999, p. 1.

32. Fyodor Dostoevsky, *Notes from Underground* (New York: W. W. Norton, 1989), p. 39.

33. Chip Berlet explores the infiltration of political conspiracism from a right-wing po- litical phenomenon into U.S. left-wing politics and rhetoric in a dated but still excel- lent 1991 study. See Berlet, *Right Woos Left* (Cambridge, Mass.: Political Research Asso- ciates, 1991). Berlet emphasizes the particular utility of Jews and Zionism in these the- orizations.

34. Sander Gilman, *Jewish Self-Hatred: Anti-Semitism and the Hidden Language of the Jews* (Baltimore: Johns Hopkins University Press, 1986), p. 289.

35. Arendt, *Antisemitism,* p. 82.

36. Ibid., pp. 112–113.

37. Nathaniel Hawthorne, *The Scarlet Letter* (New York: Signet Classic, 1999), p. 249.

Part 4

FEMINISM AND SEXUAL POLITICS

12 The President's Penis

Entertaining Sex and Power

Catharine Lumby

In an elegant essay titled "My Father's Penis," feminist author Nancy Miller recalls watching her father pottering around the kitchen when she was a child, his drawstring pajamas slightly agape. She writes:

This almost gap never failed to catch my eye. It seemed to me as I watched him cheerfully rescue the burning toast and pass from room to room in a slow motion of characteristic aimlessness . . . that behind the flap lay something important: dark, maybe verging on purple, probably soft and floppy.[1]

Forty years after the scene of these memories, Miller finds herself once again confronted by her father's penis. Her father, now stricken with Parkinson's disease, requires her help to bathe and urinate, a situation which leads her to reflect on the relationship between the phallus and the organ it represents. At first, she concludes that touching her father's penis has destroyed its mystique, writing that, while the phallus symbolizes male power ("the way my father could terrify me when I was growing up"), the penis is simply a biological accident. Months later, as her father lays dying, Miller is no longer sure it's so easy to separate symbolic power from its human form:

Had my father still been able to read, I would never have written about "the penis." By going public with the details of domestic arrangements on Riverside Drive, I was flying in the face of the parental injunction not to "tell" that had haunted my adolescence and continued well into my adult years.[2]

Miller's essay points to the complicated relationship between power and the way individuals embody it. Her father's penis is many things to her: a source of mystery, difference, sexuality, awe, physical illness, and frustration. There is, she suggests, an undeniable connection between male power and the penis, but it's not straightforward. It's a relationship that causes men, as well as women, confusion and even despair.

In the closing years of the twentieth century, U.S. citizens have been getting uncomfortably close to their president's penis. Of course, everyone knows the president has a penis—it's an essential criterion for the job, after all—but no one wants to think about it. The presidency is a highly symbolic office. The incumbent is expected to display superhuman levels of self-control, reliability, and good judgment, none of them traits normally associated with the male organ. The United States likes its presidents to have balls, but a penis is different. A penis can only get in the way of the national interest.

In traditional feminist terms, the phallus is the classic metaphor for male power. But it's important to remember that it's just that—a symbol. In human terms, the mantle of power comes with built-in anxieties—it isn't ready-to-wear and there's always someone claiming they fit the mantle better. If the phallus is a symbol, then the penis is its real life corollary. And penises are notoriously unreliable. They shrink in cold water, droop after too much alcohol and, sometimes, just want a night or two to themselves. They're also unpredictable, unreasonable, and faithless—though how their owners respond to these incitements and frustrations varies widely.

Clinton is not, of course, alone in his struggle to contain damage from the sex scandals that have dogged his career. Around the Western world, voters are demanding increasingly high ethical standards from politicians, judges, bureaucrats, and other high-ranking public servants. Royal commissions, Senate and congressional inquiries, and independent bodies set up to investigate corruption have all helped to highlight impropriety and raise public expectations about the conduct of elected and appointed public figures. The growth of news programs and products has also played a key role in encouraging the appetite for information about those in public office.

The voting public has come a long way since the United States, and the rest of the Western world, watched open-mouthed as the Watergate affair unraveled, taking a president with it. In 1972, it still seemed inconceivable to many voters that someone trusted with the highest office in the United States would cynically lie to his people. Today, we expect our politicians to lie. Ironically, at a time when it's harder than ever for politicians to escape public scrutiny, public confidence in politicians across the Western world is sinking[3]—and the media's key role in promoting this disillusionment means that journalists and media producers are commonly regarded with equal disdain.

In conventional terms, investigative reporting of the kind that brought down President Richard Nixon sits at the pinnacle of quality journalism. At its best, it requires back-breaking research, fact checking, lateral thinking, and constant monitoring to avoid litigation by people whose career and finances are at stake. Tabloid investigations into the private lives of public figures are conversely seen as the lowest form of journalism. Yet, increasingly, the kinds of issues that bring political leaders and other public authority figures, such as judges or doctors, into disrepute are very similar to the issues which have always been canvassed by the tabloid media. Matters that would have once more than likely stayed private—affairs with a secretary, drug abuse, sex with a young boy, or incidents of domestic violence—are now routinely exposed in public inquiries and canvassed in mainstream media outlets as well as the more traditionally tabloid news products.

This "tabloidization" of the mainstream media has been frequently decried by both conservative and liberal commentators for polluting the wellspring of democracy by distracting viewers from "real" political issues and distorting the purpose of public communication. As Bruce Robbins notes in his introduction to *The Phantom Public Sphere*: "The list of writings that announce the decline, degradation, crisis, or extinction of the public is long and steadily expanding. Publicness, we are told again and again and again, is a quality that we once had but have now lost, and that we must somehow retrieve."[4] What both popular and scholarly critics of the media often overlook, however, is the relationship between the growing media focus on the private lives of public figures and the politicization of issues and behaviors formerly relegated to the private, personal, and moral domain. It's a relationship, as I'll argue in this chapter, which suggests that liberals and others aligned with progressive social movements need to be cautious about the terms in which they condemn media investigations into the private lives of public figures.

Since the late 1960s, a host of alternative political and therapeutic move-
ments, including feminism and the gay and lesbian rights movement through to
the rise of 12-step programs and family therapy, have succeeded in politicizing
and publicizing behavior that was once seen as a personal or moral matter. Sexu-
ality, sexual harassment, child abuse, domestic violence, and addiction are now all
seen as matters of public interest—and, increasingly, as matters that are relevant
to the fitness of someone to hold public office. While such issues were always seen
as issues of "character," they weren't so frequently penalized or openly discussed
in the way they are today, because they often weren't the subject of public in-
quiries, judicial proceedings, or therapeutic discourse. Domestic violence and sex-
ual harassment are two of the most obvious examples here. Even two decades ago,
the allegation that a politician was having an affair with a junior colleague would
have been seen as a matter of sexual morality, not an abuse of power. Similarly,
spousal abuse was routinely understood as a domestic problem, not a matter for
the police.

It is common wisdom, on both the left and the right, that both tabloid-style
media intrusions into the private lives of political figures and the spin-doctoring
machinations of public-relations consultants are hindering democracy and dis-
tracting public attention away from the "real" issues in public life. Yet separating
tabloid-style intrusions into the private lives of public figures from legitimate in-
quiries into matters of public interest is no longer so simple in a world where a
host of attitudes and behaviors once seen as private matters are increasingly seen
in political terms. Indeed, much of the popular anxiety about the media coverage
of scandals involving public figures is arguably rooted in a more fundamental con-
fusion about when and why behavior is properly public (purely political) or per-
sonal (purely moral). And, as the Clinton/Lewinsky affair demonstrated so well,
journalists are not the only ones who are confused about where to draw the pub-
lic/private–political/personal lines: feminists, media commentators, politicians,
and scholars are just as divided.

Of course, anxiety about the relationship between what behaviors and atti-
tudes are private and which ones are public animates conservatives as much as lib-
erals, but for quite different reasons. Hillary Clinton was quite explicit in blaming
her husband's troubles on a right-wing conspiracy to drive him from office. As a
neoliberal, there's no doubt that Clinton is a more appealing president to many
feminists and that his views on gender equality have rankled many conservatives.
For right-wingers, the Lewinsky affair was and remains primarily a matter of
"character"—an event that demonstrated Clinton's fundamental immorality. U.S.

politics is heavily inflected by the desire of U.S. conservatives to promote the norms of Christian morality by denouncing adultery, homosexuality, and promiscuity. And the Lewinsky affair was certainly used by many prominent morals campaigners as an opportunity to further this agenda. But while the conservative agenda was an important aspect of the Lewinsky affair, it's not one I intend to specifically address in this chapter, since I want to focus on the more neglected question of how liberal agendas have also prepared the ground for the publicizing of sexual behavior and attitudes. It is, however, important to note the distinction between conservative and liberal agendas when it comes to the blurring of boundaries between public and private spheres and to recognize that the meeting of the two in popular debate is yet another force contributing to public confusion over where such boundaries should be drawn.

Mediating Democracy

In *The Politics of Pictures*, John Hartley argues that the mass media is now at the heart of representative democracy. He writes:

In classical Greece and Rome, assuming you were a free man—rather than a woman, slave or foreigner—you could walk into the agora or forum and participate in public life directly, as a voter, a jurist, a consumer, or as an audience of oratory in the service of public affairs. . . . But nowadays there is no physical public domain, and politics is not "of the populace." Contemporary politics is "representative" in both senses of the term; citizens are represented by a chosen few, and politics is represented to the public via the various media of communication. Representative political space is literally made up of pictures—they constitute *the public domain.*[5]

In such an era, Hartley suggests, attempting to separate politicians from their media images is futile. Political campaigns are now structured entirely around media events, and key debates are inevitably broadcast on television, ensuring that appearance, tone of voice, demeanor, and the ability to speak in short, witty grabs are, at least, as important as the substance of what is said or argued. But if politicians are becoming increasingly expert in using television to stage media events and perform for the public, the continued growth of the mass media and the blurring of the lines between information and entertainment is also bringing new kinds of stories about politicians into the public eye: stories that are harder to control or spin-doctor.

Over the past decade, North American voters have become habituated to sex scandals erupting during election campaigns, two of the most famous being Gary Hart's affair with Donna Rice and Gennifer Flowers's account of her relationship with Bill Clinton. These stories often germinate in conventional tabloid outlets like the *National Enquirer* or the *Globe*, and once they would have died there too. But the proliferation of news programs and products and the advent of tabloid prime-time current-affairs shows in the United States, driven by this increased competition, has ensured that stories about politicians' private lives are now routinely picked up and investigated by the mainstream media.

The "bimbo eruptions" that have plagued Bill Clinton's political career were all originally fueled by media sources that would once have been dismissed as trashy or marginal. The first reports of the Lewinsky scandal were infamously sparked by allegations published in *The Drudge Report*, a gossipy Internet site run by a thirty-year-old out of his Los Angeles home. *Newsweek* was the first major news organization to investigate the story, but ultimately decided not to publish it. *The Drudge Report* then reported both the story and the fact that *Newsweek* had decided not to run with it. As a result, news of the Lewinsky scandal spread and ultimately surfaced in the *Washington Post* and the *Los Angeles Times*.

Renowned U.S. journalist and editor of the on-line journal *Slate*, Michael Kinsley, commented: "The Internet made this story. And the story made the Internet. Clinterngate, or whatever we are going to call it, is to the Internet what the Kennedy assassination was to TV news: its coming of age as a media force. Or some might say media farce."[6]

But regardless of where the stories originate, the detail in which traditional news sources cover such scandals has become increasingly harder to distinguish from traditional tabloid media coverage. In the case of the Lewinsky scandal, mainstream media outlets, such as CNN, *Newsweek,* and *Time* magazine, unhesitatingly devoted intense coverage to the allegations, including speculation about whether Clinton defines oral sex as infidelity, whether the president's penis had strange identifying characteristics, and whether Lewinsky owned a dress stained with the president's semen.

There was certainly something weird (if not downright entertaining) about watching senior media commentators trying to look dignified while they speculated about what kind of sex the president preferred and which dress had semen stains. On one *Larry King Live* episode, Gennifer Flowers, the lounge singer who claimed Clinton had a long affair with her while he was governor of Arkansas, explained that Clinton liked to take chances when having sex. She offered the example that he'd once asked her to "make love" in a bathroom when Hillary and a host of official guests were only meters away on the lawn. Following this graphic interview, Marlin Fitzwater, a former White House press secretary, pondered whether the president made a distinction between "sex" and "oral sex." Wolf Blitzer, CNN's senior White House correspondent, participated in the debate but remarked uncertainly: "We're trying not to be completely in the gutter."[7]

The willingness of the conventional "quality" news media to canvas the intimate details of stories like the Clinton/Lewinsky affair is driven by complex forces, not the least of which is the broadening in the scope of which issues are considered political that I alluded to above and will discuss further below. But a factor that has been equally key in this shift in the news media is the vastly increased competition between news programs and products—a change, in turn, driven by the advent of multichannel television services, global news services, the growth of alternative entertainment media, and, most recently, the rise of the Internet. It is widely accepted that this diversification has encouraged conventionally staid news media to increasingly consider the entertainment value of both their formats and the content of stories, and one obvious consequence is the growth of stories that focus on sex, scandal, and intrigue in the private lives of public figures.

Sex scandals involving politicians undoubtedly rate well—at least initially—regardless of what viewers and readers might say publicly about the desirability of the media covering such issues. But if the blurring of the lines between entertainment and information media has provided a context for stories about the private lives of public figures, then their impact on public opinion needs to be assessed in the same light. The gradual transmutation of politics into entertainment may mean politicians are more vulnerable to having their private lives scrutinized, but it may also offer them unexpected reprieves. One of the strangest aspects of the Lewinsky/Clinton saga was that the revelations appeared to have no impact on the president's approval rating. Quite the reverse, in fact: it actually increased at the height of the crisis, from 56 percent in December 1997 to 59 percent on January 25, 1998, according to a CNN/USA Today Gallup poll. Yet only 35 percent of the same people polled answered yes to the question, "Is Clinton honest and trustworthy?" compared with 49 percent in 1997.

One plausible reason for this disparity is that voters were reluctant to convict a president of wrongdoing until all the evidence had been considered. But, given that politics is now substantially played out as media entertainment, another is that political ratings also, at least in part, have something in common with television ratings. People can hate what a program depicts but still enjoy watching it for its entertainment or shock value. As journalist Kurt Andersen speculated at the time:

For modern Americans, politics happens on television. And the titillating new story line that gooses the ratings of an old hit show (Paul and Jamie having a baby on Mad About You, *say) is now an established TV gimmick. Before the Monica Lewinsky subplot, the audience was beginning to get bored with the Clinton administration. Now they're interested again.*[8]

The backlash against the Republicans over the 1999 Senate impeachment trial may, conversely, reflect the public's boredom with the Clinton/Lewinsky scandal after a year of being bombarded with information about it. In early 1999, polls showed that voters still believed Clinton lied about his conduct with Lewinsky, but they also showed that most citizens were keen to put the matter behind them—that they were essentially sick of hearing about it.

Popular Politics

Writing in the wake of the enormous public outpouring of grief following the death of Princess Diana, cultural studies scholar Ruth Barcan argues that her funeral saw a sudden eruption of "the popular feminine" into a masculinized public sphere. It amounted, she argues, to a type of the triumph of the feminine—of all that official culture deems to be "embarrassing, excessive or trivial."[9] Barcan's alignment of the masses with an emotional feminine world and the public sphere with a masculine rational world references a large body of feminist work that has explored the way the public and private spheres have been conventionally split along gendered lines in which the feminized domestic sphere is identified with the body, intimate relationships, and emotions, while the masculinized public sphere is identified with the mind, contractual and commercial relationships, and reasoned debate. As feminist philosopher Moira Gatens has argued, this gendering of the private and public realms is tied to the very foundations of the liberal conception of civil society.[10]

While the relationship between the public and private spheres has always been far more complex and less monolithic than this simple juxtaposition suggests,[11] the separation of the private and the public certainly has a deep-rooted political significance in liberal democracies. Certainly, a common rationale offered for popular hostility to feminist initiatives is the perception that feminists are attempting to regulate areas of life that are properly individual, personal issues. It's for precisely this reason that sexual harassment legislation is one of the most vexed territories in contemporary public debate.

The feminist-driven recognition that unwanted sexual attention from employers constituted a form of sex discrimination has resulted in state and federal legislation in many Western countries outlawing workplace harassment. In simple terms, attitudes and actions that were once seen as "natural" or as private moral issues became objects of public scrutiny. This politicization of the intersection of sex, gender, and power in the workplace has, in turn, legitimated media interest in the sexual conduct of some powerful men toward their employees. Advocates of sexual harassment laws may, of course, protest that regulating the unwanted sexual advances in the workplace is an entirely separate matter to voyeuristic tabloid intrusions into properly personal matters. Yet as the Clinton/Lewinsky affair made amply clear, many people remain confused about where the public/private line should be drawn—including feminists themselves.

In early 1998, U.S. feminist icon Gloria Steinem published a strong defense of Clinton on the *New York Times* opinion page. According to Steinem, the guide to divining what is and what isn't sexual harassment is simple. You've just got to remember that "no means no; yes means yes." Paula Jones was a government employee who claims Clinton invited her to a hotel room when he was governor and asked her for oral sex. Kathleen Willey was asking Clinton for a job when she claims he touched her breast and placed her hand on his erect penis. Clinton was in a quasi-employer relationship to both these women when he made his advances. But Steinem argues that this is irrelevant. What matters is that he accepted rejection and didn't press his suit. In Monica Lewinsky's case, Steinem argues that "welcome sexual behavior is about as relevant to sexual harassment as borrowing a car is to stealing one." For Steinem, there's a clear line between behavior that is purely personal and sexual and behavior that constitutes harassment and deserves public scrutiny.[12] Yet, as the heated debate about Clinton's behavior showed, there are plenty of jurists, public policy experts, and feminists who disagree with her.

In March 1998, *Time* magazine ran a cover story on the Paula Jones sexual harassment suit that triggered Kenneth Starr's investigation into Clinton. The article argued that the law is terminally confused about what is and isn't sexual harassment.[13] What the article didn't countenance is the extent to which the media coverage of the various Clinton scandals has become inseparable from legal debates in the area. U.S. juries, which could hardly avoid being influenced by public debate on the issue, have returned well over five hundred decisions on sexual harassment since 1991. The problem is that public perception of the issue, mirrored in media coverage, is dramatically divided, as the furor over Anita Hill's allegations against U.S. Supreme Court justice Clarence Thomas demonstrated. The result is a schizophrenic pattern of rulings and settlements and a genuine lack of clarity about what is and isn't acceptable behavior in the workplace or public sphere.

For some feminists, popular debates about sex, gender, and power are always productive, regardless of how divisive they are, because they remind all protagonists that there's no single, privileged viewpoint for understanding sex and power. Other feminists remain far warier of the value of popular debate and particularly suspicious of the media's "distorting" role. But while media coverage of feminist public policy issues may often lack subtlety, it's important to recognize that it may no longer be viable to split the way an issue is played out in the public court of the media and the way it is played out in our courts and our parliaments—and indeed that the media has become an inseparable part of our public sphere.

From the availability of child care to the regulation of pornography and sexual harassment, feminism has been responsible for politicizing issues, attitudes, and impulses once considered domestic or personal. And many of the media intrusions into the private live of public figures are now justified by reference to the public interest value of sexual ethics, gender relations (in the case of domestic violence, for instance), and the way individuals balance their work and family lives.

While Bill Clinton's affair with a junior member of his staff may not have constituted sexual harassment in and of itself, it was certainly a relationship that triggered ethical questions, in feminist terms, by virtue of the power imbalance that shadows a sexual relationship between a president and an intern. But even if we were to accept the common claim that Clinton's relationship with Lewinsky wasn't a matter of legitimate public scrutiny, the fact remains that sexual harassment was at issue in the Paula Jones case, and that the triggering event for the Starr inquiry was Clinton's failure to disclose the truth about his relationship with Lewinsky in a deposition. Allegations of a conservative witch-hunt to one side, there can be no doubt that the intense public scrutiny Clinton's affair with Lewinsky received in both legal and media contexts is testament to the success feminists have had in politicizing the zones of sex, gender, and power. To then claim that the media should report such a case in purely abstract terms—that it should avoid disclosing the notorious "grubby details" of the Starr Report—is to avoid the consequences of politicizing these zones and thereby placing them on the public agenda. The details of Clinton's affair with Lewinsky became relevant because of his attempt to obfuscate a pattern of relationships with women to avoid prosecution in a sexual harassment suit and are, in this light, every bit as important as the details of Nixon's attempted cover-up of Watergate.

A growing number of contemporary feminists, however, have become increasingly wary of just how far the state has begun to penetrate the private sphere and what its real consequences are for women. U.S. feminist writer Wendy Brown sums up these concerns when she writes that "the state does not simply address private needs or issues but configures, administers and produces them."[14] Laws and public policies, in other words, don't simply police behaviors, they change the fundamental meaning we attach to those behaviors. Similarly, recent attempts to codify and regulate sexual behaviors in the workplace have had some unintended consequences, one of which is to render a whole range of behaviors potentially scandalous. Separating media interest from the public interest in this scenario isn't as simple as many feminists might wish. Indeed, the media have much in common with feminists here. The feminist project of politicizing the private sphere and its attendant issues, such as sexual harassment, domestic violence, and child care, was not simply an attempt to readjust the public sphere—it inherently, if unwittingly, assailed the basis on which we separate the private and the public. "Bad" tabloid-style media assaults on the same divide, in other words, cannot be simplistically distinguished from the "good" political motives that have fueled laws on issues which were once seen as merely personal.

Notes

1. N. Miller, *Getting Personal* (London and New York: Routledge, 1991), 143.

2. Ibid., 147.

3. J. Fallows, *Breaking the News: How the Media Undermine American Democracy* (New York: Vintage Books, 1997).

4. B. Robbins, "Introduction: The Public as Phantom," in *The Phantom Public Sphere,* ed. B. Robbins (Minneapolis and London: University of Minnesota Press, 1993), vii–xxvi. For a broader account of the "tabloidization" of US and Australian news and current affairs media in the 1990s and criticisms of it, see C. Lumby, *Gotcha: Life in a Tabloid World* (Sydney: Allen and Unwin, 1999).

5. J. Hartley, *The Politics of Pictures: The Creation of the Public in the Age of Popular Media* (London: Routledge, 1992), 35.

6. M. Kinsley, "In Defense of Matt Drudge," *Time,* 2 February 1998, 39.

7. "Larry King Live," CNN, 21 January 1998.

8. K. Andersen, "Entertainer-in-Chief," *New Yorker*, 16 February 1998, 34.

9. R. Barcan, "Space for the Feminine," *Planet Diana: Cultural Studies and Global Mourning*, Research Centre in Intercommunal Studies, Sydney, 1997, 37.

10. M. Gatens, *Feminism and Philosophy: Perspectives on Difference and Equality* (Cambridge, U.K.: Polity Press, 1991).

11. See, for instance, Nancy Fraser's account of the significance of nonbourgeois, nonliberal competing public spheres, or "counter-publics" in N. Fraser, "Rethinking the Public Sphere," in *The Phantom Public Sphere*, 1–32.

12. G. Steinem, "America's Sexual Obsessions," *Sydney Morning Herald*, 24 March 1998, 19.

13. J. Cloud, "Sex and the Law," *Time*, 23 March 1998, 28–34.

14. W. Brown, *States of Injury: Power and Freedom in Late Modernity* (Princeton, Princeton University Press, 1995), 195.

13 'Tis Pity He's a Whore

Ellen Willis

As Bill Clinton looked me straight in the eye, tightened his jaw, and denied having sexual relations with That Woman, I had a fantasy: suppose, on that historic *60 Minutes* episode in 1992, he had said, "Yes, I had an affair with Gennifer Flowers." And suppose Hillary had added, "Not every marriage is monogamous. Relationships are complicated, and ours is no exception."

Why is such candor unthinkable? After all, most of the voters who elected Clinton didn't believe his denial that he'd slept with Flowers, any more than they would believe his denial about Monica Lewinsky, five and a half years and a second victorious campaign later. There's a good chance that Americans would have supported the Clintons' right to set the terms of their marriage—even identified with it, considering the complications of their own lives. Yet declining to tell the lies that pay homage to virtue would indeed have been a daring political gamble and a shocking, radical act. It would instantly have shifted the debate from whether personal lapses from conservative sexual and familial values should disqualify a candidate for public office to a more basic issue: should public officials be required to conform to those values in the first place? Bill Clinton, who is neither a radical nor much of a political gambler, was not about to stake his candidacy on the outcome of such a debate. But by lying, he acceded to his opponents' moral framework. Had he challenged it and won anyway, he would have done himself and the entire country a favor by showing that politicians, even presidents, need no longer submit to the sexual blackmail of the right. Instead, he supplied the rope that effectively strangled his presidency.

My enthusiasm for radical candor won't sit well with those who argue that the worst feature of the presidential scandal was its contribution to a horrifying breakdown of the distinction between public and private life. Jean Cohen and Andrew Arato—responding in *Dissent* to the article where I first made the foregoing suggestion—contend that the proper public response to intrusive sexual questions is simply that they are "out of line and nobody's business." Of course, Clinton shouldn't have to discuss his sex life with the media. Nor should he have been questioned about a consensual affair as part of the discovery process in a sexual harassment lawsuit, any more than a woman who complains of sexual harassment should have to submit to being deposed about her sexual relationships with other men in the office. Nor should Kenneth Starr have been allowed to investigate Clinton's relationship with Lewinsky on the pretext that his attempt to cover up an affair he shouldn't have been asked about in the first place was relevant to the Whitewater inquiry. Nor should Starr have forced Lewinsky to testify by threatening to prosecute her and her mother on the basis of illegal tapes, or asked her questions about the minute details of her encounters with the president, ostensibly to nail down Clinton's perjury but actually to strip him naked before the world. Nor should the House have voted to release this material to the public, with utter disregard for what is supposed to be the confidentiality of grand jury proceedings (granted that Starr's leaks to the press had long since made it a joke). Clearly, what we have witnessed is the frightening spectacle of right-wing zealots abusing the power of the state to invade Clinton's—and Lewinsky's—privacy.

But public discussion of what to make of this invasion has displayed a persistent confusion—shared by queasy liberal commentators and ambivalent "ordinary Americans" alike—between sexual privacy and sexual secrecy. The two are in fact very different in their meaning and purpose. Genuine sexual privacy rests on the belief that consensual sexual behavior is an individual matter that need not and ought not be policed. Privacy will be consistently respected only in a sexually libertarian culture, for repression inevitably gives rise to a prurient preoccupation with other people's sex lives. And when privacy is respected, secrecy is unnecessary: as the actor and libertarian Orson Bean once observed, if people were brought up in a culture where eating was considered a shameful act, they might rebel against that social taboo, yet they could never truly imagine the unselfconsciousness of Americans dining in a restaurant.

Secrecy, on the other hand, is based on the need to hide one's behavior from public scrutiny and judgment. What's at stake is not only moral respectability but dignity, in a culture where bodily needs and appetites are still on some level regarded as infantile, ridiculous, and an offense to our higher spiritual natures. The widespread acceptance of secrecy ("everybody lies about sex") reflects the recognition that people must protect themselves from others' prurience; but it's also a way to avoid openly confronting the gap between our official standards of morality and dignity and our actual behavior. While the defense of privacy involves a critique of conservative sexual norms, the defense of secrecy serves to enforce them by denying their ubiquitous violation. Refusing secrecy, and the shame it implies, can paradoxically further the cause of privacy. A person's sexual orientation, for instance, is surely nobody's business. Yet by choosing to come out of the closet, often in the most public of ways, gay and lesbian activists launched us on the path toward a society in which homosexuals may enjoy their private lives without constant fear of exposure and punishment.

When the Lewinsky story broke, media commentators indulged in such an outpouring of nostalgia for the good old days of "Don't ask, don't tell"—before those feminists decided that the personal is political and oral sex made it onto *Nightline*—that you would have thought judging politicians' private lives was something new. On the contrary, candidates, especially for the presidency, have always been vetted by the family-values cops for marital respectability. Until Ronald Reagan broke the taboo, no divorced man had ever become president. (I always admired Nelson Rockefeller for divorcing his wife to marry the woman he loved, though it probably meant the end of his presidential prospects.) Open homosexuality is still beyond the pale, as is heterosexual cohabiting out of wedlock. Presidential wives are supposed to be supportive mates, preferably mothers, domestic minded, and never openly sexual.

What *is* new is the end of the trade-off that allowed politicians, in return for outward conformity, to lead a secret sexual life on the side. This conspiracy of silence, joined by the press, served to maintain strict public norms and the illusion that authority figures exemplified the morality they preached, while cutting powerful men some slack. (Needless to say, the deal has never been available to female candidates or political wives.) It also mystified sex, keeping the gritty details of respectable men's disreputable desires and practices from compromising the enforced "innocence" (that is, ignorance) of respectable women and children. The

239

undoing of this corrupt bargain is part of our society's continuing revolt against Victorian morality, sexual hypocrisy, and a sexist double standard. From this perspective, open discussion of the realities of people's sex lives—including the sex lives of public figures—is much to be preferred. If revelations of politicians' sexual proclivities cripple their ability to indulge in pious blather about the evils of "illegitimacy," I can only cheer.

Yet this assault on repression, however desirable in the long historical view, has given rise to an immediate and serious problem: while sexual secrecy has broken down, sexual privacy has yet to be achieved. In these circumstances, the readiness of the media to pass along sexual revelations becomes a weapon of outraged moralists bent on restoring the old sexual order. And ironically, the loudest defenders of secrecy are likely, once it has collapsed, to end up joining the hunt. For if the norms can no longer be upheld by concealment, then they must be upheld by punishment, and if necessary by purge. It is this imperative that explains the curious reversal of the nation's journalistic and political establishment, from its initial horror that the president's sex life should be exposed in the national media and investigated by the independent counsel to the outpouring of high moral indignation that followed Clinton's grudging confession of an "inappropriate relationship." The underlying theme remained the same: the moral authority of the president and the presidency must be preserved—an authority presumed to require an acceptable facade of sexual dignity and "family values."

There was a surreal quality to the revulsion and, even more peculiar, the sense of betrayal that Clinton's speech unleashed among Democratic politicians, administration officials, and the standard-bearers of what I think of as "high journalism"—that is, the (mostly moderate-conservative to neoliberal) commentators for the major dailies and TV networks, including the editorialists of the *New York Times* and the *Washington Post*. In the weeks leading up the president's grand jury testimony, the prevailing line in these circles was that Clinton should publicly admit and apologize for the Lewinsky affair; that the admission could not hurt him since hardly anyone believed him, anyway; that the country simply wanted to hear the truth, after which it could achieve "closure" and "move on." But as it turned out, for this same crowd there was all the difference in the world between believing the president had lied and hearing him confirm the fact. The aides and politicians who had loyally echoed Clinton's denials now felt compelled, whatever the insult to everyone's intelligence, to declare their shock. Centrist Democrats in Congress—led by Senator Joseph Lieberman, whose last claim to fame had been a moral crusade against TV talk shows—saw yet another chance to "take the values issue away from the right." And the high journalists, who resented the saturation coverage of the sex scandal as the latest affront to their role as guardians of serious public discourse (in their worldview, sex is much too interesting to be legitimate news), turned that resentment from Starr and the tabloids toward the man whose behavior, by his own admission, had made the media orgy possible.

In short, the moment the secret was really out, the logic of preserving moral authority demanded that Clinton somehow manage to say something so powerfully redemptive that he would in effect be born again, shedding his tainted public persona for a new one worthy of the presidential mantle. The specific complaints against the president's speech—that he wasn't abject enough, that he attacked Starr, that he continued to weasel out of admitting perjury—reflected a larger frustration with his failure to accomplish what even for a gifted politician was an impossible task. No apology, made under extreme duress by an admitted liar with a long-term reputation for philandering, could have sufficed; and Clinton's subsequent attempts to juice up his repentance were merely embarrassing. Soon a chorus of voices—among them the *Times* and both Democratic congressional leaders—began suggesting that the president could yet appease his critics by giving up his last shred of cover (not to mention his legal right to defend himself against a criminal charge) and confessing that he lied under oath. If Clinton had fallen for that one, he would have been as pathetic as Charlie Brown perennially kicking the football because Lucy swears that this time she won't pull it away at the last minute.

The logical resolution of the demand that the president magically turn into someone else was resignation or impeachment. And indeed, even as Starr and the congressional Republicans were doing everything they could to insure that Clinton's image was defined by cigar-fucking and dress stains, while Democrats cowered in fear of being associated with "immorality," growing numbers of high journalists and elder-statespeople types hinted or openly suggested that the president spare our sensibilities by stepping down. The logic might have been irresistible, if it had not hit a major snag: the public's refusal to get with the program.

Commentators who attributed Americans' lack of lynch-mob fervor to a "who cares, the economy's good" attitude illuminated little but their own condescension (and their membership in that minority for whom the economy actually *was* good). Conservatives like William Bennett, who mourned "the death of outrage," were closer to the mark. In fact, the electorate's feelings about Clinton mirror the contemporary standoff in the culture war, both on the issue of sexual morality and on the larger question of how we view authority. On the one hand, most people believe, or profess to believe, that Clinton's behavior with Lewinsky was morally wrong; yet they are also strongly influenced by the idea of a right to free sexual association between consenting adults. They are unhappy with his lies, but think the questions that provoked them should not have been asked. They would have preferred to fudge the contradictions with secrecy, but are reluctant to deny the president privacy—and on both counts are leery of the right's moral police.

Even more telling, perhaps, "ordinary" Americans clearly do not share the Washington elite's investment in the idea of the president as a moral exemplar, charged with validating the existing structure of (patriarchal) authority. They see him as a man elected to do a job, a politician in a political culture where lies are a taken-for-granted part of the game and sex is a perk of power. It's hardly news that the public's respect for the governing class and the establishment press is not at an all-time high. For those once accustomed to deference, its loss is an ongoing crisis, which the Lewinsky scandal exacerbated to an intolerable degree: as they see it, "cynicism" threatens to undermine democracy, unless the elite gets its house in order. Yet in fact, Americans' refusal to put their "leaders" on a pedestal is not only eminently democratic, but altogether realistic, in an age when the nation-state is steadily weakening, and the president, as Stanley Aronowitz has put it, is basically a trade representative.

Nor is this refusal merely cynical; it also involves an element of identification. The Republican strategy of bombarding the public with sexual details fizzled, not only because people saw it as gratuitous and hypocritical, but because it shifted the focus of moral disapproval from the fact of Clinton's sexual relationship with Lewinsky to the nature of their activities. In the wake of the Starr Report, the *New York Post* pronounced its revelations "kinky"; *Post* columnist John Podhoretz bragged of his superior character on the grounds that he had never used a cigar for sexual purposes or been sexually serviced while on the phone; congressmen lamented the disgrace of it all; and even the president's lawyers, complaining about the report, called its sexual descriptions "lurid." All this huffing and puffing was bound to make people nervous, inspiring discomfiting thoughts about how lurid or kinky their own sexual impulses and quirks might look in front of an audience. Nobody, after all, is a moral authority while having sex, not even with one's spouse in the missionary position under the covers. In any case the Bill Clinton of the Starr Report does not come across as an arrogant exploiter, a Sadeian libertine, the creepy exhibitionist depicted by Paula Jones. Rather, he seems needy, affectionate, attracted yet painfully cautious and conflicted, and terrified of getting caught—in short, a neurotic middle-aged married guy, ordinary to the point of banality, except that he happens to be president of the United States. That most people saw no need to get rid of him on that account speaks well for their acceptance of their own sexuality.

If it's true that Dick Morris's poll results convinced Clinton he had to lie to the public about Lewinsky, this was a fateful miscalculation, seemingly at odds with his usual political instincts. But it's consistent with a long-standing contradiction in the president's modus operandi. Bill Clinton was elected in large part because of who he was: a member of the '60s generation, an embodiment of youth and eroticism. To be sure, he was on the clean-cut, respectable end of the spectrum of '60s types, a man who from the beginning had had mainstream political ambitions. Yet there were certain influences he couldn't help inhaling: his style and body language bore the imprint of shaggy hair, rock and roll, the sexual revolution, the blurring of racial and gender boundaries. While this made the right hysterical, it made for a bond with voters who shared these formative experiences, which is to say a large portion of the "ordinary American" population. People liked him when he did things like playing the saxophone on Arsenio Hall's show, and arguably Gennifer Flowers added to his popularity more than she detracted from it.

Nonetheless, Clinton long ago bought into the idea that to win he had to live up to a presidential image that had little to do with who he really was. I suspect that consciously or not, this concern with appearances has had less to do with maintaining public support than with courting the same centrist elite that now resents his failure to slink quietly away. Clinton is a product of lower-middle-class Arkansas, who despite his Yale and Oxford education, will never be part of that elite. Instead, in the classic manner of climbers, he has internalized both its corporate neoliberal agenda and its demand for moral rectitude. Yet predictably, his efforts to wrap himself in the family-values flag—from denouncing "illegitimacy" and signing the welfare bill to backtracking on gays in the military to the ridiculous firing of Surgeon General Joycelyn Elders for suggesting that masturbation is a legitimate topic of discussion in sex education classes—never for a moment appeased either the right's crazed hostility or the establishment's more subtle disdain.

The essential quality of that disdain was perhaps best articulated by then-*Newsweek* columnist Joe Klein in a 1994 piece on the Paula Jones case. Jones's accusations, he asserts, should be of no interest to the media. They are unprovable, backed by "despicable" enemies of Clinton with dirty motives, and in any case "it can be persuasively argued" that politicians' private lives (John F. Kennedy's, for instance) are irrelevant to their public performance. But, Klein continues, the issue won't go away, because there have been so many "previous allegations of misbehavior" against the president and because "it seems increasingly, and sadly, apparent that the character flaw Bill Clinton's enemies have fixed upon—promiscuity—is a defining characteristic of his *public* life as well." That is, the dictionary definition of "promiscuous," revolving around such concepts as "indiscriminate," "casual," and "irregular," fits the style and substance of Clinton's governing in both good ways—he is empathetic, skilled at bringing people together and finding common ground, able to disarm opponents and forge compromises—and bad: he lacks principle, wants to please everyone, has trouble saying no, fudges the truth, believes he can "seduce, and abandon, at will and without consequences."

In my reading, the not-so-deep structure of this argument unfolds more or less as follows: since JFK displayed a suitable, manly decisiveness in public ("acting in a sober, measured—and inspired—manner during the Cuban missile crisis"), we can assume that he was able to contain his sexual weakness, to confine it to the bedroom, where it belonged; his expenditure of bodily fluids did not corrupt; and so the press was right to keep it quiet. With Clinton, in contrast, the media may be forgiven for breaching the proper boundary between public and private, because his own libidinal boundaries appear to be alarmingly porous. He is charming and seductive, wont to "wheedle" and "cajole." "He conveys an impression of complete accessibility, and yet nothing is ever revealed. 'I've had blind dates with women I've known more about than I know about Clinton,' James Carville once complained." In short, Bill is not only too feminine; his femininity is of the unreliable, manipulative, whorish sort. He has let sex invade the core of his being, as we all know women do (this is why it's so much worse for a woman to be "promiscuous"); and it's this erotic spillover, this gender betrayal, that explains (or symbolizes) his moral squishiness in the public realm.

I can't quarrel with the charge that Clinton is unprincipled; it's exactly this trait that makes him so useful as a trade representative. You would think the corporate elite and their allies in government and media would be more grateful for services rendered. But then, just because you use a whore, it doesn't mean you want to marry her. Clinton put his faith in a protective culture of secrecy that was designed for the JFKs, not for the likes of him; a culture that in any case was dying (though it had protected George Bush and might still have closed ranks around a president deemed to be One of Us). Ironically, despite his "femininity," Clinton also apparently subscribed to a deeply ingrained axiom of masculine conventional wisdom—that the proper response to being caught at infidelity is to deny every-thing. So he did what reporters would once, in effect, have done for him: he lied. And the combination of a take-no-prisoners right and a spill-the-beans press—not to mention the miracle of DNA testing—did him in.

The Republicans insisted that the issue was not sex, but lies. Right, and what Clinton did was not sex, but whatever. Yet in a way it's true that falsehood was at the center of this crisis—not Bill's third-rate perjury, but the larger lie that he has tried desperately to preserve with his I-am-a-humble-sinner act. The president has behaved like a victim of hostage syndrome, embracing the moral dogma of his persecutors. As a result he was defeated, even though he managed to hang on to his job. For the rest of us, the war goes on.

Jane Gallop with Lauren Berlant

I. Sexual Politics, Powerful Bodies

Lauren Berlant: We wanted to interview you for this book because you have become so famously well versed in the law and the culture around sexual harassment, along with being a distinguished theorist of sexuality. So I wonder if you could begin by reflecting on how the expertise you've gathered from the events around *Feminist Accused of Sexual Harassment* has affected your response to the Clinton/Lewinsky sexual scandal.

Jane Gallop: There were two main things. One of them was that as soon as I started writing about sexual harassment (in 1994), I said that it was going to become a right-wing rather than a left-wing issue. To me it looked like the place where moralistic right-wing forces could take up a supposedly feminist issue and turn it into an antisex issue to use as part of an attack on the left. And suddenly it was that! Ken Starr came from the Christian right, which provided a lot of the general energy behind the scandal. These were not people who actually cared about the sexual dignity of women.

I see it as connected to the way that they've picked up family values, these people who don't value the family, don't value children, who don't value a place where people can take care of each other and love each other, etc. That's what's been happening for the last 20 or 30 years: every major feminist issue that actually manages to get a large number of people to say "Yes! That's what we want!" is picked up by the right and turned around in this special way, so that sexual politics ends up being mainly a kind of antifeminist issue; it ends up being like "we must protect ladies, and we must keep them in the home and we must protect children," which means women have got to stay home and take care of their own children—all of this seems a part of their larger offensive.

Literally, the first chapter of *Feminist Accused of Sexual Harassment* ends by saying I can see that sometime in the near future that this could become an issue of the right. So it was just gratifying in a stupid way, at the same time that it was disgusting to be a theorist gratified by real people's suffering.

LB: I might make a counterargument that sexual scandal has not become an issue of the right solely; instead, what has happened in the public sphere is that issues of sexuality can get mobilized by whoever wants to profit from them. If you can take the moral high ground by claiming a more elevated relation to sexuality, you will. So, when the left lined up behind Anita Hill, for example, isn't part of the reason that, for many reasons, making a political argument against Thomas was difficult? Clinton has participated in this himself: everyone seems capable of playing a sanctimonious game where sex is concerned.

JG: Well, basically I think it has to do with the fact that we have an extremely restricted notion of morality in our culture, having lost most anything else, including a Communist enemy, to take the moral high ground against. The moral high ground continues to be the best way to wage a political battle because it looks like you're fighting for a greater good, which turns out usually to be something like purity. So I think that it's true that sex gets mobilized for all kinds of other things. I also think that there is a particular style in which the moral or religious right uses sex as an issue, and I think that it combines morality with this kind of extreme voyeurism and sensationalism. I like sensationalism, so it's very complicated, but it has to do with this sort of weird dissociation, in which the discourse of the fire and brimstone preacher is used to describe sin in such lurid detail. Something about that really seemed relevant to this case, whereas the people who were against Clarence Thomas did not seem obsessed with the details of what he had done in the same way.

LB: Partly the details were silly.

JG: And not sexy. But it seemed like the people who were horrified with what Monica and Bill were doing were completely interested in the details, and for me Ken Starr is the figure of this. Likewise, it seemed like the people who were *against* Anita Hill were obsessed with the details, which is to say again that it was the right which was obsessed. So, in both cases it was the right which was morally antisexual, sensationalist, and completely obsessed with the details of sex.

This particular form reminds me of Jim Kincaid's *Erotic Innocence*, and his description of the culture of child molesting, which is about the complete horror at and fascination with the details, about this very complicated disavowed desire that you're stuck on, etc. Ken Starr's discourse just looks like that, just wanting over and over to hear the details.

For me it's resonant because where I first learned about that kind of discourse was reading Sade. In Sade, every libertine, every pervert who's in a position of power—the judges and the confessors etc.—is always asking for more details, and you knew that the confessor was jerking off as he was asking "and *what* did he do to you then, and *where* did he put it?" Actually, Maureen Dowd had a wonderful op-ed piece in the *Times* somewhere in the middle of this, in which she wrote the whole thing with a generic "he," as in "he was so turned on by her thong," and you gradually realize that she's talking about Ken Starr. It was really fabulous; it really gets the tone of that incredible repulsion/attraction that has to do with "I know this is really bad and I can't hear enough about it." That seems to belong to the religious right's relation to sexuality, generally.

LB: Meanwhile, the right uses lurid spectacles of sex in a kind of homeopathic way. By displaying it in detail they can then say, "Look at what we have to see, we shouldn't have to see these things!" This suggests a desire for a heterosexuality that doesn't need language because it has no structural problems or excesses. This is Foucault's point, that the only time talk about sex is deemed proper is when it's elicited by the church or the law for reasons of discipline or purification. These institutions generate a scene where if you *have* to be giving details the details prove that you're a different species than the norm, and that the thing that you're doing sexually isn't what they would call . . .

JG: What goes without saying.

LB: Exactly. The Christian right and Ken Starr want to charge Clinton and Lewinsky with a kind of perversion so that it isn't heterosexuality per se that transgresses, but some other horrible thing. For example, there is the scene with the cigar.

JG: I'm sitting here thinking about that stain. The whole fascination with noncoital sex is that sex is something that's supposed to disappear, to remain invisible. You know the stain, it has the power of the scarlet letter, and it's there approximately in the same place, and like the scarlet letter it's about sex breaking out of its confines. I mean, you know adultery was a model of this, and of course this was adultery too. . . .

I see the stain not just as bodily but as related to "we're talking too much." It's about things that are supposed to be internal; it's about airing your dirty laundry in public. Call it that. Because dirty laundry is about bodily stains showing in public. What is dirty laundry? It's about the sheets; it's about your underwear. So it seems to me that there was something about the stain related to her talking about what she was doing. It was related to noncoital, nonmarital sex, and it's about sex that's not contained in its proper receptacles, whether those receptacles are institutional or bodily.

LB: Or narrative.

JG: Or narrative, right. Then, you want to keep looking at these things that have fallen out of place. Something about that is vivid to me.

LB: I became interested in the nonnarrative part when, in *Monica's Story,* she repeatedly calls their sex "fooling around." One can imagine "fooling around," but it goes nowhere, there's no plot for it. It was only in their last encounter that he came freely, and I believe her phrase for that is something like "come to completion."

JG: That's something I found really interesting and fascinating, that Bill didn't want to lose control.

LB: In the late part of their relationship she recounts that they have a conversation where he tells her about his "secret life," that's what he calls it. He says that since he was little he's had to have a secret life, and that no one knew his secret self. It was all about being a good boy in public and being bad elsewhere, even after he got married. When he turned forty, he thought that maybe he would try not having a secret life but it was really hard for him because he'd never known any other way, and because, as she says in the interview, his religion and other things made it difficult for him to be seen as mixed or flawed. So one way of thinking about the stain and leakage is that it's the secret life falling apart, the stain is the secret, and he can't contain it any longer.

JG: And then it actually results in this scandal becoming completely unable to be contained. What I see in the stain, and in the fascinating detail of him *not* coming, is that in fact this is not a story of a man whose sexuality is out of control; this is a story of a guy really struggling to stay in control, and still you see him struggling not to give it up. And then everybody basically says to him, "Give it up, give more up, we want you to come to completion, we don't want you to hold onto any shred of dignity."

And in some ways it seems that part of what it represents, when Clinton comes to completion with Monica and loses control there, and when Starr and the

American people want the details, is that at *that moment,* rather than an earlier sexual moment, the phallus loses all its dignity, all its uprightness, that's when he stops being presidential.

LB: Absolutely. I remember hearing a disgusted pundit describe on T.V. the president shuddering over the bathroom sink [as he masturbates].

JG: Wow.

LB: The message was, the president is now reduced to *that*, and it was a stunning image.

JG: This is like Irigaray's influence from a long time ago, I hardly ever think of her now, but it really is as though the body that is not the phallic body, the body that we think is horrible, is finally the body that produces fluids. The erect penis is fine, it's phallic. But the penis that comes, that's not presidential. (laughter)

The presidential stain was his undoing: it was when he could no longer tell his stories, could no longer get up there and just talk, because it wasn't about whether DNA was absolute proof or anything like that, it was about moving to this economy in which he becomes really bodily, not the phallic bodily which a man with a hard-on is supposed to be. Male sexuality can go with power, but not at that moment of what they call "spending" and losing control and all of that.

LB: I think that's great, and we can link it to his appetite for food. When Clinton was running for president the first time, people debated the meaning of his fatness as though it meant something for politics. I remember reading an article in a Salt Lake City paper at that time where a woman talks about putting her arm around him at a photo shoot and feeling his "love handles." She says, "He's a real American!" Monica talks about his struggles with weight movingly too. She retells a story he told her that, when he was little, he was too fat to get to any of the chocolate eggs before the other kids at the Easter egg hunt, which broke my little heart. One thing that disgusts people about him, I mean, people who are already averse to him, is that he is a man of appetites.

JG: The whole thing about his relation to donuts and McDonald's, and fast food—he was always struggling to be in control.

LB: He eats it and it shows, he has a big body, one that's out of control, and in some way he looks weaker because he identifies with fatness. In the *Queen of America* I show a group of paper dolls that have Clinton, Hillary, Al Gore, Tipper, and Chelsea in their underwear. These images were published by a right-wing press very early in the first administration, when there was no new news—just the old aversions—the debacle over gays in the military, the rage against Hillary's "masculinity," Clinton's unregulated sexuality, and his fatness. What seemed disgusting was that he had a *body*. George Bush didn't have a body; Ronald Reagan's body was symbolic, like a cowboy or celebrity's; Jimmy Carter was scorned for even naming lust in his heart; Gerald Ford had one, but it was constantly failing and so was a comic sight. We'd probably have to go back to FDR to find a president with a public body who was still respected. And that was a very managed spectacle, in any case.

JG: "The Presidential Body," that would make a great essay topic. There's a moment in the Barbara Walters interview where Monica relates that he would always leave his shirt untucked because of his belly, and you just feel that and it was one of the ways where Monica and Bill get connected. If the right wing in this country is still really moralistic about sex, the left is moralistic about food, that's where the new style of moralism about control is. Well-educated liberal people are supposed to be in control of the amount of body fat they have. The people who are disgusted by Clinton's fat and by Monica's aren't the right wing, they're the ones who want a yuppie president with the right amount of body fat at the helm.

Actually, I think this is also related to the place of orality in this scandal. Too much eating, talking, and *then* oral sex.

II. Heterosexuality without Disgust

LB: Let's talk about male heterosexuality a little. If that *Ms.* Magazine that we just read is any example, feminists might argue that this scandal really is a crisis about women's subordination in America, institutionally and sexually. But what strikes me, too, is the way male sexuality is represented: the aversion to Clinton is an instance of a widely held view that men are sexually disgusting.

JG: As Irigaray talks about it, our image of good sexuality, which is phallic sexuality, not male sexuality, but good, clean, and well formed and always in reserve, is always a sign of power, it's never a sign of loss of power. But any sign of male power that is involved with fluid or flabbiness, which is like flaccidity, any part of the male body that isn't phallic, is seen as disgusting. What is more phallic than the most powerful man in the world?

I think that the same horror that the culture has about female sexuality—which is that it is actually a threat to the phallus, and it gets associated with bodiliness and with fluids and with out-of-controlness and with excessiveness—also pertains to any aspect of male sexuality or male bodiliness that's not phallic, and there's such a horror at the loss of that phallic image, especially of the most powerful man in the world. Here's Clinton, whom we've elected to be the most powerful man in the world, who does not successfully manage publicly to pull that off, to contain his body with its proper phallic form.

LB: I thought, in contrast, that his election was part of a shift in styles of "normal" masculinity. It suggested that it would be possible to have an embodied president. That is, he could have the phallus and the flesh, too. This had something to do with, I'm guessing, Clinton's style of control over language as a Southern Baptist who could profess with emotion and have that be all of a piece with his passionate rationality. Then there are the stories about his charisma, the way he can light up a room just by entering it: that was a huge thing. In short, I think he was elected in part *because* he had a body and visible pleasure in the political, and even that maybe part of the reason many voters didn't care a lot about the scandal was because they already knew he had a lusty body, so they weren't surprised.

JG: Maybe we actually are in a time when people aren't horrified that he had a body, that it wasn't, in fact, just me. Maybe that's also what the right wing's interest in preserving the phallus is about, their concern about family values and its institutions. From that point of view, their take on sexual harassment is that people in power—we'll call them "people" to make them less bodily—are never supposed to lose their power, are never supposed to show that they need or want anything, which is to say that they're supposed to remain phallic. What is embarrassing to them about the tales of the boss chasing his secretary around the table and wanting something and so on is that it looks needy and is undignified; it doesn't stay looking like power. So that's when sexual harassment becomes embarrassing, because at stake is a certain image of power, which is that it can't be embodied and it can't have need.

LB: Because having a need effeminizes you, it makes you soft. It's very striking that Monica says multiple times in the book, "He had needs," and she says it in an undisgusted way.

JG: It's clearly what seduced her. That's the desire, her desire that I could completely identify with, the desire to have this very powerful man revealed as human, as needy; to feel needed by this very powerful person makes you feel powerful. That's of course the other thing that made me feel attracted to the story about Monica, which is like what I said in the book, about why I desired to sleep with those professors who were so powerful. As I said in the book, I wanted to see them naked, I wanted to see them as *like other men*, because they were so powerful. I certainly see that in Monica's desire, that's part of what I love about the story; it's hard to ignore *Monica's* desire, she's not simply the object of someone else's desire. It might be foolish desire, but it is desire, and we recognize somebody going out of her way to get what she wants. That's why I love it—it blows out of the water the image of the younger woman, the organizational subordinate woman as simply an object of desire. Whatever we think of the desire, whether it was a mistake, etc., we cannot say he imposed his desires upon her, it's just really clear.

Which is why I think that one of the reasons I like Monica's story as a fable for our times—not that it should be what happens to anybody—is that although feminism has gone a certain way toward claiming sexual subject status for women, it has only claimed sexual subject status for some women with some proper objects of desire. It's done better for lesbians than for heterosexual women. It's done better for women who are in a relation to somebody who is sort of their power equal, or basically for women whose object of desire is a nontraditional feminine object of desire, which is to say not a man or a politician. But given that vast numbers of women continue to desire what vast numbers of women desired before feminism, which is a man more powerful than them, they seem to be relegated within the discourse of feminism to object status. That becomes a really important obstacle to feminism. I've had decades of young women heterosexual students saying, "I'd like to be a feminist, but I am a heterosexual, and there just doesn't seem to be any place for heterosexuals within feminism."

LB: By which they mean . . .

JG: By which they mean that they don't read anything that gives them a positive image of themselves as feminist heterosexual subjects. Because in feminism they see so few good images of heterosexuality. There are a couple of good ones. But basically little about heterosexual women whose desires fit some kind of traditional sexual pattern, whatever that is, for example the desire for the man who's more powerful than you or older than you.

LB: Also who's everything, right? More powerful than the woman and less powerful, as in, he's just a little boy and the president of the United States, or his skin feels like a woman's but he has the strength of a man, or he's more woman than women, more manly than men?

JG: Which we might call the desire for the phallus, once again. If you read most feminism that they pick up plus the bad media image of feminism, that desire is deemed degrading to a woman, a woman with any kind of self-respect wouldn't have that kind of desire. They experience a kind of split in fact within their sense of themselves. I mean, they're college students, they've figured out a career, and they're already in my feminist courses, so they have a certain interest in feminism whether they think of themselves as feminist or not—and yet . . .

I taught a class in feminist theory last fall and on the last day of class I had them talk about what they thought of the books, and they said they learned a lot from them, but asked why every book was by a lesbian. Not every one! I said. What about Virginia Woolf? They said, everybody knows about Virginia Woolf. I said, What about Alice Walker? They said, everybody knows about Alice Walker. So they claimed that every single one of the books I had chosen was by a lesbian, while I had chosen them because to me they were good examples of women writers who were writing theory who were both into feminism and literature. I knew that it was predominantly lesbian but I didn't know it was 100 percent—based on these complicated definitions. But: they said they didn't mind; they really just wanted one book that showed them that they could be heterosexuals and be feminists and be happy.

They loved Dorothy Allison, they loved her pro-sex thing; they loved Audre Lorde on sex but they knew that she was a lesbian. One of the girls in the class whom I really loved, she was from this working-class Italian family and she spoke very directly, and she said I JUST LOVE BOYS. I think feminism is great and I love all these books, but I LOVE BOYS! Where is the discourse of feminism for that?

That is the voice of a sexual subject, but we scarcely hear anyone talk like that.

III. Oral Sex

LB: Is part of what Monica represents to you an opportunity to address this question, what does it mean to desire big men, "guy guys," the traditional male virtues, from the feminine position?

JG: This is a major question, a question I actually want to think and talk about. One of the most undertheorized things in the world is female heterosexual desire from the subject, not the object position. What makes women desire men? I'm not talking about the desire for security, I'm not talking about romance, I'm not talking about hetero love, I'm talking about some bodily desire for the male body that a woman might have. What is it? What is it psychologically? What is its specificity? One of my fantasies about it (and this is one of the reasons I'm interested in Monica) is that one of the forms it takes—and this might be simply autobiographical—is the desire to put the penis in your mouth. Now, again, it has to do with my desire. If one imagines it from the point of view of orality, you imagine it as like going back to the infant, who experiences everything through the mouth.

If you imagine—this is my fantasy, but I'll say it— the proportion of the nipple to the infant mouth turned into a relation to the adult mouth, you would probably come up with something like a penis.

LB: I had a dream the other night that I was having sex with a guy who had a huge erect cock coming out of his neck. It made things a little ungainly but it was also very sexy. Later it migrated down to the regular place: and then, he had really long nipples. So it was a regular suckfest. The dream was very happy. One day's residue I was working through there referred to a paper I'm writing about pictures of people having sex. It contrasts the work of Nan Goldin, in which couples' sexual bodies are often bruised by light or violence, to that of Laura Letinsky, whose couples are contingent but aren't bruised by anything *yet*, except perhaps disappointment. In one of Letinsky's photographs of very engaged intercourse there's a very moving penis, so to speak, red and hard, emerging from the vagina: on the penis there's a large drop of liquid from the woman's body. It's so beautiful—I'd never seen such an image. The sucking dream was entering that esthetic of liquid penetration, but orally.

JG: So why is it, then, that people resist the difference between oral sex and oral eroticism? It's because it's hard for people to see the penis as an object of desire, to see the penis acted upon, rather than acting. So many of the hegemonic images we have of oral sex are basically of the man fucking someone's mouth.

LB: Really? I can't think of any! I think it's this: the man leaning back, in the "blow me" position and enjoying not having to do anything.

JG: I think that's the main image, but when women talk negatively about fellatio they see it as that, and it's also the fantasy of *Deep Throat* basically. I see it that when women talk about it as degrading to the woman, as servicing the man, they see that everything is about the *cock*. You can find it, for example, in gay male literature, where they talk about the desire to suck cock. Also, cocksucker is the most derogatory thing you can be in this culture, which is about something else, the penis being in a very different relation, it's about what you were talking about before, the change in men, the desire for men to be something very different.

LB: I'm wondering whether the antipathy to fellatio has something to do with the image of mutuality that one finds in heterosexual sex talk. The specificity of oral sex, that it could happen anywhere in an event, that it's not just foreplay, and that it may not be reciprocated, I think that's very scary to some people, very threatening.

JG: For me, it's connected to the stain. It's about not being in a closed circuit. The image of fucking is somehow that people have genitals and they're stuck together, they're not out there separate, like goes with like, so we're not matching a mouth and a genital or something like that. Supposedly it's producing genital pleasure in both people at the same time, as opposed, say, to producing oral pleasure in one person and genital in the other; they're not in different psychoanalytic stages. As well as in your face to face, hips to hips image, you're not upside down, at different ends of the bed, or someone's not down by somebody's feet.

LB: So, did you think this too during the Clinton/Lewinsky scandal, that all this oral sex talk in the public sphere was good for sex?

JG: I thought it was wonderful! I was applauding! I had this notion that at one moment the entire nation was envisioning the same sex act at the same time, and that it was this act of fellatio, and the fact that it wasn't fucking. It wasn't that wild as a sexual practice, but the fact that in our culture sex is so completely synonymous with coitus, so that when you say sex it's supposed to mean coitus, the fact that it was dislodging it, that there would be this huge sexual relation that everybody knew about and had to talk about—people had to say, these people were having sex and they weren't fucking.

LB: That reminds me of an amazing conundrum in all of this: were they having sex? Bill said they weren't having sex because they weren't fucking, and this made sense to Monica, and meanwhile the press was saying bullshit, they couldn't have had that thought! But what you're saying is that they could have had that thought.

JG: I think that for me it opened up the discourse of what sex is! With all of the scandal and titillation, people talking about sex all of the time, it's amazing how seldom people ask the question of what is the specific practice people are talking about when they talk about sex. They just assume that it's fucking. It has always felt completely oppressive that there is this one specific act that people always talk about but don't have to specify. The idea of all these people specifying and having to discuss it, I thought it was great. It was a huge weird teach-in about sex.

IV. "It's Not about Sex"

LB: This might be a good place to return to one of the major disavowals of the Clinton/Lewinsky scandal, the claim that it was not, after all, about sex.

JG: Everyone said that it was not about sex, but about lying, and that lying matters (presumably, more than sex). And yet clearly when you read the testimony it was clear that it was about sex, otherwise why would we get so many details? There's something about this disavowal, and it seemed to me very similar to what goes on in anti-sexual harassment discourse and anti-pornography discourse, which is the assertion that it's not about sex at the same time as there's a complete focus on the sexual details. In fact, one of the women who accused me of sexual harassment said that it wasn't about sex but about power. So I feel like that there's a way here, which I associate with the right, and which has a complicated relation to the way feminism takes up sex, that ends up serving other antifeminist issues. One thing feminism says about all kinds of sexual issues is that they're not really about sex, they're about discrimination against women, they're about power differentials, they're all about exploitation. This gets picked up by people who say "it's not about sex" but then become obsessed with sexual details, so that the claim seems to be a cover story. The claim that "it's not about sex" plus an obsession with sexual details may be a marker that a group is redeploying a feminist argument in a very nonfeminist way.

LB: I think "it's not about sex but about lying" also refers to the status of sex as a discourse of truth. The need for sex to tell truth when we know that it can so easily involve dissembling informs a lot of the anxiety around sex. People can say, though, that there's an ethical revelation in Clinton's promiscuity: sex and dissembling are the same gesture for him, as he commits adultery and then can only lie about it. He breaks both moral and statutory laws that way. In addition, in his merging of the governmental with the sexual body, he betrays the American people, as though there's an inevitable analogy between Hillary and the citizenry. His lies become the truth of his sexuality and his being, and the fact that he can survive *although we know this* must contribute somewhat to what pundits call "Clinton fatigue."

JG: This is also about his secret life, the way that we believe the secret life is the real life, rather than that the secret life has a complicated relation to the public life. He is the president and he is a person: but the real stuff is presumed to be what's hidden. It's part of Derrida's critique of truth as that which is hidden, it comes out of our mistrust of surfaces, our love of depth and interiority, of hiddenness.

LB: And the corollary that language will always lie.

JG: And that the naked self is the true self. One of the things that's really interesting to me about the response of the American people is that they said, We know about this stuff, but he's doing a good job as president, and that's actually what we care about. They actually didn't fall for this: there's a kind of fantasy behind the impeachment that's sort of like Monica's fantasy, except that she was doing it for her own pleasure and not for something more displaced and more troubling,

257

the idea of undressing power, the idea of the emperor's new clothes, and the idea of seeing it meaty and quivering and flabby and naked. And feeling the power you have when you reduce someone. It's like the moment when the officers pull off the prisoner's epaulets, all that public humiliation: there's something about that that's like this very very powerful desire. In Monica's case it's explicitly sexual, and in its explicitly sexual form it seems to me much more affirming and loving than in this really political legalistic form.

It seems to me that if you want to talk about power differential in sex, it's not about the power differential that exists outside the sexual relation, which somehow doesn't change, it's about the way the sexual relation could have a power differential in it in which one person is vulnerable in the sexual relation and the other person isn't. And whether that's what's the matter with rape, for example, which has one person fearing for their life and the other person feeling completely powerful, which seems to be a pretty serious power differential in a sexual relation, or whether one imagines a situation in which basically one person is taken over and exposed and the other person remains completely in control.

LB: That's the image of sexuality in sexual harassment.

JG: It's the image of what real sexual harassment would be. The way sexual harassment is too often defined is that if you take people who have a different amount of power in the world then in their sexual relation they will inherently have a different amount of power. I think regardless of the amount of power people have in the world, that there are sexual relations in which both people are risking themselves, and there are other sexual relations where one person is not at risk in the same way. That seems to be the relation between Ken Starr and Bill Clinton in some way.

LB: I think that's absolutely right, but I want to go back to the distinction, though, between people who are taking risks and people who are not taking risks. What makes sexual harassment necessary as a concept is that people constantly misrecognize the differences between their institutional and their personal relationships. What usually happens is that people say, "it's just about us" in a kind of Romeo and Juliet way. It's our little cognitive world, and our personal desire and our privacy, and it isn't about the institution. One thing that sexual harassment law says is that it is *always* about the institution. So, for example, you might think it's just about you and whoever, but other people in the office feel constrained and under pressure to conform to the open secret in a way that circumscribes the ways they can do their work. Also, I think that sex isn't private, it's never private: it's always personal, in that persons are doing it, but it happens in a nexus of very public and institutional relations. What does it mean to say that it's something that happens "between" two people, except that the desires and fantasies you have enable you not to pay attention to the way your personal intimacies resonate in other people's immediate worlds? It's part of the intelligence of sexual harassment law to recognize that.

JG: I think the problem with that is that if sexual harassment law did what you just said, it would be good, because it would be smart. But sexual harassment law says good sex is private, but this kind of (workplace) sex is not private. It's like saying that married couples have the right to privacy but perverts don't. Which is that it doesn't say that all sex is public; if it did that, I would be all for it. It says people who have a public relation shouldn't have a private relation, whereas people who have sex should have just a private relation.

LB: The reason they had to say that was because people refused to believe that in institutional contexts their personal relationships were mediated by institutions.

JG: What you're talking about is consensual relations policy. Sexual harassment was originally about something that is completely not sexual, which is about some form of imposed sexuality that gets in the way of somebody doing their job. What you're talking about is what is increasingly understood as sexual harassment, which is all these corporations that now have policies forbidding even dating among their employees. They're trying to reseparate the public and the private. They're saying because it's so complicated to figure out how to deal with these issues there should be no sex. I see that as horrible, because it seems to me to go against the attempt to see the workplace as a place where people are people. It dehumanizes the workplace.

LB: I see what you're saying, that current sexual harassment ideology wants to return the workplace to being an uncomplicated space. In a sense, that's what feminist anti-sexual harassment work seeks to do as well, to enact a fantasy of an uncomplicated world. But it is inevitably complicated, and sometimes it is complicated because people see their intertwined romantic subjectivities as in a little autonomous bubble protected from the particular world of power and value it nonetheless floats in. When the bubble breaks, it's a nightmare. But I guess it's only sexual harassment if someone gets fired or can't do their job as a result. Still, I think of anti-sexual harassment ideology as an important pedagogical tool about all this.

JG: I don't believe it's possible to legislate a world that isn't complicated. I feel like the direction in which sexual harassment policies are headed is toward a time

when the workplace was all male and men were closeted. It's as though the peo-
ple you work with and the people you date are different species. A lot of this arises
out of the combination of women in the workplace and gay people who are out.
So it's hard to separate out people in the workplace from people we desire. So it
gets complicated. We no longer have separate spheres. So we have to deal with it.
The policy against sexual harassment that grows out of that situation says that we
have to deal with this ethically, because there's a lot of unethical behavior going
on, which is fine, but we can't deal with it by trying to return to the purity of the
world of separate spheres.

LB: This is something relevant to my response to *Feminist Accused of Sexual Ha-
rassment*, actually. I thought that what we had to return to was a notion that peo-
ple in power had a responsibility to be smarter, to be conscious about the com-
plexities of intimacy in the context of institutional hierarchies. The people with
power have to be able to say to a prospective colleague-lover: this is something
that I want; but in wanting it, I am putting you in a kind of jeopardy I'm not in.
So, to go back to your earlier discussion of risk . . .

JG: I actually do not believe that, at least in this day and age, which is different
than ten years ago, I'm not sure that people with less power are at greater risk in
a sexual relation. For example, Bill Clinton was at much greater risk than Monica
Lewinsky. He actually had more to lose and lost more. He didn't lose as much as
many people thought he would lose, but he could have lost his entire presidency,
plus the political career he'd spent his entire life building, whereas Monica, she
got a book contract and TV exposure. You could argue that there was an inequal-
ity of risk there, but it went the opposite way.

It's also true now that if you work in a university where there's a policy
against teacher/student sex, and you break that policy, the teacher is at much
more risk than is the student. The teacher could lose their job. The student can sue
and make a lot of money! So in fact I think that's not about sexual harassment,
but about sexual relations that are consensual. There's actually more risk there.

LB: On the other hand, you could say that the reason that the teacher is at more
risk is because initially the teacher wasn't at more risk. That is, if the teacher is hav-
ing sex with one of the teacher's students, the student's career there, his happi-
ness, his safety in the world depends on his autonomy, and this is what is com-
promised by his consent. Of course, everyone is compromised by their consent.
The question is whether or not the teacher should have been smarter.

JG: I resist the idea that the teacher should always be smarter. (Laughter) I think
sometimes it's good for the student to be smarter and the teacher to be stupid.

LB: I like learning from my students, but—this is especially about graduate students—the management of a career, the contingency of a dissertating subjectivity, the whole scene of professionalization involved in graduate school that we have gone through and they haven't, it's a huge transition. So that's why I think teachers should be smarter. But *Feminist Accused of Sexual Harassment* makes the opposite argument. It argues, in essence, that the student should manage things, it's the student who's supposed to be knowing and in the know, and so on, when it comes to sex with faculty.

JG: I'm not sure that I made that argument. I think that the argument I make, which is somewhat different, is that I think that teachers should risk losing control. I'm not sure I'm asking anyone to manage things. I think it has to do with the fact that I so value the loss of control. I say this as actually a very controlled person.

LB: It's interesting: I read *Feminist Accused of Sexual Harassment* as saying, "When I was a graduate student, I knew my need and made other people meet me there."

JG: I think that maybe the voice of that book was to go back on my experience and tell it as if I always knew what I was doing, which was not, I think, how I lived it.

LB: So when you got to the story of your students later, who misrecognized your practice—even though there had been a verbal contract about what your practice is as a teacher—I read that as you saying, "They should have understood. Because that's what a student should do, a student is smarter, and a student should seize the educational opportunity to learn what I'm teaching about this, about knowledge, identification, sexuality, power, etc."

JG: Yes, I certainly was complaining that they were dumb. I remember during the part of the case when I said, "My sexual preference is graduate students," I remember thinking, "These are English graduate students. Don't they know about metaphor? Don't they know about figurative language? Can't they read a trope? " I remember thinking in those disciplinary terms. I mean, what bad students they were!

LB: I actually think—and this is central to the general crisis we're talking about here—that people cannot read figuratively where sex is concerned.

JG: Yes, this is something I once said somewhere in writing, that I think that sex is the figure for the literal. Sometimes it's not sex but the body or anatomy or the naked as the literal, but sex, the body, nakedness are all involved.

LB: So what does it mean to say, "It's not about sex"? Is it to say that we're afraid of the literal, we're afraid of the simple?

JG: Maybe that's why they say, "It's not about sex." Because they have this stupid notion of sex that it is this simple, literal thing, and because they're seeing it as actually complicated, about sex and politics and secrets and all of this sort of stuff, it must not be about sex. But it's just that a notion of sex is missing here: this is just complicated.

LB: If it's figurative it isn't sex.

JG: And if it's complicated it's not sex.

LB: But it is sex.

JG: Not like I know what sex is.

LB: Queer and feminist theory were supposed to produce different conditions of possibility for sexuality in its relation to the materialities of survival and freedom, including changing what the "good life" might look like. The case that we're discussing now is about a failure to generate those stories. In the culture of discourse around Clinton and Lewinsky nobody was allowed to say publicly, "I need to lead a different kind of life, these institutions around the couple and the family do not work for me." Instead, she goes on looking for Prince Charming, he returns to his wife, has prayer breakfasts, and "acts presidential."

JG: We have this narrative, this binarized view of different genders acting in their binarized way—this is why we don't have a narrative about what heterosexual practice is. The completely active phallus and the completely receiving object of the phallus, which is probably not what coitus even is most of the time, but which is what we think it is most of the time when we don't want to think of what it is. In fact, in that image we don't really have specificity, bodiliness, and we don't have a story, because the story involves negotiations between two terms, with things going wrong and getting fixed.

LB: Another part that doesn't get represented in conventional heterosexual romance ideology is one's incoherence: there is so much of throwing your body and your trust in there and pulling it out halfway or all the way, even in long-term couples. Sometimes you know why you're inconstant, and other times you're an enigma to yourself. Ineloquence and incoherence are so central to the intimate, and yet all the standard languages of desire are very *clear*. This is definitely a context of the Lewinsky/Clinton scandal: where sex is, it not only has to be uncomplicated, but languages of intention are invariably used. It's not dignified to say, we didn't know what we were doing, we just acted on impulse, we just got some pleasure and put it in our pockets, and we felt each other up, felt mixed, and didn't think about it.

262

JG: Right, or we hoped to have pleasure but it didn't work, it was just OK. But sex is supposed to be transcendent or horrible.

LB: You're making me think that another reason "It's not about sex" is a powerful sentence is that if it *is* about sex it's hard to make meaning out of it. Sex is supposed to be meaningful.

JG: It can be bad or good, but it has to be meaningful. It ties you up into a teleological narrative: you're either living happily ever after or you're going to fall. This is the story of women's plots, which is if you make the wrong step that it has lifelong *consequences*. It gives sex enormous meaning. Part of "happily ever after" is that we have determined that these people are going to have sex repeatedly. The sex stops having meaning then because it looks just like a repetition, which it isn't. But it has no narrative meaning.

LB: Unless you decide to pay attention. Monica is a great example of someone who paid attention. She remembered *everything*. She had a diary, and she would go home and write in it, and she told her friends about everything. We had an event, we had another event, it went on for two years, it never moved from the stage of event to repetition.

JG: Maybe it didn't stop being an event because the relationship wasn't legitimate. Maybe that's a part of the pleasure of adultery: each time the relationship remains an event.

LB: I think if you live in the same town, it gets beyond the event stage pretty soon, but if you're in a long-distance affair, which their thing basically was, each "moment" can remain canonized.

JG: They lived in different worlds, they had to arrange transportation. One reason it kept being an event was that it was adultery. But more importantly, it was that there was a real risk that it would never happen again. They never settled into "this is ongoing." It was always news for her.

LB: She never knew when it would happen to her, describing herself sitting near the phone, waiting. Each instance of hailing was an event for her.

JG: The language of the event belongs somewhat to the discourse of seduction, from her point of view: will he give himself to her again?

V. Autobiography, Politics, Therapy

LB: One way you opened up your knowledge to a broader audience was by using autobiography. Because something hard had happened to you, you had to make an appeal of sorts, a brief for yourself that had the clarity of the law. This scene made you perhaps simplify something that, in another conversation, you might have been happy to keep difficult, acknowledging contradictions, incoherence, and unconsciousness, and so on. It's interesting to note under what conditions one can enter a more public language about sex and sexuality—in this case the overlapping domains of the law and autobiography, which is what you had to do in your legal brief too, I assume.

JG: There is a shadow version of *Feminist Accused of Sexual Harassment*, which is the 140-page response I wrote to the complaints—literally longer than the book, and very, very, very different. In some way, I had to write *Feminist Accused* to get that other text out of my system. What I hated about writing that other text was drawing lines, saying, no I never did anything ambiguous *in my life*. I always knew exactly what I was doing, there wasn't a shadow of an ambiguity; and that did such intellectual violence to me, to have to write that way, always completely un-ambiguous. That was the hardest part of the case—140 pages, and in three weeks. It was about not being who I am intellectually. I completely told the truth, but I found the mode of it really hard. It had to do with giving up the way I understand my experience to a legal discourse in which you're presumed guilty. I wrote the book partly to repossess my experience of the world.

LB: It would be very interesting to read Monica's testimony next to *Monica's Story*. What you're suggesting here are some of the ways autobiography can be dis-torted, so that you had to rewrite your autobiography in order to reinhabit it. The law calls you to a certain innocence that requires you not to be yourself, but to be yourself *for the law*.

JG: Basically because it was a world that says: if it is sexual, then it's guilty; and if it is innocent, then it isn't sexual. That very understanding of things just horri-fied me. That claimed a version of the sexual—that sex is evil.

LB: Evil is a different question than guilt, is that what you mean?

JG: Guilt is a discourse of the law. But although sexual harassment is a legal issue, it is such a moralized issue that it feels like it has to do with evil, not guilt. Take a term like "sexual predator." It's a word that defines someone not as guilty but re-ally evil, or amoral.

I think the notion of a sexual predator, this stuff about chemical castration, for example, it's horrifying. This might be because I just read James Kincaid's *Erotic Innocence*—just think that we live in a culture that believes that people who im-pose sex on other people are worse than people who murder other people. It's re-ally scary. He's specifically focusing on children, which is obviously the worst version of it, but it's actually larger than that. The argument he makes, which is powerful and horrifying, is that we actually care more about children's innocence than their lives. We say about children that it's worse to be violated than to be killed. That's what they used to say about women. Kincaid says that in the Middle Ages, when raped women would commit suicide, they would see that as good. It's based on this idea that purity is worth more than life.

LB: It's also about a notion of sexuality as a vascular monster that overcomes the will of reason. But it additionally enables people to talk about someone's personal history outside of morality. The nexus of unconscious, corporeal, hormonal, and intentional expression that equals your sexuality becomes material for trying to say that this person *isn't* evil because they are incapacitated by their sexuality, not rationally engendering acts but being overwhelmed by hard-wired impulses.

Contrast this to the story concocted during the sixties, when sexuality looked like a potentially beautiful thing, a site of derepression and transformation in so many domains personal and institutional. Part of what enabled that was a certain relation to autobiography. The derepression of knowledge about lives that had not been recognized as important, the legitimation of personal testimony, these stories were generated as knowledge *for* social transformation.

JG: Well, feminist studies is completely implicated in that story, and the conversation we're having is connected to the ongoing debate about whether the place of autobiography in feminist studies is just feminism turned into "the personal is the personal." The attack on autobiographical writing in feminism by feminists and nonfeminists, again, I think is missing the point, which is that just as there's bad traditional academic writing and good traditional academic writing, there's bad autobiographical writing and good autobiographical writing. This has to do with how rigorous it is, whether it's doing some work, if it's sloppy.

LB: But it's also about the therapeutic modalities of feminist work, its relation to problem solving, sexual and intellectual transformation or enlightenment, and the like. Is therapy transformative or monumentalizing? When people want to stop having a feeling, are they going to be directed toward conventions that, in a sense, destabilize them more and are less narratively satisfying, or are they going to do what they can to *stop the story*? One way of stopping the story and the feeling is to forget about it; another way is to come to terms through a fixed story about one's sexuality that one repeats ad infinitum.

This goes back to what you were saying before about the incitement for Bill to give it up more, tell his story again and again, for the law, perhaps for money, to his family and friends, and to "the American people." He'll be a professional speaker in any case, but people will turn everything into autobiography, in a way they've not at all done for previous presidents since, say, Nixon. He'll have to skirt the difference between confession and public autobiography, he will have to say that he's constantly changing for the good, and learning from his interactions. This incitement will come partly from the sense garnered in therapy culture that he would have been a better man and a better president if he'd had more self-knowledge.

JG: That's right, he needs more self-knowledge! He doesn't know enough!

LB: Or he knows enough, but doesn't want to feel responsible for his effects on other people.

JG: Yet Clinton did feel responsible for Monica. This is not the story of a happy-go-lucky guy. He tried to stop, he tried to act responsibly toward her, he tried to get her a job: he wasn't actually irresponsible toward her. His desire might have been irresponsible, but that's not the same thing.

VI. Anatomies and Destinies

LB: Let's return to the scene of Clinton and Monica writ large to ask: What's going to be its destiny?

JG: I think no one can imagine its future. No one can imagine Monica's future; we know she's going to be around for a lot more years and she's going to have a sexual life. People can't imagine that if she's going to get married, who would marry her, what it would mean, what this story would mean in terms of that. That's one thing. People can't really imagine what's going to happen to Clinton, they can't think about that. In fact, this whole thing has been about the unpredictable narrative destiny of the story. When it became clear that the impeachment was going to be pursued, people said they can't really do it or he'll get impeached. But actually something more complicated happened. He got impeached, but he was still president. That wasn't supposed to happen! It turned out that there was life beyond impeachment! That there was presidency beyond impeachment! There's something weird about being beyond impeachment. Impeachment seemed like such a horizon, which is what you can't see beyond, so when it turned out not to mean that he was being kicked out of office, it was really perplexing. It seems that there's something we're unused to thinking about, about the narrative in which you can be dragged through the mud and still be president, that sex doesn't ruin your life, that scandal doesn't ruin a public career. We're not in this narrative of when you fall, you fall. When you fall, you look silly, you fall on your ass, everybody laughs at you, Jay Leno makes jokes about you for six months, and you're still the president! Or you're still Monica, in fact going on TV, and dating, living this complicated life that's open-ended. So we seem to be out of that tragic narrative of one false step and that's the end.

LB: It could be bad, if you think that this means that no scandal can diminish his power because people are inured to scandal, there's so much of it, with the effect that Clinton can bomb Iraq and Kosovo every day and it doesn't scar his reputation. Or, it could be that people are distinguishing among kinds of scandal, such that they're not going to let something like sexuality become the outrage. Of course, they will if they're in Colorado! What if people had had to vote on this, rather than watch senators? I'm not sure that they would have voted with as much cynical realism or forgiveness as they seemed to express to reporters and pollsters. My view was that no matter what people thought about what Clinton did, the senators and congressmen were worse. It was such a partisan circus you either had to maintain your previous positions or give up on listening altogether.

JG: What struck me was the number of people I saw interviewed who identified with Clinton, who wouldn't want the private details of their sexual lives exposed. Everyone believed that at that level of detail, anyone would be humiliated. Let he who is without stain cast the first stone? Part of what's interesting is that usually in that kind of scapegoating mechanism, people disidentify with the scapegoat and throw him out, saying, "We are clearly unlike him." But people could identify with Clinton. But to have a really strong moralistic antisex culture, you have to have people who can operate through a kind of disidentification, who basically can channel whatever it is into a feeling of "I am not at all like that, get it out of my sight." That was what the right was counting on, and it really didn't happen, and it seems like we're in perhaps the beginning of a different moment than what seemed like a much more sexually moralistic moment of the last ten years.

LB: I don't have as much optimism about the relation between what people think and the way political culture proceeds.

JG: Which is worth saying. What seemed interesting to me about this is that people were just responding differently than the pundits predicted. Sometimes that was frustrating—people didn't want him to get impeached and he got impeached anyway. But it seems, ultimately, probably to be erased by the fact that he was still president.

LB: That would be a really great effect of all this.

JG: I think so too, but I'm an incurable optimist.

15 Sexuality's Archive

The Evidence of the Starr Report

Ann Cvetkovich

My disenchantment with the office of U.S. president makes me a somewhat re-
luctant commentator on the Clinton-Lewinsky affair, but I come to the topic out
of long-standing interest in the sex life of the U.S. president. During the late
1960s, at the age of twelve or thirteen, I used to have fantasies about being a sex
counselor to the Nixons. I imagined that Tricky Dick and his long-suffering wife
Pat, she of the Republican cloth coat, were still living in the benighted era of the
Hays Code and the TV sitcoms of the 1950s and hence sleeping in side-by-side
twin beds. In my first act as sex counselor to the First Couple, I would encourage
them to pull the beds together so as to emphasize sex rather than sleep. After that,
the details seem now, as then, a bit fuzzy. I do know that, as a precocious reader, I
was under the strong influence of the conduct manuals for the "sexual revolu-
tion," such as *Masters and Johnson's Human Sexual Response*, *Everything You Always
Wanted to Know about Sex*, and *The Sensuous Woman*, and since one major lesson I
had absorbed from them was the importance of foreplay, my fantasies never really
had to go all the way.

Improving the Nixons' sex life was my solution for ending the war in Viet-
nam. I was sure that Nixon's personality was impairing his judgment in doing the
right thing and ending the war in Vietnam, and there was a connection in my

mind between his unlikability and a sex life that I presumed to be lackluster. Clearly, a man so emotionally and sexually incompetent was not fit to run the country. (If the presumption that trouble in the president's sex life will lead to trouble for the nation seems crude or dubious, consider that the equations produced by my fantasy life seem to have been amply fulfilled by Bill Clinton's decision to bomb Iraq when faced with the threat of impeachment.) I wasn't entirely sure what pleasure could be had for Dick, who seemed irretrievably morose and caught in a public life for which he was temperamentally unsuited. So my real focus was on saving Pat, in hopes that she might be able to use the power of intimacy to effect the changes that the antiwar movement could not. My sense was that she was worn down and depressed by the burden of public life, torn between wanting to protect her husband and secretly knowing that many criticisms of him were valid. Pat's unhappiness was indicative of Nixon's influence not only on his wife but on the nation and the world as a whole. If he could be coached in how to give her more pleasure, he might be able to do a better job of taking care of the nation; and if Pat were happier, she might in turn be able to give her husband the satisfaction that would improve his leadership style.

This fantasy is an embarrassingly intimate text with which to enter the discussion about Bill Clinton and Monica Lewinsky, but I offer it as evidence of the simultaneously outlandish and powerful role of fantasy in constructing what we know and make of the presidency.[1] In such fantasies are registered our investments in public offices and political power, investments that circulate around a singular figure, such as the president, who personalizes or gives face to the abstract structures of state power. Eroticized or sexualized fantasies about the president are the product of a celebrity culture that makes public figures intimately available for scrutiny and speculation and that makes personality and politics indistinguishable.

Another name for the adolescent fantasies of young girls is fandom, and presidents and prime ministers occupied only a minor subgenre in my lavish and extensive fantasies about celebrities, which most frequently featured rock stars and movie stars. Fandom is itself a historically specific phenomenon, which is as much a part of the history of the 1960s and '70s as the Nixon presidency, the antiwar movement, and the so-called sexual revolution. Fan cultures were dramatically enabled and expanded by the popular culture of the 1960s that included television, rock music, and youth scenes, and the institutions of celebrity that they foster have played a crucial role in the ongoing displacement of political culture by media culture. The linkage between the sexual and the political that made it possible for me to imagine that the sex life of the president would have an impact on the war in Vietnam was also a discourse being forged in the 1960s. My fantasy life as a young fan thus constitutes an important archive for understanding the formation of versions of pro-sex feminism that continue to guide my responses, in the genres of both fantasy and intellectual analysis, to the presidency in the 1990s.[2] The very slightness or frivolousness of my Nixon fantasy—its obliqueness to the presumed dynamics of the political process, including the formation of public opinion—is also its significance.

My fantasies about the sex life of the president are a precursor to my subsequent interest in sexual politics, and they demonstrate my long-standing fascination with a simple, perhaps even crude, question: What's the connection between one's sex life and the rest of one's life? I'm not suggesting any simple equation between them—that, for example, good sex makes for a good life, or that without a good sex life, one cannot be happy—but I am curious about the multiple possible linkages between them and about how someone's sex life can be an important register of who they are and the social relations in which they are embedded.

I'm particularly wary of responses to Bill and Monica's affair that rest on the assumption that one's sex life and one's professional life, or one's private life and one's public life, should remain separate. Within the public sphere of mass media debate, for example, the range of feminist opinion has been especially limited and constrained by the presumptions of liberal notions about freedom and privacy. One option is to suggest that Clinton's sex life is a private matter and nobody's business but his own. Another strategy is to argue that Clinton's sexual freedom, as well as Monica's, is linked to the sexual freedom for which feminists have fought, and that they should be granted their freedom to engage in consenting sexual relations. A judgment against them runs the risk of resembling right-wing moralizing and anti-sex agendas.

Neither of these options is particularly satisfactory, and I seek to avoid them by addressing the president's sex life in specific material detail—including not just ejaculations, blow jobs, and come stains, but hallways and phone calls and gifts—rather than cordoning it off from inquiry through abstractions such as privacy and consent, however useful such principles might be in warding off a sexual witch-hunt. At the risk of replicating its obsessive surveillance, I take as my document the Starr Report, which offers an intriguingly concrete picture of what it's like for the president of the United States to attempt to have sex outside of marriage. Reading it prompts me to wonder in all seriousness what kind of leadership to expect from a president whose sex life is as severely circumscribed as the testimony about his affair with Monica Lewinsky reveals it to be. Implicit in my inquiry, it should be noted, is a decision to take the Clinton-Lewinsky drama seriously on its own terms rather than to view it as a displacement of more serious political issues onto a diversionary media spectacle. While I am very sympathetic to the latter strategy, the cultural text of Clinton-Lewinsky also serves as a vehicle for working out urgent matters of sexual politics.

Using the Starr Report as a document raises questions of epistemology and representation. How are we to answer questions about the sex life of the president? How would we know we had true answers to our questions if we got them? I've suggested already that fantasies about sex with the president are important cultural evidence even if not necessarily the stuff of legal inquiry. From this perspective, the Starr Report can be treated as a cultural document that occupies the same terrain as fantasy, gossip, and tabloid journalism. Given its marketing as bestseller, and its odd generic status as part legal document and part pulp novel, such contextualization seems entirely appropriate.

When I read the Starr Report, I find my thoughts turning, perhaps highly inappropriately, to slave narrative, most notably Harriet Jacobs's *Incidents in the Life of a Slave Girl*, another kind of document that exceeds the boundaries of genre and imports fictional strategies into the domain of testimony. Both must grapple with the challenge of representing sexuality in ways that will circumvent prurient interests in the service of other goals and with an ambivalence about making intimate lives public.[3] Both are produced under highly specific circumstances that need to be accounted for in order not to presume that testimony is being offered in an unmediated and authentic way. And both provide important documentation about the sex lives of powerful men. Jacobs's narrative is startling because it includes enough details to make vivid the logistics of white slaveowners' sexual relations with their slaves. What makes an impact is not so much the sexual acts themselves, but the details of Mr. Flint whispering in Harriet's ear or Mrs. Flint coming to Harriet's bed at night and mimicking her husband's seduction because she is so jealous of her husband's flirtation and suspicious of Harriet's own behavior. Through these visceral and material details of everyday life under slavery, Jacobs conveys the lived practices that lie behind more abstract representations of slavery. She draws us into the taboo world of white men having sex with slave women through an account that makes a seemingly unthinkable act literally possible. Jacobs offers glimpses of a domestic scene populated by men who barely bother to hide their desire, jealous wives who are not quite sure whether they want to know more or know less, and apprehensive slave girls doing the best they can to avoid being alone in a room with their masters. Just as the story of the Clinton-Lewinsky affair is a story about the spatial geography of the Oval Office, so too is *Incidents* concerned with the domestic architecture of the plantation household and with offering a graphic demonstration of how it was possible for sex, and even seduction, to occur within a space that would ostensibly seem to prohibit or prevent it. By some strange logic of associative thinking, I find *The Starr Report*'s hallway outside the Oval Office reminiscent of Jacobs's "loophole of retreat," the space under the roof of her grandmother's shed, where she was sequestered for seven years.

But if the juxtaposition of the two texts constitutes a form of "wrenching recontextualization" that Lauren Berlant and Michael Warner have described as an important strategy of queer reading, then perhaps this link is not entirely aberrant.[4] Although I would be reluctant to make too strong a link between Jacobs and Clinton-Lewinsky, or to imply that the latter are also slaves, both stories displace the abstractions of institutions with a visceral sense of bodies and spaces. I would be more inclined to link Clinton to both Mr. Flint, the philandering doctor who can't keep his hands off the slave girl living under his roof, and to Mr. Sands, the white congressman who fathers Jacobs's children and whom she hopes will use his political power to grant them freedom. The details of Jacobs's relationship with Sands remain vague in *Incidents*; we are never quite sure how she feels about him, or about whether the relationship was an expedient one through which she hoped to remove herself from the Flint household. Like Monica Lewinsky, she is under suspicion of using sex for power, and her need to defend against this accusation exerts a strong influence over her narrative. As Toni Morrison has pointed out, in articulating the nature of her project in the novel *Beloved*, the slave narrative, even as it appears very vivid and sensational, often "draws a veil over proceedings too terrible to relate."[5] Morrison especially emphasizes the slave narrative's inability to record "emotional memory," and she suggests that fiction may be necessary in order fully to capture this aspect of slave experience. Morrison proposes that "truth" may be more available through "fiction" than through "fact," and at the risk of wrenching her terms out of context, I find her distinction between "truth" and "fact" suggestive for thinking about ways to read the Starr Report that differ from that of a court of law intent on verifying the facts in order to expose perjury. Instead, the testimony and documents that surround the Clinton-Lewinsky affair might be read more truthfully through the operations of fantasy, through a reading that understands the text to offer only glimpses of the emotional, sexual, and social experiences it purports to describe.

Like the slave narrative, the Starr Report is a document whose conditions of production require a canny skepticism about the "realism" of the events on the page, even as it seduces the reader with the appearance of material and empirical evidence. Moreover, at various points both documents exceed their conditions of production and reception in order to provide unexpected insights into the cultural dynamics of intimacy and sexuality. Both make available, in the interstices of a generic narrative that glosses over many questions, certain details that open up questions and gaps. The details present in the Starr Report make vivid the material challenges of having sex with the president in the Oval Office. The constant surveillance that comes with the turf of being so public a person as the president makes it difficult for Monica and Bill even to speak to one another in private, much less have sex.

A number of key material details from the Starr Report acquired a fetishistic status in the media, most notoriously Monica's navy blue Gap dress with the come stains on it and the cigar that Bill reportedly inserted in her vagina. It is worth noting that one of the reasons for the amount of detail in the Starr Report is Bill's refusal to "go all the way" and engage in the kind of sexual intercourse that almost goes without saying. Because Monica and Bill did not have what "ordinary Americans" would think of as sex, i.e., penis-in-vagina heterosexual sex, a great deal of detail emerges in the Starr Report that might otherwise have remained shrouded by the default image of sexual intercourse.[6] Instead, the Starr Report offers nuanced distinctions about what parts of Monica's body Bill touched and whether she was clothed or not, and about whether, if she went down on him, she was having sex but he was not. The materiality or specificity of the evidence produces a textual encounter with the sensuous lived experience of their intimate life. At various points squeamishly revealing even for those with no qualms about sexually explicit representation, the report also becomes a fascinating portrait of the range of sexual acts that are covered over by vague terms such as heterosexuality, romance, affair. In this respect, it is compatible with the interests of studies of sexuality that insist on specificity and variation as a way of avoiding the pitfalls of abstraction that have produced simplistic versions of good sex and perverse sex.

The more famous details—the dress and the cigar—are part of a wider array on which I would like to focus my attention here, including the hallway off the Oval Office where most of Bill and Monica's "sexual encounters" occurred, the drama of Bill's (withheld) ejaculation, the gifts and notes they exchanged, and the role of White House employees in both facilitating and preventing their meetings. These details sit within the narrative of the Starr Report in an oddly materialist

273

way, providing not just legal evidence for Kenneth Starr's inquiry, but testimony—in a somewhat different, more emotionally loaded, register—to the psychodramas of middle-class heterosexuality in the wake of feminism.

The Hallway with the Door Ajar

The sexual encounters generally occurred in or near the private study off the Oval Office—most often in the windowless hallway outside the study. During many of their sexual encounters, the President stood leaning against the doorway of the bathroom across from the study, which, he told Ms. Lewinsky, eased his sore back.[7]

Although to some readers the Starr Report might seem needlessly explicit and voyeuristic in its inclusion of the sexual details of Monica and Bill's affair, it also, by acceding to the need to establish evidence that, even if they did not have sexual intercourse, they had enough sexual contact to compromise Clinton's testimony in the Paula Jones case, constitutes an extremely useful archive of intimacy. Read in the context of Laura Kipnis's materialist account of the extramarital affair, for example, it chronicles the logistics of space and time that are as much a part of any sexual encounter as the contact of one body part with another.[8] Confined to the hallway between the Oval Office and a more private study, Monica and Bill were unable to lie down, unable to take their clothes off, and forced to remain silent. "Sometimes I bit my hand so that I wouldn't make any noise," adds Monica. Moreover, Clinton at least was never able to let his attention stray too far. The door was kept ajar so that he could hear anyone coming into the Oval Office; on some occasions, they were interrupted by phone calls or visitors. In some instances, they persisted: "The President indicated that Ms. Lewinsky should perform oral sex while he talked on the phone, and she obliged" (96). During one meeting in the hallway, Clinton is distracted by the fear that someone might be outside the window. Monica testifies that "'when I was getting my Christmas kiss' in the doorway to the study, the President was 'looking out the window with his eyes wide open while he was kissing me and then I got mad because it wasn't very romantic'" (65). Spatially, then, the relationship is confined to the interstices of a public building, and the hallway in which they meet is not unlike the bathrooms and parks where gay men have public sex. Their sexual acts might more accurately be categorized according to a taxonomy of public sex, rather than according to distinctions between the hetero and the homo, or between oral, anal, and vaginal sex. The literal difficulty of finding a place or position in which to engage in any kind of sexual activity offers evidence of the degree to which Clinton's entire daily life is lived in the public eye and under constant surveillance, so much so that sexuality seems largely precluded except within the protected confines of heterosexual marriage.

The hallway is also reminiscent of Harriet Jacobs's "loophole of retreat," the space between the roof and the ceiling of a small shed, in which she spends seven years watching her family while waiting for a chance to escape safely to the North. Both prison and freedom, the garret spatializes slavery and thus provides a graphic representation of its effects. Similarly, Clinton's hallway demonstrates the constraints of the presidency—indeed, it might even drive the need for a sexuality that can represent the possibility of privacy, of an act that is not part of his professional life. Although differences between the president and the slave girl are vast, in both narratives spatial confinement makes the impact of social systems material.

Going All the Way

"I don't understand why you won't let me . . . make you come; it's important to me; I mean, it just doesn't feel complete, it doesn't seem right." Ms. Lewinsky testified that she and the President hugged, and "he said he didn't want to get addicted to me, and he didn't want me to get addicted to him." They looked at each other for a moment. Then, saying that "I don't want to disappoint you," the President consented. For the first time, she performed oral sex through completion. (115)

The famous semen-stained blue dress was not just Ken Starr's come shot, the incontrovertible evidence that the president had engaged in something approximating "real" sexual intercourse with Monica Lewinsky. As it turns out, such distinctions and hierarchies were also operating between Bill and Monica themselves, as she attempted to persuade him to go all the way and he resisted, ostensibly because he didn't trust her enough but also presumably because he was attempting to avoid precisely the version of "sexual relations" that Ken Starr was looking for. Unlike the young girls in Sharon Thompson's *Going All the Way*, who resist putting out before having secured their boyfriends' emotional commitment, Monica was determined to make Bill vulnerable enough to come.[9] In a reversal of the customary roles, she constantly pressures him to give it up. Monica plays the femme top, eager to use her sexual powers to provide satisfaction for her lover.

The erotics of postponement and substitution created by the need to avoid penis-in-vagina sexuality also give rise to what might be considered queer forms of sexuality. Most notably, for example, Bill and Monica's use of the cigar as dildo links their behavior to lesbian sex cultures, in which penetration by objects other than penises, such as fingers and dildos, is accorded the status of full-fledged sexual intercourse, not just substitute or foreplay. Of course, Monica herself seems to consider "penis-in-vagina sex" to be her ultimate goal, at one point managing to persuade Bill to touch his genitals lightly against hers. Going down on Bill seems to have been the easiest way for her to experience the intimacy of penetration without encountering his resistance.

This drama of penetration and its displacements is more an emotional than a sexual one, though. For Monica, penetration and ejaculation represent emotional intimacy, signaling that Bill trusts and even respects her enough to give her what she wants. It's not until their last two sexual encounters that he ejaculates. He has already disappointed her by breaking off the relationship and failing to get her another job in the White House after she was transferred. He is clearly struggling with the conflict between his desire for her and his understanding that it can only lead to trouble. But his submission ultimately seems more of an emotional than a sexual act, driven by his fear of disappointing Monica. He is enough of a sensitive man to be susceptible to her pleas to be given at least the experience of his orgasm if not of a fuller relationship. As a spatial sign of the increased intimacy of their last two explicitly sexual encounters in February and March of 1997, Bill and Monica actually move from the hallway into the bathroom off of the back study, risking being out of earshot of the Oval Office. It's a poignant moment in its own way, this drama of the president risking his own personal version of safe sex in order to please a woman who he knows has little power. And Monica is right in thinking that ejaculation is no small thing; Bill subsequently breaks off the relationship again, this time more emphatically. Despite changing historical circumstances, going all the way is still dangerous.

Emotional Attachment

I am not a moron. I know that what is going on in the world takes precedence, but I don't think what I have asked you for is unreasonable. . . . This is so hard for me. I am trying to deal with so much emotionally, and I have nobody to talk to about it. I need you right now not as president, but as a man. PLEASE *be my friend. (154)*

Are emotional and political relationships continuous or mutually exclusive? Does the president, as a constantly public person, have an identity as "just" a man or a friend? Although verging on the whiny, Monica's request raises a crucial question about the relative status of intimate relationships and professional ones. As if to acknowledge the affair's psychological complexity, the Starr Report's overview includes a section devoted to the topic of "Emotional Attachment." Once the relationship seems to be ongoing, Monica wants them to get to know each other. Their encounters include what she calls a form of "pillow talk" in which they return to the Oval Office to chat. Although sometimes Bill shuts her up from gabbing by kissing her, he seems to be genuinely interested in talking to Monica, eager to prove, for the sake of his own self-respect and hers, that he's not just out for pussy. The Starr Report offers the following evidence that their intimacy was more than just sexual: "They were physically affectionate: 'A lot of hugging, holding hands sometimes. He always used to push the hair out of my face.' She called him 'Handsome'; on occasion, he called her 'Sweetie,' 'Baby,' or sometimes 'Dear.'" (56). Monica recalls Clinton's pleasure with the ways that she made him feel young and that "he said he wished he could spend more time with her" (56). Although there is the drive for the come shot as proof of the intensity of the relationship, the Starr Report also indirectly verifies the reality of the relationship by focusing on the ways that it was about more than just sex. Revealing the impact of feminism on the intimate life of an affair, Monica wants more than sex, and she demands to be treated with respect as a person. Even more notable is Bill's willingness to comply, especially since his efforts to be something more than just a cad in his interpersonal relationships only seem to get him into trouble. The evidence of emotional intimacy between Monica and Bill reveals the shifts in sexual life produced by feminism, as well as the ongoing contradictions it has produced. Adding or substituting emotional intimacy for sexual intimacy does not necessarily resolve the power imbalances of an affair between a powerful public man and a less powerful woman.

Moreover, the sympathy that Monica has earned from Clinton himself because of his inability to satisfy her is gone once there is a possibility that she has failed to keep the secret of their relationship. (Perhaps he suspected even then that her claim to have nobody to talk to was a big lie.) Clinton goes so far as to say that if he'd known what she was like, he wouldn't have gotten involved with her. Knowing that she has very little bargaining power, Monica appeals to Bill on humanist grounds, suggesting that their intimacy might reside outside his professional status as president, and also on feminist grounds, suggesting that her bid for emotional recognition remains meaningful despite how "what is going on in the world takes precedence."

Monica's desire for a world outside professional connections in which her re-lationship with Bill could exist seems rather conflicted given her efforts also to capitalize on those connections. The relationship grows more complicated when it leaves the admittedly cramped space of an intimacy that seeks to remain out-side of social recognition and enters the more public domain in which Monica seeks redress both for her silence and for having fucked a man as powerful as the president. Transferred away from the White House to the Pentagon and disap-pointed by Clinton's failure to bring her back to an appointment in the White House, she applies pressure to get a good job elsewhere. The casualness of the nepotism that makes this request plausible is rather startling. Needing to distance himself from directly intervening, Clinton puts Vernon Jordan on the task; al-though it takes a little pestering from Monica via Bill to get Jordan to act, once he makes the calls to the U.N. and then, because Monica doesn't like that job and wants one in the private sector, to Ronald Perelman at Revlon, the job offers are almost instantaneous. Monica's sense of entitlement and her anger about not get-ting what she wants complicate the tale of emotional attachment thwarted by in-hospitable circumstances.

The Gift Economy

Many of the thirty or so gifts that Monica gave the president reflected his interests in his-tory, antiques, cigars, and frogs. Ms. Lewinsky gave him, among other things, six neck-ties, an antique paperweight showing the White House, a silver tabletop holder for cigars or cigarettes, a pair of sunglasses, a casual shirt, a mug emblazoned "Santa Monica," a frog figurine, a letter opener depicting a frog, several novels, a humorous book of quota-tions [about Jewish wit], and several antique books. He gave her, among other things, a hat pin, two brooches, a blanket, a marble bear figurine, and a special edition of Walt Whitman's Leaves of Grass. *(59–60)*

Both Monica and Bill were able to offer material evidence of affection, while still operating under cover of official protocols, by giving gifts. The gifts provided an excuse for her to visit the Oval Office and became a kind of secret code; Bill could signify his affection, for example, by wearing one of the ties that she gave him in public. Under pressure to destroy or to avoid accumulating any physical evidence of their relationship, the lovers create an archive that is simultaneously intimate and public. Its meanings remain invisible to others because the objects themselves have meaning largely because they are invested with sentiment.

The list of things they gave to each other reads like an odd cross between a state visit, Father's Day, and Hallmark greeting cards. The gifts are both personal and impersonal in part because they borrow from a public language of sentiment rather than expressing something more particular to the relationship. The final package Monica sent to Bill (via Betty Currie) included "a love note inspired by the movie *Titanic*" (182). Commercial culture is prevalent in other gift choices; Monica is extremely excited when Bill fulfills her request for souvenirs from the Black Dog, a popular restaurant in Martha's Vineyard, writing an e-mail to a friend to say "he not only brought me a t-shirt, he got me 2 t-shirts, a hat and a dress!!!! Even though he's a big schmuck, that is surprisingly sweet—even that he remembered!" (136). Grafted onto sanctioned public forms of gift giving, some of their choices, such as the White House paperweight or books about U.S. history, reflect their more professional identities and national sentiments. Does Bill think about Walt Whitman's sexuality when he gives Monica *Leaves of Grass,* or is Whitman representing the great tradition of American letters? The material language of Bill and Monica's affection may seem clichéd, or sentimental, or commodified, but that does not make it less real.

In the end, the gifts are subpoenaed by the investigation and considerable attention is given to the logistics of how they were collected by Betty Currie and "hidden" under her bed. Monica wrote on the box—"do not throw away!!" Fearful that others might not recognize the sentimental value of the objects, she stakes her claim to ownership in hopes that they will be of little value to others once their usefulness as evidence has ended.

The Hired Hands in the (Big) White House

Despite the apparent openness of the Starr Report, it only hints at many important stories that remain untold. Scattered throughout the text, for example, are references to the vast array of White House workers who were aware of the president's relationship with Monica and who played a role in facilitating it. Like many public figures, the president is surrounded by subordinates who are exposed to the intimate details of his life but supposedly not part of it. A more materialist approach to the lives of public figures would take this knowledge seriously, a fact often recognized by forms of gossip culture that draw on these sources (as well as by celebrities who hold their employees contractually obliged to remain silent). Among the interesting supporting characters are Evelyn Lieberman, the deputy chief of staff for operations, who gets Monica transferred to the Pentagon; and

Betty Currie, personal secretary to the president, who takes Monica's calls and sometimes escorts her into the White House on weekends. For some White House employees, it becomes a matter of state to protect Clinton from his own philandering impulses. Visits to prostitutes might have been much easier to arrange than sex within the workplace of the White House. When Monica shows up at the White House gate and raises a fuss because Clinton has been seeing Eleanor Mondale rather than taking her call, it is ultimately the guards at the gate who are reprimanded and threatened with being fired because they revealed this information.

An especially intriguing figure in the story of the Clinton-Lewinsky affair is Betty Currie. The Starr Report offers very little sense of who she is despite the fact that she plays a central role in enabling the relationship between Monica and Bill. There are only questions: Did she know what was going on in the Oval Office and the hallway and quietly pretend not to know or hear anything? What did she and Monica talk about when she escorted her into the White House or provided sanctuary for the box of gifts that became evidence? How does the fact that she is African American (information that remains invisible in the Starr Report) affect her relationship with the president? The specter of the plantation household arises again when contemplating the overdetermined role of race in the president's relations with his trusted employees (as well as his friend Vernon Jordan). These are stories that might require a different kind of investigation than Kenneth Starr's, one that would connect the intimacies of the president's sex life with the intimacies of his work life.

Sexual Healing

Because the most revealing details of the Starr Report are not its truths or its lies, it was particularly infuriating when the congressmen deliberating about the articles of impeachment invoked the rule of law as a way of explaining how they could vote for impeachment on grounds of perjury. They claimed that the actual content of the lie did not matter because, in principle, any lie was wrong. This lack of attention to the substance or detail of the testimony keeps what is valuable about it as an archive for sexual politics cordoned off behind a quantitative evaluation of evidence as merely true or false. The story told in the Starr Report is not really one that can be evaluated in a court of law; hence its excessive status as a text that can be read as gossip or scandal, but which also, if we are to take gossip seriously, gives us a cultural story. Thus, I would question the response to the affair that takes the form of suggesting that the President's sex life is none of our business. While that may be the case as far as the courts and legal inquiry are concerned, for those of us who come to the case from a cultural perspective the details of the Clinton-Lewinsky affair make it possible to analyze public life from the important vantage point of intimacy.

This reading of the Starr Report's archive yields a graphic version of sexuality, but one in which the graphic is not just sexually explicit but actually a more general category that encompasses the material specificity of everyday life. If our goal is not so much to catch Bill Clinton with his pants down and/or in an act of perjury as it is to learn something about sexual life, these material details are important. Viewing the Oval Office (and its hallways) as a site of sexual activity and not just public policymaking, and as a site where material bodies and not just symbolic figures live, offers useful perspectives on power, publicity, and domesticity. The sexual life of a public figure and national leader such as Bill Clinton raises questions about the way powerful men sustain their professional identities through a range of intimacies—with wives, mistresses, prostitutes, and assistants—that are part of the business of power. Abstract terms such as heteronormativity, adultery, nonmonogamy, and marriage don't quite capture what it is like to live inside of Bill Clinton's body, or Monica's. Or our own.

The Starr Report's evidence presents particular challenges for a feminist analysis of marital sex and adultery, sex in the workplace, and sexual harassment. For example, definitions of sexual harassment that characterize intimacy in general structural terms, such as, for example, in terms of relationships between coworkers or between teachers and students don't necessarily do justice to the intricacies of a relationship like Bill's and Monica's, which is a story of sexual frustration and limitation, as well as one of consent, seduction, and excitement. To describe their encounters as bad sex runs the risk of presupposing a judgment, whether moral, therapeutic, or political, about what constitutes good sex. But their furtive and abortive contact with each other offers testimony to a problem that no self-help solution or simple moral framework can fix. It's a story about a world in which feminism has raised expectations for both sexual and emotional satisfaction that have made neither marriage nor careers any easier. Although it may be harder for middle-aged professional men to remain oblivious to women's feelings and easier for young heterosexual women to seek empowerment through sexuality, there's still a lot of secret fumbling in the hallway. Despite historical change, erotic life still functions as both an escape from, and an avenue to, professional publicity. Perhaps because it's not in the business of offering neat solutions, the Starr Report's story, as I read it, speaks to the still urgent necessity of transforming everyday sexual lives and creating new forms of sexual experience. Unless there is room for a richer discussion of sex acts, and adultery, and sexuality and emotion, we won't be in a position to imagine (or fantasize) about makes for "good sex." From the vantage point of queer studies, perhaps we can begin to envision in "graphic" terms a visceral world of sexuality and bodily life that could rearrange the houses in which we live.

Notes

1. My claims for the value of intimacy here and throughout this article have been enabled by Lauren Berlant's work in *The Queen of America Goes to Washington City: Essays on Sex and Citizenship* (Durham, N.C.: Duke University Press, 1997), and the special issue of *Critical Inquiry* 24:2 (Winter 1998) devoted to the topic of "Intimacy."

2. For more on the social significance of young girls' fantasies, as well as on fandom more generally, see Constance Penley, *NASA/Trek: Popular Science and Sex in America* (London: Verso, 1997).

3. For considerations of *Incidents in the Life of a Slave Girl* relevant to my discussion, see Lauren Berlant in *The Queen of America Goes to Washington City*, chapter 6, pp. 221–246, and Hortense Spillers, "Mama's Baby, Papa's Maybe: An American Grammar Book," *Diacritics* (1987), pp. 65–81.

4. Lauren Berlant and Michael Warner, "What Does Queer Theory Teach Us About *X*?" *PMLA* 110 (May 1995): 343–349.

5. See Toni Morrison, "The Site of Memory," in Russell Ferguson, Martha Gever, et al., eds., *Out There: Marginalization and Contemporary Culture* (Cambridge, Mass.: MIT Press, 1991), 299–305.

6. See Henry Abelove, "Some Speculations on the History of 'Sexual Intercourse' during the 'Long Eighteenth Century' in England," *Genders* 6 (Fall 1989), 125–30, for a discussion of how this norm was installed, in the process relegating other forms of sexual activity to the status of "foreplay," and hence not "real" sexual intercourse.

7. *The Starr Report: The Independent Counsel's Complete Report to Congress on the Investigation of President Clinton* (New York: Pocket Books, 1998), p. 55. Subsequent page references will be included in the text.

8. See Laura Kipnis, "Adultery," *Critical Inquiry* 24:2 (Winter 1998), pp. 289–327.

9. Sharon Thompson, *Going All the Way: Teenage Girls' Tales of Sex, Romance, and Pregnancy* (New York: Hill and Wang, 1995).

Part 5

ETHICS AND MORALITY

16 Sex and Civility

Eric O. Clarke

> Behind the pseudo-democratic dismantling of ceremony, of old-fash-
> ioned courtesy, of the useless conversation suspected, not even unjustly,
> of being idle gossip, behind the seeming clarification and transparency
> of human relations that no longer admit anything undefined, naked bru-
> tality is ushered in.   —Theodor W. Adorno, *Minima Moralia*

Despite having the ring of an old-fashioned crankiness, the epigraph from Adorno touches on a vexing issue raised with near screeching annoyance during and after what has come to be known as the Lewinsky affair: the decline of civility in America. According to this decline narrative, Americans are just not nice to one another anymore. Across a range of situations and occasions, their behavior is downright inappropriate. No shared codes of conduct prevent us from yelling, cursing, honking, insulting, disrespecting, intentionally annoying, obscenely gesturing, or otherwise hurling abuse.

Much more than a simple plea for politeness, however, this decline narrative also comprises an entire jeremiad of elements that make up a rather mysterious thing called "public morals." The referent here for "morals," or simply "morality," lies in the realm of conduct. It is in this sense of morals as conduct that sex and the decline of civility became inextricably linked in the endless commentary on the Oval Office encounters between President Bill Clinton and intern Monica Lewinsky, the president's months-long denials and dissimulations to the public about these events, the report of the independent prosecutor, Kenneth Starr, the accompanying impeachment hearings in the House of Representatives, and the actual trial in the Senate. The president's sexual "misconduct" became the potent symbol for a nation whose "moral compass" was pointing in the wrong direction.

But what's sex got to do with it? Why, during the Lewinsky affair, did sex acquire such potent symbolic significance in relation to democratic civility, to the idea of "public morals"?[1] I suspect there are many answers one could provide. Here I would like to offer up a few problems in the relation between sex and civility, problems that are more definitional than exhaustive.

First, a telling incoherence defined the events surrounding the president's actions, the media coverage of them, and the political response: his alleged high crimes and misdemeanors both were and were not about sex. This incoherence was highlighted by the resignation of House speaker-designate Robert Livingston over stories circulating in the media that he had had extramarital affairs. If, as Republican members of the House Judiciary Committee insisted, Clinton's impeachment was not about sex, why would Representative Livingston resign not over perjury or obstruction of justice, but over infidelity? And why would he then figure his resignation as an "example" for Clinton to follow?

Livingston's resignation was only the most explicit example of the ambiguity surrounding sexual "misconduct" and legal infractions during the Lewinsky affair. More generally, this ambiguity reveals the fraught place of sex in the public sphere. On the one hand, the national media is saturated by sexualized spectacles and other putatively "nonpublic" aspects of the private sphere.[2] On the other, political leaders, news media, and conservative organizations concerned with "public morals" have derided the publicizing of sexual details from the Lewinsky scandal (along with, of course, many other examples of publicized salaciousness in the national media). Oscillating between the ceremonial (marriage), the repetitiously titillating (pornography), the officially sanctioned (monogamy), and the furtively intimate, sex hovers ambiguously between the ever metamorphosing division of private from public.

However, the incoherent vacillations between sexual misconduct and legal infraction, between "personal morality" and public interest, indicates more than dynamics particular to sexuality or sexual politics per se (although these are important factors). They also indicate the ambiguous status of morality itself.[3] In one instance, morality designates the sort of prudish restrictions on individual behavior, especially sexual behavior, that are anathema to self-determination and individual liberties. Particularly for modern societies held together more by political administration than shared ethnic identities, religious traditions, or organicist conceptions of the nation, this kind of morality often functions as a last line of defense for "tradition." This is especially true for those who view behaviors that stray from an imaginary set of norms—behaviors often gathered under the euphemism "lifestyle"—as signs of national weakness and social decline. In another instance, morality also designates the very ground on which self-determination and individual liberties (not to mention "lifestyles") would be defended: the universalism of Enlightenment moral-political principles, such as rights, whose notions of the human, of human dignity, undergird most progressive political claims. The Enlightenment moral-political legacy largely defines the terrain on which political struggle in the West is played out. The contemporary political philosopher Axel Honneth has succinctly summarized this important political valence of morality: "Morality, if understood as an institution for the protection of human dignity, defends the reciprocity of love, the universalism of rights and the egalitarianism of solidarity against their being relinquished in favor of force and repression."[4] Whether one agrees with Honneth's assessment or not, his position usefully pinpoints the moral principles that significantly, and sometimes silently, shape the grounds for progressive politics.

The tortured confluence of the restrictively punitive and the expansively protective aspects of morality has impacted contemporary lesbian and gay politics in a quite pronounced way. The political vision of national lesbian and gay organizations and publications in the U.S. is increasingly saturated by both rights discourse *and* moralizing sexual discourses. Because of this, national lesbian and gay politics has begun to capitulate to a national political imaginary that views individual moral worth as the sine qua non of enfranchisement itself. It has become increasingly common for U.S. lesbian and gay political leaders, spokespersons, syndicated columnists, and publications to tell their readers and constituencies that they must *earn* the rights they seek by conforming to a phantom normalcy. Yet this is only half the story. Because only certain rights are deemed worth having—largely marriage and military service—only those who conform to the version of social belonging these rights enshrine are deemed worthy of rights in general.[5] In this way, a conduct-based morality has crept into contemporary progressive sexual politics, and as a result has largely contoured the moral-political vision of lesbian and gay politics in general. Sexual propriety in particular has infiltrated lesbian and gay politics to such an extent that a former White House intern could effectively trump the hand of what counts as progressive sexual politics simply by extolling the pleasures of phone sex on national television.

A severely constipated vision of sexual politics, however, forms only the most pronounced moment in the strange confluence of traditional behavioral codes and protective moral-political principles. This confluence creates a more generalized atmosphere of indeterminacy. Because the oscillation between a restrictive and an expansive morality constantly shifts the ground on which individual liberties and social belonging stand, no clear standards of value can operate as the regulators of enfranchisement. On the one hand, traditional, conduct-based moralities rely on action-based attributions of value, which are then retrospectively read as signs of the inner worth of one's character. On the other, the moral-political principles that underlie social enfranchisement, such as rights, depend upon ideas of the human in general by which worth is (at least in principle) settled a priori. While notions of value ground both types of morality, the modes of judgment within which value is practiced can differ significantly. The enabling ambiguity between these modes of judgment certainly presented a challenge both to the national media's spectacularization of Clinton's indiscretions and to the legislative bodies assigned the task of adjudicating his guilt or innocence. What relevance could sex have, exactly, in this adjudication?

This compacted task of judgment was made even more tenuous by the very nature of Clinton's trysts. They were part of what we may call indeterminate erotic expression—forms of erotic expression not subordinated to already valorized aspects of social belonging defining legitimate sexual personhood, such as contractual marriage or its semblance. Indeterminate erotic expression includes, for example, chance encounters, phone sex, orgies, s/m, or indeed blow jobs in the corridors of the White House. The indeterminacy of Clinton's erotic indiscretions set in motion the mechanisms by which "public morals" and legal-juridical principles came together and demanded the intercession of a judgment ultimately unable to adjudicate between sexual misconduct and legal infraction. Its inability, I would argue, indicates not only that indeterminate erotic expression violates the propriety of traditional sexual moralities. Because indeterminate erotic expression remains largely outside the purview of rights, it also indicates the limits and failures of the way civil rights as universal moral-political principles have been conceptualized and practiced.

In this way, indeterminate erotic expression demands the intercession of judgment not in the sense of an adjudication of worth, but rather in the sense of an imaginative revaluation of ethical life. This revaluation takes place by inhabiting the contradictory space of an ambiguous moral sphere—the historically contingent instantiation of ideally universal, democratic moral-political principles. There is a pressing need to struggle over how rights are defined and practiced. Further, such a revaluation is made possible by understanding the inadequacy of an ambiguous moral sphere for generating a different order of value—which is to say, an order of value not dependent on unduly restrictive sexual proprieties. Judgment can then become a practice of value that emerges from and yet importantly *exceeds* an ambiguous moral sphere. A more expansive and ethically attuned judgment forms one of the broader possibilities emerging from specifically *queer* thought and life, possibilities that go beyond an enfranchisement constrained by moral worth.

These possibilities can emerge only if a leftist commonsense repudiation of the moral is displaced in favor of grasping and reworking the ethico-political field now inhabited by unduly restricted modes of judgment. If morality, in one of its guises, forms an inescapable ground for progressive thought and politics, then it is all the more incumbent to recognize the value determinants that saturate an ambiguous moral sphere. This is also to say, self-conscious reflection on the principles of value that mediate progressive efforts to expand enfranchisement can also lead to less proprietary notions of civility itself. This is why, I would suggest, Theodor Adorno defended something like "old-fashioned courtesy" against the pretense of an immediate transparency in social interaction. Appeals to "normalcy" or "authenticity" cannot take the place of seriously working through the forms of moral common sense that mediate public and private life. Efforts to present lesbians and gay men "as they really are," which is to say "just like everyone else," has failed to generate an equitable enfranchisement. In the end, such efforts present no more and no less than a very particular, thoroughly sanitized picture of queer life that nevertheless legitimates itself as total. Parading under the guise of authenticity, such efforts thus disable progressive thought from reoccupying and thus reworking the moral terrain it nevertheless must tread.

Notes

1. Gayle Rubin argued some time ago that sex often acquires a symbolic (and highly politicized) importance far beyond its confines, particularly in relation to "moral panics." See Gayle Rubin, "Thinking Sex: Notes for a Radical Theory of the Politics of Sexuality," *Pleasure and Danger: Exploring Female Sexuality*, ed. Carole S. Vance (Boston: Routledge and Kegan Paul, 1984), 267–319.

2. See Lauren Berlant, *The Queen of America Goes to Washington City: Essays on Sex and Citizenship* (Durham, N.C.: Duke University Press, 1997).

3. Michel Foucault presents a succinct discussion of morality's ambiguity in *The History of Sexuality,* vol. 2: *The Use of Pleasure*, trans. Robert Hurley (New York: Vintage, 1984), 25.

4. Axel Honneth, *The Fragmented World of the Social: Essays in Social and Political Philosophy*, ed. Charles W. Wright (Albany: SUNY Press, 1995), 256.

5. On the relation between moral worth and social enfranchisement, see Eric O. Clarke, *Virtuous Vice: Homoeroticism and the Public Sphere* (Durham, N.C.: Duke UP, 2000), 29–67.

17 "He Has Wronged America and Women"

Clinton's Sexual Conservatism

Janet R. Jakobsen

"He has wronged America and women," proclaims Pheda Fischer, who is described in the *New York Times* as "a 74-year-old retired nurse from Waveland, Miss." She continues, "I don't understand why the women's organizations don't get upset. Don't they have any morality? I still want him gone" (January 26, 1999, A15). The standard response to Ms. Fischer's inquiry about the morality of "women's organizations," or feminists in general, is that while they don't like what Clinton has done and find him (as supposedly does the rest of America) to rate "near rock bottom" as a "moral leader," they like his policies and so want him to stay in office. Moreover, the narrative continues, those who hound the president, both the independent prosecutor, Kenneth Starr, and congressional Republicans represent the political faction—the radical and Christian right—that is the most hostile to women's interests.[1] Thus, feminists are willing to sacrifice morality to politics. This narrative has an appeal that is both commonsensical—along the lines of "my enemy's enemy is my friend"—and ideological, along the lines of "we always suspected that feminists were fundamentally amoral and self-interested."

In this essay I will suggest, however, that the obverse is, in fact, a more accurate account of at least some feminists' response to the Clinton impeachment scandal. These feminists, myself among them, think that Clinton's policies are bad for women. These same feminists do not think that the right wing that sought to remove Clinton from office had accurately identified the moral problems in either his administration or in his personal behavior. Finally, we have questions about the moral integrity or hypocrisy of the right itself. We wonder whether Clinton's actions have been more morally problematic than those of any other postwar U.S. president with the possible exception of Jimmy Carter. To put the issue this starkly is to put it provocatively. Who, after all, wants to defend Bill Clinton on moral grounds? And yet it is important at least to engage with the question of how one understands the moral problems with Bill Clinton, because to do so provides the opportunity to explore the political effects of moral language and particularly moral language about sexuality in U.S. public discourse.

Tina Turner for President

In the fall of 1996, as presidential elections came around once again, my best friend was in line to vote in Philadelphia when a disagreement erupted between the woman in front of her and the election workers. The woman wanted to cast a write-in vote, which required a special form in these days of electronic elections. The election workers were resisting her request, apparently because it would be a hassle to find the form. My friend happily chimed in on behalf of her comrade in line, thankful for some interest in an election that seemed to offer only bad choices. Eventually, the woman won the day and was granted her constitutional right to vote, the form was procured and the line moved on. On their way out of the building, my friend and her new acquaintance conversed and eventually my friend gathered the courage to say, "If you don't mind my asking, who did you write in?" "Tina Turner," the woman responded. "Don't you think that if she were president there would be a battered women's shelter on every corner?" My friend wholeheartedly agreed, thinking that she had missed an opportunity by not voting for Tina Turner herself.

The problem for my friend and me in voting in the presidential elections was that by the fall of 1996 Bill Clinton had already demonstrated that he was not an ally to any of the causes that we care about most: the struggles against racism and sexism, and for economic justice and sexual freedom. His first term was largely lackluster on a number of these issues, and he was most successful in making the traditionally Republican economic agenda central to the Democratic party (taking over from George Bush, for example, in the fight for NAFTA). Then, in the summer of 1996 Clinton did major damage in all of these areas simultaneously with two strokes of the pen by signing both the Personal Responsibility and Work Opportunity Reconciliation Act (also known as "welfare reform") and the Defense of Marriage Act. In terms of policy, at least, Bill Clinton damaged poor people in general and poor women in particular. Clinton's rhetoric surrounding "welfare reform" continued the long tradition of demonizing poor women, particularly young women of color, for their sexuality. He had earlier undermined gay rights with his "don't ask, don't tell" policy that was supposed to be gay friendly but in practice this has led to more discharges on the grounds of sexuality than in the years leading up to its institution. And then he supported the Defense of Marriage Act, which bizarrely "defended" marriage by homophobic caveat.[2] By the time of the election, it was clear that in certain ways the policies that were enacted during his administration were at least as bad from a feminist perspective as those of the Reagan-Bush years.

Having given Clinton up as a lost cause, imagine our surprise when in the fall of 1998 and winter of 1999, as the impeachment saga unfolded, feminists were accused of moral hypocrisy for not hopping on the bandwagon to remove the president from office over his sexual misdeeds. Feminists, we were told, refused to support the president's impeachment because we liked his policies too much. The very same feminists who forced sexual harassment law on the American public were unwilling to enforce its precepts once it was one of their friends in the hot seat. Feminism's moral feet of clay had been exposed.

To someone trained in the study of ethics, as I am, these charges seemed to require some very basic moral analysis. The questions that one learns to ask when studying ethical "cases" are particularly relevant to this "case" as well: What are the basic moral principles that are at stake? How can these principles be applied to the case at hand and what is the context for their application?

Moral Principles: Sexual Freedom

Many feminists have long been suspicious of the type of right-wing sexual conservatism that was behind so much of both the Starr Report and the impeachment proceedings themselves. While this is only one among various feminist positions on the question of the president's impeachment, I will explore it in the rest of this essay because it is not the expected position in mainstream political talk about "feminists" and because it explains the apparent paradox of the hesitancy on the part of many feminists to support the impeachment.

Feminists have long argued that historically one of the major means through which women have been disempowered is by control of their sexuality. This control has been enacted in a contradictory manner: both by treating women as if they are and/or should be asexual, and by treating women as if they are nothing but their sexuality. The contradiction has made the control of women through their sexuality more effective, and it has made fighting that control more difficult.

Sexual relations are fundamentally intertwined with power relations. Sexual harassment law is based on the recognition that sexual relations involve enactments of power and thus that sex can sometimes be a means of abusing power.[3] If women are harassed and humiliated at work by being subjected to sexual aggression, if, for example, they are treated as if they are only their sexuality, then women are denied the exercise of their right to earn a living. But harassment is not the only means by which sexuality can be employed to limit women's social power. Women have also been constrained by strict standards of sexual respectability in which virtually any expression perceived as sexual could produce social ostracization. This ostracization is not just the stuff of high school angst. Rather, it can resonate in women's economic lives, particularly for those women whose livelihood depends on marriage, but also for women who might not depend on it. A loss of sexual respectability can have serious and permanent social and economic consequences. Because both an emphasis on and a denial of women's sexuality have been mechanisms for enacting gender dominance, feminists have developed a notion of sexual freedom in which women are free to express their sexuality while also being free from sexual harassment as well as sexual dangers like rape.

The connection between sex and power is not just a matter of gender relations, however. As with gender domination, the major mechanisms of racial domination in the United States historically have included sexual harassment and abuse and the accusation that people of color lack sexual respectability and hence deserve to be socially segregated and ostracized. Historians like George Mosse have also shown how sex, and sexual respectability in particular, have been central in the maintenance of class hierarchies. Like the complex question of sexual freedom that is enacted both through the right to express one's sexuality and the right to say no to unwanted sex, the problem of sexuality as a vector of domination in different kinds of social relations has challenged feminists to complicate their notions of sexual freedom. So, for example, feminists have developed concepts of reproductive freedom that include rights to freedom from unwanted pregnancy and rights to the freedom to have children regardless of race or class status.

The various social movements with which feminism has been historically intertwined—antiracist, economic justice, lesbian, gay, and queer rights, environmental issues—have over the course of their histories developed a variety of meanings for freedom. These visions of freedom are often complicated, and they are distinct from the traditional, conservative notion of freedom as autonomous individualism. For example, Katie Cannon has pointed out that African American communities, and African American social movements in particular, have been a central source for American understandings of freedom. Cannon argues that African American concepts of freedom rarely focus on the type of individualism that is a marker for modern capitalism.[4] Rather, African American concepts of freedom have been more focused on freedom for the community as a whole. Free blacks, for example, argued for the abolition of slavery in part because they recognized that they could not be truly free while others were enslaved. Cannon writes of a freedom that is fundamentally moral and communally, not individually, based. For other feminists, freedom has been similarly grounded in relationships. If the value of autonomy depends on the denial of the labor of others, which makes certain forms of action and agency possible, then from this feminist perspective both moral agency and freedom must recognize their implication in relationships. Sexual freedom would involve a recognition of the relational implications of sexual acts, and thus would encourage honesty and respect for one's partners.

Conservatives will respond, however, that sexual freedom is precisely the problem, that sexual freedom is not a moral principle but a sign of the very immorality that currently threatens America. Bill Clinton, in this conservative view, exemplifies the dangers of pretending that sexual freedom could have any connection to morality. For conservatives, the logical outcome of social movements claiming sexual freedom is—Bill Clinton. And while feminists (including Hillary) may deserve Bill Clinton, the rest of the country should be protected from him and people like him.

There are two clear problems with this conservative view. First, there is rarely any explanation of why sexual freedom is the height of immorality, while other types of freedom—political and economic freedom, freedom of speech and thought—are not only expressions of high moral principle, but are, in fact, the central values of the American nation. Second, how is Bill Clinton the paradigmatic example of sexual freedom in action? He has not expressed or employed the principle of sexual freedom in either his personal actions or his policies. In fact, Bill Clinton is a sexual conservative.

With regard to the first of these points, the most common conservative defense is the putative consequences of sexual freedom: unwanted pregnancy, sexually transmitted disease, AIDS, broken homes, children without fathers (and from there it is a short slide to poverty and crime). Yet, when it comes to political and economic freedom, the argument about consequences is deemed irrelevant. Freedom of speech is so important, conservatives argue, that it must be protected on college campuses regardless of consequences. Even hate speech must be protected regardless of the harm inflicted on individual students or the damage done to the community as a whole. Consequences, even when damaging, must be disregarded to uphold the higher principle of freedom of speech because this freedom is one of the foundations of our democracy. Sexual freedom is frivolous in comparison to this foundational freedom. Thus, we face horrible consequences for the sake of frivolous and self-indulgent passions. Sex just is not, or should not be, that important.

And yet, sex was important enough to impeach the president. Here we have one of the central contradictions of American thinking about sex. Sex is both frivolous, a private concern, *and* sex is central to American public life. In the course of this article, I will suggest that sexual freedom is not only an important personal freedom and individual right, it is also fundamentally tied to the other forms of freedom and equality on which American democracy is supposedly based. I will also suggest that Bill Clinton's affair with Monica Lewinsky was not an expression of a new sexual freedom associated with the social movements of the 1960s and 1970s. Instead, Bill Clinton merely enacted the long-standing tradition of heterosexual monogamous marriage as duplicitous (at least for powerful men).

One final objection must be addressed before moving on to consider the context of this case, which is the claim that this case is not really about sex at all. The president was impeached for lying under oath in the Paula Jones sexual harassment case and for obstruction of justice in trying to cover it up. It just happens that the lies were about sex. While technically correct, this is a difficult position to maintain. (The president was excoriated for focusing on legal technicalities that could obscure the "real" truth.) Not only is the Starr Report obsessively filled with sexual details, even the House managers for the Senate trial admitted that many senators associated the perjury charge with sex, and thus the managers tried to focus their strategy on obstruction of justice.[5] We also have to ask why these charges in particular led to the impeachment of the president.[6] Ronald Reagan was also accused of potentially obstructing justice, not in a sexual harassment case, but rather in providing support for the Contras in Nicaragua. These were serious charges, yet there was never any serious move for impeachment. Why impeach the president this time, when the crimes were not crimes of state? Why were accusations with regard to lying about sex powerful enough to set the impeachment in motion? Why did the revelations about wrongdoing with regard to campaign finance that were breaking at the time of the impeachment hearings seem to bounce out of the public consciousness virtually immediately, even as we remained transfixed by all-Monica-all-the-time on cable television?[7] It is also important to think through the American people's position on lying, which is, it seems, a complicated one. If we compare public reactions to the Reagan and Carter presidencies, then we see that the more honest of the two was staggeringly less popular with the American people. In one sense the destruction of Jimmy Carter's presidency centered on questions of belief, his own sincere belief in Christianity and his scrupulous honesty, which made him believable—but also laughable—before the American people. His Christian belief and his honesty were among a complex of characteristics that made Carter seem less than traditionally masculine, and the Iranian hostage crisis confirmed this failure in masculinity and ultimately led to the end of Carter's presidency. Clinton's lies, however, never undercut his popularity with the American people, perhaps in part because they were the type of lies that confirmed his conventional masculinity.

Finally, if this case were only about lying and not about sex, it would be hard to explain the political pressure that led Representative Robert Livingston to resign from the House and from his position as Speaker-elect when his own extramarital affairs were revealed. Livingston was never accused of lying (although he did not reveal these affairs publicly until forced to do so), and he was never accused of lying under oath or of obstructing justice. His resignation makes clear that the political environment created by the Clinton impeachment was fundamentally and irrevocably about sex. Finally, for the purposes of this paper, the claim that Clinton has "wronged America and women" and that feminists are moral hypocrites is based fundamentally on sex. Feminists should have been the first to the ramparts against Clinton, not because he lied, but because the case in which he lied was about sex.

The Context: Morality and the Culture Wars

The charges against feminism, as well as those against Clinton, invoke the complicated terrain of contemporary U.S. culture and politics, including the effects of the "culture wars" over issues of race, gender, and sexuality that have been going on since the social movements of the 1960s and 1970s.[8] According to some of his critics, Clinton is the embodiment of the destructive force of these movements, a clear example of the negative effects of liberated gender and sexuality, which also involved displaying all too much comfort with the crossing of any type of social boundary, including racial boundaries. This comfort led many to think of Clinton as America's first "culturally black" president. This analysis explains how conservatives in Congress could be so angry at a president who had supported much of their legislative agenda and had himself brought the country to the right on certain issues of economic and social policy.

For example, on December 20, 1998, the day after President Clinton was impeached by the House of Representatives, in an article in the *New York Times* attempting to comprehend the Republican "urge to impeachment" despite strong public opinion against such a move, former congressman Father Robert F. Drinan is reported as saying: "And more and more I think it's cultural. These people say that Clinton is responsible for abortion and homosexuality. They just dump on him." Later in the same article, former senator Lowell P. Weicker, importantly identified by the *Times* as "one of the first Republicans in 1974 to urge the impeachment of Richard M. Nixon, and who supports Mr. Clinton's impeachment," is reported as saying that "the President's strong showing in the polls was a testimony to the way women and minorities viewed the Republican Party rather than Mr. Clinton himself. 'If you are women, if you are a minority, why would you want to kick out a man that you perceive as your friend and put yourself in the hands of a political party governed by the religious right?'"[9]

It seems clear that both Drinan and Weicker are right about the perception on the part of many of the opponents of impeachment that what was driving the impeachment process was a deep set of cultural issues that had in the past few decades been fought over vociferously, often under the banner of the "culture wars." There is an important distinction between Drinan's and Weicker's comments, however. Drinan is clear that the right has identified Clinton with a particular set of cultural issues. It would be a mistake, however, to presume that, as Weicker apparently does, Mr. Clinton is thereby your friend "if you are women, if you are a minority." (The tortured nature of Weicker's syntax is just another example of how difficult it is to think of these various issues as interconnected.) This supposed friendship on the part of Clinton is certainly suspect if you're a minority woman and poor. What Weicker is also missing is that those who oppose impeachment (without necessarily supporting the president) were often as concerned about the type of charges against the president and the method by which the inquiry was undertaken as they were about those on the right who promoted impeachment. As Orlando Patterson wrote in a *Times* editorial: "One reason African-Americans have so steadfastly stood by the President, in spite of his having done so little for them, is that their history has been one long violation of their privacy."[10] Put perhaps most succinctly by Julian Bond, "They had the guy and went looking for the crime. We've seen that before." Thus, many African American activists and scholars, including many African American feminists, were opposed to the president's impeachment.

What concerned many opponents of impeachment was not that Clinton had been their friend in policy terms, nor even that Clinton was threatened by those who also threatened "women" and "minorities," but rather that the means employed—lurid sexual accusation—have been employed time and again to prevent the exercise of various forms of freedom. Sexual freedom is central to the possibility for other forms of freedom in America in part because the language of sexual accusation is so often used to prevent the exercise of various freedoms or to undermine social movements for freedom. This type of sexual accusation is often made in highly moralistic language, the type of language that has been central to the conduct of the culture wars.

The culture wars, ostensibly over cultural issues such as, "obscene art," "teenage pregnancy," or "honor in the White House," also have a means of maintaining American social hierarchies through the use of moral language. The language of morality has been particularly central for those conservatives who wish to maintain the social hierarchies that the new social movements coming out of the 1960s and 1970s have attempted to transform. It is very difficult in the contemporary political climate simply to assert these hierarchies as positive—simply to say, for example, that women are "unequal" to men (although such statements, as Newt Gingrich was all too happy to remind us in his famous remarks with regard to women in the military, remain part of the political landscape). It is both more possible and more effective to say that shifts in gender relations produce dangerous moral problems. The stir raised by economist Gary Becker's *A Treatise on the Family* is a case in point.[11] In a relatively familiar refrain, this time backed by an impressive array of numbers, Becker argues that women's gains toward economic equality have led to higher divorce and illegitimacy rates and to a lack of respect for men as husbands. The idea that men could or even should find some means of gaining respect from the women in their lives other than through the economic subordination of those women is not part of Becker's analysis. While Becker himself does not advocate a simple return to the "traditional" family, the implication of his analysis, taken up more explicitly by a number of news articles on his research,[12] is that women's equality poses a social and moral problem. Similarly, it is no longer plausible in mainstream discourse to make direct moral claims based on race—to say, for example, that African Americans are inherently immoral. It is, however, commonplace to make moral claims about sexual behavior that have the same effects. One of the reasons that proponents of traditional morality are so contentious in their moral assertions is that they are used to being able to proclaim on the moral worth of others, yet they then sometimes find themselves in the uncomfortable position of being charged with immorality. Racism and sexism are moral as well as social problems. The outrage expressed by some persons at being called "racist" or "sexist" (which in contemporary debates seems sometimes to be a bigger trauma than being the object of racism or sexism could ever be) is indicative of the shock caused by being on the other end of moral exchange.

The use of moral language about sexuality in particular is often a means of making connections among issues like gender, race, and class. For example, in contemporary discourse sex has importantly come to be identified as a "behavior" in contrast to the supposedly immutable characteristics of race or ethnicity. So, for example, in the debate over "welfare reform" in 1996, there was much talk, including by Clinton himself, about "teenage mothers," and this talk invoked a particular image: the young, urban, poor woman of color. Here, a moral discourse about sexual *behavior* did much of the work that directly racist discourses have done in the past, and yet race need not even be mentioned. In this instance, moral language about sexuality enabled the formation of public policy with distinctly racist effects directed primarily at poor women.

The contemporary political tendency to accomplish social goals through moral language focused on cultural issues is one of the ways the disjunction between the presumption of Clinton's "friendship" with "women and minorities" and his policies has been obscured. The president's detractors have not seemed to notice that socially his policies have been bad for many African Americans and people of color, particularly in economic terms. Rather, conservatives are offended by the cultural affront of President Clinton's apparent comfort with African American people and with an African American public presence in his administration. There was a sense in the general discussion of the impeachment that it had something to do with race relations. The white supremacist ties of Trent Lott and Bob Barr have been remarked upon in the major media (and denied by both Senator Lott and Representative Barr), but the major connection offered between this cultural comfort with (if not full acceptance of) white supremacy and the impeach-ment proceedings is mostly made in terms of a more general cultural war.[13] It is easier to understand why issues of race are relevant to impeachment when they are considered in the context of the ways that race and sex have been linked throughout American history. In particular, from the lynching of African Ameri-can men to accusations that African American women are never sexually re-spectable, sex has been used as a means of monitoring, adjudicating against, and often punishing persons so as to maintain racial boundaries and racial domina-tion. It is quite possible that such ties were at work in this case as well, that the perception that Clinton was "culturally black" (so named by Toni Morrison) fu-eled the hatred of Clinton by white southerners like Barr. Clinton was himself a white southerner, and his cultural comfort (fraternization even) with African Americans did violate basic racial boundaries. To attempt to reinforce such bound-aries and punish such violations through sexual regulation is nothing new. It is important to consider such ties between race and sex precisely because they pro-vide a context for understanding the relationship between Bob Barr and Trent Lott's ties to white supremacy and the main discussions of Clinton's sexuality.

This set of connections is part of what makes sexuality so central to con-temporary American politics (despite the fact that conservatives regularly pro-claim it to be trivial and worthy only of being ignored). These connections also provide one of the reasons why sexual freedom is important not just to feminist concerns, but to a wide range of social issues. Sexual freedom is an important part of American freedoms more generally, because it is crucially connected to various freedoms across social issues.

The other major moral contention that has been central to the "culture wars" is how morality itself works. Conservatives denigrate feminist understand-ings of morality as amoral at best. The issue is posed by conservatives as being one between an "absolute" and a "relative" morality. Repeatedly, conservatives in both the House and Senate proclaimed their morality to be absolute and that of their opponents to be relative and, therefore, worse than no morality at all. As with most such oppositions, however, the two sides are rarely as neatly divided as the rhetoric might imply. The speech made by Representative Jim Leach, one of the Republican moderates in the House who were the last to commit their votes for impeachment, is a particularly poignant example of the effects of the push for the language of absolute morality. Leach was first elected in the 1970s before the con-servative turn that marks the contemporary Congress and has been a serious mod-erate. He has also been a major opponent of Clinton's, trying vigilantly to pursue questions of financial misconduct, particularly with regard to the electoral process. He was, it seems, genuinely undecided until the end and did not support all of the articles of impeachment. Part of his speech in deciding to support the first and second articles of impeachment (in his words, "those dealing with perjury") ran as follows:

In the final measure, what is at issue regarding possible impeachment of the President is a question of relativism versus absolutism. Relatively speaking, there is little doubt that other Presidents have had inappropriate relationships, including one with an individual who, as a slave, not only worked for but was owned by the President. There is also no doubt that other Presidents have lied about public matters, perhaps more serious than adultery; the U.S. role in the Bay of Pigs invasion, the true nature of Gary Powers's mission to Russia in a U-2 spy plane and the details of the arms-for-hostage transaction that was at the heart of the Iran-Contra affair, to name a few. On the other hand, none of these circumstances involved Presidential fabrications made under oath. . . . What distinguishes President Clinton from his predecessors in this regard is that relatively speaking, the acts under review may not represent as great umbrages to our system as certain others, but lying under oath amounts to an absolute breach of an absolute standard. It makes it impossible to justify a vote against impeachment.[14]

That this use of the concept of an absolute principle might seem strained should not be surprising, given that absolutist morality forces all of the complexity of moral life within its terms and boundaries. Why does Leach need to use "absolute" twice in his final statement, that Clinton committed "an absolute breach of an absolute standard"? Here Leach's efforts to distinguish Clinton's actions from the standards that have obtained for presidential behavior in the past are caught in precisely the type of legalism and failure of common sense of which conservatives accuse both "relativist morality" and Clinton. He must relativize Thomas Jefferson's sexual relationship with his slave, Sally Hemings, and slavery itself moves into the moral passive voice as a system of labor which apparently carries no particular moral valence (Hemings "not only worked for the President"). Commonsensically, it would seem that misleading the American people about military operations that involved international incidents or that were themselves in violation of the law would be more serious than lying in a civil lawsuit that was later dismissed. But Leach must wash away those actions as irrelevant and morally unimportant in order to maintain the coherence of absolutist language in what is, in fact, a morally and legally complicated situation.

Many people's mistrust of absolutist morality comes from the fact that life rarely seems to fit into such simple terms. One of the rhetorical strategies employed against this experience of moral life is the appeal to the protection of children. For example, Randy Tate, head of the Christian Coalition, proclaimed after the verdict of the Senate trial, "Children now have the lesson that lying, cheating and breaking the law are permissible on the pathway to success."[15] This is a typical strategy on the part of the right for dealing with the contradictions of simultaneous social conservatism and support for free enterprise. For example, the right has long opposed "hate speech" codes on college campuses as a fundamental infringement on freedom while supporting all kinds of Internet restrictions in the name of children. More than this, though, the reference to children works and is necessary because this type of absolutist morality makes more sense to children than to adults who know that life is not so simple.[16]

Many contemporary cultural critics, including some feminists, have become suspicious of any use of moral language at all, because such language is so frequently used to show that women are not and can never be moral in the way that men are. Because moral language can be used to reinforce social hierarchies, it often seems to be about drawing boundaries where someone—women, people of color, homosexuals—has to be on the outside so that those on the inside can confirm their sense of themselves. Despite these suspicions, however, it has not been so easy to forgo moral language altogether. Any activity has its own norms.[17] The question then becomes not whether or not one uses moral language, but what kind of language does one use and how does it work? In order to acknowledge that one is making moral claims, it is not necessary to make them in classical or absolutist moral terms.

Certainly, absolutist morality is never as absolute as its invocation sounds. Virtually everyone would acknowledge, for example, that there are times when moral principles, including absolute moral principles, come into conflict. This conflict sometimes leads to the abridgement of one or another (absolute) moral principle. The most obvious such case is that of war. "Thou shalt not kill" would seem to be the most fundamental of absolute moral principles (the one which is included in virtually any religious or moral system), yet organized killing in the form of war is also common across the world. While there are those who maintain this principle as unimpeachable and refuse any type of killing, the vast majority of Americans, particularly those conservatives who advocated absolutist morality as the basis of Clinton's impeachment, are willing to abridge this principle in the case of war and often also with regard to capital punishment. William Bennett, the virtual dean of the new conservative morality, argues, in fact, that war is itself a moral crucible, the place where the highest moral virtues are forged, and those who oppose war, like the participants in the 1960s and 1970s U.S. antiwar movement, are harbingers of moral decay within a society.[18]

Absolutist morality has difficulty recognizing the type of moral complexity in which moral principles like "thou shalt not kill" are abrogated for various reasons or in which moral principles are themselves complex (as I have suggested sexual freedom is). Not all of the moral perspectives that have been developed in new social movements are relativist (just as not all absolutist moralities are completely absolutist). But, for advocates of absolutist morality, like House whip Tom DeLay, the supposedly relativist morality against which they rail is not just a different kind of morality, it is tantamount to no morality at all.

The slippage from the accusation of relativist morality to the accusation of amorality makes invisible the fact that many of the new social movements have been organized around moral notions, specifically around moral notions of freedom: from freedom riders in the civil rights movement, to women's or gay liberation, freedom has been a central concept to U.S. social movements. This is not surprising given the centrality of freedom to American politics, but freedom is also one of the most complicated moral concepts in American history. As historian Eric Foner has carefully traced in *The Story of American Freedom*, as freedom has been such an organizing principle in American politics, it has carried many different meanings that have been contested time and again.[19]

It is this history of American freedom with which feminists who support sexual freedom are engaged. Feminists have developed concepts of sexual freedom that run counter to the type of absolutist morality promoted by conservatives, but sexual freedom in the context of feminist ethics also makes important moral claims that cannot simply be dismissed as "relativist." The impeachment debate did not deal seriously with the concerns of feminist ethics or sexual freedom from a feminist perspective. While the impeachment may have been driven by dislike (and even hatred) of alternative moralities, Bill Clinton was no proponent of feminist ethics or feminist social policy, nor were his actions particularly indicative of sexual freedom. The accusation that feminists responded to the impeachment proceedings in terms that were amoral at best was just another American public conversation carried on without significant input from feminists. Feminists are once again the objects of, but not subjects in, American public discourse.

304

Clinton and Sexual Morality

The problem with Bill Clinton is not that he is the embodiment of the decades of liberation with which he is identified by conservatives. He has not brought atheism, moral relativism, and sexual liberation to the White House, but rather church-going Christianity, moral rigidity, and sexual conservatism. Traci West has provided a careful ethical analysis of Clinton's statements with regard to welfare reform and found him using the typical conservative language with regard to recipients of welfare, stating, for example, that mothers who receive welfare benefits "expose" their children to "poverty and welfare, violence and drugs." And he uses an anecdote of a welfare recipient who states that welfare recipients should be forced to work because "if you don't make us do it, we'll just lay up and watch the soaps." In repeating this anecdote, Clinton uses one woman's statements to morally incriminate welfare recipients as a whole.[20]

Clinton's particular view of "morality" on the issue of welfare stands in contrast to that of Ronald Reagan. Reagan's expressed views of poor people were those of a simple morality play, in which poor people were simply immoral. For Clinton, the supposed tie between poverty and immorality is not a permanent condition for the poor, but one that can be changed through self-improvement. While Clinton is supposedly more liberal, he maintains a tie between poor women and their supposed immorality. His liberalism consists simply in the belief that poverty is not indicative of a permanent condition, but could be "reformed." Hence, welfare "reform" can be accomplished through the "personal responsibility" signaled in the name of the welfare reform act. It was Clinton's rhetoric of reform that ultimately won the day and accomplished what is arguably the most extensive change in the structure and function of government of the post-Reagan era. For poor women, Clinton's supposed liberalism, when combined with sexual conservatism, has proven to be worse than was Reagan's. If feminists have failed in solidarity, it is not in failing to ride into the fray to accuse Clinton of sexual harassment. They have, rather, remained much too silent, in the major media at least, about Clinton's use of a discourse of sexual conservatism to undercut economic possibilities for millions of poor women.

If the use of sexual morality by conservatives to reinforce social hierarchies is nothing new, neither is Clinton's personal sexual behavior anything new or surprising. That all of Washington was shocked and appalled that a powerful white man entered into a sexual liaison with a woman not his wife and much his

junior in terms of age and power seems disingenuous at best. The issue is not sim-
ply the hypocrisy that was brought to the fore by the revelations of affairs by
Henry Hyde and Robert Livingston. Rather, Clinton's affair with Monica Lewinsky
was business as usual. Why was everyone so surprised to find out on August 17
what no one apparently knew before—that a powerful man had dallied with a
much younger woman? Some conservatives were confirmed in what they had
known all along, but what they had seemed to know all along was that Clinton
was a personally evil person. No one acknowledged that, when it comes to ques-
tions of gender, age, sex, and power such behavior is the rule in Washington (and
the rest of the country). The conservative focus on Clinton as an evil individual
meant that when Livingston's affairs were revealed, the mechanisms of accusation
used against Clinton had to be turned against Livingston. The liberal response of
charging conservatives with hypocrisy maintains this focus on individuals be-
cause it doesn't acknowledge that Clinton's and Livingston's behaviors were part
of the same system of sexual conservatism.

One of the aspects of patriarchal sexual morality that makes it confusing is
that patriarchy includes not just the stringent morality of sexual prohibition
that is currently enunciated as a conservative Christian morality, it also in-
cludes the acceptance, if not incitement, of sexual encounters of powerful per-
sons with various "subordinates." These contradictory prohibitions and incite-
ments can be held together and, in fact, work together because of their speci-
ficity of object. Everyone knows of the famous "double standard," commonly
referred to in everyday American life, in which some "girls" are the type that
"boys" marry and some are the type to have sex with. Within this system,
"girls" are charged with the task of protecting their own sexual respectability in
the hope of remaining in the first category, while boys are not held responsible
or rendered unmarriageable because of their sexual availability. It is not surpris-
ing that a system of sexual power relations would contain this contradictory
prohibition and permission, because both sides of the contradiction reinforce
the privilege of those who are already empowered.

The entire system works on the basis of an open secret. Everyone knows that
the double standard is in operation, but also denies it—as if boys who marry are
just as respectable as the girls they marry, whatever their sexual histories. This re-
spectability centered on marriage and patriarchal family structure, like legitimacy,
allows for and even incites white men of power to cross the boundaries of re-
spectability.[21] White men of power and privilege can expect that sexual favors, be-
yond those of married respectability, will be part and parcel of their assumption

306

of power. Once again, the secret is an open one, where the general knowledge of power and sexual access is part of the culture in which men of privilege participate. Yet its secrecy allows for individual men to disassociate their own sense of respectability from their sexual activities beyond its boundaries.

Participation in this culture is encouraged, if not enforced, as part of the masculinity of privilege. Take, for example, the incident in which Senator John McCain, whose political persona turns on the moral righteousness of his identity as a Vietnam P.O.W. and who has taken a nonpartisan and morally articulated stand for campaign finance reform, related an "offensive" joke about Hillary Rodham Clinton, Chelsea Clinton, and Janet Reno (the joke was apparently so offensive that a press that has seemed unable to suppress any salacious detail of the Clinton-Lewinsky affair refused to print it). The press asked why McCain would do something so out of character. McCain himself claimed not to know why he did it. He made a mistake, he said. But why this mistake? One which he himself didn't understand? The disassociative aspects of the patriarchal culture of power to which this joke belonged meant that in the world outside the open secret, in the world of public respectability, it was inexplicable, but in the world of powerful masculinity, it was requisite. Thus, the telling of this joke secured McCain a place among those who might think that his "morality" would make him unfaithful to conventional masculinity, even as he couldn't explain it to the public. His mistake was in terms of the when and where rather than the what of his actions. His mistake was saying publicly what's known, but unspeakable. Had he merely related this joke at a private dinner among his peers, it might have served him well, but at a public dinner for the press it violated the pact of open secrecy.[22]

Clinton, in engaging in the affair with Monica Lewinsky, was also participating in the culture of powerful masculinity into which he had been educated and then elected, while simultaneously maintaining, at the cost of intricate denials and distinctions à la the *Sixty Minutes* performance with regard to Gennifer Flowers, the sexual respectability of his public marriage persona. Clinton's task was to maintain both of these forms of sexuality as part of the same form of masculinity. He could not admit to any of his alleged sexual liaisons, or settle with Paula Jones, and maintain his public respectability and moral authority.

Sexual conservatism in the United States has traditionally relied on both the proscription of sexual behavior outside the bounds of heterosexual monogamous marriage and the violation of that proscription by powerful and privileged males. And it must be remembered that if this is the system of power around sexual relations, then both the expression of the prohibition by those who are powerful and the violation of that prohibition by those very same persons is conservative of the system as a whole. Clinton's hypocrisy in pronouncing negatively on the sexuality of "teenage mothers" and then violating the bounds of heterosexual monogamy himself was in this sense no different from that of countless other conservative politicians. It certainly was not an expression of sexual freedom.

The value of sexual freedom promoted by some feminists is intended to change this system as a whole. Sexual freedom will not be of value if it does not challenge both sides of sexual conservatism: both sexual prohibition and the sexual access that powerful men can assume with regard to women less powerful than themselves. Feminists have argued that sexual equality would require that all parties to sexual engagements be able to enter into them freely. While the working out of an entire sexual ethics is beyond the scope of this essay, an ethics in which sexual freedom is a positive value is very different from a sexual ethics in which some persons express their power by "freely" engaging in sexual relations. The former requires respect for one's partners, honesty, and agreement on the terms of engagement. Clinton's behavior did not display any of these characteristics, but was business-as-usual patriarchal sexuality.

Clinton's treatment of his wife is wholly in keeping with the logic of this system. By all reports, he lied to his wife. Do Bill and Hillary have some kind of agreement between them that places the basis for their marriage on some terms other than patriarchal monogamy? While we cannot say for sure, we certainly have no evidence that this is the case, and we will never have any such indication in public. Whatever their private relations, Hillary Clinton agreed to play the role of betrayed wife in public, and she was embraced to a certain extent for so doing. The "woman wronged" is a staple in conservative discourse and has been used for the justification of all kinds of dominating projects. It does not provide women much access either to empowerment or freedom. Certainly one of the reasons that the president's overall approval ratings remained high throughout the drama is that he has in some sense fulfilled the role of privileged masculinity over his feminist wife. He has not been emasculated by being married to a feminist, but instead has cheated on her in time-honored fashion. In the meantime, his wife has become more conservative. Mrs. Clinton's own movement toward conservatism can be traced through a number of issues, including her recent move toward supporting the death penalty in preparation for her Senate run in New York. There are alternative scenarios to playing out the role of woman wronged, but it is virtually unimaginable that they should be played out publicly in the contemporary United States while the enforcement of sexual conservatism remains politically powerful. What would it have been like if Hillary had said that she did not care whether Clinton had pursued a relationship like the one he had with Monica Lewinsky? What if she had said they had an agreement about sexual relationships that this relationship did not violate? What if she said that she too had such relationships?

Hillary Rodham Clinton's recent statements that she and Bill Clinton have a deep bond that transcends whatever happens, and that she blames his upbringing for his actions, are hardly statements that indicate her empowerment. Much of the media commentary was hard pressed to explain why Hillary would go into the matter in an interview, now that the matter is closed. A *New York Times* editorial suggested that she may need to shore up her feminist support by showing that she is angry at Clinton.[23] The questions of how exactly these statements are supposed to be positively feminist is intriguing if not baffling. The mother-blaming that is implied in her statements about his upbringing by his mother and grandmother is more recognizably conservative than feminist. Being angry at men is hardly the first and only principle of feminist politics. Women's empowerment is central, and very little in the entire impeachment saga has made much of a contribution to such feminism.

As with his treatment of Hillary, Clinton's treatment of Monica Lewinsky is not indicative of sexual freedom. He treated her coldly and refused to engage with her fully, even when she requested that he do so. The great irony is not only that Clinton is in fact a sexual conservative, as I have shown, but that the sex was bad—infrequent, furtive, guilty, withholding. As Adam Gopnik pointed out in the *New Yorker*, it is only when Clinton's treatment of Lewinsky improved, when he fully responded to her, that he moved into the territory that allowed Kenneth Starr to develop his report. Gopnik argues that the Starr Report is structured as a novel:

Yet, bizarrely, what offends this narrator is that the sexual relations did become reciprocal and engaged—that the hero aroused the heroine as much as she aroused him, that he touched and caressed and praised and eventually gave her pleasure, several pleasures. For, as the hero becomes more sympathetic as a human being—less contemptuous, more remorseful about his own behavior, more generous sexually—he also (according to the narrator) incriminates himself ever deeper. . . . This is because the narrator is obsessed by a luridly abstract document—a definition of sexual acts—drawn up by the hero's enemies, which in effect criminalizes any reciprocal acts. . . . The selfish acts are the safe ones: the reciprocal acts are criminal. (42)

Gopnik's point is that it matters both to the Starr Report and the larger narratives of the impeachment drama that the sex between Clinton and Lewinsky is bad sex (in fact, my own title for the impeachment play itself would be "All This over Bad Sex?"). The sex itself shows not only Clinton's own sexual conservatism, but also demonstrates a sexual ethic he shares with Starr. What matters is not the treatment of women in sexual relations, but the legalistic "legitimacy" of particular sexual acts—a legitimacy determined by relations among men in which women are only supporting players.

Throughout the ordeal, Lewinsky has refused to play the role of Clinton's victim, despite the fact that such claims might have won her both better treatment from Kenneth Starr and more sympathy from the American public. Lewinsky stood her ground and refused to paint herself as a victim. It is not clear to me, as Gopnik claims, that Lewinsky is "on the far side of the sexual revolution" (40). But, perhaps it is just that the "sexual revolution" of the 1960s and 1970s did not provide fully for sexual freedom. While Monica Lewinsky is obviously more comfortable with sex than is Clinton, her choices still reflect those of traditional patriarchal power relations.

Did feminists fail Monica Lewinsky by not vociferously claiming that she was exploited and Clinton should be impeached? Certainly we have failed her by not arguing against the "Monica is a tramp" line. The *20/20* expose of her relationship with a high school teacher portrayed her as the one who behaved in an inappropriate manner, with no commentary on the high school teacher's role or on his continuing involvement in a relationship with a student that lasted five years, and that supposedly made him feel "uncomfortable." Neither is it a particularly feminist position to say that Monica was merely "sleeping her way to the top." The problem with many of these analyses is the inability to speak about structures of power. We need a much more finely tuned vocabulary of power—one that can talk about the social relations and culture of power. We are not "enablers." As Wendy Kaminer has pointed out, we do not have a "personal" relationship with the president, but we are participants in a sexist culture.[24]

It *is* possible to hold a morally consistent position with regard to both political policy *and* sexual ethics and not want to participate in the impeachment drama. The impeachment drama did *not* provide some new moral ground for conservatives who were finally willing to take feminist concerns seriously and discipline one of their own—a conservative white male—for his mistreatment of women. The impeachment drama did not display any concern for the well-being of Monica Lewinsky or Hillary Rodham Clinton. Both women were hounded and humiliated, threatened with jail, and harassed by the special prosecutor and the press, if not by Bill Clinton. The impeachment drama replayed an old, old story—one in which women have little power and no good choices. It was, after all, a conflict between white men over the sign and symbol of "woman"—nothing particularly new there. Moreover, the impeachment of Clinton did not contribute to sexual harassment law and may, in fact, have made questions of harassment more difficult to pursue, thus undermining possibilities for legal redress. Nor did it lead to the development of a personal sexual ethics in which women might have some measure of the sexual autonomy and decision making allotted to powerful men. That not all feminists joined in the outrage at Bill Clinton does not express a betrayal of feminist principles, but rather a belief that there were no feminist principles promoted on either side of the aisle or the drama.

Has Bill Clinton wronged America and women? The answer would have to be yes, but then that was already true in the summer of 1996, not because of Clinton's personal sexual behavior, but because of his policies—his signing of both the "welfare reform" act and the Defense of Marriage Act during that summer. In that sense, my friend's acquaintance was right: better to write in Tina Turner for president.

Notes

1. Much of the media coverage of Starr has focused on his Christian upbringing and ties to the Christian right. See, for example, Michael Winerip, "Starr Report Recalls Outlook of a Preacher in Rural Texas" (*New York Times,* September 13, 1998, 1A). While it is certainly important to consider the ties of powerful political figures to the organizations of the radical right, this imputation of Mr. Starr's puritanical investigation to his religious heritage did allow for a certain disavowal of sexual conservatism on the part of the mainstream media, making the *New York Times'* repeated calls for censuring the president look like a reasonable moderation, regardless of the constitutional viability of such a move.

2. For an extended analysis of both welfare reform and the Defense of Marriage Act, see Jakobsen, "Family Values and Working Alliances: The Question of Hate and Public Policy," in *Welfare Policy: Feminist Critiques,* ed. Elizabeth Bounds, Pamela K. Brubaker, and Mary Hobgood (New York: Pilgrim Press, 1997).

3. I am using an understanding of power relations in which power itself is not a moral problem but rather an inherent part of human interaction. Power is, in fact, necessary to moral possibility, because human agency (and therefore moral agency) depends on

the power to act. Moral problems are involved in power relations either through an abuse of power or in situations of domination in which one party to the relationship is so circumscribed as to have very few options for how to act. For a full explanation of the moral implications of this view of power, see my "Introduction" to *Working Alliances and the Politics of Difference: Diversity and Feminist Ethics* (Bloomington: Indiana University Press, 1998).

4. Katie Cannon, *Black Womanist Ethics* (Atlanta: Scholars Press, 1988).

5. Certainly, for the public conversation, the sexual detail in the Starr Report was as or more important than the question of perjury. As the *New York Times* reported: "One ratings service found that more people read the sections about sex than those about perjury" (Lisa Napoli, "The Post-Lewinsky Winner Is the Web" September 28, 1998, C7).

6. "'The senators seem to relate the perjury charge to sex, and the President's twisting definitions,' said Representative Ed Bryant, a Tennessee Republican. 'It's an easier sell job with obstruction of justice. It's about a cover-up'" (Eirc Schmitt, "Obstruction Charge Drove Managers' Witness Choices," *New York Times,* January 28, 1999, 1A).

7. See Alison Mitchell, "Republicans Drop Bid to Investigate Clinton Campaign," (*New York Times,* December 4, 1998, A1).

8. For example, the *New York Times* reports that the 1998 convention of the Christian Coalition was marked by "specula[tion] that the libertine legacy of the 1960's still held sway over American culture" (Laurie Goodstein, "Christian Coalition Laments Lack of Widespread Anger about President's Behavior," September 20, 1998, 34A). For a reading of the impeachment proceedings in their entirety as part of a "culture war," see Maureen Dowd, "'Honour in a Shallow Cup'" (*New York Times,* December 13, 1998, WK15).

9. *New York Times,* December 20, 1998, WK6.

10. Orlando Patterson, "What Is Freedom without Privacy?" *New York Times,* September 15, 1998.

11. See Gary Becker, *A Treatise on the Family* (Cambridge, Mass.: Harvard University Press, 1991).

12. See, for example, John Tierney's column "Do Daddies Get as Good as They Give?" *New York Times,* August 5, 1999, B1.

13. For example, Bob Herbert commented on Barr's acknowledgment that he was a keynote speaker for the white supremacist group, the Council of Conservative Citizens, as an indicator of the general extremism of the Republican leaders of the impeachment proceedings ("The Capitol Hill Mob," *New York Times,* December 13, 1998, WK15).

14. "Impeachment; Excerpts from Comments by Republicans Who Have Decided to Impeach," *New York Times,* December 17, 1998.

15. *New York Times,* February 13, 1999, A9. A cartoon in the *New York Times* "Week in Review" section similarly analogizes thinking about Clinton's impeachment to childhood morality by showing a mother about to spank her son in the kitchen as the son proclaims, "I'll gladly accept a censure, you know" (Wayne Stayskal, *New York Times,* December 13, 1998, 6WK). This analogy confuses not only the complexities of adult moral life with childhood moral understanding, but makes the issue of impeachment about "punishing" the president rather than about crimes against the state. This fundamental confusion between impeachment as a political concern and the issue of punishment remained central to the public discourse throughout the trial.

16. See, for example, the work of developmental psychologist Lawrence Kohlberg in *The Philosophy of Moral Development: Moral Stages and the Idea of Justice* (San Francisco: Harper and Row, 1981), and *The Psychology of Moral Development: The Nature and Validity of Moral Stages* (San Francisco: Harper and Row, 1984).

17. For a full discussion of norms and questions of power, see Janet Jakobsen, "Queer Is? Queer Does? Normativity and Resistance," *GLQ: A Journal of Lesbian and Gay Studies* 4.4 (1998).

18. Bennett argues that "war has always been the crucible—that is, the vessel as well as the severest test—for our core beliefs" (*Imprimis,* a publication of Hillsdale College, 1998, 4).

19. Eric Foner, *The Story of American Freedom* (New York: W. W. Norton, 1998).

20. Traci West, "Agenda for the Churches: Uprooting National Policy of Morally Stigmatizing Poor Single Black Moms," in *Welfare Policy: Feminist Critiques,* ed. Elizabeth Bounds, Pamela K. Brubaker, and Mary Hobgood (New York: Pilgrim Press, 1997), pp. 133–153.

21. Abdul JanMohamed has clearly mapped these prohibitions and permissions with regard to nineteenth-century sexuality "on/of the racial border." Looking specifically at the slave-holding United States, JanMohamed shows how that system of sexuality maintains an ethic of sexual prohibition across the racial border for everyone except the male slaveowner who crosses the racial border in an open secret—open in that it was widely known and hence culturally accepted (crossing the border in this case is not a personal failing), and secretive in order to disassociate any persons born from such crossings from the legitimate inheritance of the offspring of the slaveowners' marriage. See Abdul R. JanMohamed, "Sexuality on/of the Racial Border: Foucault, Wright, and the Articulation of 'Racialized' Sexuality," in *Discourses of Sexuality: From Aristotle to AIDS,* ed. Domna Stanton (Ann Arbor: University of Michigan Press, 1992). Clinton finds himself in a somewhat different situation, but nonetheless in the midst of a patriarchal culture that has a similar set of secrets and dissociations. The question of con-

temporary sexuality is not only one of legitimacy and inheritance per se, but rather, as George Mosse has shown, one of "sexual respectability," in which "respectability" is a marker for bourgeois class power and privilege. This shift to respectability allowed, for some, openness to class mobility while maintaining sexuality as a normative control in relation to that mobility—those who are and those who would be bourgeois must produce themselves as sexually respectable, hence, insuring stability of class distinction despite mobility. See George Mosse, *Nationalism and Sexuality: Middle-Class Morality and Sexual Norms in Modern Europe* (Madison: University of Wisconsin Press, 1985).

22. That such sexuality and its disavowal are a common part of Washington life was illustrated by Maureen Dowd's casual reference to it: "That is why this trial is so loony. Congress has an illustrious history of politicians having affairs with younger female aides and lying about it. The House managers pretend to be outraged that Mr. Clinton lied to Sidney Blumenthal about Monica. As if members of Congress never lie to aides intending that the lies be repeated?" (*New York Times,* February 7, 1999, WK17).

23. *New York Times,* August 4, 1999, A18.

24. *New York Times,* September 27, 1998.

18 Sexual Risk Management in the Clinton White House

Anna Marie Smith

As Clinton leaves office, his aides mention time and time again that he is concerned about his historical legacy. Feminist historians will look back at the Clinton administration and give it a mixed review. On the one hand, Clinton will be remembered for a few key initiatives on late-term abortion, family leave, and the earned income tax credit. His partnership with Hillary Rodham Clinton will be compared to that between the Roosevelts. Women and minorities also won a substantial number of the appointments to the Clinton administration. On the other hand, Clinton abandoned many of his best nominees, presided over a dramatic increase in the gap between the rich and the poor, and supported a draconian welfare law that virtually eliminated the statutory entitlement to poverty assistance.

Above all, feminists will remember the Clinton-Lewinsky affair as a moment in which sexual harassment policy was turned inside out. Many of us have struggled for years to pass policies in our workplaces and to enact laws in our legislatures that reflect a feminist position on sexual harassment. We have had to confront some of our most recalcitrant male colleagues in meeting after meeting to make our point clear. No, we are not against sex, sexual expression, or freedom of speech. We insist that a person's right to equal opportunity in the workplace is violated wherever she/he is faced with unwanted sexual conduct. If a woman has been subjected to unwanted sexual behavior that is so severe that she could not do her job or that she could not pursue her studies properly, or if she has been effectively coerced into accepting sexual conduct as part of a quid pro quo exchange, then she has been denied one of her basic rights. From a feminist perspective, the key question is this: Is the adult[1] worker consenting to the sexual conduct in question, and is that consent freely given, or is her/his consent produced by the coercive dimensions of her/his workplace status? The feminist perspective is absolutely agnostic on the moralistic questions that may arise. We do not care—and we should not care—whether or not the adults involved are male, female, transsexual, married, single, divorced, straight, or gay; whether the worker complainant holds a "decent" job or works on the street; whether the sexual practice is "tasteful" and "normal" or "tacky" and "perverse," or whether sexual relations took place in an "appropriate" private venue or in a "pristine" public place.

In the Clinton-Lewinsky affair, as in the Thomas-Hill hearings, feminists lost control of the public discourse on sexual harassment. To take but one example, the taboo on adultery looms large in the Clinton-Lewinsky records. Starr and the Republicans seem to have assumed that the public would be outraged by their allegation that the president had abused his power specifically to conceal an adulterous sexual liaison. The fact that every single sexual moment between Clinton and Lewinsky was fully consensual for both parties was hardly given any emphasis at all.

In the end, the pro-impeachment camp was bewildered by the fact that the American people were not really fazed by something as banal as extramarital sex. The ghosts of Chappaquidick and Gary Hart's *Monkey Business* cruise did not rise again. For all the apparent failures of Starr and the Republicans to mobilize popular opinion against Clinton in defense of "moral decency," however, feminists will look back at the Clinton years as a turning point in official discourse on marriage and the family. In his trademark "triangulation" style, Clinton picked a theme right out of the Republicans' repertoire—family values—and made it his own. At the same time, however, the neoconservative policies that he approved made it more difficult than ever for working-class and poor families to stay together.

In the following essay, I want to explore the ironic logic of two juxtapositions. First, Clinton constructed himself as a pro-family and pro-marriage leader, even as his policies had severe anti-family effects, and even as he continued to pursue his sexual fetishistic interest, namely extramarital casual sex. Second, the Clinton-Lewinsky affair began at a particularly intense political moment for the White House, namely during the government shut-down of 1995, and continued

316

in an administration that had just shifted toward a much more restricted policy vis-à-vis access to the Oval Office. In the midst of what his own aides regarded as a dramatic intensification of time and space management, Clinton carved out the space for a secret sexual liaison that took place just out of sight and just beyond the earshot of the White House staff. While some may regard the actual setting of the affair as an irrelevant detail, the fact that one of the most infamous extramarital affairs of the century was conducted in a workplace should be central to feminist discourse on the case.

The Clintons: Images, Policies, and Policy Image

The Clinton-Lewinsky affair can be located within a complex and contradictory tradition—the regulation of sexuality through the deployment of marriage as a form of social control. By using the terms "regulation" and "social control," I do not mean to indicate that this tradition has taken the form of a totalistic conspiracy-like system that has been successfully and uniformly imposed upon subordinate groups by a dominant class or an omnipotent state. There is a long tradition in early modern and modern Western societies of promoting popular heterosexual marriage to bring an otherwise unruly bachelor population into a disciplined condition and to prevent the social problems associated with a large wanton bastard population. As many researchers in the field of the politics of sexuality acknowledge, however, the promotion of heterosexual marriage and the nuclear family on the part of governments, religious institutions, social movements, and experts in the medical, psychological, and psychiatric professions has sometimes had a significant effect among the bourgeoisie as well as the working class, has often resulted in incoherent ad hoc policies or even failure rather than perfect social control, and has always been enormously differentiated across various classes, races, immigrant peoples, and colonial subjects.[2]

The Clinton administration's position with respect to gender, family values, and marriage is quite complicated. Clinton clearly owes his electoral achievements in part to gendered policies and images. When Clinton succeeded in his 1996 reelection bid, the voting data demonstrated that while male voters were almost evenly divided between Clinton and Bob Dole, 43 to 44 percent, women supported the incumbent by a 59 to 35 percent margin. Several analysts hailed the emergence of a new key voter, the white middle-class suburban "soccer mom," and contended that Clinton's vigorous defense of women's rights was a winning factor. Leading feminists such as Gloria Steinem had in fact asked women to cast their vote for Clinton on the grounds that there were significant differences between his positions and those of Dole and the Republicans, and that where Clinton had wavered, he had done so only because he did not have a strong enough progressive support base.

For all the media's emphasis on the gender gap, it should be remembered that other feminist analysts differed sharply with Steinem. This is not to say that there was no basis whatsoever for the feminist pro-Clinton argument. Clinton had in fact vetoed the ban on late-term abortions, and had ensured that the unpaid family leave law, the Violence Against Women Act, and the ban on assault weapons were passed. He had expanded the earned income tax credit by increasing the subsidy for the 15 million low-wage full-time working recipients and by extending the eligibility requirements to include an additional 4.5 million workers. Clinton had also appointed an impressive number of women and minorities to offices in his administration.

But Katha Pollitt calls this record of positive achievements for women a "short [and] narrowly tailored list."[3] Clinton had actually abandoned many of his women appointees, such as Zoë Baird, Lani Guinier, and Joycelyn Elders, when their views, or even the right's distorted constructions of their views, threatened to contradict his moderate image. Clinton had constructed himself as a firmly pro-choice leader, but he had done nothing to improve access to abortion. Eighty-four percent of American counties lack abortion facilities, and states are free to impose mandatory counseling and waiting periods for all women and parental approval for women under the age of eighteen. The states are also allowed to exclude coverage for abortions by Medicaid, the health-care plan for the poor. Clinton had promised to support gay rights, but he had capitulated on the issue of gays in the military, given no power to his AIDS "czar," distanced himself from his gay supporters, enthusiastically embraced the myth that children should only be raised by married heterosexual couples, and signed the 1996 Defense of Marriage Act, a bill that allows states to ban gay marriages. Clinton's welfare reform policies have yet to make a major impact on the poor. However, given the overrepresentation of women and minorities among the poor in the United States, it is reasonable to suggest that the elimination of welfare entitlements will have an especially large impact on women, blacks, and Latinos during the next economic down-turn.

Clinton has had the good fortune to occupy the White House during an economic recovery, and it should be recognized that some of the fruits of the current upswing in employment and wages have in fact benefited even the poorest to some extent. The gap between the rich and the poor nevertheless remains larger in the United States than in any other Western country. The current economic recovery has not transformed the fundamentally anti-egalitarian nature of American society, and, insofar as it depends upon market speculation and an increase in household debt and is not being used to fuel massive investment in public education, it will not lay the foundation for more equality in the future. If poor people are locked into low-paid jobs with no union protection and little opportunity for advancement, then it is simply common sense that they will encounter serious difficulties in holding their families together as decent housing, adequate food, and basic health care remain beyond their reach.

Clinton also vigorously worked with the Republican-led Congress to secure the passage of the North American Free Trade Act that will have devastating effects on workers and unions over the long term. Progressive critics are divided on the question of Clinton's decision to prioritize balancing the budget, but all contend that he has maintained an excessively generous level of military expenditures. Many of Clinton's otherwise promising policies remain empty rhetoric: his pledges for support for the inner cities are meaningless without a substantial jobs creation program and the increase in the minimum wage still leaves a family of four under the poverty line. Although Clinton did sponsor legislation that established uniform achievement standards for children from wealthy and poor school districts alike, the Republicans reduced his already insufficient education spending initiatives, thereby ensuring the further deterioration of the public elementary and secondary school system. Finally, Clinton has failed to act positively in key issue areas such as the environment and campaign finance reform and has abandoned his own moderate proposals to reform the American capitalist health-care system.

Feminist critics also point out that Clinton's leadership style has had a restrictive effect on the feminist movement itself. Wherever he is confronted by a credible source of opposition, Clinton's instinct is to appropriate his antagonists' arguments and to neutralize them. Fighting the Gingrich-led resurgence of Republican popularity, Clinton adopted their balanced budget, pro-free trade, anti-immigrant, anti-welfare, and pro-law and order policies. With respect to feminist leaders, Clinton offered them government appointments and an unprecedented degree of access to the White House. Feminists and progressive leaders who did nevertheless criticize Clinton for supporting welfare reform were marginalized and censored at the 1996 Democratic convention by Clinton's campaign staff. The Reverend Jesse Jackson, for example, joined Patricia Ireland, the president of the National Organization of Women, to protest against the passage of the 1996

319

Personal Responsibility Act. It was only when Clinton faced impeachment hearings during fall 1998 and wanted to shore up his support among blacks that Jackson was brought into the White House for extensive consultation.

Frances Fox Piven contends that Clinton's neutralization strategy has in fact had an enormous impact on women's organizations and social-welfare advocacy groups. She argues that progressive activists have placed too much emphasis on what she calls the "insider strategy" and have virtually abandoned their political independence insofar as they have muted their criticism of the administration.[4] Pollitt further argues that this pattern of incorporation and neutralization has seriously weakened the feminist movement as activists' energies have been directed away from grassroots mobilization to lobbying and fundraising for Clinton and moderate Democrats, many of whom ultimately supported welfare reform and other anti-egalitarian policies. Although she admits that Republican administrations certainly would have pursued a more reactionary agenda, Pollitt concludes that they would not have occupied the sort of imaginary "middle ground" that Clinton has staked out, and therefore would not have been able to neutralize the progressive opposition within and outside Congress to such an enormous degree.[5]

Given the fact that Clinton's policies were not in fact remarkably pro-women in any sense, the gender gap cannot be explained in terms of his actual political agenda and concrete achievements. Zillah Eisenstein contends that Clinton was particularly adept at borrowing feminist and feminizing symbols during his 1996 electoral campaign. He presented himself to the voters as a "caring and sharing" leader: he claimed that he "felt the pain" of the voters, and offered initiatives on popular symbolic issues such as teen smoking, school uniforms, violence on television, gun control, and crime. These initiatives, however, were conceived in the sort of low-cost manner that suited the downsized government tone of 1990s American public discourse.[6] Clinton also gained from the Republicans' failure to anticipate the importance of women voters. The 1995 government shutdown, the blatant extremism of Gingrich, Pat Buchanan, and the Christian Coalition, and Dole's own masculine Washington style made it relatively easy for the president to construct himself as the Republicans' feminine "other." Elizabeth Dole, Susan Molinari, and Colin Powell were pressed into service at the 1996 Republican convention to give Dole's candidacy a more women- and minority-friendly feel, but their gestures never effectively counteracted the Republicans' reputation.

Eisenstein argues that more than anything else, it was Clinton's marriage that allowed him to emerge as a credible pro-woman leader. By staking out the pro-choice position, and by constructing himself as the supportive spouse of an empowered and articulate woman, and as the loving father of an intelligent and independent daughter, Clinton cloaked himself in feminized images and thereby won the political cover he needed to pursue the anti-welfare and anti-egalitarian aspects of his agenda. When his health-care initiative seemed destined for failure, it was Hillary Rodham Clinton who took the largest share of the blame. Throughout the health-care debate, it was Hillary who became the masculine and aggressive "policy wonk," while Bill remained the master of the compassionate personal narrative. When rumors about his adultery began to circulate during the 1992 campaign, and the most sordid details of his sexual encounters with Monica Lewinsky became public in 1998, Hillary proved to be his most valuable asset as she came to his defense and "saved" their marriage.[7]

Sexual Management beyond the "First Marriage": The Role of Clinton's Staff

While the "First Marriage" operated as the president's most important symbolic counterweight to the sex scandals, the official record reveals that it was his staff who attempted to come between Clinton and ruinous sexual "excess" on the mundane, behind-the-scenes level. The Starr Report includes a full transcript of Monica Lewinsky's testimony that she gave before the grand jury on 6 August 1998 and 20 August 1998. Lewinsky also gave a deposition before the independent counsel on 26 August 1998. From these documents, we can get a glimpse not only of Lewinsky's version of her affair with Clinton, but her remarkably consistent account of the activities of the White House staff.

In July 1995, Lewinsky began an internship in the correspondence division of Chief of Staff Leon Panetta's office in the Old Executive Office Building in the White House complex. She saw Clinton at various public functions and began to flirt with him. On 15 November 1995, they had their first private meeting and sexual encounter. It is significant that their affair began exactly at that time. Newt Gingrich, Republican Speaker of the House, was at the height of his popularity in 1995. His neoconservative "Contract with America" seemed unassailable while Clinton had failed to introduce his promised health-care reform program. Congressional Republicans won majorities in both bodies in Congress in 1994 and continued to dominate national politics. Clinton's approval ratings sagged, and he had to insist on the continuing relevance of his office.

Situated in this particular political environment, the 1996 budget was subject to tremendous antagonism and delay. There was a great deal of hostility between the Republican congressional leaders and the White House, such that the Office of Management and Budget (OMB) could not wield its normal consensus-building powers. Clinton decided that he could not accept the congressional budget and therefore vetoed the appropriations bills. Because the Republicans could not muster a two-thirds vote in both bodies, a stalemate ensued. The failure of the appropriations bills meant that the entire government machinery literally ground to a halt. Offices were closed and civil service employees were placed on "furlough": they were sent home without pay for an indefinite period. The federal government was literally shut down between 14 November 1995 and 20 November 1995.

Essential employees were the only staff members who were allowed to continue working during the furlough. The White House staff of 430 people was reduced to ninety for the duration.[8] A special atmosphere must have prevailed in the White House in these conditions. Clinton had embarked on an enormously risky path: he would only win the stalemate if public opinion turned against the Republicans for having shut down the government. If that happened, he would emerge as the senior statesman who could rescue the country from Gingrich's extremism. In the end, Clinton's gamble ultimately did pay off, and the showdown with the Republicans helped him to triumph over Dole the following year. In mid-Novermber 1995, however, no one could have predicted this outcome with confidence; things certainly could have gone the other way. Although Clinton himself may have actually preferred the excitement of this moment to the days in which he had been forced to watch the rise of Gingrich from the sidelines, it was a dangerous time. Clinton's aides and Cabinet members closed ranks and stood by their leader in the midst of great uncertainty. Meanwhile, the egalitarian effects of the disaster-time culture that prevailed in the White House were quite substantial. Unpaid interns were not only instantly promoted as they were asked to perform the tasks of the absent salaried administrative assistants, they also found themselves working shoulder-to-shoulder with heretofore remote senior officials.

Lewinsky, who normally worked during her internship in the Old Executive Office Building in the White House complex, reported in her testimony that during the furlough she was assigned to answer phones in Leon Panetta's West Wing office in the White House [730–31] (25–6).[9] Given her subsequent actions, it is highly ironic that Lewinsky was in Panetta's White House office at the time. Clinton's first chief of staff, Thomas "Mack" McLarty, ran what presidential experts regard as a fairly loose operation. After several errors, coordina-

SEXUAL RISK MANAGEMENT IN THE CLINTON WHITE HOUSE

tion failures, and scandals involving the firing of the Travel Office staff and the use of FBI files, Clinton replaced McLarty with Panetta in July 1994. One of the hallmarks of Panetta's leadership style was a much more restrictive space and time management style where access to the Oval Office was concerned. The list of aides and advisors who could easily meet with the president was shortened. Fewer meetings with the president were scheduled, and fewer people attended each meeting. Increased focus was brought to the president's daily considerations; an issue had to be studied and analyzed before it could be raised with him. Investigative journalist and presidential specialist Elizabeth Drew noted the effects of Panetta's controlled environment:

Walk-in privileges to the Oval Office were drastically reduced; not even his national security advisor, his legal counsel or his confidant [George] Stephanopolous [Senior Adviser for Policy and Strategy] could get to the president except through Panetta. No decision papers went directly to the president; even those from the National Security Council went first through Panetta's review. No longer were policy decisions made by seminar. And perhaps most significantly, hierarchy and clear lines of authority and responsibility were established.[10]

For all of Panetta's efforts, the furlough disrupted everything. Lewinsky found herself placed in a highly favorable position to pursue the president. In her testimony, she stated that her relationship with the president changed from flirtation in public ceremonies to actual sexual interaction on 15 November 1995. Associate Independent Counsel Karin Immergut questioned Lewinsky on the transition.

Q: I wanted you to explain sort of how it came about.
A: It was during the furlough. I was up in Mr. Panetta's West Wing office answering phones. The President came down several times during the day. There was continued flirtation and around 8:00 in the evening or so I was in the hallway going to the restroom, passing Mr. Stephanopoulos' office, and he [Clinton] was in the hall and invited me into Mr. Stephanopoulos' office and then from there invited me back into his study. [730–31] (25–6)

It is at this point that Clinton and Lewinsky had their first private meeting. Although their actual interaction is rather brief, they acknowledged their mutual attraction and kissed for the first time. Later that evening, around 10 P.M., Clinton went into Panetta's office and invited Lewinsky to meet him five minutes later in Stephanopoulos' office. From there, they went into Clinton's back study where they could be alone. They kissed, and Lewinsky performed oral sex on Clinton.

The furlough conditions also provided the opportunity for their next encounter.

Q: When was the next time?
A: On the 17th of November.
Q: And could you explain how that contact occurred?
A: We were again working late because it was during the furlough and Jennifer Palmeri [special assistant to the chief of staff] and I, who was Mr. Panetta's assistant, [sic] had ordered pizza along with Ms. Currie [personal secretary to the president] and Ms. Hernreich [deputy assistant to the president and director of oval office operations].

And when the pizza came, I went down to let them know that the pizza was there and it as [sic] at that point when I walked into Ms. Currie's office that the President was standing there with some other people discussing something.

And they all came back down to the office and Mr.—I think it was Mr. Toiv [deputy white house press secretary], somebody accidentally knocked pizza on my jacket, so I went down to use the restroom to wash it off and as I was coming out of the restroom, the President was standing in Ms. Currie's doorway and said, 'You can come out this way.'

So we went into his back study area, actually, I think, in the bathroom or in the hallway right near the bathroom, and we were intimate.

At that point they kissed.

Q: And how did that encounter end?
A: I said I needed to back [sic] and he said, "Well, why don't you bring me some pizza?" So I asked him if he wanted vegetable or meat.

Lewinsky brought some pizza to the Oval Office area.
Q: Could you describe what happened when you returned?
A: Yes. I went back to Ms. Currie's office and told her the President had asked me to bring him some pizza.

She opened the door and said, "Sir, the girl's here with the pizza." He told me to come in. Ms. Currie went back into her office and then we went into the back study area again. [734–6] (29–31)

The pretext worked. Clinton and Lewinsky gained private time together and were able to have another sexual encounter. Again, Lewinsky's remarkable access to the president arises directly out of the governmental crisis situation. A complete unknown at the bottom of the White House hierarchy, Lewinsky suddenly found herself answering phones for the president's chief of staff and ordering a pizza with his assistant, the president's personal secretary, and a presidential assistant. Then Lewinsky had a legitimate reason to approach the Oval Office: she needed to tell Currie and Hernreich that the pizza had arrived. Up until the furlough, Lewinsky had had to admire the president from afar as she stood with the rest of the interns in rope lines and reception crowds. In November 1995, however, she found herself sharing "study break" snacks with the president's closest personnel, and moving with full authorization through the hallways and outer offices next to the Oval Office.

Lewinsky had previously applied for a paid staff position in the White House. She accepted a job offer for a position in the correspondence division of the Legislative Affairs Office at the White House on 13 November 1995. She continued to work as an intern for two weeks, and then took up her staff appointment on 26 November 1995. On several subsequent occasions, she followed strategies for meeting with Clinton that they had clearly worked out together. Sometimes she would create a pretext for meeting with him in the Oval Office by carrying folders that she described to others as "papers" for him. At other times, they would either set up meetings by telephone or Clinton would invite her into the Oval Office after meeting her "accidentally" in another White House office or hallway.

Lewinsky indicates in her testimony at several points that when she visited Clinton at the White House, he always escorted her out of the Oval Office—a room with large, uncovered windows—to the back study, the adjoining bathroom, and the rear hallway for their sexual encounters. Immergut questioned Lewinsky on Clinton's choice of locations for their sex acts.

Q: *Why did you choose the hallway?*
A: *Because I believe it was—it was really more the President choosing the hallway, I think, and it was—there weren't any windows there. It was the most secluded of all the places in the back office. Well, that's not true. The bathroom is the most secluded, I guess, because you can close the door.*
Q: *And did you sometimes have sexual encounters in the bathroom?*
A: *Mm-hmm. [. . .]*
Q: *Okay. Did you notice whether doors were closed when you were physically intimate with him in the back study or hallway?*
A: *No, he always—well, I'm not sure about the door going in the dining room but I know that the door leading from the back hallway to the—into the Oval Office was always kept ajar to that he could hear if someone was coming.* [754–6] (49–51)

Lewinsky also related that she would often enter Clinton's study or the Oval Office through one door and exit through another so that the Secret Service guards would not be able to tell how long she had been there.

As a member of the Legislative Affairs staff, Lewinsky was given a "blue pass," which allowed her to enter the hallways surrounding the Oval Office. The added mobility that came with the position was crucial to their affair. In one of her responses, Lewinsky not only details the White House rules that restrict the movements of interns, but indicates that Evelyn Lieberman, deputy chief of staff, had first become suspicious about Lewinsky's behavior while she had been an intern—that is to say, quite early on in her flirtation with Clinton.

A Juror: *So that interaction that you had with Evelyn Lieberman was when she was telling you what?*
The Witness: *She stopped me in the hall and she asked me where I worked, in which office I worked, and I told her Legislative Affairs in the East Wing. And she said, "You're always trafficking up this area. You know, you're not supposed to be here. Interns aren't allowed to go past the Oval Office." [. . .] I went back to Evelyn Lieberman, to Ms. Lieberman, and I—I said, "You know, I just wanted to clarify with you that I work here, I'm not an intern. So, you know, I am allowed to go past the Oval Office." I don't think I said that, but I had a blue pass. And she looked at me and said, "They hired you?" And I was startled and then she said, "Oh well, I think I mistook you for someone else or some other girl with dark hair who keeps trafficking up the area."* [1066–7] (265–6)

Lieberman's suspicions clearly became the basis for further steps that were taken to protect Clinton from scandal. Lewinsky was stopped only once by Clinton's Secret Service agents. This occurred on 7 April 1996, during an important turning point in their affair.

A Juror: *Ms. Lewinsky, I wondered if you ever had any trouble with the Secret Service in trying to be near the President.*
The Witness: *No. The only time that I remember was when I went to see him on the last time in '96, I guess it was April 7th, Easter. And when John Muskett [Secret Service uniformed officer] was outside and he said he was going to check with Evelyn [Lieberman] if I could go in and then I don't remember exactly how it happened, but I sort of—I don't remember the exact discussion, but it ended up he ended up [sic] not talking to Evelyn and I went in.* [1098] (297)

Lewinsky had in fact been fired from her staff position on 5 April 1996, and had been transferred to a position in the Pentagon. The Starr Report evidence includes a 16 October 1996 memo written by a staff member in the White House named "John" that was addressed to Lieberman. ("John" could be John Hilley, an assistant to the president, director of Legislative Affairs, and Lewinsky's supervisor.) "John" had had a meeting with Lieberman the previous day in which she had made several suggestions for improving the management of his office. In the memo, he details changes that he had already made during the earlier months of 1996 with respect to White House personnel. "John" states, "I've also enclosed a brief memo on our correspondence operation. It was in bad shape when I came in. We got rid of Monica and Jossie not only because of 'extracurricular activities' but because [sic] they couldn't do the job." [2828] (710)

In her testimony before the grand jury, Lewinsky described a 7 April 1996 telephone call with Clinton in which she informed him that she had lost her position in the White House. According to Lewinsky, Clinton was not only upset that she had been transferred, but saw her transfer as a deliberate attempt on the part of his aides to protect him from scandal. In Lewinsky's account, Clinton acts as if he had not been consulted about her transfer to the Pentagon.

A: . . . I told him that my last day was Monday. And he was—he seemed really upset and sort of asked me to tell him what had happened. [782] (77)

Lewinsky arranged to meet with Clinton at the White House and used the pass that she possessed as a member of the Legislative Affairs staff to gain entry to the Oval Office. Associate Independent Counsel Michael Emmick's line of questioning appears to have been designed to bring to light any special favors with respect to employment that Lewinsky subsequently received from Clinton. Lewinsky's answers, however, portray not a manipulative schemer, but the actions of a man trapped between his interest in pursuing a sexual relationship with Lewinsky and the interest of his politically savvy staff. The romantic gloss that Lewinsky's account expresses—Clinton emerges as a heroic David promising to battle against the Goliath of his staff to make room for their relationship—may of course be a product of Lewinsky's fantasy that was not shared by Clinton himself. Indeed, because Clinton never responded directly to detailed questions about their encounters, we will probably never know exactly how he felt about the whole situation.

Q: What I am going to ask you about . . . was your discussions with the President about the termination and about what the future would hold for you.
A: He told me that he thought that my being transferred had something to do with him

and that he was upset. He said, "Why do they have to take you away from me? I trust you." And then he told me—he looked at me and he said, "I promise you if I win in No-vember [1996] I'll bring you back like that." [783] (78)

Lewinsky then had a telephone conversation with Clinton on the following Friday, 12 April 1996.

Q: Tell us about what the two of you talked about.
A: He told me that he had asked Nancy [Hernreich] and Marsha Scott [deputy director of personnel] to find out why I had been transferred, and that he had learned that Evelyn Lieberman had sort of spearheaded the transfer, and that she thought he was paying too much attention to me and I was paying too much attention to him and that she didn't necessarily care what happened after the election but everyone needed to be careful before the election. [784–5] (79–80)

Lewinsky signed an immunity agreement with the Office of the Independent Counsel on 28 July 1998. According to her handwritten notes for her oral proffer agreement, she states that when she informed Clinton about her transfer, he in-dicated to her that

Evelyn Lieberman spearheaded the transfer because she felt that the President paid to [sic] much attention to me and vice versa. Ms Lieberman told the Pres. [sic] that she didn't care who worked there after the election, but they needed to be careful until then. [paragraph break] After the election, Ms. Lewinsky asked the Pres. to bring her back to the WH. In the following months, Mr. Clinton told Ms. Lewinsky that Bob Nash [assistant to the president and director of presidential personnel] was handling it and then Marsha Scott became the contact person. Ms. L. met with Ms. Scott twice. In the second meeting, Ms. Scott told Ms. L. she would detail her from the Pentagon to her (Ms. Scott's) office, so people could see Ms. L.'s good work and stop referring to her as "The Stalker." Ms. Scott told Ms. L. they had to be careful and protect the Pres. Ms. Scott later rescinded her offer to detail Ms. Lewinsky to her office. [709–10] (6–7). (Emphasis in the original)

Lewinsky returned to these latter details in her testimony, stating that in early 1997, Nash and Scott were assigned the task of considering Lewinsky for a posi-tion in the White House but ultimately did not follow through.

Beginning in April 1996, there was a break in the interactions between Clin-ton and Lewinsky. Either Clinton followed the wishes of his staff and chose not to pursue Lewinsky, or the politically sensitive efforts of his staff prevailed. In any event, Lewinsky did not see Clinton again until late February 1997, well after his 1996 reelection. Lewinsky clearly made an attempt to see the president at this time. The Starr evidence includes a 24 February 1997 memo from Currie to Clinton entitled "Items of Interest." It includes only two sentences, "Monica Lewinsky stopped by. Do you want me to call her?" [3162] (711)

Lewinsky testified before the grand jury that she was called to the White House by Currie to attend Clinton's weekly radio address and to collect her Christmas presents from him on 28 February 1997. As is already well known, Currie was the intermediary between Lewinsky and Clinton when their affair resumed, for Lewinsky had been transferred to the Pentagon, and Clinton's aides had clearly developed concerns about their interaction. In Lewinsky's terms, "Betty always needed to be the one to clear me in so that, you know, I could always say that I was coming to see Betty." [775] (70) Having a meeting with Currie as a cover story was especially crucial since, according to Lewinsky's testimony, a member of Clinton's staff kept a list of his visitors and circulated it to the rest of his staff. [1061] (260) Currie not only ferried messages back and forth between them; she also told Lewinsky when Clinton's aides would be absent from their posts in the White House. According to Lewinsky, for example, Currie let Lewinsky know that Hernreich had yoga classes on Tuesday nights. [778] (73)

Lewinsky indicated in her testimony that the concerns of Clinton's aides had not dissipated as a result of his reelection. Stephen Goodin [aide to the president] saw Lewinsky waiting in Currie's office after the radio address on 28 February 1997. He immediately convened an unscheduled meeting in the Oval Office with Currie and Clinton. According to Lewinsky, she later learned from other White House staff that Goodin had told Currie and Clinton that they could not allow Lewinsky to be alone with the president at any time. After Goodin left the Oval Office, Currie did accompany Lewinsky, and the three of them entered the president's back office. However, either sympathizing with Lewinsky or refusing to accept chaperon duties as part of her employment contract, Currie only partly implemented the Goodin plan, and Clinton and Lewinsky were able to begin what ultimately became the last phase of their sexual interactions. Immergut questioned Lewinsky on this point.

Q: Okay. And why did Betty come in the back office with you?
A: I later found out that—I believe it was Stephen Goodin who said to Ms. Currie and the President that the President couldn't be alone with me, so Ms. Currie came back into the back office with me.

Q: *And then what?*
A: *And then left.* [750–51] (45–6)

Questioned later by Emmick, Lewinsky reaffirmed that just prior to her meeting with the president that day, she had seen Goodin, Clinton, and Currie go into the Oval Office together. A few weeks later she learned that Goodin had stated to Currie and Clinton at that time that "she [Lewinsky] can't be alone with him [Clinton]" [766–7] (61–2).

Emmick also pursued a line of questioning about Lewinsky's ability to evade Clinton's aides.

Q: *Where are the aides at the time you are having your encounters, if we can call them that, with the President?*
A: *Most of the time they weren't—they weren't there. They weren't at the White House.*
Q: *And how was that arranged ?*
A: *When I was working in Legislative Affairs [in the White House], I don't think—I don't know if it was ever verbally spoken but it was understood between the President and myself that most of the—most people weren't in on the weekends so there was—it would be safer to do that then. And then after I left the White House, that was sort of always a concern that Betty and I had just because she knew and I knew that a lot of people there didn't like me.* [767] (62)

Emmick brought Lewinsky back to the same theme at a later point.

Q: *Any discussion with the President about trying to make sure that there are fewer people around when you were to visit?*
A: *When I worked in Legislative Affairs, I think that was sort of the understanding that the weekend was the—there weren't a lot of people around. And there were times when I think that the President might have said, oh, there are too many people here because there was some big issue or some big event happening maybe.* [778] (73)

Clinton as a Sexual Subject: Maiden in the Tower or Shame-Ridden Fetishist?

It goes without saying that every president of the United States enjoys the protection of one of the most tightly controlled security systems in the world. Space and time management for the Clinton administration had in fact been even further intensified before the affair began. The errors incurred under the McLarty regime had been extremely costly; it could be argued that Panetta's management style saved Clinton from even worse disasters. It should also be noted that during his first term, Clinton not only had to deal with the issues of the day; he also had to prepare to fight the most expensive electoral campaign in the history of the country. Given the fact that a presidential contender now has to raise hundreds of millions of dollars every year for his own campaign funds and his party's "soft money" funds, political campaigns are now permanent and almost all-encompassing phenomena: virtually every minute and every public gesture counts. Election experts estimate that a record amount of $1.6 billion was raised and spent on the 1996 election. Eight hundred million dollars were spent on the presidential election alone, a figure that is three times greater than the 1992 spending level.[11] It makes sense, then, that Clinton is constructed in the official record as a prized race horse whose movements had to be scripted down to the smallest detail by his handlers.

There is also little evidence that Clinton shared Lewinsky's romantic view of their interactions. Lewinsky clearly saw herself during the affair as a heroine who was rescuing her lover from imprisonment—that is, Clinton's containment within the spatial and temporal rules imposed by his office—by using her erotic energy. While she may have regarded the interactions between Clinton and his staff as a David and Goliath tale, she constructed a different story where her relationship with Clinton was concerned: in her discourse, he takes on the role of the powerless maiden locked in the tower, and she becomes the heroic knight valiantly making every effort to liberate the trapped lover.

It appears that the idea that Clinton would eventually leave his wife and form a lasting partnership or even a marriage with Lewinsky was entirely the product of her own imagination. It is nevertheless plausible that Clinton did in fact see himself as torn between his sexual desire and his political ambitions. He may indeed have regarded his staff as denying him gratification when they fired Lewinsky; he may have even complained to her in a plaintive voice, "Why do they have to take you away from me?"

But we also have to consider the possibility that Lewinsky's testimony suppresses the logic of desire that was at work in this scenario. In her account, the furtive nature of their encounters was a *faute de mieux*—a secretive arrangement that would always be second-best since it meant that their interactions had to remain brief sexual encounters in the Oval Office. True, the political costs for a Democratic president of having any sort of extramarital affair in the era of the

"Contract with America" were enormous. We should note, however, that other presidents—including George Bush—have had little difficulty in accommodating their extramarital affairs.

Three factors made Clinton's pursuit of sexual gratification especially dangerous. First, his particular fetish was not extramarital heterosexual intercourse with a long-term partner or sex with a trustworthy sex-trade worker—it was casual sex with women who were not prostitutes. Second, the evidence suggests that Clinton was not at peace with himself about his fetishistic interests. As we already well know from campaigns to promote safer sex where transmission of the HIV virus is concerned, shame can be deadly, for the only individuals who take precautions are the ones who can affirm their sexual interests in advance. The closeted married man stopping for sex with a male stranger in a public bathroom at the mall or in a rest area off the interstate highway is probably not carrying a condom. Similarly, Clinton's own sense of shame must have made it more difficult than it need have been for him to create viable opportunities for the pursuit of his sexual interests. Third, it is perhaps the case that Clinton actually enjoyed taking the risk that he would be caught in the act. We know that he finds political risk-taking peculiarly exhilarating, and that he certainly did not experience any difficulties in achieving an aroused state during his interactions with Lewinsky—some of which occurred just out of the sight and just beyond the earshot of his aides. Taking these factors together, it makes sense that Clinton did not do what he could have done to save himself from unnecessary scandal. He could have affirmed his fetishistic desires to his wife and closest aides. Then he could have made arrangements to see trustworthy and security-approved sex trade workers on a regular basis. He could have even asked them to stage casual sex scenes with simulated risk-taking. Given his wealth and authority, he certainly would have had access to some of the best prostitutes in the business and, as long as their contracts were fair and fully honored by their client, there would have been no contradiction between such an arrangement and Clinton's ostensible support for feminist demands.

If Clinton actually did have an interest in casual sex where the risk of discovery was actually part of the sexual scene, then Lewinsky's account inverts the situation entirely. She believed that Clinton really loved her and that if his official duties, political ambition, interfering staff, and overbearing wife had not been in the way, the two of them would have gone off together into the sunset. Lewinsky's romantic discourse is structured by what Foucault calls the "repressive hypothesis," namely the assumption that prohibition represses genuine desire, and that the dismantling of a prohibitionary structure would therefore allow for the authentic expression of the self.[12] If Clinton had pursued Lewinsky from the perspective of a risk-taking casual sex fetishist, however, it was precisely the pressure of the office, the possibility of interruption and even the nearby movements of White House personnel and his spouse that made the scene work for him. The space and time management techniques deployed by his staff become not a police mechanism that threatened to extinguish romantic love but an erotic backdrop, a virtual sex toy. This is one of the elements of the ubiquitous phenomenon of sex in the workplace that rarely receives any attention: prohibition and taboo do not necessarily threaten the erotic; in some cases, they are the condition of possibility of the erotic.

The Antifeminist Impact of the Scandal

The one virtue of Kenneth Starr's own perverse and fetishistic pursuit of the most minute details about the Clinton/Lewinsky affair is the fact that his report absolutely lays to rest any lingering doubts about Lewinsky's consent. Part of the struggle that we will have to wage as feminists with respect to the damage that this entire scandal has done is to specify yet again exactly what we mean by sexual harassment. Consensual extramarital sex and consensual sex in socially "taboo" spaces like the workplace have absolutely nothing to do with sexual harassment. Again, sexual harassment only occurs in situations in which unwanted sexual behaviour is so severe that it makes it impossible for the complainant to perform her/his work duties, or to gain access to an otherwise available resource such as an educational experience—or unwanted sexual behavior is clearly offered as part of a quid pro quo exchange. Unless we maintain our distinct position, feminist opposition to sexual harassment will be interpreted by the moralistic right as simply one more contribution to the patriarchal campaign to protect traditional heterosexual marriage. Feminists must also insist not only on the difference between consenting adults and coerced victims, but also on the responsibility of the subject who actively pursues sex in the workplace. Sexual desire is not an independent force that exceeds an individual's control. The fact that social taboos eroticize workplace sexual expression does not absolve anyone from their obligation to respect their coworkers' rights.

Consistency was never one of Clinton's virtues, especially where ethical questions are concerned. We need not embrace the reactionary idea that marital fidelity is a prerequisite for public office to acknowledge that one of Clinton's most serious failures to conduct himself in a consistent and honest manner does in fact revolve around marriage. Monogamous patriarchal heterosexual marriage is currently being widely promoted in the United States by policy experts, politicians, religious leaders, and right- and left-wing communitarians alike as a solution to poverty and to antisocial behavior among the "underclass." Clinton, the very same leader who signed the key piece of pro-marriage welfare law—the Personal Responsibility Act (1996)[13]—decried the "national epidemic" of teen pregnancy on numerous occasions and approved the Republican Congress's anti-lesbian and -gay Defense of Marriage Act (1996), was not only a notorious philanderer, but was himself in a situation in which his marriage was being used in a (vain) attempt to keep him in line and out of trouble. And when we consider the actual policies of the Clinton administration, it is also highly ironic that this president claimed that his right to privacy was violated by the independent prosecutor's investigation,[14] since his welfare and anti-terrorism policies[15] have received very poor marks from human rights experts. Of course, consistency is no virtue when it produces a right-wing result. During the 2000 presidential campaign, the leading contenders tried to outdo each other by trumpeting their "personal character," showcasing their support for "faith-based" institutions, proclaiming their "family values" credentials, and reducing women to the role of adoring and submissive wives. It is clear that the Clinton/Lewinsky scandal will cast this kind of antifeminist shadow on American political discourse for years to come.

Notes

I want to acknowledge the importance of the work of Zillah Eisenstein and Katha Pollitt with respect to the development of this chapter. Many of my arguments were presented in a paper that I delivered at the Democracy-Sexuality-Citizenship Conference in Berlin on 9 October 1998; my thanks to Sabine Hark and the Heinrich Boell Foundation for their support.

1. Since child labor has been banned in the United States, and sexual harassment laws apply exclusively to the workplace, the relevant legislation and court decisions on sexual harassment anticipate an exclusively adult class of complainants.
2. See, for example, Jeffrey Weeks, *Sex, Politics and Society: The Regulation of Sexuality since 1800* (New York: Longman, 1981).
3. Katha Pollitt, "We Were Wrong: Why I'm Not Voting for Clinton," *Nation*, 7 October 1996, 9.

4. Barbara Ehrenreich, "Frances Fox Piven," *The Progressive,* November 1996, 34.

5. Pollitt, "We Were Wrong," 9.

6. Zillah Eisenstein, *Global Obscenities: Patriarchy, Capitalism and the Lure of Cyberfantasy* (New York: New York University Press, 1998), 63–65.

7. Ibid., 58.

8. Office of the Independent Counsel, *The Starr Report: The Independent Counsel's Complete Report to Congress on the Investigation of President Clinton* (New York: Simon and Shuster, 1998), 70–71.

9. *The Starr Evidence: The Complete Text of the Grand Jury Testimony of President Clinton and Monica Lewinsky* (New York: Public Affairs, 1998). Pagination from the original copy of the testimony and supporting documents as submitted by the Office of the Independent Council, 9 September 1998, and released by the U.S. Congress, 21 September 1998, is given in square brackets; pagination from the unabridged Public Affairs edition of the testimony is given in round brackets.

10. Elizabeth Drew, quoted in Theodore J. Lowi and Benjamin Ginsberg, *Embattled Democracy: Politics and Policy in the Clinton Era* (New York: W. W. Norton, 1997), 247.

11. "Money Votes," editorial, *Nation,* 11 November 1996.

12. Michel Foucault, *The History of Sexuality,* vol. I (New York: Vintage, 1980).

13. On the relationship between welfare "reform" and the reduction of poor women's right to privacy, see Gwendolyn Mink, *Welfare's End* (Ithaca, N.Y.: Cornell University Press, 1998).

14. See the following passages of Clinton's testimony before the grand jury on 17 August 1998: [477] (467), [529–30] (519–20), [545] (535), [553–4] (543–4), [559] (549), [599] (589).

15. Human rights activists have criticized Clinton for signing the 1996 anti-terrorism law that bans any person resident in the United States—citizens and aliens alike—from supporting the activities of a "foreign terrorist organization." The law also grants the secretary of state the power to determine which organizations fit into this category based on a vague definition involving the use of violence. The concept of "supporting" such organizations is defined quite broadly; otherwise, lawful advocacy and fundraising activities on behalf of a named organization are now classed as felony offences punishable by up to ten years in prison. Pro-African National Congress anti-apartheid activism could have been criminalized under this law, and yet it leaves the most serious terrorist threats to American social order, such as domestic anti-abortion violence and the right-wing militias, completely untouched.

Contributors

Lauren Berlant is Professor of English at the University of Chicago. She is author of *The Anatomy of National Fantasy: Hawthorne, Utopia and Everyday Life* (University of Chicago Press, 1991), and *The Queen of America Goes to Washington City: Essays on Sex and Citizenship* (Duke University Press, 1997), as well as the editor of *Intimacy* (University of Chicago Press, 2000). She is co-editor of *Critical Inquiry*, Contributing Editor of *Public Culture*, and on the editorial boards of PMLA and Modern Fiction Studies.

Eric O. Clarke is an Associate Professor of English at the University of Pittsburgh, where he teaches nineteenth-century British literature and queer theory. He is the author of *Virtuous Vice: Homoeroticism and the Public Sphere* (Duke University Press, 2000).

Tyler Curtain teaches critical and queer theory in the English Department at the University of North Carolina at Chapel Hill.

Ann Cvetkovich is Associate Professor of English at the University of Texas at Austin. She is the author of *Mixed Feelings: Feminism, Mass Culture, and Victorian Sensationalism* (Rutgers University Press, 1992), and co-editor, with Douglas Kellner, of *Articulating the Global and the Local: Globalization and Cultural Studies* (Westview, 1997). She has published articles in *GLQ* and the collections *Lesbian Erotics; Butch/Femme;* and *Art, Activism, and Oppositionality*. She is currently at work on a book about trauma, sexuality, and lesbian publics.

Simone Weil Davis is an Assistant Professor of English at Long Island University's C. W. Post campus. Her first book, *Living Up to the Ads: Gender Fictions of the 1920s,* is part of the New Americanists series of Duke University Press.

Lisa Duggan is Associate Professor of American Studies and History at New York University. She is co-author with Nan D. Hunter of *Sex Wars: Sexual Dissent and Political Culture* (Routledge, 1995), and author of *Sapphic Slashers: Sex, Violence and American Modernity* (Duke University Press, 2001). She is on the Board of the Center for Lesbian and Gay Studies at CUNY, and is a consulting editor of *The Journal of the History of Sexuality*.

Jane Gallop is Distinguished Professor of English at the University of Wisconsin—Milwaukee. She is the author of a number of books, including *The Daughter's Seduction, Thinking through the Body*, and, most recently, *Feminist Accused of Sexual Harassment.*

Marjorie Garber is William R. Kenan Jr. Professor of English at Harvard University and Director of Harvard's Center for Literary and Culture Studies. She is the author of three books on Shakespeare and of a number of works on cultural theory and criticism, including *Vested Interests: Cross Dressing and Cultural Anxiety, Vice Versa: Bisexuality and the Eroticism of Everyday Life, Dog Love*, and *Symptoms of Culture*. She is also general editor of the CultureWork series with Routledge, and co-editor of several of its collections of essays: *Media Spectacles, Secret Agents: The Rosenberg Case, McCarthyism and Fifties America, Field Work*, and the forthcoming *One Nation Under God? Religion and American Culture.*

Janet R. Jakobsen is Director of the Center for Research on Women at Barnard College. She is the author of *Working Alliances and the Politics of Difference: Diversity and Feminist Ethics* (Indiana University Press, 1998). She is co-editor of *World Secularisms at the Millennium*, a special issue of *Social Text,* and co-author of *Love the Sin: Sexual Regulation in the Name of Religion and How It Could be Otherwise* (forthcoming) with Ann Pellegrini. Her current book project is *The Value of Freedom: Sex, Religion, and America in a Global Economy*. Before becoming an academic she was a policy analyst and lobbyist in Washington, D.C.

James R. Kincaid is Aerol Arnold Professor at the University of Southern California, and has not, malicious rumors to the contrary, been fired or even indicted. He is author of a good many things in Victorian literature and culture, in theory, and recently in what he thinks of as "ideological comedy," and studies of the stories we tell and have told about children, sex, and the erotic. His books include *Child Loving: The Erotic Child and Victorian Culture* (Routledge, 1992); *Annoying the Victorians* (Routledge, 1995), and *Erotic Innocence: The Culture of Child Molesting* (Duke University Press, 1998).

Laura Kipnis is Professor of Radio–TV–Film at Northwestern University and is the author of *Bound and Gagged: Pornography and the Politics of Fantasy in America* (Duke University Press), and *Ecstasy Unlimited: On Sex, Capital, Gender and Aesthetics* (University of Minnesota Press).

Tomasz Kitlinski and **Pawel Leszkowicz**, whose identities are mutating, interchangeable, and possibly conspiratorial, spent 1998–99 observing Monica Lewinsky as Fulbright scholars at the Transregional Center for Democratic Studies, New School University. **Joe Lockard**, a unitary academic narrator at University of California—Berkeley, is a member of the Bad Subjects Collective.

Catharine Lumby is the Director of the Media and Communications Studies Program at the University of Sydney. She is the author of *Bad Girls: The Media, Sex, and Feminism in the '90s* (Allen and Unwin, 1997), and *Gotcha: Life in a Tabloid World* (Allen and Unwin, 1999).

Micki McElya is a doctoral candidate in American History at New York University studying the postbellum American South and the history of sexuality. She is currently at work on a dissertation, "Monumental Citizenship: Reading the Mammy Commemoration Controversy of the Early Twentieth Century," which explores race, gender, and citizenship in the 1920s United States.

Toby Miller teaches Cinema Studies at New York University. He is the author of *The Well-Tempered Self: Citizenship, Culture, and the Postmodern Subject; Contemporary Australian Television; The Avengers; Technologies of Truth: Cultural Citizenship and the Popular Media;* and *Popular Culture and Everyday Life.* He is also co-editor of *SportCult; Film and Theory: An Anthology,* and *A Companion to Film Theory.* He edits *Television & New Media* and is a co-editor of *Social Text.*

Frederick C. Moten teaches in the Department of Performance Studies at the Tisch School of the Arts, New York University. He has published work on the relation between politics and sound in the black radical tradition and is currently completing a book on this issue called *Event Music.* **B Jenkins,** recently deceased, was a longtime educator and political activist from Kingsland, Arkansas, and Las Vegas, Nevada. She was most recently ombudsperson for the State Industrial Insurance System of Nevada.

Dana D. Nelson is Professor of English and Social Theory at the University of Kentucky and author of *The Word in Black and White: Reading Race in American Literature, 1638–1867,* and of *National Manhood: Capitalist Citizenship and the Imagined Fraternity of White Men.*

Anna Marie Smith is Associate Professor of political theory, feminist theory, and lesbian and gay studies in the Department of Government, Cornell University. She is the author of *New Right Discourse on Race and Sexuality, Britain 1968–1990* (Cambridge University Press, 1994), and *Laclau and Mouffe: The Radical Democratic Imaginary* (Routledge, 1998).

Sasha Torres is Director of the Program in Film and Media and the Second Decade Society Faculty Development Chair at Johns Hopkins University. She is the author of *Black, White, and in Color: Television, African Americans and the Production of National History* (forthcoming), and the editor of *Living Color: Race and Television in the United States* (Duke University Press, 1998). She is a co-editor of *Camera Obscura* and serves on the editorial boards of *Gay and Lesbian Quarterly, Aztlan,* and *Meridians.*

Ellen Willis teaches journalism and directs the Cultural Reporting and Criticism program at New York University. Her articles on cultural and political issues have been collected in two books: *Beginning to See the Light* and *No More Nice Girls.* Most recently she is author of *Don't Think—Smile! Notes on a Decade of Denial* (Beacon Press, 1999).

Eli Zaretsky is Professor of History on the Graduate Faculty of the New School for Social Research. He is author of *Capitalism, the Family and Personal Life* which was translated into fourteen languages, and the editor of William I. Thomas Florian Znanecki's *The Polish Peasant in Europe and America.* His overall history, *Secrets of the Soul: Psychoanalysis, Modernity, and Personal Life,* will be published by Alfred J. Knopf and Hanser Verlag.